GW00578100

A HANDBOOK OF

DEVON PARISHES

A COMPLETE GUIDE

FOR LOCAL AND FAMILY HISTORIANS

HELEN HARRIS

HALSGROVE

First published in Great Britain in 2004

Frontispiece photograph: *Dartmouth viewed across the Dart from Kingswear*

British Library Cataloguing-in-Publication Data
A CIP record for this title is available from the British Library

ISBN 1 84114 314 6

HALSGROVE
Halsgrove House
Lower Moor Way
Tiverton, Devon EX16 6SS
Tel: 01884 243242
Fax: 01884 243325
email: sales@halsgrove.com
website: www.halsgrove.com

Printed and bound by CPI, Bath

INTRODUCTION

Towards the end of 2002, chance remarks that I heard caused me to realise the limitations of knowledge that exist in our large county of Devon – even among people born here – about parishes remote from the ones where they live. Then, for those who come from elsewhere, either to visit or to settle, Devon's size and labyrinth of roads may be somewhat bewildering. At about the same time I also became aware that 2004 would mark 50 years since the first publication of W.G. Hoskins' *Devon*, a book which, with its gazetteer, has been for me a constant and cherished work of reference for nearly half a century. It seemed that perhaps time might be ripe for another, updated, gazetteer of the county's parishes. Whilst seeking to follow a pattern similar to that set by Hoskins, and to include basic items of historical knowledge that I had gained from his writings, I wanted to be able to provide details of locations, road accessibility, and topography, together with some general information about the towns and villages, parish churches, industries, railways, and any other matters of local interest which might be useful in the 21st century. Early in 2003 I raised the subject with Simon Butler of Halsgrove – whose own community history series was approaching an important milestone – and was delighted to receive a positive reply. My work started forthwith.

The sun shone on me during my travels of investigation during 2003's glorious summer, and it was a pleasurable task to revisit the many parishes known to me over the years. I have been in every parish in the county and into as many of the churches as possible. On the summer's hottest days I found welcome refreshment on pushing open churches' heavy ancient doors to find coolness and tranquillity within, and I became very conscious of how these historic buildings in their continuing use are valued and lovingly cared for. Sadly it was not possible for me actually to enter every church, many these days have to be kept locked when not in use – happily a minority – and the reasons for that are understood. Space limitations for a book of manageable size have also restricted the amount of church detail that I could include, but I have tried to draw attention to main features of interest.

This study concerns civil parishes, which in most cases correspond to the ecclesiastical ones. Deviations, where they occur, are noted. Of ancient origin, parishes remain viable and convenient units in which to consider the different areas of our countryside. Many ecclesiastical parishes originate from the 11th century, and became closely linked with the manorial system. Religious houses, in the form of monasteries and minsters of canons, had existed from the late 7th century, and as time advanced numerous churches were built by the Saxons, often of wood. Administratively, the county was divided into over 30 Hundreds, each comprising approximately 100 households. By the 11th century some of the religious houses were becoming churches and these, together with the growing number of others, gradually acquired responsibilities for their surrounding areas of habitation, which became known as parishes (meaning 'the area around', e.g. a church). Many of the smaller churches were established by lords of manors, for themselves and their tenants, sometimes on an earlier Saxon site and often near the manor house, and thus manor and parish boundaries mainly coincided. Most of Devon's parish churches were in place by the 11th and 12th centuries, and the system of parishes was fully operational by the end of the 13th century, with the church having jurisdiction in parish matters. By the 16th century, however, the government of parishes was not just ecclesiastical, but also acquiring secular responsibilities and influences. As these increased, and with the creation of parish councils in 1894, and subsequent legislation, civil parishes have become recognised units of local government.

Devon has 422 civil parishes, plus the island of Lundy, and the three conurbations of the City of Exeter and the Unitary Authorities of Plymouth and Torbay. These three are divided into wards, and include some former country parishes which have now been brought within the boundaries.

In order to provide an approximate location, each parish entry is referenced by a letter and number which correspond to a grid square on the outline map (p.5). The respective district authority of local government, and the comparative population (Pop.) figures for 1901 and 2001 are given. Access routes are noted, and distances from main towns. These are given as direct distances ('as the crow flies'), so actual road distances will be rather longer. Altitudes are given in feet, as such figures are still used by many people and generally by those locally, and are more easily visualised on a parish basis than by applying metric with decimal points. For those who prefer metres the conversion is: 1foot = 0.3048 metres.

My main written sources, apart from my own previously published works, have been as follows:

Shorter, A.H., Ravenhill, L.D., and Gregory K.J., *Southwest England*, Nelson, 1969
Hoskins, W.G., *Devon*, Collins, 1954, (particularly for names mentioned in Domesday)
White's Directory of Devon 1878
Orme, Nicholas, 'The medieval parishes of Devon', *The Devon Historian* 33 (October 1986)
Orme, Nicholas (ed.), *Unity and variety*, University of Exeter Press, 1991
Orme, Nicholas, *English church dedications* (Devon & Cornwall), University of Exeter Press, 1996

Griffith, Frances, *Devon's past: an aerial view*, Devon Books, 1988
Bone, Mike, and Stanier, Peter, *A guide to the industrial archaeology of Devon*, Association of Industrial Archaeology, 1998
Information provided in the churches, including leaflets obtainable at many on their historical features.
(Several of the works noted under particular parishes may no longer be on sale, but most can be referred to in the Westcountry Studies Library, Exeter.)

I also acknowledge with gratitude:
Co-operation from Devon County Council, including providing me with a map showing all named parishes, and with the 2001 census figures.
Exeter City Council, Plymouth Unitary Authority, and Torbay Unitary Authority, for maps showing their wards.
The Diocese of Exeter for providing me with a map of the parishes of the diocese and lists of the churches.
The Westcountry Studies Library for notes on relevant books on parishes, including the handlist of Devon parish histories: *Abbots Bickington to Zeal Monchorum*, 1994, compiled by Ian Maxted, County Studies Librarian, to mark the centenary of parish councils.
(And all the above for answering queries on the telephone)
Mr John Pike for making available to me his notes on the churches of Torbay.
Mr A.B. George, and Mr D.L.B. Thomas, for the loan of certain items of information.
In addition, I thank numerous people whom I have had the good fortune to meet on my visits to parishes and their churches, many of whose names I do not know, who have talked and shown much kindness.

In addition to societies mentioned under particular parishes, readers are recommended, as appropriate, to the following:
The Devonshire Association for Science, Literature and the Arts
The Devon History Society
The Devon Family History Society
Devon Archaeological Society
Devon Wildlife Trust
South West Maritime History Society

In Devon there is to be found a very wide variation of land type and scenery. The wild, rugged, and mainly unspoilt north coast differs greatly from that in the south, which is generally softer and more developed. Also different are the two moors: Dartmoor, which is mainly granite, and Exmoor with its rocks of Old Red Sandstone. There is the broad belt of sometimes bleak and lonely Culm Measures land which stretches across from east to west, north of Dartmoor; the steeply-rising, flat-topped Blackdown and Haldon Hills, composed largely of Greensand; and the contrasting colours of grey Devonian limestone, white crystalline limestone of Beer, and the New Red Sandstone at points along the South Devon coast and extending inland through Crediton. To add movement to the scene there are the countless streams, glorious rivers, and broad estuaries that complete the fascinating diversity of the county of Devon.

Helen Harris

All photographs are by the author, except where otherwise acredited

Slight discrepancies between spellings of certain place-names and family names may be apparent as such details are subject to change over time; throughout the book the author has used the spellings included in her source materials.

LOCATION MAP

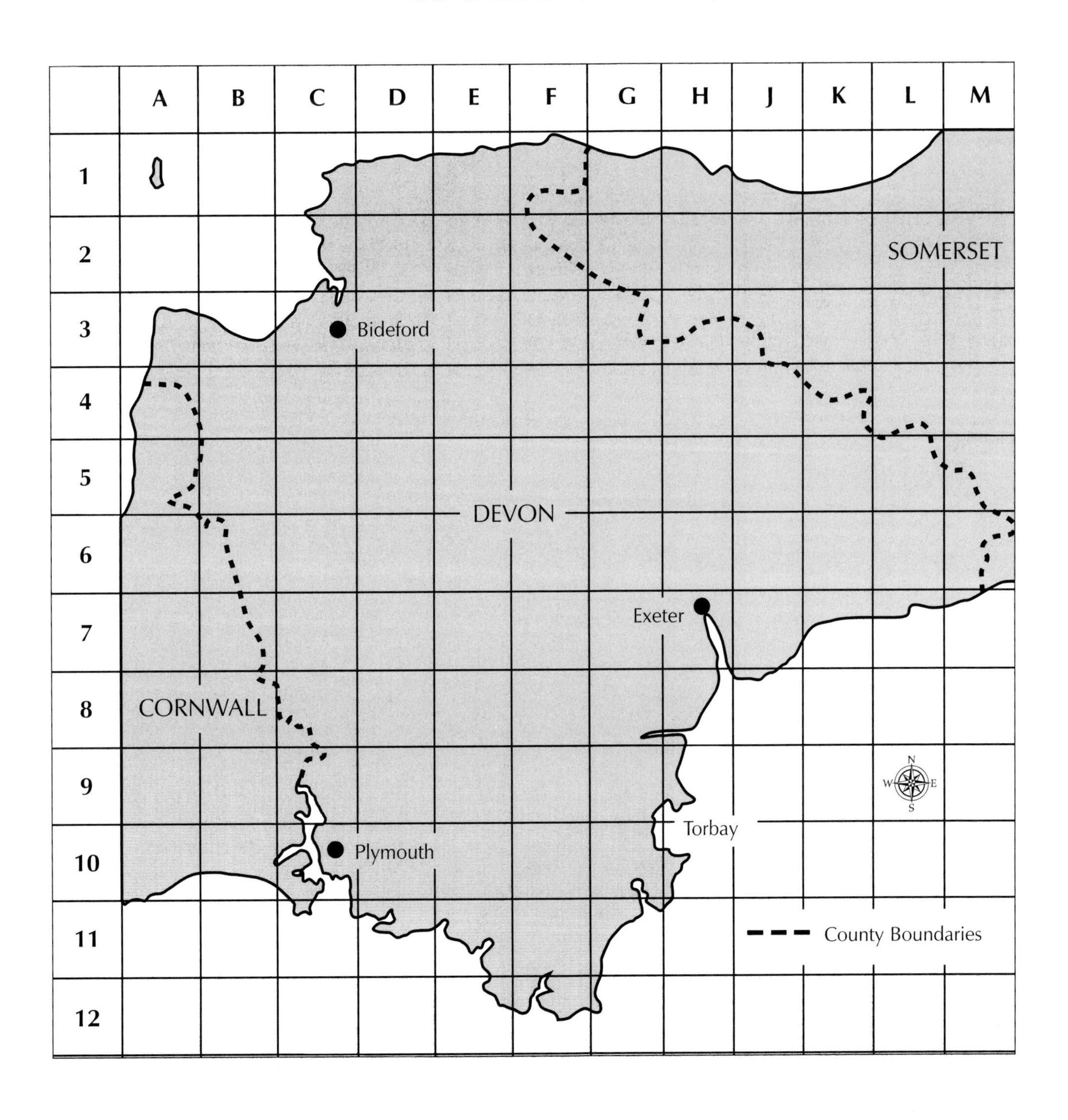

ABBOTS BICKINGTON (B4) Torridge Pop. 35 (1901: 61)

Located 1½ miles NE of Venn Green (Milton Damerel) on the Holsworthy-Bideford road (A 388), this small parish is bordered on the north-east by the River Torridge.

From the 12th century until the Dissolution the parish was part of the lands of Hartland Abbey. Culsworthy was named in Domesday.

The church (St James) is one of the smallest in Devon, with seats for just 45. It was built c.1300 on an earlier foundation. The tower has a tiny neat spire. From the churchyard there are wide views eastward, and to Dartmoor.

ABBOTSHAM (C3) Torridge Pop. 434 (1901: 451)

Abbotsham's pebble and rocky beach. Hartland Point far right.

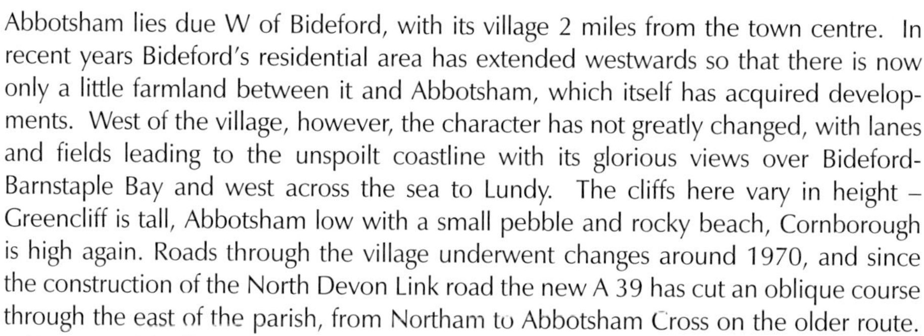

Abbotsham lies due W of Bideford, with its village 2 miles from the town centre. In recent years Bideford's residential area has extended westwards so that there is now only a little farmland between it and Abbotsham, which itself has acquired developments. West of the village, however, the character has not greatly changed, with lanes and fields leading to the unspoilt coastline with its glorious views over Bideford-Barnstaple Bay and west across the sea to Lundy. The cliffs here vary in height – Greencliff is tall, Abbotsham low with a small pebble and rocky beach, Cornborough is high again. Roads through the village underwent changes around 1970, and since the construction of the North Devon Link road the new A 39 has cut an oblique course through the east of the parish, from Northam to Abbotsham Cross on the older route.

Known originally as Hama, in 981 Abbotsham was one of several endowments granted to Tavistock Abbey. Perhaps because of its remoteness, in the 12th century the manor of Abbotsham was rented out to farmers rather than being held in hand by the abbey, and later, at the Dissolution, unlike many other Tavistock properties, it was not granted to the Russell (Bedford) family.

The church (St Helen) is known to have existed well before 1246, and it contains a 12th-century font. There has been subsequent rebuilding, and restoration in the 1870s. The structure of Abbotsham Court dates partly from the 16th century.

ABBOTSKERSWELL (G9) Teignbridge Pop. 1515 (1901: 451)

The small parish of Abbotskerswell is located immediately S of the town of Newton Abbot, of which it is a sought-after residential area, with the road to Totnes (A 381) running southwards on the western side. The name is due to its having been held at the time of Domesday by the abbot of Horton in Dorset, differentiating it from neighbouring Kingskerswell which was held by the king. Kerswell is a corruption of carsewell, carse being Saxon for cress, for which the local stream was apparently renowned.

The fairly substantial village is situated in the north of the parish. The church (St Mary the Virgin) is of ancient origin. The present building is of mainly 15th-century construction with remains of an earlier building in the chancel. The church house dates from the 16th century. There was a small Cluniac priory here for some years from 1119.

ALFINGTON see OTTERY ST MARY

ALL SAINTS (M5) East Devon Pop. 498

The small civil and ecclesiastical parish of All Saints is located due N of Axminster, bordered by Axminster, Membury, Chardstock and Hawkchurch. The evidently cherished and well-kept church (All Saints) is located beside the minor road east of the hamlet of Smallridge. It was built in 1840, and enlarged eastwards in 1850.

ALPHINGTON (H7) Exeter City (Pop. 1901: 1103)

Located 1½ miles S of Exeter city centre, Alphington was formerly a separate village but since 1971 has been part of the extended city. The marshy area which separates it from the River Exe, to the east, has now been mostly developed into the large Marsh Barton industrial estate. The Alphin Brook flows through on its course to join the Exe.

The parish is today a conglomeration of routes which link with the A 38, the A 30 and the road into the city. The main railway passes through the east of the parish. Alphington formerly had a halt on the Teign Valley railway which opened in 1903 to connect with the already existing Teign line at Ashton; it closed in 1958.

The church (St Michael & All Angels) dates from at least as early as the 12th century. The present building is of 15th-century construction. There is a fine 12th-century font of Beer stone and a 15th-century rood screen.

ALVERDISCOTT (D3) Torridge Pop. 281 (1901: 241)

Alverdiscott, 4 miles E of Bideford, is located at a staggered crossroads on the B 3232 cross-country road from Torrington to Barnstaple. Parish boundaries are mainly across land, which is moderately high, rising to 500 ft near Windmill Cross.

The church (All Saints) dates from the 15th century, largely rebuilt in 1866. It has a Norman font.

Webbery was a Domesday manor, and was anciently occupied by a family of the same name. The house was rebuilt around 1820. Stoneycross is a hamlet.

ALWINGTON (C3) Torridge Pop. 381 (1901: 316)

This mainly farming parish extends from the River Yeo, tributary of the Torridge, northwards to a remote stretch of the North Devon coast west of Bideford, where the red sandstone cliffs of Peppercombe provide a colourful feature. The finding of flint arrowheads on land in the parish suggests possible habitation from Stone Age times.

The church (St Andrew), which reputedly occupies the site of an earlier structure or preaching place, dates mainly from the 15th century, with later rebuilding. The nave arcades are of Lundy granite, and the church contains much carving, including modern work. Near the altar is the Portledge pew. Portledge was the home of the Coffin family from the time of Henry II until the 20th century, and the church contains several memorials to the Coffins – and Pine-Coffins as they became after the marriage of Dorothy Coffin to Edward Pyne in 1671. After some years as a hotel, Portledge, with its 16th-century house and estate, is now in private ownership and is not normally open to the public.

Alwington supported Methodism with growing numbers from the early 19th century. The present Methodist Chapel celebrated its centenary in 1997.

The ancient Yeo Vale House, rebuilt in Georgian style in the late 18th century, still retains its 15th-century gatehouse. The former chapel at Yeo was rebuilt in the early 19th century beside the road to Tuckingmill, where the ruins are now seen.

Further reading: Alwington Parish Council, *Alwington, a millennium experience,* 2001

APPLEDORE see NORTHAM

ARLINGTON (E1) North Devon Pop. 98 (1901: 217)

Arlington is centred 6 miles NNE of Barnstaple, immediately east of the tortuous A 39 Barnstaple-Lynton road. Its boundaries are almost entirely defined by waters that combine westwards as the River Yeo, flowing to the Taw at Barnstaple.

The undulating land includes the park of Arlington Court, home of the Chichester family from the 14th century until 1947 when it was given to the National Trust. It is now opened to the public. The present house was built in the 1820s.

The church (St James) dates from the 15th century, rebuilt (apart from the tower) in 1846. Ecclesiastically the parish is united with East Down. Twitchen, in the east, was a Domesday manor.

ASHBURTON (F9) Teignbridge Pop. 3909 (1901: 2628)

Situated SE of Dartmoor and within the area of Dartmoor National Park, Ashburton lies close beside the route of the A 38 expressway between Exeter and Plymouth.

The parish shares boundaries with no fewer than ten others: Buckfastleigh, West Buckfastleigh, Holne, Buckland-in-the-Moor, Widecombe-in-the-Moor, Ilsington, Bickington, Torbryan, Woodland, and Staverton. The ancient town is located near the parish boundary on the south-east, with the River Ashburn, or Yeo, flowing through on its way to join the Dart 3 miles downstream. A beautiful, largely wooded stretch of the River Dart forms the western boundary. Although the town stands at around 200 ft, hills rise all around. Those on the eastern boundary reach 579 ft. A knoll (round hill) at the back of the town attains 500 ft, and northwards the land rises towards the moor to several high points including 1450 ft on the northern boundary near the summit of Rippon Tor. This is a most lovely part of Dartmoor with very fine views in all directions.

Tower of St Lawrence Chapel, Ashburton's former Grammar School.

While the moorland bears many signs of prehistoric inhabitation, the town itself has a considerable history. Before the Norman Conquest it was part of the estates of the bishops of Exeter and continued so until the early 17th century when it was sold. The town had a market from the 12th century and was created a borough in 1238. The church (St Andrew) is located in the centre of the town and dates mainly from the 15th century, but also includes remains of 14th-century work, notably in the chancel. The granite-built tower is very fine. Various alterations were carried out when the church was restored c.1840. (Buckland-in-the-Moor, with its church of St Peter, is united with Ashburton ecclesiastically, although a separate civil parish.) Just east of St Andrew's stands the Methodist Church, dated 1835, with its bold Ionic columns. A short distance farther eastwards along the main street is the old grammar school with its tower, known as St Lawrence Chapel. This was given to the town in 1314 by Bishop Stapledon of Exeter, with the original Guild of St Lawrence, headed by the Portreeve and Burgesses, being charged with its care and that of a charity school. The building, which is now listed Grade 1, continued as a school into the 20th century. It is now in the care of the Guild of St Lawrence in modern form, created in 1985 as a successor to the original, and is still the annual meeting place of the Portreeve, Court Leet and Baron Jury. It is also made available to the public for the town's museum and archive.

In 1305 Ashburton was one of four towns located around the edge of Dartmoor that were designated as Stannary Towns, to which tin, extracted and smelted in the respective quarters of the moor, had to be brought for assaying, weighing and stamping and the paying of dues to the Crown. This was necessary before it could be sold, for which buyers came to the sessions from far afield. The requirement officially ended in the early 19th century but mining of 'black' tin, taken away for smelting elsewhere, and the mining of copper and other minerals, continued for some years, particularly in the area of Owlacombe, in the east, where working continued until 1930.

Ashburton also featured in Devon's woollen trade. There were several early water-powered woollen mills in the locality, some serving at different times as corn mills, and in Kingsbridge Lane in the town there stood the woollen mill of John Berry & Sons, its site now a car park.

In 1872 Ashburton became the terminus for the branch railway along the Dart valley from Totnes, which also had stations at Staverton and Buckfastleigh. This was a busy line in its day, bringing in coal and other requirements and serving the wool industry. The line closed to passengers in 1958 and for goods in 1962, although the Totnes-Buckfastleigh line was bought by the Dart Valley Light Railway Company and developed as a tourist attraction. Continuation to Ashburton was inhibited by the construction of the modern dual-carriageway A 38, and particularly the Dart Bridge interchange.

Further reading: Pilkington, Francis, *Ashburton, the Dartmoor town*, Devon Books 1989
Various, *The book of Ashburton*, Halsgrove, 2004
Museum: Ashburton Museum, 1 West Street

ASHBURY see NORTHLEW

ASHCOMBE (H8) Teignbridge Pop. 77 (1901: 125)

Located 8 miles S of Exeter, Ashcombe, whose name means 'valley of the ash', is a parish of steep ascents on the south-eastern edge of the Haldon Hills. The small village stands at over 300 ft, embraced by arms of the high ground which rise on the west to 750 ft and on the east to 800 ft. The Dawlish Water rises in these hills and flows south-eastwards through the village and combe, which are served by minor roads branching from the B 3192 between the A 380 and Teignmouth.

The parish was owned before the Norman Conquest by Radulf, or Ranulf. The church (St Nectan), which replaced an earlier Celtic building, was originally dedicated by Bishop Bronescombe in 1259, and the list of rectors is unbroken from 1280. The medieval structure was almost completely rebuilt 1824–5, but still contains many interesting features including ancient bench ends and an Elizabethan lectern. It is a peaceful place of beauty and simplicity.

ASHFORD (D2) North Devon Pop. 273 (1901: 148)

Ashford is a small parish, attractively situated on rising ground overlooking the Taw estuary, just N of the A 361 Barnstaple-Braunton road.

The original church (St Peter) was dedicated in 1338–9. There is a small tower and broach spire. The building was reconstructed in 1854 but with early finely carved woodwork retained. The font is Norman. There are fine views from the churchyard to Chivenor and the estuary. The parish is united ecclesiastically with the Barnstaple parish of Pilton.

Further reading: Bosley, Alan, *The jubilee book of Ashford village*, 2002

ASHPRINGTON (G10) South Hams Pop. 428 (1901: 479)

Ashprington village centre.

Ashprington (anciently Aisbertona) is located immediately S of Totnes, from which it is served by minor roads. The meandering course of the tidal River Dart forms the eastern boundary, and Bow Creek, watered by the tributary Harbourne River, that on the south. From these banks the land rises to hills which reach 440 ft north-west of the village, and 469 ft in the north. Stretching along the frontage of the Dart is the partially wooded parkland of Sharpham House, a mansion built between 1770 and 1826. It now houses a college, while farming, dairying, and vineyard businesses occupy other areas.

It is known that there was a church here in 1143. The present church building (St David) dates from the 15th century, but the slender tower with its tower stair jutting out on the north side is older, dating possibly from the 12th century. The red sandstone font is also of the 12th century, the arcades are of Beer stone. The church was restored in 1880 and 1889 and the carved pulpit dates from 1909.

Painsford is an ancient mansion in the south-west, close to the Harbourne. Tuckenhay is a hamlet on Bow Creek, partly in Ashprington and partly in Cornworthy. On the Ashprington side there was a corn mill, and a paper mill that worked from 1830–60, as well as quays from which much stone from local quarries was shipped away. There are also likekilns close by.

ASHREIGNEY (E4) Torridge Pop. 446 (1901: 540)

Ashreigney parish is bounded by the River Taw on the east and stands on the high ground that rises from the Taw valley (and the A 377 road) and stretches to that of the Torridge on the west. Taw tributaries form parts of the north and south boundaries, which continue westwards over land to the A 3124 Exeter-Torrington road that divides the parish from Dolton.

The church (St James) – located in the village – was built in the 15th century and restored in 1889.

Earlier known as King's Ash, the parish took the name of Ashreigney from the Reigny family who were former lords of the manor. Goodcott, Hook, and Riddlecombe were Domesday manors, and Hanford Barton was known c.1200.

ASHTON (G7) Teignbridge Pop. 174 (1901: 150)

Ashton, 7 miles SSW of Exeter, is located on the western slopes of the Haldon Hills,

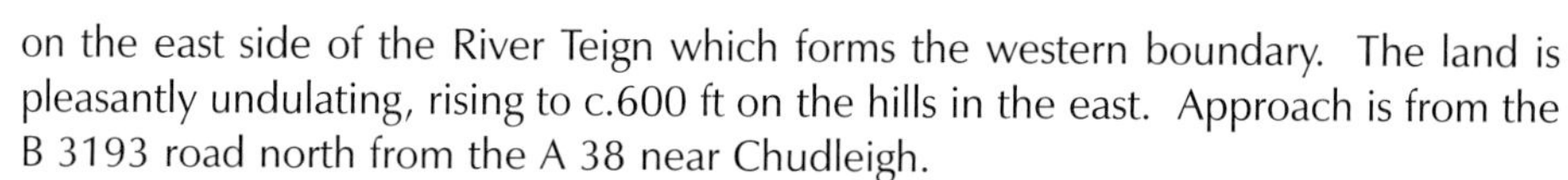

St John the Baptist Church, Ashton, dates from the 13th century.

on the east side of the River Teign which forms the western boundary. The land is pleasantly undulating, rising to c.600 ft on the hills in the east. Approach is from the B 3193 road north from the A 38 near Chudleigh.

The church (St John the Baptist), situated on the hillside, dates from the 13th century, carefully restored early in the 20th century. It contains many interesting and beautiful features. These include a very fine carved rood screen, an Elizabethan pulpit with sounding board, and wall paintings.

Lower Barton, formerly called Place, just below the church, was the home of the Chudleighs from the early 14th century to 1745. George Teign Barton, in the south, dates from the 16th and 17th centuries and was so-called because a medieval chapel of St George stood on the site.

Ashton was the terminal station on the initial Teign Valley railway, constructed from Heathfield, north of Newton Abbot, in 1882. The line was extended from here to Exeter in 1903. The section north of Christow closed in 1958, while some traffic continued in the south until 1965.

ASHWATER (B6) Torridge Pop. 651 (1901: 758)

Part of Ashwater village with its triangular green.

The fairly large parish of Ashwater has its village centre 6 miles SSE of Holsworthy and is approached by minor roads from the A 388. The eastern parish boundary is marked by the River Carey, elsewhere its course is more indirect, following in the north-west the upper reach of the Claw. The border is shared with no fewer than ten neighbouring parishes.

The village surrounds a triangular green, and the church (St Peter) stands nearby. The structure dates from the 14th and late 15th centuries. It contains a Norman font, and some interesting tombs.

Quoditch is a hamlet in the north-east of the parish.

ATHERINGTON (D3) North Devon Pop. 391 (1901: 453)

The road to Atherington rises fairly steeply from the Taw valley, with the village standing 7 miles SSE of Barnstaple on the crossroads of the B 3227 Torrington-South Molton road and the B 3217. The River Taw forms the eastern boundary and the A 377 Exeter-Barnstaple road runs within the parish alongside the river.

The church (St Mary) stands prominently in the village, its tower seemingly bent on piercing the clouds. It is believed to have been built between 1202 and 1272, the north aisle being extended in 1579. There is the remaining section of a magnificent rood screen on the north side, which is unique in Devon, being the only one still having a rood loft. The carving of it, c.1530–40, was led by John Parry of Northlew, assisted by two Chittlehampton men. At some later date the central section across the church was replaced by a screen that is more open and less ornate. The font is 15th century. The church was restored and partly rebuilt in 1833. The altar is of the 1950s.

AVETON GIFFORD (E11) South Hams Pop. 772 (1901: 657)

Aveton Gifford's church of St Andrew, rebuilt after its wartime destruction.

Aveton Gifford parish surrounds the upper tidal limit of the River Avon as it reaches the conclusion of its flow from the heights of Dartmoor and through steep valleys. Here it emerges into the estuary and heads for the sea. From a narrow projection south-west of the Avon the parish extends north with hills that reach 556 ft near the northern boundary.

The village is located in the south, immediately north of the Avon. The A 379 Plymouth-Kingsbridge road passes through, although the village is now bypassed on the west. Minor roads include the waterside route to Bigbury, usable only at low tide when ford crossings of small creeks are passable. From the 16th century Aveton Gifford was one of south Devon's many fishing settlements.

The church (St Andrew), which stands high above the village to the north-east, dates from 1250, although the original building, apart from the Early English porch and 14th-century font, was destroyed by a bomb in 1943, during the Second World War. Rebuilding was completed in 1970. An early rector was Walter de Stapledon who later became Bishop of Exeter and was involved in the building of the Cathedral.

Further reading: Shaw, C.C., comp., *A history of the parish of Aveton Gifford*
Doughty, Ken, ed., *Aveton Gifford, a heritage*, Parish project group

AWLISCOMBE (K5) East Devon Pop. 507 (1901: 464)

The village of Awliscombe is situated 2 miles NW of Honiton on the A 373 road to Cullompton, 8 miles distant. Lands of the parish extend a short distance south of this road, westwards to the fringe of Hembury fort, but most stretch northwards, to the slopes of the Blackdown Hills and an altitude of 850 ft. The River Wolf flows southwards through the parish and village to join the Otter.

Believed to have been built on a former pagan site, the church (St Michael & All Angels) dates from the 13th century. The roof was later reconstructed and the church restored in 1837 and again in 1887. It contains much fine work, including a 14th-century Beer stone screen.

The name is believed to be derived from 'owls' combe' on account of the number of owls that bred in the area and were heard at night.

AXMINSTER (L6) East Devon Pop. 5626 (1901: 2933)

Norman doorway in the east wall of Axminster church.

Axminster, Devon's most easterly town, shares a brief length of its parish boundary on the east side with Dorset. The River Axe flows through the parish from north-east to south-west, joined at this lower point by the Yarty. The valley here, a mile south-west of the town, broadens out and constitutes an area of land common to the parishes of Axminster and Kilmington. The terrain to the south-east rises steeply, reaching 670 ft near the county border.

Several routes meet at Axminster, notably the A 358 (Fosse Way) coming up from Axmouth and continuing to Chard and the A 30, and the A 35, proceeding from the east and going on westwards to Honiton, which now bypasses the town on the south. Axminster is also served by a railway station on the (formerly Southern) service from Waterloo, although the former branch from Axminster to Lyme Regis no longer exists.

The town originated in Saxon times, probably in the 7th century, doubtless due to the convenience of the nearby Fosse Way, built by the Romans. Further evidence of the Romans, including paving, was found during construction of the bypass. A minster was founded here in the early 8th century and a busy market town developed. Until 1204 it was a royal estate, but then passed to a succession of individuals. These included Reginald Mohun who gave it to the Cistercian Newenham Abbey which became established just south-west of the town. After the Dissolution the manor passed into other hands. Only traces of the abbey's walls remain at Higher Newenham, where a farmhouse was built c.1600.

Of Saxon origin, the fine church (St Mary) is situated in the town centre. It is a cruciform building dating from the 12th century. The chancel is of the 13th century when also the central tower was rebuilt. There is a Norman doorway in the east wall. At Woodbury there is also the small church of Holy Cross.

The author of *The Worthies of Devon*, John Prince, was born in the parish in 1643.

The name 'Axminster' has long been synonymous with carpet manufacture. The industry was founded here by Thomas Wilton in 1755. The original factory was destroyed by fire in 1826–7 and although it was rebuilt, the industry was moved to Wilton, near Salisbury, in 1835. The replacement factory of 1827, comprising a group of stone buildings, can still be seen near the town centre. Carpet-making was re-established in the locality by the Dutfield family in 1937, and still continues as Axminster Carpets.

Further reading: Dudley, Angela M.W., *The book of Axminster*, Barracuda, 1988
Berry, Les, and Gosling, Gerald, *The book of Axminster with Kilmington*, Halsgrove, 2004
Chapman, Geoffrey, *The history of Axminster to 1910*, Marwood, 1999
Local societies: Axminster Historical Society

The Axe Valley Branch of the Devonshire Association
Museum: Axminster Museum, Church Street

AXMOUTH (L6) East Devon Pop. 493 (1901: 643)

The parish of Axmouth is bordered on the west by the estuary of the River Axe and on the south by cliffs and landslips of the English Channel coast. A tributary of the Axe flows westwards through the north. Land rises to a level of 455 ft, with the Iron Age hill fort on Hawkesdown Hill (c.400 ft) occupying a commanding site just north-east of the village. Approach, for the 5½ miles SSW from Axminster, is by the A 358 road, continuing as the B 3172 following the crossing of the A 3052.

Axmouth has a long history. It was probably a port in Roman times at the southern end of the Fosse Way to Lincoln, which is still followed here by today's road. Saxons inhabited the area from the 7th century, and later the parish was owned by King Athelstan, Edward the Confessor, and William I. Several factors eventually caused adverse effects to the port; a shingle ridge accumulated cross the river mouth, causing silting and narrowing of the outlet. Efforts to redevelop and revive the port in the early 19th century proved unsuccessful, and then, in 1868, the branch railway from the London & South Western line was constructed to Seaton – on the west side of the estuary. This led to greater prominence for Seaton which grew into a small resort, at Axmouth's expense. A compensation was the construction, in 1877, of one of the earliest concrete bridges in the country across the mouth of the Axe. A three-span structure, of concrete cast to resemble stonework, it is scheduled as an Ancient Monument and now carries pedestrians only, a new bridge having been built on the upstream side in 1989–90 for the B 3172 road.

The church (St Michael) belonged in medieval times to the abbey of Mont St Michel. The present building dates from c.1150, and retains some of the Norman structure. It was enlarged in the 13th and 14th centuries, and the present tower was built in the 15th century. Restoration was carried out in 1889. Axmouth, Stedcombe, Bruckland, and Charton were all separate estates before 1066, and Bindon – south-east of the village – also existed before the Conquest.

The Axe estuary is rich in bird life, offering feeding grounds for migrants in passage and species that over-winter here.

Further reading: Pulman, George P.R., *The book of the Axe,* Kingsmead Reprints, 1969

AYLESBEARE (J6) East Devon Pop. 527 (1901: 225)

Aylesbeare, 7½ miles E of Exeter, lies between the A 30 and the A 3052 Exeter-Lyme Regis road and is approached from both, also from the B 3184 and B 3180 which connect the two, and by minor roads. The land rises eastwards to Aylesbeare Hill and Aylesbeare Common on the pebble-bed ridge, to altitudes of 481 ft marked by a tumulus, and to 526 ft in the south-east. A stream that rises on this high ground flows westwards through the village to join the River Clyst.

The church is of ancient foundation, the first recorded incumbent named in 1261. The present building (the Blessed Virgin Mary) dates from the 14th and 15th centuries, although the base of the tower is believed to be earlier. Evidently well cared for, the church in 2003 was undergoing a programme of renewal of its roof, and restoration of the tower.

The manor was held in early times by the Courtenays as part of the barony of Okehampton.

Further reading: Senar, Howard, *Aylesbeare, a Devon church and parish*, 1996

BAMPTON (H3) Mid Devon Pop. 1598 (1901: 1657)

Bampton, which originated in Saxon times, is a fairly large parish and small town located 6 miles N of Tiverton. The town stands at the junction of the A 396 Exe valley road from Tiverton and the B 3227 (formerly the A 361) from South Molton to Taunton. The River

Batherm flows through the town on its way to join the Exe 1½ miles downstream. In the north-west and north-east the county border with Somerset briefly forms the boundary, between these points Bampton shares a parish boundary with Morebath, marked for a stretch by the Batherm and a tributary. Bampton's western boundary is defined by the curving River Exe. The country here is dramatically undulating with many points reaching over 700 ft, and 914 ft being attained at the boundary on Bampton Down in the south-east and 947 ft and 969 ft in the north-east.

The town has a broad main street. Formerly a busy market town it also had two fairs, with great sales of cattle and sheep. The fair held on the last Thursday in October still continues, with many horses and ponies brought down from Exmoor; although the scale has diminished in recent years large numbers of people gather for the event. Bampton was also a centre of the woollen cloth industry until this declined in the early 19th century.

The River Batherm flows through the town of Bampton on its way to join the Exe.

The church (St Michael & All Angels) dates from c.1300, rebuilt and enlarged in the 15th century and restored in 1872. There is also the small church of St Petrock at the hamlet of Petton in the north-east. Shillingford, between Petton and Bampton, is another hamlet where formerly there was also a small ancient chapel, but this no longer exists. There are the remains of the motte and bailey of Bampton Castle, dating from the 12th century, on the north side of the town, to the east of the turning to Morebath. On the town's south side large quarries were worked into the 20th century.

Bampton was formerly served by the Exe Valley Railway, completed from Tiverton to Morebath in 1884. Direct travel to Exeter was also made possible when the line from the city to Tiverton was opened in the following year. The line closed in 1963.

Further reading: Francis,T.J., *A short history of Bampton,* 1991
Seward, Caroline, *The book of Bampton,* Halsgrove

BARNSTAPLE (D2) North Devon Pop. 20724 (1901: 9698)

Barnstaple, 7 miles inland from the North Devon coast, stands on the widening estuary of the River Taw. Comprising waters from both Dartmoor and Exmoor and from countless tributaries, the Taw is the only major Dartmoor river to flow in its own right to Devon's north coast, following a long course that covers half the county's breadth. At the north end of the town the Taw is joined by the Yeo, originating from the Exmoor foothills near Blackmoor Gate.

The town boundary also includes the ancient parish of Pilton to the north (apart from West Pilton) and the largely residential areas of Newport to the south and Sticklepath on the rising ground west of the Taw, each of which has its own church. The town itself lies mainly east of the river, the two sides being connected by the

The Square, Barnstaple, c.1910.
COURTESY THE BOOK OF BARNSTAPLE

16-arch Long Bridge of ancient origin. It is believed that there may have been a crossing here in Roman times or possibly earlier, probably slightly upstream. Documentary evidence exists for a bridge – perhaps partially a causeway – in the 13th century, and there are various subsequent references. The present bridge, which apparently dates from the 15th century, was widened c.1800, in the 1830s, and in the early 1960s.

Barnstaple originated in Saxon times, its name identifying it as the staple, or trading post of Bearda. Pilton was of earlier importance, having become a burh in the early 10th century before the honour was transferred to Barnstaple. This probably happened at a time that coincided with the town's early coinage of 979–1016. The borough belonged to Edward the Confessor, and at Domesday was one of four boroughs in Devon. Whether an early castle existed here is uncertain; the present 60 ft high Castle Mount more probably dates from the early 12th century, concurrently with the building of walls around the town (no longer existing).

For long regarded as the capital of north Devon, Barnstaple has for centuries been a centre of enterprise and a port, known also by its Latinised name: Barum. In medieval times exports included products of the town's considerable woollen industry. After this ended c.1600 Irish wool was brought in and distributed to places inland. Unlike Bideford, with its stronger currents, Barnstaple suffered from silting which eventually prevented access by large vessels. Nevertheless, in the 19th century timber from various overseas countries was brought in by sailing vessels to Rolle Quay at the Yeo confluence, or off-loaded at Appledore. Emigrants were often carried on outward voyages. Barnstaple's quay until the 1870s was by the Strand, and the original Exchange, re-built in the early 18th century and known as Queen Anne's Walk (now containing the Heritage Centre) marks the point where merchants agreed their deals on the Tome Stone. Subsequently trading boats used the slightly downstream Castle Quay, and Rolle Quay. Shipbuilding was important at Barnstaple at least from the 1700s to the early 20th century. Later work included the building of reinforced concrete ships under government order during the First World War, in a shipyard on the west bank. Latterly, dredging of sand and gravel continued for the local cement and building industries. Fishing has been a traditional, but declining pursuit.

Barnstaple has long been known for its potteries, and Brannams Pottery, making Barum Ware and originally in Litchdon Street, still functions on the town's outskirts at Roundswell, where terracotta ware is a speciality. Besides the timber industry, cabinet-making developed and expanded during the 19th century, the factory of Shapland & Petter on the Taw's west bank, just below the bridge, was a familiar feature until its recent re-location. Amongst the town's other industries, which included glove-making, was lace manufacture, introduced during the 19th century and involving factories. One was begun by a Mr Boden from Derby in 1825 and the part of the town around his works took on the name: Derby.

Until the mid 20th century Barnstaple had several areas of poor, congested housing. In the 1950s and '60s these were demolished and new estates built on the town's outskirts, notably on the south and east, and the town's internal road system was modernised.

Transport has, in general, seen great changes. In 1854 the London & South Western Railway reached Barnstaple, with its station on the river's west side. In 1873 a second rail connection came with the opening of the (later Great Western) line from Taunton, for which Victoria Station was built on the east. An extension from the LSWR station to Ilfracombe was opened in 1874, necessitating a curving iron bridge downstream of the Long Bridge, and a Town Station on the east bank. From here, between 1898 and 1935, the narrow gauge Lynton & Barnstaple Railway also operated. A rail link between the GWR and the first LSWR station was constructed in 1887, but this, together with the GWR line, the one to Ilfracombe, and the iron bridge, have all gone in later years. Only the service between Exeter and the station on the west remains. Meanwhile, more roads have been built, notably the North Devon Link road, opened in 1987, which bypasses Barnstaple to the south. Plans are afoot for a further town bypass with a new bridge on the downstream side, to relieve town congestion.

Barnstaple's main Anglican church (St Peter) is set in the heart of the town. Dating probably from the 13th century, it was enlarged in the 17th century and underwent changes in the 19th century. It has a twisted spire. Beside it is the 14th-century St Anne's Chapel, originally a chantry and later the grammar school; the playwright John

Gay was a pupil. Holy Trinity Church, with its tower, dates from the mid 19th century. The church at Pilton (St Mary), dating from the 13th century, was originally the church of a small priory. It contains many interesting features. St John the Baptist Church, Newport, was built in the early 20th century. The modern church of St Paul, Sticklepath, was opened in 1957.

The town has many other fine and interesting buildings. Barnstaple Pannier Market, in the town centre close to Butchers' Row, still presents a busy scene on Fridays, although the cattle market sadly closed following the foot-and-mouth epidemic of 2001. So ended a centuries-old tradition. However, another longstanding establishment, Barnstaple Fair, still exists and draws people in from far and wide when it opens on the Wednesday before 20 September each year.

Further reading: Stone, Avril, *The book of Barnstaple*, Halsgrove, 2002
Stone, Avril, *The book of Barnstaple vol 2*, Halsgrove, 2003
Lamplugh, Lois, *Barnstaple: town on the Taw*, Phillimore, 1983
Museums: Museum of North Devon
St Anne's Chapel & Old Grammar School Museum

BEAFORD (D4) Torridge Pop. 393 (1901: 428)

Beaford, 4½ miles SE of Torrington, is bordered on the west by the River Torridge and extends eastwards to include Beaford Moor. The Torrington-Exeter road (A 3124) runs through the parish and village. Beaford village is attractive, several of its houses being thatched. The church (All Saints) is of 15th-century construction, its tower rebuilt, with a small spire, c.1910. There is a Norman font.

Woodleigh (or Woolleigh), in the north-west of the parish, was a Saxon estate. The name comes from 'wolves clearing'.

The Beaford Centre (arts) is located on the western edge of the village.

Local society: Beaford Local History Group

BEAWORTHY (C6) West Devon pop. 236 (1901: 246)

Beaworthy, 8 miles WNW of Okehampton and 1 mile SE of Halwill Junction, is a parish of unusual shape, lying NW-SE and narrowing to a prominent 'waist' in the centre, where the land attains an altitude of 917 ft at Castle Cross on Broadbury Down. Earthworks at this crossroads site, now occupied by the large radio mast, are possibly Roman or Romano-British. The western boundary is closely aligned with the straight A 3079 road between Thorndon Down and Halwill Junction, a course that was also taken, with deviations, by the London & South Western Railway's route from Meldon Junction near Okehampton to Holsworthy, opened in 1879 and closed in 1966. The railway brought into being the centre still known as Halwill Junction (see HALWILL).

Beaworthy's church of St Alban contains remains of earlier, Norman, structure.

The quiet village is situated in the north of the parish, with the small 14th-century church (St Alban). The building contains remains of the earlier, Norman, structure. It was largely rebuilt in 1871. Priestacott and Patchacott are hamlets.

BEER (L7) East Devon Pop. 1381 (1901: 1118)

The parish of Beer is bounded on the south and south-east – on either side of the prominent chalk cliff of Beer Head – by the English Channel. The large and attractive village fronts on to the south-east section of coast. Land levels rise at various points to a maximum 488 ft. Road approach is from the A 3052 between Sidmouth and Lyme Regis, via the B 3174 which connects along the coast with Seaton.

Important in Beer's geology and history are the Beer Quarry Caves, which are accessed from a valley about a mile inland. The rock here, known as Beer Freestone, consists of a unique seam of fine white crystalline granular limestone, lying beneath overburden. It was worked by the Romans, who were attracted to it by its similarity to that of Rome, and employed by them in various structures. Its use continued by the Saxons and Normans in the construction of numerous churches including Exeter Cathedral, and it features in many other notable buildings elsewhere in England. Extraction continued up to the early 20th century. The extremely interesting disused workings are opened to visitors, with conducted tours.

Beer has also had two other long-standing activities: fishing and lacemaking. (Smuggling could be classed as a third, with the quarry tunnels used for storage.) Beer fishermen have always been highly able, with skills passed down in families from one generation to another. A continuing local tradition is the pulling up of all fishing boats every night on to the shingle beach. Sadly, there are now doubts as to whether this form of family fishing will survive, as numbers of men and their boats are dwindling severely. Lacemaking, done largely in the past in cottage doorways, is believed to have been introduced into Devon by Flemish refugees in the 16th century. By the end of the 17th century Beer was among several east Devon centres of the trade, but by the 19th century depression had set in. This was recognised by Queen Victoria who commissioned Beer and Branscombe lace for her wedding dress, and it has also been used in more recent royal robes. The intricate close work, hard on the eyes, produces fabric of great beauty.

Houses and cottages in the village are mainly built of either Beer stone or black flint, sometimes incorporating both. Alongside the street runs Beer Brook, a stream from three springs given to Beer by Lady Rolle – initially to carry smelly fish waste away to the sea. The Rolles succeeded the Walronds at Bovey House in 1796, the Walronds having owned it from c.1300.

The church (St Michael) dates from the late 1870s, replacing an earlier chapel. Beer was united with Seaton as a civil parish up to 1894, and ecclesiastically until 1905.

Further reading: Scott, John, and Gray, Gladys, *Out of the darkness* (re. the quarry)
Chapple, Arthur J., *Beer in time and tide*, 1987

BELSTONE (E6) West Devon Pop. 257 (1901: 236)

Belstone parish, on the northern edge of Dartmoor, is somewhat pear-shaped, the west boundary being mainly defined by the East Okement River and the east by the Taw, with the land of Belstone Common narrowing towards the apex and rising steeply southwards, to include Belstone Tor (1508 ft).

Bronze Age remains on the moor include the Nine Stones cairn circle, and other cairns, some obscured by tinners' workings. Irishman's Wall, crossing the parish moorland east-west, is relatively modern, built in the early 19th century and intended as the northern boundary of a large enclosure that was never completed, foiled by the objections and actions of the commoners.

Copper was worked in the parish in the 19th century, at the small Taw River Mine, west of the Taw on the slopes of Belstone Cleave, which closed in 1892, and Greenhill, close to the old A 30 road in the north-east.

The village itself stands fairly centrally, at 992 ft. It is accessed by minor roads from the A 30 east of Okehampton. The church (St Mary) is of ancient origin, with priests recorded from 1260. The building dates from the 13th century, restored in 1887 and re-furnished in the 20th century. The sturdy granite pillars and granite font are of the early date, the rood screen, with the figures of Christ, his mother, and St John, is a memorial to the fallen of the First World War; its woodwork is by Herbert Read of Exeter.

Further reading: Walpole, Chris and Marion, *The book of Belstone,* Priv. pub., 2002

BERE ALSTON see BERE FERRERS

BERE FERRERS (C9) West Devon Pop. 3066 (1901: 1955)

The parish of Bere Ferrers, which includes the small town of Bere Alston, is roughly triangular. Its eastern boundary is defined by the River Tavy, culminating in its entry to the Tamar at the triangle's southern apex. The Tamar forms the boundary on the west and north-west, a meandering loop forming the Hooe mini-peninsula, and another loop causing the between-rivers northern boundary to be short. Approach is from the A 390 Tavistock-Callington road, via the B 3257 and minor routes.

In the 12th century the manor was acquired by the Ferrers family whose house stood on the site of Bere Barton, near the water's edge. Close by is the church (St Andrew). The 12th-century font was probably from the original church. The present building is of 14th and 15th centuries construction, with later additions; the 14th-century east window glass is among the oldest in Devon. The church's 14th-century rebuilder, Sir William de Ferrers, endowed a collegiate church for a community comprising an archpriest, four other priests, and a deacon.

Bere Ferrers is situated at the confluence of the Rivers Tamar and Tavy.

Bere Alston, which became a borough c.1300 with a market, is the busiest part of the parish and has its own church (Holy Trinity), built in 1848.

Mining was important in past centuries. Silver-lead lodes running north-south were worked at times from the late 13th century to the 1880s. Smelting was done locally, mainly at Weir Quay, to which in the 19th century ores from overseas were shipped up the Tamar waterway for the smelters.

Favourable conditions for early growth aid the production of fruit and other market garden crops which developed in later times. An advantage for this industry that gave swift transport to London was the establishment of a second main railway route to Plymouth in 1890, with stations at Bere Alston and Bere Ferrers. Although the main line connection from Bere Alston ceased in 1968, the parish is still served by the Tamar Valley line running from Gunnislake (Cornwall) into Plymouth.

The beautiful Tamar Valley is, in this reach, a notable area for wintering birds, including avocets.

Local society: Bere Local History Group

BERRYNARBOR (D1) North Devon Pop. 749 (1901: 589)

Berrynarbor borders on North Devon's Bristol Channel coastline between Watermouth and Sandy Bay, and extends south to include the hilly country that rises to 886 ft on Berry Down, with the steep-sided Sterridge Valley. Numerous tumuli on Berry Down are an indication of early habitation. Berry, in the name, was acquired from the Berry family by whom the manor was held from the 13th to the 18th century; they built their manor house close to the church c.1450.

The church (St Peter), which includes elements from the 12th and 13th centuries, was mainly constructed in the 15th century. Surprisingly at this distance, the internal structure includes stone from Beer Quarries in east Devon, which must have entailed a rather long overland journey, or, more probably, sea voyage. East Hagginton was a Domesday manor. Watermouth Castle was built in the early 19th century in Gothic style.

The parish is served in the north by the A 399 coastal road between Ilfracombe and Blackmoor Gate, and east-west in the south by the A 3123.

BERRY POMEROY (G9) South Hams Pop. 973 (1901: 1193)

Berry Pomeroy lies immediately E of Totnes, and extends from the broadening River Dart, in the south, northwards to the boundary with Ipplepen. From the Dart the land rises steeply to a hill of 338 ft; farther north the land is more gently undulating, but reaches 400 ft north-east of the village. The A 385 road from Totnes to Paignton (4 miles distant) passes through from west to east, just south of the village. The church (St Mary) was rebuilt in the 15th century and later further reconstructed. It has a very fine screen. In addition the village still has its manor house, church house, tithe barn, and pond.

In the centre of the parish, in a wooded setting high above the Gatcombe Brook, are the impressive remains of Berry Pomeroy Castle. The parish was anciently owned by the de la Pomerai family, but there is no evidence for a castle here before a member of that family built one on this site in the 14th century. The castle that resulted was more of a grand residence than a defence. In 1548 the manor was sold to the Seymours, the family of the Dukes of Somerset by whom it is still owned. This was the family of Jane Seymour, third wife of Henry VIII, and of her brother Edward, Lord Protector following Henry's death, during the minority of King Edward VI. It was probably the Lord Protector's son who, in the 16th century, built the house whose ruins stand within the courtyard. The family lived here for some generations, during which William, Prince of Orange, was entertained following a Parliamentary meeting held in a house at Longcombe, in the parish. By the late 17th century Berry Castle had been abandoned as a dwelling and was falling into decay. Since 1977 it has been in the care of English Heritage.

Further reading: Seymour, Deryck, *Berry Pomeroy Castle*, 1982

BICKINGTON (G8) Teignbridge Pop. 311 (1901: 215)

Bickington general view, c.1962.
COURTESY THE BOOK OF BICKINGTON

The hilly parish of Bickington, 15 miles SSW of Exeter and 4½ miles W of Newton Abbot, is situated on the south-eastern fringe of Dartmoor National Park on the old A 38 road, with the modern expressway running close and almost parallel to the north of the former route. The village is set nearby on the south-west, on the ancient pre-turnpike road. The east-flowing River Lemon passes through the parish, with the land rising fairly steeply to north and south.

The church (St Mary the Virgin) dates from the 15th century. It stands in the village, its tower a familiar landmark to travellers. Bickington's civil and ecclesiastical boundaries do not fully coincide – the ecclesiastical parish is slightly the larger, with extended areas on the north-east and south-west.

Besides farming, other occupations have been followed by Bickington people, in particular work in the woollen industry. Bickington Mill, in the valley, was powered by water conveyed in a leat from the River Lemon. It ceased producing cloth in 1857 and a few years later was converted for making flock from rags, which continued until the Second World War. The building was demolished in 1953. There was also a bone mill at Chipley, as well as a flour mill at Lemonford. Small limestone quarries were operated in the parish.

Further reading: Hands, Stuart, *The book of Bickington*, Halsgrove, 2000

BICKLEIGH (near Plymouth) (D9) South Hams Pop. 4312 (1901: 296)

Bickleigh's Ham Green viaduct, on the former Plymouth-Tavistock railway line, is now a cycle track. Piers that carried the 1858 structure remain.

Bordering the north of Plymouth, Bickleigh is bounded on the east by the River Plym in its wooded valley, and on the west by the lower Tavy to its confluence with the Tamar, the latter as a result of boundary changes in 1974 in which Bickleigh absorbed the rural part of Tamerton Foliot. To the north the parish meets the boundary with Buckland Monachorum at the beginning of Roborough Down. The A 386 Plymouth-Tavistock road runs north through the parish, with Bickleigh village a mile to its east and Roborough village bypassed. The northern area is included in Dartmoor National Park. The southern part now has residential and industrial developments, while, just east of Bickleigh village, are the Bickleigh Barracks of 42 Commando Royal Marines. Also in the parish is the route of the former GWR railway from Plymouth to Tavistock, opened in 1859 as the South Devon & Tavistock Railway. It closed in 1962 and is now a cycle way.

The church (St Mary the Virgin) is of ancient foundation. There was a church on the site in 1288, the manor having been given to Buckland Abbey in 1278. A vicar was recorded in 1546. The tower dates from the 15th century, the main building being rebuilt and restored in the 19th century. There is a Norman font which was unearthed in the churchyard in 1909, as well as the one in current use which dates from 1589. In 1963 the patrons, Lord and Lady Roborough, gave a new east window, a modern design depicting 'Resurrection' by Edward Payne, and also the reredos, granite altar, sanctuary paving, and granite communion 'rails'. There is also the church of St Anne at Glenholt.

There was a quay at Maristow, on the Tavy, in the 13th century; the Maristow estate is in the hands of Lord Roborough. Warleigh, close to Warleigh Point, where the Tavy joins the Tamar, was named in the 12th century when lived in by Sampson Foliot. A viaduct carries the Tamar Valley Railway across the Tavy at this point.

BICKLEIGH (near Tiverton) (H5) Mid Devon Pop. 239 (1901: 207)

Ancient Bickleigh Bridge carries the A 396 Exeter-Tiverton road over the River Exe.

Bickleigh is a somewhat T-shaped parish, narrow in the south and widening in the north. It extends on either side of the beautiful Exe valley, 4 miles S of Tiverton. The A 396 Exeter-Tiverton road passes through, crossing the river by the 5-arched Bickleigh Bridge, built in the 1630s and widened in 1772. Land rises on the west to 440 ft and on the east to 550 ft.

The village stands on the hillside east of the river. The church (St Mary), which dates from the 14th century, was largely rebuilt in 1848; a 12th-century doorway and font remain from earlier. Bickleigh Castle, on the west bank of the Exe, was actually a fortified and moated manor house, dating from the 12th century when it was the home of the Bickleighs. The house was mainly rebuilt after passing to the Courtenays in the early 15th century, although there are remains of the earlier structure including a small chapel. The fine early 15th-century gatehouse was reconstructed in the 17th century by the then owners, the Carews. After years as a farmhouse it was restored in the 20th century.

A noted Bickleigh character of the past was Bampfield Moore Carew, son of the rector in the early 18th century who ran away and became a gypsy – and eventually their 'king'. He was transported to Americas but eventually returned to England and joined Prince Charles Edward's army in 1745, before settling back at Bickleigh where he died in 1758.

The former Exe Valley Railway passed through the parish. Opened from Exeter to Tiverton in 1885 it had a station at Bickleigh, just north of the bridge. The station was, however, named for Cadeleigh to save confusion with Bickleigh near Plymouth. There was also a halt at Burn, close to the Exe 2 miles to the south. The line closed in 1963. Near Bickleigh Mill, where 'Devonshire Centre' offers attractions for visitors, a half-mile stretch of the track has been restored at the Devon Railway Centre, on which a small steam-driven train is operated.

BICTON (J7) East Devon Pop. 280

The small parish of Bicton, which lies along the northern border of East Budleigh, 10 miles SE of Exeter, is approached by the B 3178 road from the A 3052. It predominantly comprises Bicton Park, home for generations of the Rolle family, with Bicton Common on the east. The present impressive house, which dates from the 18th century, is now an agricultural college. The park and very fine gardens, with other attractions, are open to the public.

The present church (St Mary) was built in 1850. The ruins of the earlier church, including the tower, are nearby, converted to a Rolle family mausoleum. The parish is united ecclesiastically with All Saints, East Budleigh.

BIDEFORD (C3) Torridge Pop. 14,407 (1901: 8754)

The ancient port of Bideford stands astride the tidal north-flowing River Torridge as it widens to join the sea, its west and east banks connected by the 24-arch Long Bridge. The first bridge on this site, of wood, is believed to have been built in the later years of the 13th century, before which the crossing was by a ford slightly upstream, which reputedly gave the place its name 'by the ford'. In the late 1530s the first stone bridge was built, partly enclosing the earlier wooden structure, the variations in the size of the arches being accounted for by the differences in lengths of timber originally used. Repairs and widening of the bridge were carried out at stages during succeeding years, the latest such major operation being in 1925. In 1967 the bridge suffered a collapse at the western end, necessitating repairs and causing a spell of extreme inconvenience to traffic. In 1987 the new downstream high level Torridge Bridge was constructed to carry the A 39 road. Hills rise on either side of the river, up which the town has developed over the centuries, with the main town area on the west and the part known as East-the-Water on the east.

Bideford was given by William II to the Grenvilles, and the family held great influence until the mid 18th century. In the 13th century Bideford became a borough,

Bideford's ancient 24-arch Long Bridge. The modern Torridge Bridge can be glimpsed on the right.

The 100 ft Kathleen & May, *the last schooner to operate from a British port, is now moored at Bideford.*

and was granted a market and fair. Overshadowed as a port by Barnstaple in earlier times, from the reign of Elizabeth I Bideford's overseas trade gained in importance, boosted by Sir Richard Grenville's colonisation of Virginia and Carolina, which opened up trade in tobacco and other products with America that continued for 200 years. Grenville sailed in his ship the *Revenge* with Drake in his pursuit of the Spanish Armada and was mortally wounded in 1591. The tobacco trade with Virginia and Maryland reached its height in the early 18th century, surpassing Barnstaple's trade and bringing much wealth to the town. Irish wool, and salted cod from Newfoundland, were among other goods brought in.

The original church (St Mary) was built on the site of a Saxon church in the 13th century. In the 19th century, the structure having become dangerous, it was mainly demolished and rebuilt, with just the earlier tower and Norman font remaining.

Bideford Quay, on the west bank, certainly existed from 1619, and probably earlier. It was widened in the early 20th century and in 2002–3 underwent further constructional work designed to obviate flooding during exceptionally high tides.

The town has several fine houses dating from the trade boom of the early 18th century, notably merchants' houses in Bridgeland Street, and another that became the Royal Hotel in East-the-Water (where Charles Kingsley is believed to have written part of Westward Ho!). Kingsley's statue stands on the river's west side, at the north end of the Quay.

During the 19th century Bideford's port activities revived. Many emigrants sailed out from the Torridge to settle in America. Boat building and repairing were thriving industries on East-the-Water quays, where other commerce also developed. Such trade has, however, greatly declined in later years, particularly since the closure of the railway which served Bideford from 1855 until the late 1900s, with its station on the east bank. Most of the formerly busy area on the east has been redeveloped, with the remaining trade concentrated on the west bank's Town Quay. Exports are now mainly of ball clay brought here from the works at Meeth and Peters Marland and destined for the potteries of Spain, Finland and other continental countries. Small quantities of fertilisers are brought in. A few fishing boats also operate from Bideford. Of marine historical interest is the 100 ft schooner *Kathleen & May*, moored now on the Torridge's east bank, just below the bridge. Formerly involved in the coastal trade, she was the last merchant schooner to operate from a British port; visitors are welcome and boarding is possible at certain times.

Bideford had potteries from medieval times until the early 20th century, making a variety of products from floor tiles to jugs, mugs, bowls, and plates. Another past item of interest was the narrow gauge Bideford, Westward Ho! & Appledore Railway, which started on Bideford Quay and was in operation from 1901–1917. Various light industries have been established in more recent times, and the town is a centre for holidaymakers.

Further reading:	Grant, Alison, *The book of Bideford*, Barracuda Books, 1987
	Fielder, Duncan, *A history of Bideford*, Phillimore, 1985
	Christie, Peter and Grant, Alison, *The book of Bideford*, Halsgrove, forthcoming
Local societies:	Bideford Community Archive
	Bideford Branch of the Devonshire Association
Museum:	Burton Art Gallery and Museum, Kingsley Road

BIGBURY (E11) South Hams Pop. 582 (1901: 260)

Bigbury parish includes a short length of sea coast, and the west side of the Avon mouth and estuary from which it extends northward. The land is hilly throughout, rising to c.400 ft. Approach is from the A 379 Plymouth-Kingsbridge road and the B 3392. The old village is located fairly centrally, 4½ miles in direct distance WNW of Kingsbridge and 13 miles ESE of Plymouth. To its north-west is the hamlet of St Ann's Chapel, which had an ancient chapel near a holy well. The resort village known as Bigbury-on-Sea is on the coast, closely opposite Burgh Island from which the parish probably derived its name. There was formerly a fishermen's chapel here, dedicated to St Michael, but no longer existing.

Bigbury church (St Lawrence) is of early origin, the present building with its tower and short spire dating from the 15th century. By the mid 19th century it had become somewhat ruinous, and was largely rebuilt in 1872.

BISHOPS NYMPTON (F3) North Devon Pop. 932 (1901: 893)

The large parish of Bishops Nympton, centred 3 miles SE of South Molton, is bounded on the west by the River Mole and on the south by a tributary, the Crooked Oak Brook. The River Yeo, which briefly defines the boundary on the east, flows westwards through the parish to join the Mole. The parish owes its name to having been an estate of the bishops of Exeter.

The church (St Mary the Virgin) is a long building of 15th-century construction. The main body was restored in 1869 and the tower in 1877. There is a Norman font. Incumbents date from 1207.

Ash Mill, on the Crooked Oak, Bish Mill on the Yeo, and Newtown which developed on the former main road to Taunton, are hamlets. The Lower Mole Mill, on the South Molton parish boundary, was used for wood, and later corn. (Now residential.)

The A 361 North Devon Link road, constructed in the 1980s, runs through the parish. In former times Bishops Nympton was served by the railway from Taunton to Barnstaple, opened in 1873 and closed in 1965, sharing its station, 2½ miles NE of the village, with Molland.

BISHOPS TAWTON (D2) North Devon Pop. 1176 (1901: 2632)

Bishops Tawton parish lies S of Barnstaple on the east bank of the River Taw, which forms the western boundary. The A 377 road from Exeter, crossing the river at New Bridge (the present bridge replaces a 14th-century structure), enters the parish in the south, and bypasses the village street and square, in its final stretch before joining the A 39 and A 361 North Devon Link road. The railway also passes briefly along the parish edge before reaching Barnstaple.

The northern section of the parish is largely suburbanised, as Barnstaple has extended. Southwards, however, the character is distinctly rural and agricultural. Just south of the village is Codden Hill, rising to 630 ft, a familiar landmark that is visible for some miles.

In medieval times Bishops Tawton belonged to the bishops of Exeter, who enjoyed great wealth and had a palace here. Remains of it can be seen near the church. The present church (St John the Baptist), which has a medieval spire, dates from the 14th century, restored in the 1860s and undergoing further remedial work in 2003. There is an Anglican chapel at Herner, built in 1888.

Hall, in the south of the parish – the present house was built in the 1840s to replace an older one – was the home of the Hall family before 1461 when it passed through marriage to a branch of the Chichesters. Little Pill, just north of the village, was a mansion in the 14th century.

An ancient doorway in the west wall of the church dates from c.1138, but the surrounding decorative work is older and may be of pre-Christian origin.

BISHOPSTEIGNTON (H8) Teignbridge Pop. 2423 (1901: 1076)

Bishopsteignton is a triangular-shaped parish, with its base, or southern boundary, defined by the northern shoreline of the Teign estuary. The village is in the south, 3½ miles ENE of Newton Abbot and 2 miles W of Teignmouth. Land levels rise northwards, to 811 ft on Little Haldon in the east (where a tumulus indicates early human presence) and to 764 ft at the northern apex on the south-eastern extremity of the Haldon Hills. The A 381 Teignmouth-Newton Abbot road runs east-west through the south of the parish, as does the main railway, closely following the shore. The village is situated just north of the A 381, approached by minor roads which continue as a network northwards. Luton is a small village towards the north, whose church (St John) is united ecclesiastically with Ideford.

The bishops of Exeter owned Bishopsteignton from before the Norman Conquest (hence the name). It was one of the richest manors, with a palace sited north-east of today's village. The church (St John the Baptist) dates from the 15th century but was largely rebuilt in 1815 when the tower, formerly central, was rebuilt at the west end.

An ancient doorway on the south side of the west wall dates from c.1138, but the surrounding decorative work is older and indicates earlier influence from Celtic or possibly pre-Christian times. To the west of the church, above the churchyard, are remains of a sanctuary chapel dedicated by Bishop Grandisson in the 14th century to provide refuge for felons who had accepted life banishment, where they might shelter on their way from Exeter to sail from Teignmouth.

BITTADON (D1) North Devon Pop. 45 (1901: 54)

The small parish of Bittadon lies E of the old Barnstaple-Ilfracombe road (B 3230), 5 miles N of Barnstaple and 4 miles S of the coast. The land rises to 750 ft, and tumuli in the north indicate prehistoric habitation.

There is no actual village. The little church (St Peter) is remotely situated near farms. It is of uncertain date, rebuilt in the 1880s, well-kept, and evidently cherished. It contains a 13th-century font.

The church has a Norman font and Jacobean pulpit.

BLACKAWTON (G10) South Hams Pop. 647 (1901: 946)

Blackawton is located 4½ miles W of Dartmouth and 6 miles NE of Kingsbridge, served entirely by minor roads that extend from those which connect the two towns. The large village is, therefore, somewhat remote. The land is hilly, much of it in the 400-500 ft range, and reaching 647 ft just north of the village. The stream called the Gara flows through on its way to the sea at Strete.

Blackawton was one of the South Hams parishes that were evacuated of their inhabitants between December 1943 and late 1944 to enable allied forces to carry out exercises in preparation for the D-Day landings in Europe. People had just a month to remove from their homes and farms.

The church (St Michael) dates from at least as early as the 14th century, the high altar having been dedicated by Bishop Grandisson in 1333. The original church remains the core of the present building which was enlarged in the late 15th century. There is a very fine Norman font, and a Jacobean pulpit. The rood screen was removed for safe keeping during the wartime evacuation and afterwards replaced.

Local society: Blackawton & Strete History Group

BLACK TORRINGTON (C5) Torridge Pop. 509 (1901: 652)

Black Torrington is bounded on the north by the River Torridge and on the west by a tributary, the Whiteleigh Water. Elsewhere the boundary, sometimes following streams, reaches a southerly point just north of Halwill Junction. Black Torrington village is roughly in the centre, a mile N of the Hatherleigh-Holsworthy road (A 3072).

The church (St Mary) dates from Norman times, with the earliest recorded rector from 1278. The building was probably originally cruciform. Part of the original north transept remains while most of the present building dates from the 14th and 15th centuries. The granite arcades and font are late 14th century. The tower was built and the south aisle added c.1500. The chancel was rebuilt and enlarged 1901–2. The Revd John Russell, hunting parson and breeder of the Jack Russell terrier, was rector here from 1879 until his death aged 87 in 1883.

Coham House, in the north, has been the home of the Coham and Coham-Fleming families for many generations. East and West Chilla are hamlets in the south.

The church of St James the Apostle contains Norman work.

BONDLEIGH (E5) West Devon Pop. 123 (1901: 125)

Bondleigh is situated 7½ miles NE of Okehampton, between North Tawton and Winkleigh, served by minor roads from the A 3072, A 3124 and B 3220. The River Taw runs northwards through the centre of the parish, with the land rising on either side to over 500 ft of pleasant countryside.

The church (St James the Apostle) contains Norman work but is mainly the product of rebuilding c.1500, and reconstruction in the 17th century.

BOVEY TRACEY (G8) Teignbridge Pop. 6929 (1901: 2658)

Granite 'rails' of the former Haytor Granite Tramway add to the scenic interest of Bovey Tracey's Yarner Woods.

The town of Bovey Tracey, 10 miles SSE of Exeter, is situated close to the eastern edge of Dartmoor, with the northern and western lands of the parish extending to within the area of Dartmoor National Park. To the south-east is low-lying heathland, the site of a Civil War skirmish in 1646. The town is reached from the Drumbridges interchange on the A 38 expressway by the A 382 road which continues north to Moretonhampstead and the A 30. The B 3387 to Haytor and Widecombe across the moor proceeds westwards from the town.

The River Bovey flows south-eastwards through the parish. From here the land rises fairly steeply westwards to the eastern slopes of Haytor Down, reaching 1300 ft and taking in the woods of Yarner National Nature Reserve.

Bovey has a long history. It gained its full name from the de Tracey family, Henry de Tracey having created it a borough in the early 13th century. There are three Anglican churches. The church of St Peter, St Paul, and St Thomas of Canterbury, on the east side of the town, is of mainly 15th-century construction but with a 14th-century tower. The north aisle was added in 1858. Pillars are of Beer stone and there is a fine screen. Nearby is the Church House, built c.1500. The second church (St John) is on the west side; built in 1853 it is noted for mosaics which adorn the chancel. There is also the church of St Catherine at Heathfield. Elsford, Hawkmoor, Pullabrook, and Woolley were Domesday manors.

Bovey Heathfield is interesting geologically. Beds of lignite here have been mined at times from the 16th century. Deposits of pottery or ball clay, derived from decomposed moorland granite eroded and removed here by natural forces, led to the establishment of local potteries and brickworks. There was also a small copper mine in Yarner Woods, and micaceous haematite – a form of iron ore used in the manufacture of rust-resisting paint – was extracted by adits (tunnels) into the hillside on the east side of the Moretonhampstead road at Kelly, Hawkmoor, Shaptor, and Plumley. Of these, Kelly Mine, near Lustleigh, which was worked between the 1790s and 1946, has been undergoing a programme of restoration, including its dressing floors, buildings and machines, by the Kelly Mine Preservation Society.

Development of the village of Bow on the ancient road west from Crediton caused a change in the parish name from earlier Nymet Tracey.

From 1820 to the late 1850s the Haytor Granite Tramway (see ILSINGTON) was routed through the town on its way to the Stover Canal. After this closed Bovey Tracey was connected to the main railway at Newton Abbot when the Moretonhampstead line was opened in 1866, which utilised the route of the former tramway south from Bovey. Besides serving commercial needs the line became very popular and brought many visitors to the area to enjoy its natural beauties. After the Second World War traffic declined however and the line closed to passengers in 1959 and for freight a few years later.

Local society: Bovey Tracey Heritage Trust
Museum: Heritage Trust Archive at the old station

BOW (F5) Mid Devon Pop. 1093 (1901: 660)

Nymet Tracey church, in the parish now called Bow. The 14th-century porch was built probably inside a wider Norman one.

The parish of Bow was originally called Nymet Tracey. (Nymet means sacred place, or grove, and the manor earlier belonged to the de Tracey family). Nymet Tracey – still a hamlet – was the heart of the parish, with many houses here until their destruction by fire in the early 19th century, and is where the church (St Bartholomew) is situated. However, following the grant in the 13th century of a weekly market and three-day fair, commerce developed along the ancient road that runs east-west a mile to the north, and here the village of Bow subsequently became established. The road is today the A 3072, which connects Okehampton and Hatherleigh with the A 377 road and Crediton.

Standing on the hillside immediately east of the west-flowing River Yeo (tributary of the Taw), Bow is a busy village, with a high level walkway and several old houses. In one of them King Charles I spent the night of 29 July 1644 on his travels during the Civil War.

There is an unsubstantiated local tradition that the original church was built by William de Tracey as a penance for the part he played in the murder of Thomas à

Becket in 1170. Certainly there are remains in the present structure of late 12th-century building work, with enlargement in the 13th century. The chancel was rebuilt in 1859 and again in 1889. The south porch dates from the 14th century and was probably built inside a wider Norman arch. On it is an undated sundial. There is a fine font (14th century) and carved screen. The church's earlier dedication was to St Martin, changed to St Bartholomew in the late 19th century.

The site of Hillerton in the south was named in a Saxon charter of 739, and at Hilldown the Traceys are reputed to have had a castle, which was more probably a fortified manor house.

The railway line to Okehampton, which runs westwards south of the village, was constructed in 1865.

BRADFORD (C5) Torridge Pop. 359 (1901: 280)

Bradford lies mainly N of the A 3072 road between Holsworthy and Hatherleigh but also extends S in the area of Brandis Corner. The parish's eastern boundary is defined by a tortuous length of the River Torridge, and a tributary, the Whiteleigh Water. Its name suggests a 'broad ford' across the Torridge.

The church (All Saints), mainly dating from the early 14th century, retains a Norman doorway and a smallish neat font from an earlier 12th-century church. The north aisle was added in the 16th century and the tower repaired and raised. By the 19th century the church was ruinous and restorations were carried out in 1869 and 1875–89. There is open bench seating.

Bradford, Dunsland, Henscott, and Lashbrook were all mentioned in Domesday. Dunsland was home successively of the Arscotts, the Bickfords, the Cohams, and the Dickinsons. The fine house, built around 1500, was later enlarged, embellished and restored. After falling into disrepair during the Second World War it was again carefully restored, but in later years was sadly destroyed by fire.

Near Henscott, home of the Henscotts from the early 13th century until 1572, is a small roughly circular earthwork which overlooks the Torridge.

From the 12th to the 19th century Bradninch was a borough and market town.

BRADNINCH (H5) Mid Devon Pop. 1916 (1901: 1521)

Bradninch is a somewhat sprawling parish extending NW from the River Culm as it flows southwards to join the Exe, with the Culm mainly forming the south-east parish boundary. The land rises from the valley to a series of hills, achieving 850 ft on the western boundary. The railway and the M5 motorway both pass along the eastern boundary but without a station or direct access point; Bradninch is best approached either from the B 3181 road at Hele, from Cullompton, or from the A 396 via Silverton.

The former borough and market town dates from the 12th century, when it was held by Reginald, natural son of King Henry I in the earldom of Cornwall. In 1337 it became a part of the Duchy of Cornwall (property of the sovereign's eldest son) to which it still belongs. Borough status ceased in 1835. The woollen and lacemaking industries flourished here until a decline set in during the late 18th century. From 1762, however, paper mills were established at Hele, a settlement on the south, where paper manufacture continues.

The church (St Disen – or probably more properly St Denis) dates from the 15th –early 16th centuries, restored in 1845. It is noted for its beautiful screen. The manor house, originally built in 1547, reconstructed in 1712, has a fine interior. King Charles I slept here in July 1644 when it was his army's headquarters in the Civil War. In October 1645 the town was the Fairfax headquarters.

Further reading: Taylor, Anthony, *Portrait of Bradninch, a Duchy town Heritage,* 1981
Local society: Bradninch Local History Society

The ancient 'broad stone' which gave the parish of Bradstone its name.

BRADSTONE (B7) West Devon Pop. 63 (1901: 105)

The small parish of Bradstone, reached by minor roads N from the B 3362 Tavistock-Launceston road, is named from a 'broad stone' now seen incorporated in a hedge between a field and a lane above the manor farm. Its original significance is unknown, but may have marked a boundary, trading site or burial place. Rising high from the east bank of the River Tamar, and including the crossing point of the river by Greystone (formerly Greyston) Bridge – a 14th-century structure built on the site of an earlier one – the parish was certainly in a strategic position in times when the Saxons were pressing Celts back across the Tamar.

Before the Norman Conquest Bradstone belonged to Godwin, Earl of Wessex, and his son Harold. By 1085, as recorded in Domesday, it was held by Baldwin, a Norman sheriff and lord of Okehampton Castle, who received it from William I. Later it passed to a succession of families, including the Cloberrys from the late 14th to mid 18th centuries.

The church, dedicated to St Nonna – a Celtic saint, mother of St David – dates from the 13th century, the tower and north aisle being added in the 15th and 16th centuries. It is now redundant, in the care of the Churches Conservation Trust, and the parish is united ecclesiastically with Kelly. The manor house, near the church, is currently undergoing restoration. Its oldest fabric dates from the 16th century, with further work in the 17th and early 18th centuries. The fine gatehouse was built in 1601. Behind the house is an extensive range of farm buildings, including a 17th-century stable bearing signs of earlier work. The others date from the 19th century.

The gatehouse of Bradstone Manor was built in 1601.

BRADWORTHY (B4) Torridge Pop. 1082 (1901: 847)

The large and somewhat remote parish of Bradworthy, 7 miles N of Holsworthy, consists of moderately high, fairly level country that rises to over 700 ft. Its slight valleys are mainly along the borders. These are defined by the infant River Tamar on the west, the early stage of the Torridge in the north, and a short length of the Waldon (which rises in the parish) in the south-east. Elsewhere the boundary passes over land, in some cases following one or other of the small streams with which Bradworthy abounds.

Bradworthy's village square is one of the largest in the Westcountry.

The occurrence of prehistoric tumuli (burial mounds) suggests inhabitation from early times, and the prevalence of numerous small hamlets and the central village with its generous large square (one of the largest in the Westcountry) are indications of Saxon occupation. The settlement is believed to date from c.720. There were several Domesday estates: Alfardisworthy, Ash, Brexworthy, Horton, Instaple, and Kimworthy, and the parish has numerous other farms of early date. Much of the farmland is reclaimed moor, which tends to waterlog in winter and to dry out in summer. Generally, however, the parish has a pleasing ambience, still somewhat free from modern hustle, where one can experience a kind of wild quietness and the proximity of natural elements. Tamar Lake, at Alfardisworthy, on the parish's western border, originally the reservoir for the Bude Canal, is a particularly delightful location for wildlife.

The 16th-century church (St John the Baptist) stands near the Square. The font, dated at around 1200, is suggestive of an earlier church on the site. Apart from a small south transept and a small bay opposite on the north, the church is rectangular with no narrowing at the chancel, and no chancel step. In fact the nave aisle appears to slope very slightly down towards the east end.

Further reading: Cecil T. Collacott – various small works on Bradworthy
Local society: Bradworthy Local History Society

BRAMPFORD SPEKE (H6) East Devon Pop. 307 (1901: 374)

With its village 4 miles N of the centre of Exeter, Brampford Speke lies mainly to the west of the River Exe, although the river is not a rigid boundary. It may be approached by a minor road which leads off the A 377 road to Barnstaple ¼ mile past Cowley Bridge. In past times the village had a halt on the Exe Valley railway which opened in 1885 and closed in 1963.

The area has a long recorded history. Barrows in the north indicate the presence in the hills of a Bronze Age population. Written evidence exists from 739AD, when the area featured in a gift to the bishops of Sherborne. In 944 the area of Brentefordland (eventually Brampford – 'the ford by the brambles') which at this time also included

Upton Pyne, was sold by Edmund, King of Wessex, to Athelstan, Earl of East Anglia. The estate further changed hands in Saxon times and after the Norman Conquest during which it was divided into separate parishes. From c.1200 until 1709 it was held by the Spekes, and subsequently by other families and eventually the Northcotes.

The village is pleasant, with buildings in cob and thatch. The church (St Peter) originates from the 12th century when it was given to the monks of Exeter's St Nicholas Priory. The early church was extended in the 13th century and largely rebuilt in the 15th century. In the mid 19th century it was enlarged and, except for the tower, again rebuilt.

In 1847 a matter of contention arose when the patron appointed the Revd George Gorham to the living. Bishop Philpotts of Exeter refused to institute him because Gorham did not hold to the doctrine of baptismal regeneration. The case was taken to the Dean of Arches Court, and, on appeal, to the Privy Council. In the end the bishop was over-ruled and Gorham instituted.

Further reading: Orme, Nicholas, 'The history of Brampford Speke', *Transactions of the Devonshire Association,* 121, 1989. (Professor Orme is the author also of the brief Guide to St Peter's Church, Brampford Speke.)

BRANSCOMBE (K7) East Devon Pop. 527 (1901: 627)

The attractive parish of Branscombe, 4 miles E of Sidmouth and 2½ miles W of Beer, is bounded on the south by the English Channel coast, with cliffs that have been subject to landslips at various times. Such has been the erosion that part of Berry Camp, a defensible enclosure believed to date from the 1st millennium BC, has over years tumbled from the cliff top. Extending inland, on the eastern side, is the gentle combe with a stream that flows into the sea at Branscombe Mouth. The name may be due to the possibility of Brandwell, a local figure, having been a patron saint.

The northern boundary is marked by the A 3052 road, from which various minor routes lead south. There is no actual village, but a series of hamlets and houses located along the various routes. The church (St Winifred) is situated in the south. Cruciform, it includes traces of a Saxon building, the main structure being Norman, with later additons and alterations. It has a three-decker pulpit.

The parish evidently gave its name to the Branscombe family, whose home until the late 14th century was Edge Barton, 1½ miles inland on the western slopes of the combe. Walter Bronescombe, Bishop of Exeter 1258–80, was one of its notable members. The Branscombes were followed at Edge Barton by the Wadhams, of whom Nicholas Wadham was the founder of Wadham College, Oxford. Hole, slightly nearer the sea, dating from the 13th century, was the home until the 17th century of the Holcombs.

Branscombe was one of the places noted in the past for its lacemaking. At a time when the trade was facing depression Queen Victoria commissioned lace from Branscombe and Beer for her wedding dress.

Further reading: Butters, F.C., *Branscombe: the parish and the church*, 1970
Local Society: Branscombe Project Group

BRATTON CLOVELLY (C6) West Devon Pop. 399 (1901: 499)

Bratton Clovelly's former National School, with the church of St Mary.

Bratton Clovelly, 11 miles N of Tavistock and 8 miles WSW of Okehampton, is bounded by the River Thrushel to the south, and adjoins the parishes of Germansweek, Beaworthy, and Sourton in the west, north and east respectively, with land rising northwards to 915 ft at Castle Cross on the Okehampton-Holsworthy road (A 3079).

The impressive church (St Mary) is believed to have been built in 1375. Signs of mural paintings can be seen on the internal north wall and there is a fine Norman font.

The name 'Breazle' of a stream and farms is an example of Saxon significance. Guscott was a Domesday manor. 'Clovelly' derives from the Clavilles, 13th-century holders of the manor of Bratton. Chimsworthy farmhouse is mainly Elizabethan.

BRATTON FLEMING (E2) North Devon Pop. 942 (1901: 511)

Chelfham viaduct, on Bratton Fleming's southern boundary, carried the narrow gauge Lynton & Barnstaple Railway.

Bratton Fleming parish, which narrows towards the west, is almost entirely bounded by streams: on west and north by the River Yeo, by the Stoke Rivers Water in the south, and the River Bray on the east. The village, 6 miles ENE of Barnstaple and served by an unclassified road from Barnstaple to the A 399, occupies a hillside position, with the land rising from c.600 ft at the south-west end of the village street to 900 ft at the other end, a mile to the north-east.

The church (St Peter) is of early origin, its first recorded rector named in 1212. The present building dates from the 15th century, largely rebuilt 1855–61. There is a north aisle. The Fleming in the name was that of the early owning family whose seat was at Chimwell (now Chumhill). Benton and Haxton were Domesday manors. Several tumuli on the east side – on Bratton Down and Berry Hill where the land rises to over 1000 ft – are evidence of early human habitation.

The route of the former narrow-gauge Lynton & Barnstaple Railway, opened in 1898 and closed in 1935, passes through the parish, in which there was a station. Restoration is in progress on sections of the line (there is a visitor centre at Woody Bay Station). This work has included a major operation, completed in 2000, on the 390 ft long, 72 ft high, eight-arched Chelfham viaduct across the Stoke Rivers valley in the south-west of the parish.

BRAUNTON (C2) North Devon Pop. 7510 (1901: 2135)

Braunton's Great Field is one of very few remaining examples in England of the ancient open field system of cultivation.

The large parish of Braunton is one of widely varying character in its topography, with many features that are of considerable interest.

Located on the north side of the Taw estuary, the parish's south-west sector consists extensively of mud-flats, sand-dunes, and marshes, progressing inland to soils of high fertility. In the north-west the land rises steeply to 518 ft on Saunton Down, from where one of Devon' finest views – southwards across Barnstaple-Bideford Bay – can be enjoyed. Inland from the large village of Braunton the terrain changes again, with green valleys and hills ascending to 780 ft on the Metcombe Down boundary with Marwood.

Situated beside the river Caen as it flows from the north to the estuary, Braunton has a long history. Its name originates from St Brannoc, a Celtic saint of whom little is known. He is believed to have been an abbot and confessor, and he was clearly associated with a minster that could have been founded here as early as the 6th century. Charters of 867 and 973 refer to the settlement in various spellings of 'Brannoc's minster'. Later the name became Brannockstowne, and eventually Braunton. The 13th-century church, with its tower and small spire, enhanced c.1500, is dedicated to St Brannock (or Brannoc), whose remains are reputed to repose below the high altar. Sadly, in 2003 the church suffered a severe fire due to arson, necessitating costly restoration. There is also the church of St Anne at Saunton.

Braunton Great Field is one of very few remaining examples in England of the ancient open field system of cultivation. The Anglo-Saxon system in which villagers had their communal fields of one-acre strips generally gave way in Devon to small hedged fields long before the Parliamentary Enclosures of the 18th century. Braunton was a royal manor until the 13th century, when portions were given away to other lords causing local divisiveness. With village farms having scattered strips in the open field, as well as grazing entitlement on Braunton Marsh and Down, situations were often complicated, and it is probably due to this diversity of ownership that the system remained intact. In modern times the number of strips – divided by unploughed banks known as landscores – has decreased due to interchanges and amalgamations, but the field's historical and archaeological value is now recognised country-wide as an outstanding feature of agrarian history.

The long and attractive beach of Saunton Sands is backed by the broad area of great ecological importance known as Braunton Burrows, which narrows southwards to Crow Point jutting into the estuary. In 2002 Braunton Burrows was officially named as Britain's first biosphere reserve, an area of outstanding environmental and scientific importance, by the United Nations Organisation for Education, Science and Culture (UNESCO), thus giving it World Heritage status.

Braunton has grown considerably in recent years, largely as a residential place for Barnstaple commuters, but many interesting buildings are retained in the village and in outlying areas in the long-established hamlets of Saunton, Ash, Beer Charter, Buckland, Fairlynch, Incledon, Lobb, and Luscott. The ruin of ancient St Michael's chapel surmounts Chapel Hill, where a look-out was kept and prayers said for seafarers, and, somewhere beneath the sands of the burrows are remains of the chapel of St Anne, possibly near the lighthouse at the point of the former way across the estuary to Appledore. Saunton's small church, built in the early 20th century, was given the same dedication.

Today's Barnstaple-Ilfracombe road (A 361) passes through Braunton, where the B 3231 branches off as the coast road to Saunton and Croyde. From 1874 until 1970 the railway also passed through, with a level crossing in the main street, and a station.

Further reading: Grant, Nicholas, 'The lost life of St Brannoc of Braunton' *The Devon Historian 65,* October 2002
Museum: Braunton & District Museum, Church Street

BRAYFORD (E2) North Devon
Pop. 353 (1901: High Bray 219, Charles 220)

Brayford is a recently created civil parish combining the two ecclesiastical parishes of High Bray and Charles, which stand to the east and west respectively of the River Bray, and off the A 399 road, 6 miles NNW of South Molton. Both villages are situated at high levels of between 600 and 700 ft. High Bray occupies a summit position while Charles is approached by a short but steep minor road.

The village of Brayford, with its large quarries, lies in the valley, at a point in the north where the tortuous wooded route begins to broaden and rise towards downland of the type which forms the northern area of High Bray, where altitudes rise to 1564 ft on the boundary with Challacombe. Several prehistoric tumuli occur in the northern section, on Bray Common, Fullaford Down, and Whitefield Down. The Devon-Somerset county border forms the boundary on the east, and a tributary of the Bray that on the south-east. To the west, on Mockham Down, in the northern area of Charles, is a large oval earthwork, probably a small Iron Age hill fort.

The church at Charles (St John the Baptist) was rebuilt in 1875. The author R.D. Blackmore wrote much of his book *Lorna Doone* while staying here with his uncle who was the rector in the late 19th century. High Bray church (All Saints) was rebuilt in the early 16th century and restored in the late 19th century. Mockham Farm, in the west, was a Domesday estate, as were Gratton and Whitefield in the east; Maxworthy existed from c.1100.

BRENDON (F1) North Devon Pop. 159 (1901: 262)

The large, roughly square parish of Brendon is bordered on east and south by the Somerset county boundary, in the north by the East Lyn River, and on the west by the Hoaroak Water. The B 3223 Lynton-Simonsbath road runs southwards through the west of the parish, and an unclassified road from this follows the deep East Lyn valley – in which the village is situated – and connects east with the A 39.

Badgworthy, Cheriton, and Lank Combe were small Domesday estates. The early church was near Cheriton, but at some time in history was replaced by the one that stands beside the road that descends into the village (St Brenden or Brendon). It was completely rebuilt and enlarged in 1873 but retains a Norman font.

The high ground in the south, where there are tumuli and hut circles, rises to 1390 ft on Brendon Common.

BRENTOR (C7) West Devon Pop. 423 (1901: 105)

Brentor is reached by either an unclassified road north from Tavistock, or from the A 386 Tavistock-Okehampton road, turning off at either Mary Tavy or Lydford. Covering an area of Dartmoor's western foothills, the parish is bordered by the River Burn on the east, by the Lyd in the north, and by a somewhat indirect boundary on the west.

The village centre of North Brentor was originally part of Lamerton parish, transferred to Brentor in 1880.

Brent Tor, from which the parish is named, is a prominent familiar landmark seen from many miles away, a knoll consisting of intrusive igneous rocks rising to 1130 ft, on which stands the tiny church of St Michael. This church, built initially c.1140 by Robert Giffard, using the volcanic stone of the tor, is the parish church. It is still used for certain services while the Victorian Christ Church at North Brentor is a more convenient venue for general worship.

Earthwork ramparts dating from the 1st millennium BC encircle the slopes of the tor, indicating its likely early function as a hill fort. And further archaeological investigations, carried out recently on the northern slope, have revealed considerable remains of buildings dating possibly from the 1st millennium AD.

The manor belonged to Tavistock Abbey, whose abbot in 1232 granted an annul three-day fair at Michaelmastide, to be held at the church of Brentor. At the Dissolution the manor became part of the estates granted to John Russell.

Brentor had some small manganese mines during the 19th century, one of which, on Bowden Down, later also produced ochre.

Brentor's tiny parish church of St Michael on its igneous knoll is a prominent landmark for miles around.

Further reading: Greeves, Tom, 'Was Brentor a Dark Age centre?', *Dartmoor Magazine 71*, Summer 2003
Local Society: Brentor Archive Group

BRIDESTOWE (D7) West Devon Pop. 552 (1901: 457)

(Including lands common to the parishes of Bridestowe and Sourton.)

The village of Bridestowe is situated 6 miles SW of Okehampton, on the western fringe of Dartmoor and just south of the A 30 dual carriageway. In earlier times the road to Cornwall ran through the village, until a bypass was provided in the 1970s. Then, in the 1980s, this was overtaken by the present major road. Also, the Tavistock-Okehampton road (A 386) runs south-north through the parish. Land to the west of this road is mainly agricultural, towards the boundaries with Lewtrenchard, Thrushelton and Bratton Clovelly, but to the east, in company with Sourton, the joint common lands rise to border the Forest of Dartmoor and include Great Links Tor 1924 ft.

There are Bronze Age hut circles and an enclosure on the moor, and also possible barrows on the lower levels. Earthworks in Burley Wood are signs of an Iron Age fort and enclosure, and also of a fortified Norman castle, probably dating from the 12th century. Battishill, Combebow, Ebsworthy (home of the Ebsworthys), Fernworthy, Kersford, and Way are all recorded in Domesday. The manor of Bridestowe was held in the 12th century by the Pomerai (Pomeroy) family. Later on upon the scene came Bidlake (home of the Bidlakes), Millaton (home of the Millatons), Crandford, and Leawood where dwelt the Shilstons, followed by the Calmadys and, up to current times, the Calmady Hamlyns.

Bridestowe Station, 1920s.
COURTESY THE BOOK OF BRIDESTOWE

The church (St Bridget) has records of rectors from 1259. The present building is of 15th-century construction, severely restored in the 1870s.

Bridestowe has had its share of industries. Tinning is exemplified by a streamworks near the source of the River Lyd. Later, in the latter part of the 19th century, lead and copper were mined at Wheal Fanny or Crandford mine. The London & South Western Railway was completed through the parish from Okehampton to Lydford in 1874, and in 1879 the Rattlebrook Peat Railway had a siding at Bridestowe Station from which it made the 5-mile ascent to the peatworks located just outside the parish border. There were also limestone quarries at Combebow and Watergate. Originating some centuries ago, they were worked extensively in the 19th century and the remains of kilns still exist.

Further reading: Cann, Richard, *The Book of Bridestowe*, Halsgrove, 2002

BRIDFORD (G7) Teignbridge Pop. 473 (1901: 404)

Bridford, 7 miles SW of Exeter and 4 miles E of Moretonhampstead, is located within a wide bend of the River Teign, which forms the boundary on the north and west. It is reached by minor roads from either the Teign valley road (B 3193) or the B 3212 from Exeter to Moretonhampstead. This is a parish of steep slopes and high ground. The village itself, in the south-east, is at 750 ft, and westwards altitudes rise to points at 1035 ft and 1100 ft. The land that rises from the Teign in the north is steep and deeply wooded. In the south the northern part of Kennick reservoir, constructed in 1884, falls within the parish.

The church (St Thomas à Becket) is of ancient foundation, dedicated by Bishop Bronescombe in 1259. The present building dates from the early 14th century, reconstructed c.1500. It has a very fine rood screen, dating from c.1530. Extensive work in progress on the tower is intended to correct problems and to make it waterproof, to be followed by roof renewals and other repairs.

Laployd Barton, in the south (earlier Lapflude) was the home of the Lapfludes from the early 13th century to 1523.

Lead was mined on a small scale in the parish in the 19th century, and a barytes mine was in operation on the east from 1855, or earlier, until the late 1950s. Bridford is one of the parishes situated on the granite extension east of the main Dartmoor mass, and as such comes within Dartmoor National Park. Blackingstone Quarry on the west has been worked for granite over many years.

Local society: Bridford Local History Society

BRIDGERULE (A5) Torridge Pop. 570 (1901: 375)

Bridgerule, 4 miles west of Holsworthy, is named from its ancient bridge over the River Tamar. Having earlier comprised two civil parishes, East and West Bridgerule, it is now one, the western boundary leaving the river to enclose the section on the west.

The 15th-century church (St Bridget) stands ½ mile E of the main village. It contains a Norman font and a stoup from the earlier 12th-century building. In the churchyard is the grave of the Revd Frank Hawker Kingdon, vicar here for 70 years. He died in 1958 aged 98, his wife Jessie having died in 1927. Tackbeare was a Domesday manor.

In past times the parish was served by the Holsworthy-Bude railway, and by the southward, Launceston, branch of the Bude Canal (see HOLSWORTHY).

BRIXHAM (H10) Torbay Unitary Authority (Pop. 1901: 8092)

The fishing port of Brixham is situated on the southern arm of Tor Bay, with its sheltered harbour on the arm's northern shore. Eastwards the promontory narrows to the heathland and Devonian limestone point of Berry Head, exposed to the elements of the English Channel with rocky cliffs that provide nesting sites for many seabirds. Now incorporated with its neighbours in Torbay, Brixham is approached from the Paignton side by the A 3022 road, and from the Dartmouth direction by the A 379.

The land that reaches out to sea at Berry Head has yielded varied evidence of man's early activities. There are remains of a fortress with a high rampart that is believed to date from the Iron Age, within which Roman coins have been found. Its exact extent has become somewhat confused due to construction on the site of one of the coastal forts built as defences during the Napoleonic War. And a short distance west of Berry Head, at Shoalstone Point, remains of bones and Celtic pottery have been discovered. The area is truly a peninsula as the neck of land between Broadsands Beach and Galmpton Creek on the River Dart is less than 1½ miles in direct distance, while the length of coastline between the two is nearly 20 miles.

Brixham's Saxon settlements occupied the higher ground, forming part of a Saxon estate which covered the whole of the peninsula. After the Norman Conquest however it became divided. Fishing, together with boat building and other associated activities, has been Brixham's main industry for centuries. The harbour formerly extended farther inland to what is now the town. Brixham suffered, as did other places, from the decline that followed the First World War, but recovered in mid-century as one of the country's main fishing ports with a lead in operating beam trawlers. More recently, however, falling fish stocks and European quota cuts have caused much concern. The fish quay is a focal point in the town, as it was in 1688 when William of Orange landed here; the event is marked by a statue.

Brixham has two churches. The older one (St Mary) is at Higher Brixham. It is believed to be the third on the site in this area where the Saxons settled but there are no remains from then. Foundations of the second, Norman, church have been found within those of the present building which dates from the 14th century, with a 15th-century tower. The church was enlarged in 1825 and later restored. The first reference to a vicar was in 1290. All Saints Church in Lower Brixham was built in the early 19th century, consecrated in 1824 and subsequently enlarged. The first incumbent was Henry Francis Lyte, writer of the hymn 'Abide with me'. Following severe storm damage in 1877 the church was rebuilt, carried out in Lyte's memory.

Berry Head lighthouse, 1906.
COURTESY OF THE BOOK OF BRIXHAM

From 1868 Brixham had a railway station when a 2-mile branch was opened from Churston on the Paignton-Kingswear line. Much used in its day for fish transport, it closed in 1963.

The small Berry Head lighthouse, just 15 ft tall and sited 191 ft above sea level, supplied a long-felt need when it was inaugurated in 1906. Its beam still tells seafarers that the shelter of Torbay is at hand.

Further reading: Ellis, Arthur C., *Brixham,* Brixham Museum Society, 1992
Horsley, John E., *A short history of Brixham*, Devon Books, 1988
Pearce, Frank, *The book of Brixham*, Halsgrove, 2000
Museum: Brixham Museum, Bolton Cross
Local society: Brixham Museum and History Society

BRIXTON (D10) South Hams Pop. 1207 (1901: 652)

Brixton is bordered on the west by the City of Plymouth while on the south Cofflete Creek and the Yealm estuary form the boundary, with the land between the two forming a small peninsula which terminates at Steer Point. The eastern boundary is defined by the Silverbridge Lake. The A 379 Plymouth-Kingsbridge road runs eastwards through the village and land to the north is mainly agricultural, rising in place to rather more than 300 ft.

The church (St Mary), which stands close to the road through the village, dates from the late 15th century, restored in the late 19th century. In addition to Brixton itself, Chittleburn, Halwell, Hareston, Sherford, Spriddlestone, Winston, and Wollaton were all estates named in Domesday. From the 14th to the 18th century Spriddlestone, on the west, was home to a branch of the Fortescue family.

From 1898 the Plymouth to Yealmpton branch railway ran through the parish, with a station for Brixton, and one at Steer Point. It closed in 1930 but reopened for a time during the Second World War for the benefit of people who had moved out of Plymouth to escape the bombing.

BROADCLYST (H6) East Devon Pop. 2830 (1901: 1900)

Broadclyst is a large parish of fertile and beautiful land that extends eastwards from Exeter's north-eastern boundary and borders several parishes as far as Clyst Hydon, in sight of the Blackdown Hills. The land is mainly low level in the south but rises to 539 ft on the northern boundary. The River Clyst flows southwards through the parish and close to the village, and the Culm forms the boundary on the north-west. The M5 motorway runs through the north-west of the parish as does the former A 38 (now A 3181) which passes through the village. There are woodlands in the west including those of Killerton.

The village of Broadclyst is said to have been burnt by the Danes in 1001; of more certain fact is a serious fire that occurred in 1870 which destroyed 62 dwellings. The fine church (St John the Baptist) is of ancient foundation, believed to have been rebuilt c.1400. The tower dates from the 16th century and has recently been restored.

Columbjohn was one of several farms dating from before the Norman Conquest. Held by John de Culm in the 13th century it passed to the earls of Devon who held it until 1539. Around 1600 it was bought by Sir John Acland who built a new mansion. The family lived here until after Sir Arthur Acland bought Killerton nearby.

Sir Thomas Acland rebuilt the house there in the 18th century, to which the family then moved, Columbjohn being demolished except for its Elizabethan gateway. During the Civil War Columbjohn was a garrison of the king, but later the headquarters of Fairfax when his army was at Silverton.

Among many farms that date from shortly after Domesday is Churchill, in the east, from which the Churchill family took its name in the 12th century. Another was Killerton on the west, marked by the wooded Dolbury Hill on which are earthworks believed to date from the Iron Age. The Killerton estate was bought by Edward Drewe in the 16th century. After selling to the Aclands the Drewes moved to another of their properties, at Broadhembury. In the mid 20th century Sir Richard Acland passed Killerton House and park to the National Trust, and it is now the Trust's regional centre of administration. The Anglican chapel (The Holy Evangelists) was built in 1842 to replace the earlier one at Columbjohn. A small chapel of ease (St Paul) built at Westwood, in the west of the parish in 1873, is now redundant.

Local society: Broadclyst History Society

Broadhembury – Broadhembury takes its name from the Iron Age Hembury Fort in adjacent Payhembury.

BROADHEMBURY (K5) East Devon Pop. 654 (1901: 554)

Broadhembury is a fairly large parish that straddles the A 373 Cullompton-Honiton road, approximately 5 miles from each town. The spacious and attractive village is situated a mile north of this road. It has several houses of cob and thatch, and the Drewe Arms, dating from c.1500, was possibly originally the church house. The parish name derives from the proximity of Hembury Fort (see PAYHEMBURY).

The rolling hill country rises from c.300 ft in the south-west to 897 ft on the north-west boundary and 922 ft on North Hill in the north. The River Tale flows through the parish.

The church (St Andrew) was dedicated in 1259 by Bishop Bronescombe, although there may have been an earlier structure on the site. The present fine building dates from c.1500, the tower from 1480. Rigorous restoration was carried out in 1850. In 1930, when plaster was removed, the 15th-century painting of the roof timbers was discovered. The Revd Augustus Toplady, writer of the hymn 'Rock of Ages' was vicar here 1768–78.

Brictric, Thane of Gloucester, a Saxon nobleman, was lord of the manor before the Norman Conquest. Later the manor changed hands, and from 1240 to the Dissolution belonged to Dunkeswell Abbey. Owners from 1603 for nearly three centuries were the Drewe family who established a large house at Grange, the former abbey farm, and most of the present village. The present house at Grange is largely the 17th-century original, with later alterations. The Priory, in the north-west of the parish, stands on the site of a 12th-century monastic cell of the Cluniac monastery of Montacute in Somerset.

Broadhembury church's 15th-century font.

BROADHEMPSTON (G9) Teignbridge Pop. 641 (1901: 441)

Broadhempston, 4 miles SE of Ashburton and 4 miles NNW of Totnes, and served by minor roads from the A 38, A 384, and A 381, is a hilly parish watered by the little River Hems (tributary of the Dart) which, with a tributary stream, defines the boundary on the west and south-east respectively. Land rises from the Hems to points of over 400 ft, including Beacon Hill in the north-east at 464 ft.

The village is pleasant and large, with the fine church (St Peter & St Paul) which stands on the west side. This originates from the 14th century, but the present building, except for the earlier tower and chancel, dates from the early 15th century. It was partially restored in 1877 and the screen in the early 20th century. Ecclesiastically the parish is united with Woodland, where there is the church of St John the Baptist.

Beaston, Bickerton and Forder Green are hamlets within the parish. In the time of Edward the Confessor the manor of Broadhempston, then called Hamestone, belonged to Ordulf; after the Norman Conquest it was granted by William I to his half-brother Robert, Earl of Mortaigne, in whose family it remained until the reign of John.

BROADWOODKELLY (E5) West Devon Pop. 218 (1901: 222)

Situated 7 miles NNE of Okehampton and 1½ miles SW of Winkleigh, Broadwoodkelly is fairly remote, and the village small and quiet. No main road passes through, and no river, but there is a network of minor roads and lanes from the A 3124 and several streams which flow westwards to become tributaries of the Okement and ultimately the Torridge.

The church (All Saints) dates from the 15th century; it was restored in 1868.

The manor of Broadwood was held by the Kellys from the 12th to 14th centuries. Brixton, Ingleigh, and Middlecott were named in Domesday.

BROADWOODWIDGER (C7) Torridge Pop. 548 (1901: 593)

Broadwoodwidger is a fairly large parish of open hilly farming country north of Lifton that tapers towards the north, stretching from the River Carey in the west to the Thrushel on the east, and including the lower valley of the Wolf. At this stage the waters of the Wolf have been impounded by the dam of Roadford Reservoir, completed in 1990, and now forming a large lake. (See also GERMANSWEEK).

Approached from the modern A 30 road, or its former route, by minor roads, the village stands at high level, with a village green. The church (St Nectan) is of early origin. The oldest parts – the nave and north wall – date from the 13th century. The south aisle was added in 1531, with the arcade of granite columns and arches. The sanctuary is light with clear glass, while in the west wall is a small window depicting the patron St Nicholas. The bench ends are finely carved, one bearing the date 1529, the same date as the rood screen. The large font is Norman. The church was restored in 1871 and further work carried out in more recent years. The pulpit dates from 1901. Outside, opposite the south door, is a massive rare fern-leafed beech tree, believed to be c.400 years old. It bears both fern-shaped (serrated) and normal beech leaves. Beside it is a large granite cross brought some years ago from a farm where it had been supporting an out-building.

The view from the churchyard is impressive, overlooking the Wolf valley and south-eastwards to Dartmoor. The parish includes the hamlet of Kellacott and Rexon. Downacary, Moor, and Norton were recorded in Domesday. Witherdon was a manor of the Bidlakes.

Part of Broadwoodwidger parish is now flooded by Roadford Reservoir. The dam (left) was completed in 1990.

BRUSHFORD (E5) Mid Devon Pop. 59 (1901: 59)

The tiny parish of Brushford, which lies between Winkleigh and the A 377 Exeter-Barnstaple road, is bounded on the south and east by the River Taw, here flowing north-eastwards, and a tributary. The land is undulating, rising to 578 ft.

There is no actual village. The church (St Mary), which dates from Norman times, was restored in the 1870s. It stands in a field, close to Brushford Barton Farm.

BUCKERELL (K5) East Devon Pop. 270 (1901: 240)

Buckerell, 2½ miles W of Honiton, lies to the north of the River Otter which forms the southern boundary. The village connects by minor roads to the A 30 in the south and the A 373 Honiton-Cullompton road in the north. From c.200 ft on the southern boundary land rises to the 597 ft Buckerell Knap on the north-east and to 739 ft on the boundary just south of Hembury Fort in the north-west. The parish includes the hamlet of Weston in the south-east.

The church (St Mary & St Giles) dates from at least as early as 1200 when it was in the ownership of Dunkeswell Abbey. The present building dates from the early 15th century.

BUCKFASTLEIGH (F9) Teignbridge Pop. 3661 (1901: 2781)
WEST BUCKFASTLEIGH South Hams Pop. 293

For administrative purposes the parish is divided, Buckfastleigh West having become a separate civil parish in 1894, and under present arrangements they fall into different districts. They are considered here, however, as one, corresponding to the ecclesiastical parish.

Situated on the south-eastern fringe of Dartmoor, the parish of Buckfastleigh rises for 5½ miles from the River Dart and its tributary the Mardle, to an altitude of 1690 ft at Petre's Bound Stone on the boundary with Dartmoor Forest. Rocks vary from Devonian limestone, in which occur extensive scientifically-recognised caves, to moorland granite. Much of the parish is rural, with winding lanes, streams, woodland and grassland. Farming is predominantly pastoral. Prehistoric features exist on the moor, and in Hembury Wood are substantial remains of an Iron Age hill fort. There were workings for tin on the moorland, and copper was mined, notably at Brookwood.

The ruins of Holy Trinity Parish Church, 1992. The 800-year-old church was destroyed by fire on 21 July 1992. COURTESY THE BOOK OF BUCKFASTLEIGH

For centuries the town was involved in the woollen industry. Former weavers' cottages can be seen in Chapel Street, near remaining sections of one of the local mills, which closed in 1973. Tanning, fellmongering, and engineering have been other industries. Numerous 'courts', comprising cottages that previously housed workers, are now seen as tastefully modernised dwellings.

The parish also includes the village of Buckfast, actually the older of the two settlements. Here a Benedictine abbey was founded by King Canute in 1018. Absorbed into the Cistercian order in 1147 the life of the abbey continued until the Dissolution of the Monasteries in 1539. Three and a half centuries later Benedictine monks came again to Buckfast, and in succeeding years built a new abbey church on the site. It was consecrated in 1932 and completed in 1938. Modern associated developments have followed.

Buckfastleigh's ancient parish church of Holy Trinity, sited on the hill above the town, is now a restored ruin, with its spire remaining as a noted landmark. In 1992 the church was tragically destroyed by arson. Its remains, dating from the 13th century, have been carefully conserved and are still consecrated, and freely open for visitors. Recent archaeological investigations within the remains have revealed the existence of much earlier ecclesiastical structures, which have yet to be fully assessed. A new parish church of visionary design (St Luke) has now been built down in the town, consecrated in 2002. It occupies the site of a former chapel-of-ease, also St Luke's, built in the 1890s, and is a striking example of architecture designed to meet the aspirations and needs of church life in the modern age.

Buckfastleigh acquired a railway station in 1872 when the branch from Totnes to Ashburton was opened. The line closed in 1958 but the length to Buckfastleigh was subsequently bought and re-developed as a popular tourist attraction. It now operates in the season from Buckfastleigh Station along the Dart valley to Totnes as the South Devon Railway.

Further reading: Harris, Helen, *The church on the hill*, Halsgrove, 1996
Coleman, Sandra, *The book of Buckfastleigh*, Halsgrove, 2003
There are also various works on Buckfast Abbey
Local society: The Buckfastleigh Society

BUCKLAND BREWER (C3) Torridge Pop. 777 (1901: 644)

Buckland Brewer, 4½ miles SSW of Bideford, stands between the A 39 and A 388 and is approached from the unclassified road to Bradworthy. It is a hilly parish with the village occupying a lofty position. The River Yeo, on its way to the Torridge, forms the boundary on the north-east, and a tributary, the Duntz, that on the east. The routes of the south and western boundaries are more irregular.

'Brewer' in the name relates to the Brewer or Briwere family, founders of Dunkeswell and Torre Abbeys c.1200.

The church is of Norman origin, its tower rebuilt in 1309 and the main building in the late 1800s. It has a Norman doorway. In the churchyard, adjoining the main building, is the church house, believed to have been a chapel to St Stephen, restored in 1880. The church's dedication (St Mary & St Benedict) is perhaps a reminder of the parish's association also with Tavistock's Benedictine abbey, Orleigh, in the north, having been part of an original endowment of Tavistock Abbey in the 10th century. It was, however, sold to the Dennis family c.1200. Later it was sold again to John Davie, a Bideford merchant.

Galsworthy, in the west, was a manor in Domesday, and Vielstone, in the south, a medieval manor.

BUCKLAND FILLEIGH (C5) Torridge Pop. 170 (1901: 182)

Buckland Filleigh is a small parish bounded on the west by Shebbear and on the south by Sheepwash, with Peters Marland lying to the north and Petrockstow to the east. Its name is derived from Sir Simon de Filleigh, who held it in the reign of Henry II.

A considerable proportion of the parish is occupied by the parkland and woods of Buckland House. This was owned by the Fortescues from the 15th to the 19th century, the present house being built by the twelfth and last of the line of Fortescues to live here – a Colonel Fortescue who sold the property in the 1840s.

The church (St Mary & All Saints), dating probably from the 15th century but restored, including reroofing, in the 1890s, is located in the park, near the mansion.

BUCKLAND-IN-THE-MOOR (F8) Teignbridge Pop. 94 (1901: 87)

Buckland-in-the-Moor church on Dartmoor has the words MY DEAR MOTHER on its clock face.

Buckland-in-the-Moor is a fairly small scattered parish bounded on the north and west by Widecombe, and in the south and east by Holne and Ashburton, with the boundaries defined on the west and south by the Rivers West Webburn, Webburn, and Dart. From deep woods bordering the rivers land rises north-eastwards to the open moorland of Buckland Common, with Buckland Beacon at 1282 ft. There are fine views from this point, where one of the rocks is inscribed with the Ten Commandments and other scriptural verses. The writing was done in the 1920s and re-cut in 1995.

United ecclesiastically with Ashburton, the granite church (St Peter) is ancient. Basically it dates from the late 12th century, and retains early features including the south wall of the nave, the south doorway and the font. Rebuilding and enlargement were carried out later, and the wagon roof and fine rood screen date from the 15th century. The church was restored and further adorned in the 18th century. On the outside of the tower is a clock, given in the 1930s, which has, instead of the usual numerals, the letters: MY DEAR MOTHER, and the chimes play the tune of 'All things bright and beautiful'. The village is small, but has attractive thatched granite houses.

BUCKLAND MONACHORUM (C9) West Devon Pop. 3634 (1901: 1717)

A busy station. COURTESY THE BOOK OF BUCKLAND MONACHORUM

Buckland Monachorum is bounded by the River Tavy on the west, the Walkham on the north, and the Meavy valley on the south-east. The southern boundary runs across Roborough Down. Included in the civil parish are: Yelverton – a separate ecclesiastical parish since 1935, Milton Combe, Crapstone, and Clearbrook. While the western boundary, following the deep course of the meandering lower Tavy, is mainly wooded, the central area comprises open downland, with numerous small settlements, many of them modern. The village is reached by minor roads from the A 386 between Plymouth and Tavistock.

Over the down there are signs of probable Iron Age and possibly even earlier inhabitation. Recent investigations on a northern section of Roborough Down have revealed evidence of land use that suggest considerable farming activities in medieval times, in the form of banks and likely farmstead walls.

Buckland Abbey. COURTESY THE BOOK OF BUCKLAND MONACHORUM

The name 'Buckland' derives from 'Bocland', meaning land booked by Charter. After the Norman Conquest the manor was given by William I to his niece's husband, Baldwin de Brion, and successively held by the earls of Devon. In 1275 Amicia, Countess of Devon (widow of the 7th Earl) founded the Cistercian Buckland Abbey as a monastery (hence 'Monachorum' in the name) in memory of her husband Baldwin de Redvers. After the Dissolution Buckland Abbey was sold, in 1541, to Sir Richard Grenville. In 1581 it was bought by Sir Francis Drake who was seeking a property appropriate to his recently acquired prestige. In the years following his defeat of the Spanish Armada in 1588 Drake provided Plymouth with a supply of water from

Dartmoor; the open channel of Drake's Plymouth Leat, constructed in 1591, can in places still be seen. On his death at sea in 1596 the estate was inherited by his brother Thomas, and remained in the Drake family until 1946. The National Trust now owns Buckland Abbey, where Drake's Drum, carefully preserved, is on show.

Buckland church (St Andrew) was built on the site of an earlier Saxon one around 1490. Records of rectors and vicars date from 1271. There are various interesting old buildings near it in the village, including Lady Modyford's School (1702). There is also the church of the Holy Spirit at Milton Combe, dedicated in 1878.

Developed as residential areas from the 19th century are Crapstone, Clearbrook (its first cottages established for workers at nearby mines) and Yelverton. Yelverton (from 'Elford Town') grew to the extent of needing its own church. A wooden church was opened in 1895, replaced by a stone building (St Paul) in 1912. Yelverton's Roman Catholic Church (Holy Cross) in Dousland Road, was opened in 1923.

Several mines existed in the parish in past years. Virtuous Lady Mine (reputedly named after Queen Elizabeth I), near the Walkham-Tavy confluence, produced copper between 1558 and the 1870s. Others, for copper, tin, arsenic, and lead, in the valleys and on the down, were mainly 19th-century workings.

During the Second World War Harrowbeer aerodrome for fighter aircraft was developed at Yelverton, necessitating removal of Rock Methodist Church's spire and the reduction of other buildings. The airfield closed in 1950.

Further reading: Hamilton-Leggett, Pauline, *The book of Buckland Monachorum*, Halsgrove, 2002
Gill, Crispin, *Buckland Abbey*, City of Plymouth, 1951
Gill, Crispin, *Yelverton*, Grey House Press, 1984
Rowe, Alan, *Buckland Monachorum, a west Devon down and its History*, 1999

Local society: Yelverton & District Local History Society. (Covers Buckland Monachorum, Horrabridge, Meavy, Sampford Spiney, Sheepstor and Walkhampton parishes.)

BUCKLAND-TOUT-SAINTS (F11) South Hams Pop. 178 (1901: 37)

Buckland-Tout-Saints lies immediately N of Kingsbridge on either side of the A 381 Kingsbridge-Totnes road. The village is to the east. The hilly land rises to 500 ft in the north. The parish takes its name from the Toutsaints family, holders of the manor in 1238. The church (St Peter), built on its new site in 1779, replaces an ancient chapel close to Buckland House. A pleasant building, it was restored in the 19th century. The parish is united ecclesiastically with Charleton.

Large slate quarries in the parish were worked until the late 19th century.

Further reading: Cove, Patricia, *Buckland-Tout-Saints: a parish history*, 1984
Cove, Patricia, *Buckland-Tout-Saints, parish, people and homes*, c.2000

BUDLEIGH SALTERTON (J7) East Devon Pop. 4801 (1901 with East Budleigh: 2653)

The small parish and town of Budleigh Salterton lies on the English Channel coast 4 miles E of Exmouth and on the W side of the mouth of the River Otter, S of East Budleigh of which it was a part until 1894. Originally the then village was known just as Salterton, or Salterne, because of the long tradition of salt-panning at the estuary, from at least as early as the 13th century. From the beginning of the 19th century the fishing village started to develop into a town and as a quiet watering place, with its pebble beach specially favoured by the discriminating and the retired, rather than as a 'bucket and spade' resort for families. Houses from the early years of the development still add their character to the town.

The church (St Peter) is relatively modern – built in 1893. There is also the church of St John at Knowle.

From the 400 ft West Down Beacon above the cliffs west of the town fine views can be enjoyed out over Lyme Bay, on clear days from Portland Bill to Berry Head. Budleigh Salterton was the setting for Millais in his famous painting *The boyhood of Raleigh*.

In 1897 Budleigh Salterton was reached by a branch line from the London & South Western Railway via Sidmouth Junction and Tipton St John's (sic). This was extended a further 4 miles to Exmouth in 1903. The branch was closed in the 1960s.

Further reading: Cann, Richard, *The book of Budleigh Salterton*, Halsgrove, forthcoming
Museum: Fairlynch Arts Centre and Museum, Fore Street

BULKWORTHY (B4) Torridge Pop. 83 (1901: 92)

The 15th-century church of St Michael, Bulkworthy, one of Devon's smallest parishes. The steps lead to a priest's chamber over the porch.

Bulkworthy is located on the east side of the River Torridge which forms the parish's western boundary, north of the Holsworthy-Bideford road (A 388), 2 miles west of Stibb Cross.

A tumulus (prehistoric burial mound) is evidence of early dwellers, and farming has been the continuing tradition.

The well-kept church (St Michael) was built 1414–22. There is a Norman font. There is no tower but a bell cote for two bells, dating from the early 18th century. External steps on the south side lead to a priest's chamber over the porch. Nearby stands the former large tithe barn.

BURLESCOMBE (J4) Mid Devon Pop. 911 (1901: 684)

A 19th-century representation of the Last Supper on the reredos of Burlescombe church. A tapestry version, worked in the parish for the millennium, is displayed at the east end of the north aisle.

Burlescombe village is located 8 miles ENE of Tiverton and 5 miles SW of Wellington, and immediately NW of the M5 motorway. The main railway line runs through the parish, just north of the village and south of the hamlet of Westleigh, where the large limestone quarries are a dominant feature. Consisting of Carboniferous limestone (but not of the Mendips type) the stone was used in the last century on a large scale for road building, but production is now reduced according to demand. The land is open and gently undulating, rising from c.250 ft to over 500 ft.

The interesting church (St Mary the Virgin) originates from the 14th century, although there was certainly an earlier one in the charge of the abbess of Canonsleigh Abbey (see below). The 14th-century building was centred on the nave, later extended with addition of the south aisle and, in the 15th century, the north aisle. It is built of Westleigh stone, with dressings from Beer and Ham Hill. The church's length is 77 ft – the same as the height of the tower. It contains impressive monuments to members of the Ayshford family, whose home was Ayshford, in the south-west of the parish, from the early 12th century until 1689. Ayshford, Canonsleigh, Fenacre, and Appledore were all Domesday manors. Between 1161 and 1173 a house of Austin canons was founded at Canonsleigh (south-east of the quarries). In 1284 this was passed to canonesses of the same order, and the nunnery continued until the Dissolution. There are some structural remains on private premises at Canonsleigh Farm.

The Grand Western Canal (see TIVERTON) also passed through the parish, limestone from the quarries having been the main commodity carried to Tiverton.

Local society: Canonsleigh Local History Group

BURRINGTON (E4) North Devon Pop. 538 (1901: 669)

Burrington parish rises from the west bank of the River Taw, 12 miles SSE of Barnstaple. The river forms the eastern boundary, with tributary streams defining those to north and south. The undulating land attains an altitude of 662 ft at Burrington Moor Cross, in the west of the parish. Both the Exeter-Barnstaple road (A 377) and the railway, having crossed the Taw, run within the parish near the north-east border.

The church (Holy Trinity) is of early foundation, with incumbents recorded from 1277. The present building dates from the 16th century. There is a fine granite arcade, and wagon roof with carved bosses. The rood screen is very beautiful, dating from the early 16th century. The font is Norman. Restoration was carried out in 1869.

BUTTERLEIGH (H5) Mid Devon Pop. 114 (1901: 83)

Butterleigh is a small parish standing at high level (350-625 ft) on the east side of the Exe valley, 3 miles SSE of Tiverton and 3 miles W of Cullompton, and accessible by minor roads from the A 396. The River Burn, tributary of the Exe which it joins at Burn, forms the southern boundary.

The well-kept and welcoming church is of early origin, given when newly built by Brian de Boterleigh to Exeter's St Nicholas Priory in the late 12th century. All that remains from the period is the font, the church having been rebuilt in the 14th century and dedicated in 1319. It underwent further rebuilding in the 17th century and was restored in 1861.

Cadbury's Norman font was rescued from a churchyard ditch in the 19th century, restored and replaced in the church on a floor of Tavistock stone.

CADBURY (H5) Mid Devon Pop. 136 (1901: 187)

Cadbury is located on the A 3072 Crediton-Tiverton road, 5½ miles SSW of Tiverton. The parish takes its name from Cadbury Castle, an Iron Age fortified hilltop rising to 829 ft immediately south of the A 3072. In 1086 it was given to Cada. The land here is steeply undulating and spectacularly beautiful, with fine distant views from high points.

The church (St Michael & All Angels), situated ¼ mile south of Cadbury Cross on the A 3072, dates certainly from the 12th century, in which it was given to St Nicholas Priory in Exeter. The earliest recorded date of a vicar is 1244. Ecclesiastically the parish gives the name (Cadbury) to the surrounding deanery. The present building is of mainly 15th-century construction, restored between 1840 and 1857. At that time the Norman font was rescued from the churchyard ditch, restored, and placed in its present position on a floor of Tavistock stone, and the cross – seen near the top of the churchyard – which was broken in three places at its early site beside a farm – was repaired and re-erected.

Fursdon has been the home of the Fursdon family continuously since at least as early as the 13th century. (It is, at certain times, opened to the public.) Bowley, south of the village, was a farm in Saxon times.

Further reading: Fursdon, David, *Fursdon: home of the Fursdon family*

The cross in Cadbury churchyard was broken into three pieces on its former site beside a farm until repaired and re-erected here.

CADELEIGH (H5) Mid Devon Pop. 187 (1901: 167)

Cadeleigh, in the hill country 4 miles SSW of Tiverton, is approached by a 2-mile winding road from Bickleigh on the River Exe, or from the north by other minor roads from Tiverton. The (Little) River Dart, flowing to join the Exe, and a tributary stream form the boundaries on east and north, others are mainly over land. Altitudes rise steeply, attaining 770 ft in the east.

The village is situated fairly centrally. The church (St Bartholomew) probably originated in the 12th century, rebuilt in the 15th century. The Leach monument is a huge feature in the north aisle.

In the days of the Exe Valley Railway Cadeleigh had a station outside the parish and 2 miles from the village. It was at Bickleigh, but called Cadeleigh to avoid confusion with Devon's other Bickleigh, near Plymouth.

CHAGFORD (F7) West Devon Pop. 1470 (1901: 1397)

By whichever way Chagford is approached, the traveller needs to negotiate some narrow and often twisting roads and lanes, so that care is essential to avoid head-on confrontation with an on-coming vehicle. But the effort will soon be found well worth-while, as Chagford is a most delightful, interesting and friendly small town.

Chagford is best reached by the B 3206 road, west from the A 382 which connects Whiddon Down (just off the A 30) with Moretonhampstead. Although no river runs actually through the town, the parish is blessed with them. The River Teign flows eastwards through the north, its two components – the North Teign from its origins on the moor's high blanket bog, and the smaller South Teign, from Emsworthy – having united near the ancient Holy Street mill. The River Bovey, from its moorland source, winds through the south of the parish. South of the town are the hills of Nattadon and Meldon, and westwards the land rises on Dartmoor, achieving altitudes of 1432 ft at Kestor rock on Chagford Common and 1605 ft on Water Hill where the Forest boundary is met.

Ancient occupation of the area is evident from the abundance of Bronze Age remains on the moor, comprising cairns and burial chambers, stone rows and circles, hut circles and enclosures. The Celts and Saxons have left their marks too, in place names: Kagefort, that became Chaggesford and eventually Chagford, was the Saxon name for the gorse-growing crossing of the river (now marked by Chagford Bridge), and the number of places with 'worthy' (an enclosure) in their names, also in the pattern of small fields formed where land was taken in from the waste. Many of the parish's farms are old; Middlecott, Rushford, Shapley, and Teigncombe were named in Domesday. There are numerous others in this largely unspoilt area where a sense of antiquity prevails.

The open-air swimming pool at Chagford is open during the summer for the delight of residents and visitors.

Chagford town is centred on its Square, with streets radiating from it. Nearby is the church (St Michael) which dates from 1261, succeeding, it is thought, an earlier Saxon one. Some of its structure remains in the present mainly 15th-century building. It includes a chapel dedicated to St Katherine, patron saint of tinners. Several past rectors were of the Hayter-Hames family of Chagford House who have done much for Chagford in later centuries. Methodism came to Chagford when John Wesley preached in the area in 1743; the Baptists and Bible Christians as well as Methodists have had chapels here.

Contrary to what may appear as a wholly rural character, Chagford has been notable in industrial ways. In 1305 it became one of the four Stannary Towns to which tin worked on Dartmoor was brought for the official sessions of weighing, assaying, stamping and paying of dues to the Crown before being sold. It was much involved with the woollen trade, from the times when wool was spun and woven in homes and finished in tucking mills, to the factory era of the first half of the 19th century, when Mr Berry from Ashburton had four woollen mills here, making Chagford a very busy place. In subsequent years water power was utilised by ingenious pioneers for generating electricity.

Chagford had an early market in the town Square, close to the feature known as the Market House which was built in 1862 to replace the earlier Shambles. Later the sales were moved to a field behind the Three Crowns Hotel whch stands opposite the church; dating from the 16th century it was originally the town house of the Whyddon family.

For a small town Chagford has an exceptionally wide range of useful shops. It also has a delightful open-air swimming pool at Rushford which is open in summer.

Further reading: Hayter-Hames, Jane, *A history of Chagford*, Phillimore, 1981
Rice, Iain, *The book of Chagford*, Halsgrove, 2002
Local society: Chagford History Society

CHALLACOMBE (E1) North Devon Pop. 130 (1901: 195)

The large Exmoor parish of Challacombe is bounded by the Devon-Somerset county border on the east, and by the River Bray on the west. From Blackmoor Gate – crossing place of roads, and livestock market centre in the north-west – the land-based northern boundary runs eastwards, and is marked at the summit point of 1575 ft by Five Barrows, a line of round barrows which appear prominently on the skyline. The group of early burial sites, and others in the vicinity including Chapman Barrows close by on the south, are believed to date from the early Bronze Age. The southern boundary is marked near its summit of 1564 ft by Shoulsbarrow Castle at 1528 ft. This roughly rectangular earthworks represents the remains of an Iron Age hill fort, a defensive position from times when local warfare prevailed.

With the parish's northern area largely comprising Challacombe Common – some of which has undergone agricultural reclamation in later years – and the south including Shoulsbarrow Common, cattle and sheep production have long been the main farming enterprises. Red (North) Devon cattle have been traditional, although other breeds now appear. The native Exmoor Horn sheep, also Devon Closewools (developed from crossing the Exmoor Horn and Devon Longwool) are still prevalent, in company with other introductions.

The B 3358 Blackmoor Gate-Simonsbath road runs through the parish from west to east. The village is situated in a steep-sided valley, on a tributary of the Bray. The church (Holy Trinity) is located at the end of a narrow lane at Barton Town, a mile west of the village. It is the result of rebuilding in 1850, although the tower is of earlier date, with further restoration in the 1870s, and further extensive work in 2003. Of the farms, Barton Town, Whitefield Barton, Radworthy, and Wallover Barton, were small Domesday manors.

Attractive buildings in the centre of Chardstock village.

CHARDSTOCK (M5) East Devon Pop. 777

Chardstock's pleasant village, located 4 miles N of Axminster and 3 miles SSW of Chard, is approached by minor roads from the A 358 which connects the two towns. The parish, which originally comprised the cattle pasture area of Chard, was transferred from Dorset to Devon in 1896; it is bounded on the north and east by the Somerset county border, and just touches Dorset in the south-east. The land is undulating, rising to 799 ft in the north-west. A tributary of the River Axe flows southwards through the parish.

The large and well cared-for church (St Andrew), which dates from c.1400, was mainly rebuilt in Victorian Decorated style in the 1860s. It has two pulpits – a Jacobean one on the north side of the nave, and a Victorian one on the south, which has a Devon marble base and wrought iron superstructure. There is a large Victorian font near the north door. Chardstock Court, dating from the early 14th century, was the manor house of the bishops of Salisbury.

Further reading: Wood, P.J. and Carter, R.W., *A history of the parish of Chardstock,* 1999

CHARLES see BRAYFORD

CHARLETON (F11) South Hams Pop. 511 (1901: 455)

Charleton is located 1½ miles SE of Kingsbridge, on the A 379 Kingsbridge-Dartmouth road. The village falls into two separate parts – West Charleton and East Charleton. The parish is surrounded on two sides by the tidal waters of the Kingsbridge estuary and Frogmore Creek, which form the western and south-eastern boundaries. Land rises to 362 ft on the north-west.

The slate-built church (St Mary) at West Charleton stands on the parish's extreme west. It dates from the 14th century, enlarged, with addition of the tower, in the 15th century. It was largely rebuilt in the mid 19th century. The parish is united ecclesiastically with Buckland-Tout-Saints.

Slate quarries in the south produced much material for local building from the 13th century, including for the tower of Dartmouth Castle. The five-arched Charleton Bridge across Bowcombe Creek on the road towards Kingsbridge (formerly known as Bowcombe New Bridge) was built c.1831 by the engineer J.M. Rendel, who also designed a drawbridge which occupied the east arch to enable vessels serving mills and quarries upstream to pass beneath. The drawbridge was replaced by a swing bridge in 1845, rebuilt in 1873, and c.1900 was removed and replaced by the present arch. (See Keith S. Perkins: 'Rendel's hydraulic drawbridge at Bowcombe Creek' in *The Devon Historian 32*, April 1986).

CHAWLEIGH (F4) Mid Devon Pop. 621 (1901: 649)

Chawleigh is situated in the hill country E of the River Taw valley, approximately midway between Exeter and Barnstaple. The boundary is defined in the west by the Taw, in the north mainly by the Little River Dart, on the south partially by another tributary, and on the south-east across land.

The village stands on the B 3042 road which connects from the A 377 Barnstaple main road eastwards to Witheridge. The A 377 and the railway both run along the western border and Eggesford Station is actually just inside Chawleigh parish. Formerly, after construction of the railway in 1854, a livestock market was developed at Eggesford Station.

The church (St James) is of 15th-century construction and has a number of fine and interesting features, including a rood screen and parclose screen, and blue ceiling to the chancel, with bosses. There is also an interesting lych gate. Rectors are recorded from 1277. Duckham, in the south-east, was a Domesday estate, and Chenson, in the south-west, a medieval mansion.

CHERITON BISHOP (F6) Mid Devon Pop. 662 (1901: 455)

Situated 9 miles W of Exeter and 12 miles E of Okehampton, Cheriton Bishop is a parish of somewhat sprawling outline. In the west it extends and narrows to an elevation of 852 ft within a mile of Whiddon Down, north from here it is briefly bounded by the River Yeo; the northern boundary is fairly direct, and then another extension in the south-east takes it along tributaries to a point just ½ mile north of the River Teign. The old A 30 road from Exeter westwards – a very ancient route – forms a length of the southern boundary, while the modern dual carriageway road passes immediately north of the village. Cheriton Bishop village is just north of Cheriton Cross on the old A 30, and farther west along the road is the ancient hamlet of Crockernwell.

The area of Cheriton Bishop was inhabited by Celts, followed by Saxons; 'Cheriton' in early times meant 'church town' and the bishops of Exeter were pre-16th century lords of the manor. The church (St Mary) is believed to have originated in the 11th century; most of the present building dates from the 15th century, with some rebuilding in the 1880s. Part only of the finely coloured rood screen remains. The font is Norman.

Crockernwell – also Eggbear, Lambert, and Medland, respectively south, west and north of the village – were named in Domesday. Earlier still, the name of Treable, in the west, is Celtic, and Grendon – slightly farther north – was mentioned in a Saxon charter of 739.

CHERITON FITZPAINE (G5) Mid Devon Pop. 854 (1901: 678)

Cheriton Fitzpaine is a large and hilly parish, 4½ miles NNE of Crediton and 7 miles SW of Tiverton, situated to the north of the A 3072 Crediton-Tiverton road. The boundary on the west is defined mainly by the Holly Water, tributary of the River Creedy; another tributary, Shobrooke Lake, flows through the south. In the north and north-east the boundary attains altitudes of 752 ft and 764 ft, and in the south-east extends across the A 3072 to reach 818 ft. From this road a wonderful view north-westwards across Cheriton Fitzpaine and farther parishes can be obtained.

The village is located fairly centrally. The meaning of 'Cheriton' in the name is Anglo-Saxon for 'church town' and signifies a date earlier than 1066. Fitzpaine was the name of the 13th-century holders of the manor. The church's list of rectors dates from 1274. The nave of the present church (St Matthew) was built in the 14th century, and two aisles added in the 15th century. It includes pillars of Beer stone. There is a large red sandstone arch between the nave and chancel dating from the 14th century. The church was re-roofed and restored in 1883–5.

Chilton, Coddiford, Coombe Barton and Lower Dunscombe were Domesday estates. Upcott, on the north-west, was the home of the Upcotts in the 13th century, subsequently that of Nicholas Radford, and from the 15th century was the seat of a branch of the Courtenay family.

Chittlehamholt square, early 1900s.
COURTESY THE BOOK OF CHITTLEHAMHOLT, WITH WARKLEIGH AND SATTERLEIGH

CHITTLEHAMHOLT (E3) North Devon Pop. 161

Chittlehamholt stands on a ridge between the valleys of the Rivers Taw and Mole which form the parish boundaries to west and east and unite at Junction Pool – the parish's southern extremity. The village itself stands at 500 ft, on the minor road along the ridge which was a main route to Barnstaple before the valley road (now the A 377) was constructed as a turnpike in the early 19th century. The railway from Exeter to Barnstaple, opened in 1854, also follows the route of the meandering River Taw.

Until 1885 Chittlehamholt was part of Chittlehampton parish, and originally known as Chittlehamptonholt on account of it being a clearing in woodland to which parishioners could come to cut timber. The church (St John), which originally contained a gallery with total seating for 300, was built in 1838.

Snydles was a Domesday manor.

Further reading: Lethbridge, Richard, *The book of Chittlehamholt, with Warkleigh and Satterleigh*, Halsgrove, 2002

CHITTLEHAMPTON (E3) North Devon Pop. 820 (1901: 1342)

Chittlehampton 6½ miles SE of Barnstaple and 5 miles W of South Molton, is situated in pleasant farming country that descends on the west to the valley of the River Taw. The Taw, and a tributary, the Hawkridge Brook, in fact form the parish boundary on this side, while the River Bray defines it on the east.

The village, which is of Saxon origin, is located fairly centrally, on high ground, and is dominated by its exceptionally beautiful church and tower. The church is dedicated to the Celtic St Heiritha, who was born in the locality, probably in the early 8th century, and, it is believed, was a religious convert. As a young girl she was martyred by villagers with haymakers' scythes, traditionally at the east end of the village, and where she died water sprang up. The well is still preserved and it has been credited with having healing powers for those with eye afflictions, which led to the site becoming a place of pilgrimage. Heiritha is said to have been buried initially near her place of death, and a church built over, but due to a decree of Henry VIII her remains were moved to a grave outside the building. It is possible that a former small chapel forming part of the present church marks the site.

The existing church, with its four-pinnacled tower, is the result of total rebuilding carried out from around 1470–1520. The tower was last to be completed. At various times this has suffered from storm damage, with pinnacles having to be restored, latterly as recently as 1999 following the falling of two pinnacles in 1998. Modifications, mostly involving the building's interior, were carried out in 1872.

There is also the church of the Good Shepherd at Umberleigh, near the small village close to Umberleigh Bridge over the River Taw, and also a railway station on what is now known as the 'Tarka Line' to Barnstaple. Brightley Barton, also in this vicinity, has a medieval moat and a house dating from the 16th century. A stone cross at nearby Brightley Cross may have been erected as a guide for pilgrims to Heiritha's well. Whitestone, South Bray, North Newton, and South Newton were Domesday manors.

Aerial views, Chittlehampton.
COURTESY THE BOOK OF CHITTLEHAMPTON

Further reading: Chittlehampton Book Group, *The book of Chittlehampton*, Halsgrove, 2001

CHIVELSTONE (F12) South Hams Pop. 286 (1901: 385)

Chivelstone is Devon's most southerly parish, culminating in Prawle Point (meaning 'a lookout'), a prominent landmark of the South Devon coast from whose wild rocky cliffs the land rises to 454 ft. Chivelstone's 'church town' is but a hamlet near the centre of the parish. A chapel at Chivelstone was among the properties of Totnes Priory in 1288 and part of the priory of Bisham, Berkshire, in 1495. It was seized by the Crown at the Dissolution. The chancel of the present church (St Sylvester) dates from the 14th century and the nave from the 15th century. The carved oak pulpit and screen are from the 15th century. There is a sanctuary ring in the main door for the benefit of fugitives. The original dedication was to St Mary, the change being made in the mid 18th century to the more unusual one that is unique in England.

More sizeable hamlets are nearby South Allington, Ford, in the north, and East Prawle in the south. All, including Chivelstone, were Domesday manors.

The parish is served only by minor roads which extend south from the A 379 between Kingsbridge and Dartmouth.

CHRISTOW (G7) Teignbridge Pop. 802 (1901: 520)

Christow is a somewhat triangular-shaped parish, 7 miles SW of Exeter, situated on the west side of the River Teign which forms the eastern boundary. The B 3193 road north from the A 38 near Chudleigh runs close to the river through the parish and the village stands near it on the west. Land in the parish, which is included in Dartmoor National Park, rises to over 900 ft at various points including 947 ft on Christow Common in the north. Parts of Tottiford and Kennick Reservoirs (constructed respectively in 1861 and 1884) lie on the western boundary.

The original church was dedicated in 1084, and among patrons in subsequent years was Tavistock Abbey, from 1464 until the Dissolution. The present church (St James) is of 15th-century construction, built mainly of granite, with a particularly fine tower. The carved and painted screen also dates from the 15th century. The font is Norman. Some rebuilding, including that of the chancel which was also extended, was carried out in 1862.

Canonteign was a Domesday manor and the impressive Canonteign Barton or Old Canonteign was the Tudor manor house. In the Civil War it was garrisoned for the king, and taken by Fairfax in 1645. It was relegated to a farmhouse after Sir Edward Pellew (an illustrious naval commander who became the 1st Baron Exmouth) bought the manors of Christow and Canonteign in 1812 and built himself a new house in the park.

Lead, silver, zinc and copper were mined in the parish in the mid 19th century, at Canonteign (where large waste tips remain near the road), at Reed in the north, and in the south at Hyner where barytes and other minerals were also produced. Water from nearby waterfalls was used in washing the ore. Micaceous haematite, a form of iron ore, was worked at Shuttamoor, in the south-west, for some years around 1900. There was also a large quarry at Scatter Rock on Christow Common where basalt was extracted up to 1950. The stone was conveyed to the former Christow Station on the Teign Valley Railway, an extension from Ashton to Exeter in 1903 which closed in 1958.

Further reading: Clark, Stafford, *A history of the parish of Christow*, Devon, 1989

CHUDLEIGH (G8) Teignbridge Pop. 3846 (1901: 1820)

The small town of Chudleigh, 10 miles SSW of Exeter, stands on either side of the old road to Plymouth, now the B 3344, with the modern A 38 expressway by passing west of the urban area. It was on account of this ancient route that Chudleigh developed, eventually becoming an established coaching stop as the land levelled out to the south-west of the Haldon Hills. The area of the parish is fairly large and of varied character, extending in the north-east to over 750 ft on the Haldon ridge, and

Chudleigh stands on the former main coaching road, but is now bypassed by the A 38 expressway.

bounded on the west and north by the River Teign and a tributary. The A 380 road to Newton Abbot and Torbay keeps company with the boundary on the south-east, and the parkland of Ugbrooke House, seat of Lord Clifford and opened seasonally to the public, occupies an area in the south of the parish.

Already having a place of Christian worship from before the Norman Conquest, Chudleigh was chosen in 1080 by Bishop Osborne of Exeter as the site for a rural palace, slight remains of which are apparent in an orchard near Rock Road. The bishops held influence until 1550, and it is believed to have been Bishop Bronescombe who dedicated the red sandstone dressed church in 1259. That building, which was cruciform, may have been a replacement of an earlier simpler one. Further developments followed in the first half of the 14th century, including rebuilding in the perpendicular style, construction of the tower, and dressings of Beer stone. In the 16th century the south transept was replaced by a south aisle, with granite arcades. The church, which is dedicated to St Mary & St Martin, was extensively restored in 1843, from when the font and pulpit date, and further in 1870. There is a gallery at the west end. The very fine rood screen dates from the 15th century; it has undergone restoration at various times including delicate repainting in the late 20th century.

Chudleigh was a centre of the woollen industry in past centuries. In 1807 the town suffered a severe fire which destroyed 166 houses, most of them thatched. There was a limestone quarry at Chudleigh Rock south of the town.

From 1882 Chudleigh had a railway station on the Teign Valley line, situated close to the present A 38 south roundabout. This reached from Heathfield, on the Newton Abbot-Moretonhampstead line, as far as Ashton until 1903, when it was continued to Exeter. Closure came as traffic dwindled between 1950 and 1965.

Further reading: Crockett, Anthony, *Chudleigh: a chronicle*, Devon Books, 1985
Local society: Chudleigh Amenity Society

CHULMLEIGH (E4) North Devon Pop. 1308 (1901: 1158 + Cheldon 46)

The civil parish of Chulmleigh includes the small parish of Cheldon which ecclesiastically is united with Chawleigh.

Chulmleigh rises from the east bank of the River Taw which forms the western boundary. Roughly half way between Exeter and Barnstaple – approximately 20 miles from each – the small town is situated a little over a mile east of the A 377 road. The southern boundary is defined by the Little Dart River, tributary of the Taw, and a short stretch of the River Mole, and that in the north by another tributary. The land is undulating, rising to over 700 ft; it is mainly agricultural and carries a network of roads. The occurrence of tumuli on Horridge Moor indicates early human presence, and an earthwork north of Stone Barton may have been the site of an Iron Age fort.

Possibly there was a Celtic settlement here before the Romans arrived. The name is due to a Saxon, Ceolmund, who settled on the 'leigh' (sheltered clearing). At the time of Domesday Chulmleigh belonged to Baldwin, and subsequently was possessed by the Courtenays from the late 12th century until 1539. It became a borough in 1253 and had a weekly market and two fairs a year for centuries up to c.1850. Chulmleigh was also a centre of the woollen industry, notably woolcombing, until c.1800. Before the Exeter-Barnstaple turnpike road (now the A 377) was constructed along the Taw valley in the early 19th century, the town of Chulmleigh was on the main coaching road northwards, which brought an amount of trade. This declined when the new road came, and also the railway, opened in 1854. Markets for livestock moved to new auction places set up at stations on the line, and travellers bypassed the town, which remains pleasant nevertheless.

The church (St Mary Magdalene) was in early times a collegiate church with seven prebends. It was wholly rebuilt in the 15th century, and the tower completed after 1500. Further rebuilding, involving the chancel, was carried out in 1860 and the tower was restored in 1881. There is a very fine rood screen running the full width of the church. Cheldon's small church (St Mary) dates from the 15th century.

Colleton Barton, in the west, is a very fine house dating from c.1612, with a gatehouse and chapel above, licensed in 1381.

Further reading: Mair, Jack, and Bass, R.C.M., *Chulmleigh: a short history and walk around guide*, 1986
Barton, Roger, *Chulmleigh*, Beaford Centre, 1997
Local society: Chulmleigh and District Local History Society

CHURCHSTOW (F11) South Hams Pop. 408 (1901: 311)

Churchstow parish is situated immediately NW of Kingsbridge, served by the A 381 road coming from Totnes, 4 miles NE, and the A 379 from Modbury and Plymouth on the W. The village is near the northern boundary, at a point where the line dips between arms that reach out to touch the River Avon on the north-west and on the north-east. The land is hilly but mostly below 400 ft.

Churchstow's St Mary's Church, built 13th–15th century, is of more ancient foundation.

The church (St Mary) which stands near crossroads just north of the village, is of ancient foundation, built on the site of a rural oratory. The manor was a possession of Buckfast Abbey and included the area that is now Kingsbridge, which grew after the abbot gave it borough status in the 1220s. The present church building, constructed of local slate, was built between the 13th and 15th centuries. Nearby is the Church House Inn, dating from the 16th century.

Leigh, in the north-east, which has an impressive gatehouse, and Norton, on the east, were Domesday manors. Sorley, in the north-east, was mentioned in a Saxon charter of 947.

The Kingsbridge branch railway from the main line ran south through the east of the parish. It was opened in 1893 and closed in 1963.

CHURSTON FERRERS (H10) Torbay Unitary Authority (1901: 532)

Churston Ferrers lies between Paignton and Brixham on the south side of Torbay, with the A 3022 road passing through and the A 379 leading off to Kingswear. Since 1864 Churston has had a railway station (initially called Brixham Road) when the Dartmouth and Torbay Railway from Paignton opened this far in 1861. It was completed to Kingswear in 1864. The railway closed from Paignton in 1973 but is now operated by the Dart Valley Company running steam trains.

Both Churston and Galmpton – which forms the main village and has grown in later years – were named in Domesday. The church (St Mary the Virgin) is of 15th-century construction with an earlier tower of c.1300. It was restored in the 1860s. There is also the chapel of the Good Shepherd at Galmpton.

At Greenway near Galmpton Creek on the Dart is a former home of Dame Agatha Christie, the novelist, now owned by the National Trust.

Further reading: Tregaskis, Jean H., *Churston story 1088–1988*, 1990

CLANNABOROUGH (F5) Mid Devon Pop. 57 (1901: 42)

Clannaborough, 6 miles WNW of Crediton, is a most unusually shaped parish, being long, narrow, and curved. The short northern boundary adjoins that of Down St Mary, the eastern boundary touches Copplestone and wraps around Colebrooke, tapering in the south and touching Hittisleigh, while on the west the other long boundary is shared with Bow.

The parish lies south of the A 3072 road between Copplestone (on the A 377) and Bow. There is no village. The church (St Petrock) is of 16th-century construction, restored in the 1850s. The Barton was a Domesday manor and Appledore and Walson Barton were Domesday estates.

CLAWTON (B6) Torridge Pop. 326 (1901: 389)

Clawton parish stretches to the River Tamar in the west, and is watered by a Tamar tributary, the River Claw, which rises on the cold lands of Claw Moor to the north-east. The village centre lies on the main road (A 388) to Holsworthy, 3 miles to the north.

The church (St Leonard) is situated beside the minor road west of the village crossroads. There has been a church on the site for nine centuries and the present building retains Norman features in the chancel north window and the font. The tower and the arcades of the north and south aisles were built in the 14th century, the arches of Polyphant stone date from the 15th century. Steps rising from the south aisle led to the former rood loft; the screen no longer exists. Unusual etchings, portraying angels, adorn the walls of the sanctuary. The previously thatched nave roof was restored in 1873. More recently the church has undergone further restoration work which is yet to be completed, to combat the effects of prevailing winds and rain.

St Peter's Church at Clayhanger, near the Devon-Somerset border, originates from the early 13th century.

CLAYHANGER (J3) Mid Devon Pop. 114 (1901: 149)

The small, rectangular, hilly parish of Clayhanger, 8 miles NNE of Tiverton, is bounded on the north and east by the Somerset county border. The B 3227 South Molton-Taunton road passes to the north. Altitudes are mainly from 500 ft-600 ft, but attain 770 ft on the southern boundary and 900 ft in the north.

The church (St Peter) is of early 13th-century origin, restored and partially rebuilt (apart from the tower) c.1880. The early 13th-century font is of Ham stone. Donningstone Mill was a Domesday manor and the centrally situated Nutcombe Manor was the home of the Nutcombe family from at least as early as the 13th century until the 19th century.

CLAYHIDON (K4) Mid Devon Pop. 419 (1901: 413)

Clayhidon is situated on the southern slopes of the Blackdown Hills, on the Somerset border which forms its boundary on the north and east, 13 miles ENE of Tiverton and 4 miles SSE of Wellington. The River Culm flows westwards through the south of the parish. Land levels rise to achieve over 900 ft in the north, on the unclassified road running along the ridge that forms the boundary. This is an area of very fine views.

The village is located centrally, at 750 ft. The church (St Andrew) dates from the 15th century, restored c.1850. Bolham and Hole were Domesday manors.

Further reading: Clayhidon LH Group, *Clayhidon, a parish on the Blackdowns*, 1999
Local society: Clayhidon Local History Group

CLOVELLY (B3) Torridge Pop. 472 (1901: 621)

The parish of Clovelly has three distinct types of character. There is the coastline stretch of tall steep cliffs, largely wooded, with the unique village of closely sited cottages and the still-cobbled narrow street leading down to the sea – a mecca for tourists for whom it probably provides their main abiding impressions of Devon. A mile or so inland, close to the busy Bideford-Bude road (A 39) is the more 'practical' Higher Clovelly, which also has its old buildings but modern ones too, and means of shopping for necessities including petrol, and in addition an important archaeological site. And then, south of the road is a quieter open area of farms, many of them representing dwellings from the 13th and 14th centuries. This is a part of the parish, bounded mainly by streams, where visitors to attractions below seldom venture.

The archaeological site – Clovelly Dykes – is evidence of early habitation and strategic importance. Covering over 20 acres the complex earthworks constitutes one of Devon's most impressive hill forts of the Early Iron Age.

Clovelly was, for many generations until 1724, home of the notable Cary family, one of whom, George – sheriff of Devon in 1587 – developed the village and harbour as a coastal haven. The manor was bought from the Carys by Zaccary Hamlyn, who built Clovelly Court in 1740 and also created the scenic Hobby Drive to the east. Cliff-top walks were also cut on the land to the west, with summer-house-type shelters at intervals. One path leads down to a cove, Mouth Mill, where a stream rushes to the sea, with a limekiln close by. (There is another limekiln at Clovelly quay.) The property remained in the hands of the Hamlyns and their successors into the 20th century, when it was formed into the Clovelly Estate Company.

Fishing was the main occupation for Clovelly people. This continued on a busy scale into the early 1900s. The village was noted for its herring catches in the season, which ran from September or October to mid January. Boats with drift nets put out from the harbour, each with two men aboard, some of whom came from Bideford or Appledore. Herrings were gathered into a 'maise', each of 500 herrings – 100 maises a day was regarded as a good catch. Buyers came from the surrounding area to buy the herrings, traditionally sold as 120 herrings for 10 shillings – a penny a fish. The main bulk, loaded in baskets, was taken up Clovelly's back lane on donkeys – the means of transport then for all goods both taken up and brought down – and carried away latterly by lorries. The fishermen reckoned to make sufficient cash for their support until Easter, after which some turned to line-fishing for whiting, trawling for flatfish, or catching mackerel for quick consumption. Some, though, just ceased fishing and used their boats for taking visitors on pleasure trips. Clovelly's lifeboats have been manned valiantly since the first boat was provided here in 1870.

The church (All Saints) is of early cruciform origin, with remains of Norman work, including the tower, in its mainly late 15th–early 16th-century structure. There is a fine Norman doorway, believed to have been moved to its present south position from a different site. The font is thought to be Norman and the earliest recorded rector is named in 1262. Close to the church stands Clovelly Court, the gardens of which are opened to the public.

Sightseers to the village itself are catered for with a large car park, visitor centre, and small shopping and other facilities.

Further reading: Ellis, Sheila, *Down a cobbled street*, Badger Books, 1987
Ruthven, Angela, *Clovelly and its story*, Aycliffe Press, 1982

CLYST HONITON (H6) East Devon Pop. 295 (1901: 262)

Clyst Honiton (or Honiton Clyst), 4 miles E of Exeter, is situated to the east of the River Clyst. The old A 30 road (now unclassified) passes through, and, south of it, the modern A 30 constructed in the 1990s. Much of the land between the two is now that of Exeter International Airport. Established in 1937, the area involved was increased during the Second World War when Exeter became an RAF station, and further developments since the war have led to its present status.

The ancient church (St Michael & All Angels) was rebuilt in 1870, although the 13th-century font remains. From pre-1066 Clyst Honiton belonged to the Dean and Chapter of Exeter; Holbrook dates from that period and for a long time was the home of the family of the same name.

Further reading: Retter Frank, *An east Devon farm and its village,* Obelisk, 1985

CLYST HYDON (J5) East Devon Pop. 277 (1901: 286)

Clyst Hydon, 9 miles NE of Exeter and 8 miles W of Honiton, lies on a minor road which connects with the Fenny Bridges access point on the A 30 and with Westcott, south of Cullompton on the B 3181. The upper stage of the River Clyst flows through the east of the parish, briefly defining the boundary on the north-east and, with a tributary, in the south. Altitude rises from c.100 ft in the east to 500 ft in the north-west.

The village is located centrally, the spacious and well-kept church (St Andrew), is somewhat 'tucked away' but worth seeking. Dating from the 15th century, with the north aisle added in 1855, it has an open ringers' gallery and box pews. Also included, on a 150 ft spur in the south-east, is the hamlet of Aunk which is probably of Celtic origin and was an estate pre-1066.

CLYST ST GEORGE (H7) East Devon Pop. 633 (1901: 241)

The parish of Clyst St George lies to the E of the River Clyst, which forms the western boundary, in its final meandering stage before joining the Exe estuary. The A 376 Exeter-Exmouth road passes through close to the village, also the branch from it to Woodbury (B 3179).

The church (St George) originates from at least as early as the 14th century. It was rebuilt in the 1850s and again in 1952 after being gutted by fire during a wartime air raid.

Marsh Barton, in the south, was granted by Henry de la Pomerai to the Sokespitches in the late 12th century, and held by them continuously until 1803.

CLYST ST LAWRENCE (J6) East Devon Pop. 105 (1901: 113)

Clyst St Lawrence, 8 miles NE of Exeter and 5 miles S of Cullompton, is served by minor roads from the M5 via the B 3181 on the north-west, or from the A 30 in the south. The land rises from c.100 ft to 283 ft in the west. The River Clyst flows through the parish and village from north to south.

The ancient church (St Lawrence) dates from at least as early as 1203, the present building being of 15th-century construction. The granite font of c.1200 is retained. The manor was anciently held by the Valletorts, later by the Pollards, and Heles.

CLYST ST MARY (H6) East Devon Pop. 590 (1901: 157)

A bridge across the Clyst at Clyst St Mary was recorded as early as 1238. The eastern section seen here is of later reconstruction.

Clyst St Mary is a narrow, low-lying parish located E of Exeter and extending east from the River Clyst as it proceeds on its course to the Exe estuary, with the tributary Grindle Brook running through. The ancient bridge across the Clyst was recorded in 1238, with rebuilding in 1310 when two further arches, making five in all, were added, also the raised causeway. In 1549 the parish was the scene of the final defeat of rebels in the Western (Prayer Book) Rebellion, when they were routed on Clyst Heath and the village burnt by Lord Russell.

The church (St Mary) is situated at the end of a lane leading south from the A 3052 Sidmouth road, in the former park of Winslade House which is now an office complex. The church building, which dates from the 12th century, stands on the site of an earlier one. The first recorded incumbent was in 1283. The building was radically changed in a Victorian restoration when it was enlarged and 'turned around' through 90 degrees. This meant that the former south transept became the nave, and the altar was moved from the east to the north. At times the church has suffered from water damage and in 1991 was severely damaged in a fire. Subsequent rebuilding has resulted in improvements to the structure and fittings. The parish is united ecclesiastically with Holy Trinity, Woodbury Salterton.

Recent times have brought changes to Clyst St Mary due to the construction and strategic effect of the M5 motorway close to the parish's western boundary, and other developments. These include the establishment here of the permanent site of the Devon County Show.

Further reading: Axford, Jean, *About Clyst St Mary*, 2000

COFFINSWELL (G9) Teignbridge Pop. 196 (1901: 201)

Coffinswell, 2½ miles SE of Newton Abbot and 3 miles NW of Torquay, is approached by minor roads from those which connect the two towns, with its attractive village set centrally in a slight dip in the hills. In the north-west the parish boundary cuts through the ancient earthwork of Milbur Down hill fort (shared with the parish of Haccombe with Combe), an Iron Age site believed to have been more of pastoral than defensive significance. A small Roman site has also been identified to the south-east. Excavations were carried out in 1952, see *Devon Archaeology Field Guide No.1* (1987).

Coffinswell church (St Bartholomew) originates from the 12th century. The tower and much of the present building survive from the 13th century, with additions in the 14th and 15th centuries. The font, of Caen stone, is Norman. Court Barton, near the church, was the manor house.

COLATON RALEIGH (J7) East Devon Pop. 606 (1901: 474)

Colaton Raleigh, 10 miles ESE of Exeter, stretches from Colaton Raleigh Common in the west, where land rises to just over 500 ft, to the River Otter which forms approximately the eastern boundary. The village is situated on the B 3178 road between Newton Poppleford on the A 3052 and Budleigh Salterton on the coast.

The manor was in the hands of the Raleigh family from the 13th to the 16th century. Place Court, on the south of the village, was possibly the early manor house. The church (St John the Baptist) is of ancient foundation and has a Norman font; it was rebuilt, except for the 15th-century tower, in 1875.

COLDRIDGE (E5) Mid Devon Pop. 338 (1901: 374)

Coldridge, approximately 16 miles NW of Exeter, is bounded on the west by the River Taw which also, due to turns in its course, forms the boundary on the north-east and north. This results in a squarish 'peninsula' in the north, with the river on three sides and the land within rising to 427 ft at Hawkridge. Land on the southern boundary attains 634 ft. The village itself stands at 450 ft, arranged around a square and with fine views. The church (St Matthew), with its impressive tower, occupies a prominent position. It is of 12th and 16th-century construction, with traces of the earlier Norman building, and contains many features of interest including carving. The font is thought to date from the early 13th century.

The B 3220 road from Winkleigh to the A 377 Exeter road passes through the parish, south of the village. Leigh is a hamlet in the south.

The church of St Andrew at Colebrooke near Crediton.

COLEBROOKE (F5) Mid Devon Pop. 411 (1901: 650)

Located 5½ miles W of Crediton and connected by minor roads to the A 377, Colebrooke is an undulating parish with its village standing high on the south side of the valley of a tributary of the River Yeo. The large hamlet of Coleford, with several thatched houses, lies in the valley, ½ mile north. Just north-east of the village is the junction where the former London & South Western Railway (later Southern Railway) route to Plymouth takes a westward turn while that for Barnstaple continues north. (The Plymouth line was opened as far as Okehampton in 1865, a length which is still used for quarry traffic and other occasional trains. The Barnstaple line opened in 1854 and is still functional.)

The church (St Andrew) is large and light, of 14th and 15th-century construction with a Breton rood screen and a fine tower, its pinnacles and bellchamber windows restored in 1925–6. Whelmstone Barton in the north-west was recorded in 1249; in 1374 a chapel dedicated to St Mary was here. Landsend, in the west, formerly a mansion, also had a medieval chapel.

Greatly treasured in Colyton is the 9th-century cross. Originally it stood outside until broken up and used in the tower by Norman builders. The pieces were recovered and re-assembled in the 1930s and the cross re-erected inside the church.

COLYTON (L6) East Devon Pop. 2964 (1901: 1982)

Colyton is a fairly large, sprawling parish with an extremely tortuous western boundary. The small town of Colyton, 4½ miles SW of Axminster, stands in the south-east, close to the confluence of the River Coly and the Umborne Brook, with the neighbouring village of Colyford a mile south. Near here the Coly joins the Axe, and the parish's western boundary follows approximately the south-flowing Axe in its broad valley. Land rises over rolling hills towards the west and north, reaching 706 ft near Widworthy in the north-west. The town is served by minor roads from the A 35 in the north, the A 358 on the east, and the A 3052 Sidmouth-Lyme Regis road in the south.

Saxons were established in the area from at least as early as the 7th century and Colyton was important enough in 1208 to be granted a seven-day fair by King John. The town is pleasant, with several fine old houses that date from the 16th and 17th centuries, including the Great House built in the 16th century by a local merchant, John Yonge, for his family residence.

A Saxon church, or succession of churches, existed here from c.700. The present church (St Andrew) is a glorious building that has evolved from one possibly dating from the 12th century. Alterations and additions proceeded from the early 14th century, culminating, before the Reformation, with the superimposition of the octagonal lantern tower on the Norman square tower (probably inspired by that on Bruges Town Hall). Beer stone is much in evidence in the church including fine carving in screens and monuments. Greatly treasured is the Saxon cross, dating from the 9th century; during the reign of King Alfred it stood outside the church until the Norman builders broke it up and used it in the tower construction. Following a serious fire in 1933 the pieces of the cross were rescued and put together again, and the cross brought to its present position inside the building. There is also the church of St Michael at Colyford.

The prevalence of several farms in the parish that have 'hayes' or 'hayne' in their names, from the medieval word meaning enclosure, indicate their likely origin from c.1300. Some were up-graded in style in later centuries. Colcombe Castle, ½ mile north of the town, was a seat of the Courtenays, early lords of the manor. The original house, dating from the 13th century, eventually fell into decay but was bought and rebuilt in the 16th century as a residence of the Pole family. During the Civil War it was a headquarters of Prince Maurice. Gatcombe in the south, and Farwood Barton in the west were Domesday manors.

From 1868 Colyton was served by the Seaton branch of the London & South Western Railway from Seaton Junction. This closed in 1966 but in 1970 the 3-mile line from Seaton to Colyton was adapted for carrying trams, and the Seaton Tramway now operates along the attractive valley, with amenities at Colyton Station.

Further reading: Robin, Jean, *The way we lived then*, Ashgate, 2000
Local society: Colyton Parish History Society

COMBE MARTIN (D1) North Devon Pop. 2650 (1901: 1521)

Combe Martin is located on North Devon's Bristol Channel coast, between Sandy Bay to the west and the cliffs of Holdstone Down to the east. The hills and their adjoining coastline are spectacular. Girt Down incorporates Little Hangman (716 ft) on Hangman Point, and a mile east Great Hangman (1044 ft). Holdstone Down rises to 1146 ft at Holdstone Barrows – a name that indicates early human presence. The village itself stretches NW-SE along the River Umber valley, with a village street on the A 399 that is amongst England's longest.

The beautiful church (St Peter) is partly of 13th-century construction, but mostly of the 15th century, with a fine rood screen of that date. Following 1066 the manor was given by William I to Martin de Tours – hence the name, combined with 'combe' denoting a valley running up from the sea. Interesting farms in the parish include Challacombe, on the western slopes of Girt Down, which was a medieval manor.

Silver-bearing lead ore was mined in the parish in the 13th century – when men were brought to work in the industry from Derbyshire and Wales – in the late 16th century, and from c.1796–1813, followed by various short-lived attempts at revival. There are remains of a ruined engine house and chimney on Knap Down, just north of the village. Small quantities of coal were brought into the cove, some of it used for lime burning. Hemp was formerly grown locally, from which shoemakers' thread was spun in the village. Market gardening has been a busy industry, taking advantage of the fertile soils and shelter and warmth of the deep valleys. Much of it has been worked in strip fields that run from properties up the valley sides, resulting from the early field systems.

In modern times Combe Martin has become increasingly attractive to visitors, and in summer is busy with the holiday trade.

Further reading: Combe Martin Local History Group, *Out of the world and into Combe Martin*, 1989
Beaumont, G.F., *The story of Combe Martin*, 1981
Local society: Combe Martin Local History Group
Museum: Combe Martin Museum, The Parade

The church of St Nicholas at Combe Raleigh dates from the 1200s, reconstructed in the 15th century.

COMBE RALEIGH (K5) East Devon Pop. 206 (1901: 223)

Combe Raleigh occupies a small hilly area on the northern side of the valley of the River Otter, a mile N of Honiton. The river itself forms part of the southern boundary, while a tributary flows south through the village. Land rises towards the north, attaining altitudes of over 870 ft.

The church (St Nicholas) dates from the 13th century, with a list of rectors from 1261. The parish was then owned by the Raleighs. The present building is of 15th-century construction. Close to it is a medieval house called the Chantry.

COMBPYNE ROUSDON (L6) East Devon Pop. 231 (1901: Combpyne 101, Rousdon 46)

Situated 2½–5 miles S of Axminster, Combpyne Rousdon is bounded on its southern edge by the rocky English Channel coastline on which the effects of landslips are prominent. Land rises steeply from the coast, reaching 589 ft on Combpyne Hill in the north-east. Rousdon was formerly a tiny separate parish in the south, the house, built in the 19th century for Sir H.W. Peek, was the home from 1937 of All Hallows School (now closed). The A 3052 Sidmouth-Lyme Regis road passes through the south, with an unclassified road proceeding from it northwards towards Axminster.

Combpyne lies in a valley, stretching along a northward minor road. The church (St Mary the Virgin) is believed to date from 1240, subsequently somewhat altered. Its list of vicars dates from 1278. The building, which has a saddleback tower, was restored in 1877. In early days the manor was held by the Coffin and Pyne families.

COOKBURY (C5) Torridge Pop. 158 (1901: 146)

Cookbury lies 5 miles E of Holsworthy, N of the Holsworthy-Hatherleigh road (A 3072). The church, (St John the Baptist and the Seven Maccabees) retains its 13th-century tower and chancel; the small north aisle dates from c.1500, with traces of earlier work, and the south transept was added in the early 16th century. The tower has a small, squared pointed cap. In 1982 the church was classed as redundant, and in 1987 was designated a chapel-of-ease. It was restored in 1992 and is now united with Bradford.

In the 13th and 14th centuries, Stapledon farmhouse was the mansion of the Stapledons, the family of Walter de Stapledon (1261–1326) who became Oxford professor of canon law, Bishop of Exeter 1307–26, founder of Stapledon Hall (later Exeter College) at Oxford, and Lord High Treasurer to Edward II.

The copelan stone at Copplestone. The carved granite pillar dates from the 10th century and gave its name to the Coppleston family as well as to the village.

COPPLESTONE (F5) Mid Devon Pop. 894 (1901: N/A)

Copplestone is a civil parish only, formed in the late 20th century from small portions of the parishes of Down St Mary, Crediton Hamlets, and Colebrooke. It is located at the junction of the A 377 Exeter-Barnstaple road and the A 3072 which forks west for Okehampton and Hatherleigh. The railway also passes through, with a station.

The name is derived from *copelan stan*, a 10 ft high carved granite pillar dating from the 10th century, which marks the former meeting point of the three parishes. In recent years, due to the growth of traffic through the village, the stone was moved (not without controversy) to a new safer position a few feet away. The stone was referred to in a charter of 974 and gave the name to the Coppleston family who lived in their estate here until the 17th century.

Ecclesiastically, Copplestone – which has a small church (St Boniface) at Knowle, dedicated in 1953 – comes within Down St Mary parish.

As a boy Ernest Bevin, who rose to become Foreign Secretary in 1945, lived at Copplestone in a house called Lee Mount, on the east side of the A 377 just north of the village. In 2002 a plaque commemorating his time there was placed on the house by the Devon History Society.

CORNWOOD (E10) South Hams Pop. 988 (1901: 870)

Cornwood is a large parish situated on the southern edge of Dartmoor, with its northern area lying within the Dartmoor National Park. This wild moorland, which shares a boundary with the Forest of Dartmoor in the north, reaches over 1500 ft at several points, and 1615 ft on the north-west boundary with Shaugh Prior. The north-east boundary is defined by the upper reaches and continuing flow of the River

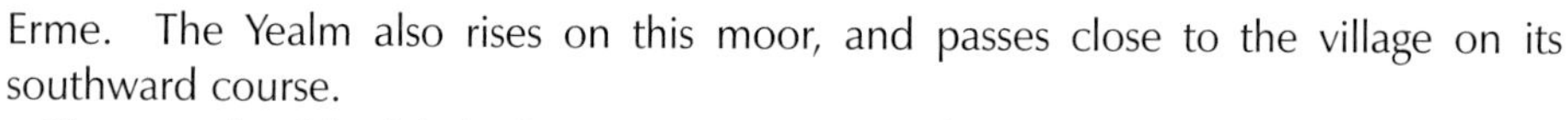

Cornwood village centre.

Erme. The Yealm also rises on this moor, and passes close to the village on its southward course.

The moorland is rich in Bronze Age remains of every description, including the southern stretch of the longest known stone row, of 2¼ miles, which continues northwards over the moors of Harford and the Forest. It was also a scene of tinners' workings, on the banks of both the Erme and the Yealm, and there are remains of tinners' mills. The extraction of china clay has been a continuing industry with workings on Heddon Down and at Cholwich Town. At Cholwich Town, settled by the Cholwich family in the early 13th century and inhabited by them until the 19th century, the substantial farmhouse, built c.1600, is now closely surrounded by clay-workings.

Cornwood village, 9 miles ENE of Plymouth and 3 miles NW of Ivybridge, is located south of the moorland, 2½ miles N of the A 38 expressway. From this the parish is served by a network of minor roads, including a route from Ivybridge through to Yelverton which, particularly near the village, is narrow and twisty. There are several ancient farmhouses that were settled in medieval times. Hele was the home of the influential Hele family. Fardel was a Saxon estate and a Domesday manor, Blachford was also a Domesday manor.

The church (St Michael & All Angels), which stands on rising ground south-west of the village, dates from the early 13th century and the tower is of that time. The first rector is recorded in 1257, and the church and three altars were re-dedicated by Bishop Grandisson in 1336. The present building dates mainly from the 14th century. The north transept contains an altar brought here from a former chapel at Lutton. The reredos is of Derbyshire alabaster and Italian marble.

The main line railway passes through the south of the parish. Cornwood formerly had a station to which in past times traction engines brought blocks of clay for dispatch.

Further reading: Various, *The book of Cornwood and Lutton*, Halsgrove, 1997

CORNWORTHY (G10) South Hams Pop. 368 (1901: 329)

Part of the former cloth, and later paper, mill at Tuckenhay in Cornworthy parish.

Cornworthy's northern boundary follows the southern bank of the River Dart in its beautiful meandering tidal course, and also Bow Creek, with tributary streams mainly defining the others. From the waterside lowlands levels rise over hills, reaching 600 ft in the south-west. Cornworthy village is in the north, approached by minor roads from the A381 Totnes-Halwell road and the A 3122 from Halwell to Dartmouth.

The present church (St Peter), which is not the first to occupy the site, dates from the 14th century. It is obviously lovingly cared for. The Norman font, of red sandstone, remains from the earlier building, and is the oldest feature in the church. The pillars are of granite, supporting arches of Beer stone and granite. The screen suffered 17th-century vandalism. The box pews and pulpit are Georgian. A quarter of a mile west of the church is the 14th-century gatehouse of an Augustinian priory of canonesses founded in the 12th century. Allaleigh, in the south-west, was the ancient home of the Hawley family of Dartmouth.

The hamlet of Tuckenhay on Bow Creek, through which flows the River Harbourne, joined here by its tributary the Wash, is partly in Cornworthy and partly in Ashprington. One of the buildings was in earlier times a cloth mill which became a paper mill c.1829 and continued in production until the mid 20th century. It now comprises holiday apartments.

CORYTON (C7) West Devon Pop. 86 (1901: 205)

Named Curigtown in Saxon times after the Celtic St Curig who, it is believed, came this way teaching Christianity in the 6th century, Coryton, 6 miles NW of Tavistock, is bounded on the south by the River Lyd and on the west by the Lew. They unite near the former Coryton railway station on the old line from Lydford to Launceston (opened in 1865, closed in the 1960s).

Situated on the hillside above the pleasant open Lyd valley and accessible by minor roads from the unclassified Tavistock-Lewdown road, and the A 386, is the church (St Andrew). Dedicated by Bishop Bronescombe in 1261 it was restored in the late 1800s.

A slate quarry, on the edge of Eastcott Down, was in use as early as 1300. Although not the hardest of slates, with its slightly pink colour it was sought for roofing houses and churches both near and far. The quarry was worked latterly during the 19th century and until 1917. A small mine produced manganese in the 19th century.

Further reading: Newman, Thomas, *The history of Coryton*, 1940

COTLEIGH (L5) East Devon Pop. 229 (1901: 186)

Cotleigh is a small parish 3 miles ENE of Honiton, standing high on the hills W of the Umborne Brook, tributary of the River Coly, which forms the eastern boundary. Land rises farther west to c.600 ft. The village is approached by minor roads from the A 30 in the north and the A 35 in the south.

The church (St Michael) dates from the 13th century. It was restored and the chancel completely rebuilt in 1867.

Looking across Lynmouth Bay to the cliffs and high ground of Countisbury on the edge of Exmoor. Foreland Point is on the left.

COUNTISBURY (F1) North Devon Pop. 66 (1901: 279)

Countisbury is the most easterly North Devon parish on the Bristol Channel coastline across which, from the lofty heights on a reasonably clear day, Porthcawl on the Welsh coast can be seen, and often steam rising from the Port Talbot steelworks farther west.

On leaving Lynmouth the A 39 road makes a long and steep ascent of Countisbury Hill, rising 1000 ft in less than 2 miles. At the top are heather moors, and magnificent views in all directions. The dramatic coastline extends north to Foreland Point – over 700 ft in altitude – with its steep cliffs and lighthouse. In contrast, the parish's southern boundary follows the mainly wooded valley of the East Lyn River. Between them, Kipscombe Hill on Countisbury Common attains 1125 ft, and Old Barrow Hill, farther east, 1136 ft. The name of the latter, and various tumuli, indicate early inhabitation, while, just to the north-east of Barrow Hill are earthwork remains of a Roman signal station or fortlet, part of a chain established during the advance in the 1st century AD. Another earthwork, *arx Cynuit* (probably the origin of the name Countisbury), a mile west of the village was the site of a defeat of the Danes by Odda of Devon, in 878.

The ancient church (St John the Evangelist) was rebuilt between 1796 and 1846. Ecclesiastically the parish is united with Lynmouth, where there is the church of St John the Baptist.

CREACOMBE see RACKENFORD, WITHERIDGE

CREDITON (G5) Mid Devon Pop. 6837 (1901: 5266)

The town of Crediton, 7 miles NW of Exeter, stands on the A 377 Exeter-Barnstaple road which follows the town's long main street. The A 3072 road to Tiverton connects here as do various minor routes. The River Creedy runs north-east of the town and the Yeo to the south; they unite just to the south-east.

A large surrounding rural area was separated from the town as the civil parish of CREDITON HAMLETS (see there) in 1894.

Crediton has a long history. It was the birthplace c.680 of Winfrith, who became known as St Boniface. He took Christianity to central Germany where he founded the monastery of Fulda. His name is revered in the town. A minster was established here in 739, and the first diocesan church built in 909. This served as the cathedral when, in 933, a see was also established with a succession of nine bishops culminating in the 11th century with Leofric, who obtained permission from the pope to remove the see to Exeter in 1050. Crediton's parish church (Holy Cross) was subsequently made collegiate, until dissolved in 1547 when it was bought by the parishioners. The very fine building, of local New Red Sandstone, stands close beside the road through the town. It is cruciform, reshaped c.1500, and with a notable clerestory. Archaeological

Crediton was the birthplace of St Boniface who took Christianity to Germany. His statue stands in the town's park.

investigations carried out just north of the church in 1984 have revealed remains of a timber building, possibly Anglo-Saxon, which may relate to the earlier monastery.

Around 1238 Crediton was created a borough but its importance as such was short-lived. The woollen industry brought prosperity for the town – and particularly to the families of Davie, Northcote, and Tuckfield – from the early 16th century, until it shared Devon's decline in the industry in the late 18th century, at a time when several fires caused serious devastation. Crediton today is the centre for business and shopping for the large surrounding area, with industries that include graphics and pharmaceuticals. There is a monthly Saturday stall market. The railway to Barnstaple (opened to Crediton in 1851) passes through, with a station on the south side of the town.

Local society: Crediton Area History and Museum Society
Crediton Branch of the Devonshire Association

CREDITON HAMLETS (F & G, 5 & 6) Mid Devon Pop: 1307

The large civil parish of Crediton Hamlets was separated from the town in 1894. It extends west, south, and east of the town to border the parishes of Sandford, Copplestone, Colebrooke, Hittisleigh, Cheriton Bishop, Tedburn St Mary, Whitestone, Newton St Cyres, and Shobrooke, and is watered by the River Yeo in the north, and tributary streams.

The land is mainly rich and fertile, including red soils and, although altitudes rise, particularly towards the west conditions are temperate, and 'early' for crops. The A 377 Exeter-Barnstaple road passes through the north and the area is served by a network of minor roads. Also passing through is the railway to Barnstaple, with a station at Yeoford, a small village where there is also the Anglican chapel of Holy Trinity.

Downes, home of the Buller family from 1726, was the birthplace of Sir Redvers Buller, the general who served in South Africa during the Boer War and was responsible for relieving Ladysmith. (There is a statue of him, mounted on horseback, in Exeter.) Fordton, Uton Barton and Court Barton at Venny Tedburn – all south of the town – and Spence Combe in the north-west, were ancient mansions. There are remains of an Early Iron Age fort at Posbury in the south-west.

CRUWYS MORCHARD (G4) Mid Devon Pop. 472 (1901: 523)

Cruwys Morchard is located 5 miles W of Tiverton, on the Tiverton-Witheridge road (B 3137), a parish of hills, woods and streams with most of the land at 500-600 ft and rising to 800 ft in the south. The boundary is defined on the east by the Little Dart River and on the south-east by a tributary stream. The Holly Water marks the boundary on the south-west and the River Dalch that on the north-west.

There is no village. Cruwys Morchard House in its small park has been the home of the Cruwys family since at least as early as the time of King John, and although the male line died out in the early 19th century the son of the heiress took his mother's maiden name, so that the Cruwys name continued. Close to the house is the church (Holy Cross) which dates from the early 14th century with a 16th-century south aisle. In 1659 the church suffered a severe fire which necessitated internal renewal and repairs to the tower. Hill, Ruckham, and Yedbury were Domesday manors. The parish includes the hamlet of Pennymoor.

Further reading: Tull, Christopher S., *Cruwys Morchard, church, parish and people*, 1973, based on Cruwys, Margaret C.S., *A Cruwys Morchard notebook*, 1939

Cullompton's main street carried the main A 38 trunk road until by-passed by the M5 c.1970.

CULLOMPTON (J5) Mid Devon Pop. 7609 (1901: 2922)

Cullompton, 11 miles NNE of Exeter and 5 miles SE of Tiverton, is situated in the valley of the River Culm which flows southwards on the east of the town. From c.150 ft in the valley, land rises westwards to 500-600 ft and to lesser altitudes on the east.

The town has a wide main street that was formerly the A 38 road (now the B 3181) which was the main trunk road until the construction c.1970 of the M5 motorway which now by-passes the town on the east, with an appropriate access point. The main railway passes through, but there is no longer a station.

Cullompton has a long history. The lands of 'Columtune' were bequeathed by King Alfred to his son Ethelward and in 1020 were given to Gytha, wife of Earl Godwin and mother of King Harold. Later the manor was owned by the earls of Devon and in 1278 Amicia (Countess of Devon in her own right) willed it to the abbot and convent of Buckland Monachorum (see that parish). The abbot gave the town a leat which flowed along the main street until 1962.

For long a market town, Cullompton was for centuries a centre of the woollen industry, which brought prosperity. There were several mills, including three corn mills on the east side of the town, powered by a leat from the Culm. The church (St Andrew) is large and extremely fine. It was a collegiate church before the Norman Conquest. The present building is of mainly 15th-century construction, with a splendid rood screen of similar date, and a south aisle added in 1526 by John Lane, a wealthy woollen merchant. Restoration, including that of the chancel, was carried out in 1849. There is also an Anglican chapel at Langsford.

The town suffered a major fire in 1831 which caused great destruction. Still to be seen in the main street, however, are the house known as the Walronds, dating from 1603–5, and the Manor House, a 16th-century building enlarged c.1718, which is now a hotel. There are several 'courts' of former workers' houses leading off the street. At the north end are almshouses dating from 1522, now converted to homes for the elderly. Churches include the Baptist Church, established c.1700, St Boniface Roman Catholic Church built in 1929, and the Methodist Church, dating from 1785. John Wesley first preached in the town in 1748.

All Saints' Church, Culmstock, is noted for the yew tree which has flourished from the top of the tower for 200 years.

Further reading: Various small works dealing with different aspects of Cullompton's history written or edited by David Pugsley.
Various, *The book of Cullompton*, Halsgrove, 2001
Local society: Cullompton Local History Society

CULMSTOCK (K4) Mid Devon Pop. 851 (1901: 766)

Culmstock, 9 miles E of Tiverton and 5 miles SSW of Wellington, is bounded on the north by the Somerset county border. The River Culm flows through the south of the parish and on it stands the village. Land here in the Culm valley is of 250-300 ft altitude, but rises to over 850 ft on the western extremity of the Blackdown Hills in the north. Culmstock Beacon on these hills is still an occasional site for celebratory bonfires. The parish lies to the east of the A 38 and M5, from which it is approached by minor roads.

In earlier times Culmstock was a market town, and a local centre of the woollen cloth industry. By the 17th century the making of fine serge was of major importance, with fulling mills and many employees. Even after Devon's decline in the 19th century the work continued at Culmstock in the Millmoor factory, in both spinning and weaving, powered by waterwheel. The structure was rebuilt in the late 1870s by Fox Brothers of Wellington but was closed in the 1960s. It has now been converted to dwellings but still retains the waterwheel. There are former weavers' cottages near the church.

The waterwheel is still in place at Culmstock's Millmoor factory, used for spinning and weaving wool for cloth until the 1960s.

The church (All Saints) originates from at least as early as the 14th century, while stones in the chancel indicate the existence of an earlier Anglo-Saxon building. The chancel and vestry were probably built in the 13th century, the nave, south aisle, tower and porch in the 14th century. Alterations in the 19th century included raising of the roof and building of the clerestory, which enhances light and sound, and addition of the north aisle. Culmstock church is famous for the cherished yew tree that grows from the top of the tower, it is believed to be 200 years old, nurtured by lime in the mortar.

The parish has several hamlets: Prescott to the south-west, and in the north Nicholashayne, Northend and Upcott where there is a Baptist chapel originally built in 1715. At Spicelands there is a Friends' Meeting House dating from 1670.

Further reading: Culmstock Local History Group, *Culmstock: a Devon village*, 1982
Local society: Culmstock Local History Group

DALWOOD (L5) East Devon Pop. 388 (1901: 346)

The village of Dalwood, 3½ miles NW of Axminster and 5½ miles E of Honiton, lies in the valley of the Corry Brook, tributary of the River Yarty, to which the parish extends briefly on the north-east, while on the north-west it reaches to the Umborne Brook, tributary of the River Coly. The southern boundary dips just south of the A 35 road, from which the village is approached by minor routes. The land is undulating, rising from 100-200 ft in the valley to 628 ft on Dane's Hill east of the village. Dalwood parish, like its northern neighbour Stockland, with which it was closely associated, was transferred to Devon from Dorset in 1842. The church (St Peter) is of 15th-century construction, restored in 1881.

Further reading: Chapman, G.M., *Dalwood, a short history of an East Devon village*, 2nd ed., 1990

DARTINGTON (F9) South Hams Pop. 1917 (1901: 627)

Dartington parish is bounded on the north-east by a wide loop of the River Dart and extends westwards to the Harbourne which marks the short south-west boundary. Land in the east is mainly low-lying, below 300 ft, but on the north-west levels rise to 500 ft. The A 384 Totnes-Buckfastleigh road passes through, with Dartington village approximately 2 miles from the former and 3½ miles from the latter, and the A 385 branches west from this at Shinners Bridge to join the A 38 near South Brent.

Possessed by the Martins from the 12th to 14th century, in 1384 Dartington was granted by Richard II to his half-brother John Holland, who later became Duke of Exeter. Making Dartington his seat he developed the Hall and its various buildings which included the great hall. Changes of ownership followed and by the 16th century the property was in the hands of the Champernownes, who held the manor until the 20th century. During this time alterations were made and certain parts become ruinous. In 1925 a large part of the estate was bought by Mr and Mrs Leonard Elmhirst as an experiment for reconstruction of rural life. A company was formed, embracing various enterprises, and a school, and the great hall restored. Numerous houses were built in current style during the 1930s, and the gardens developed. Dartington is now recognised as an arts centre.

Dartington's ancient church close to the Hall was demolished in 1873, apart from its tower. A replacement church (St Mary) was built beside the turning to Dartington Hall on the A 384. This included material from the old St Mary's and newly cut limestone from the Shinners Bridge quarries. The original font, altar, pulpit and restored screen were installed in the new building. The fine star vaulting in the porch has also been retained as have the white Beer stone arcades, raised on Portland stone bases to accommodate the loftier roof. There is also the small church (St Barnabas) at Brooking, Tigley Cross, built as a chapel-of-ease in the 19th century.

Local society: Dartington Rural Archive

DARTMOOR FOREST (D and E, 6-9) West Devon Pop. 1619 (1901: as Lydford: 2812)

The wild granite upland of Dartmoor occupies a large part of central Devon and is the source for many of the county's rivers. It is now wholly within Dartmoor National Park.

Until 1987 the Forest of Dartmoor was part of the parish of Lydford, and together they constituted Devon's largest parish by far. Since the separation Dartmoor Forest on its own still maintains that majority, covering approximately 56,000 acres.

'Forest' used in this context does not denote a covering of trees. Dartmoor was an early hunting ground of Saxon kings and became subject to forest law under the Normans; 'forest' used in this connection defines a royal hunting ground. Forest law had indeed been extended to the whole of Devon in the 12th century but in 1204 King John granted a charter of disafforestation to the county except for Dartmoor and Exmoor, which were still reserved for his pleasure. The same charter provided that summer grazing rights on the moor, to which Devonians had become accustomed, were to continue.

On 1239 the Forest of Dartmoor and manor of Lydford were granted by Henry III to his brother the Earl of Cornwall. In 1337 Edward III granted to his son Edward the Black Prince, among other possessions, the castle and manor of Lydford and the chase of Dartmoor, since when the Forest, as it has continued to be known, has remained part of the Duchy of Cornwall, vested in the sovereign's eldest son. Developments within the Forest were not prevented provided they did not interfere with royal hunting. Certain privileges and obligations attached to such settlements.

The West Dart River, near Dunnabridge.

The Forest is surrounded by 26 border parishes, 22 of which share an actual boundary with it. (Now plus Lydford.) By ancient law the tracts of common land pertaining to these parishes – and also forming a large part of Dartmoor – were known as the Commons of Devon. Certain farms in these parishes carried grazing rights, subject to conditions, on the Forest besides on their own commons.

Dartmoor has supported habitation for thousands of years. Farming probably originated c.4000BC when the area was more wooded than now. Probably around 2500–2000BC successors of those early people built the stone rows, of which over 60 are known, followed by large cairns, ritual stone circles, hut circles and other features. Lengths of low banked boundary walls, known as reaves, were made probably around 1700-1600BC. (See Fleming, Andrew, *The Dartmoor Reaves*, Batsford, 1988.)

Probably due to climate deterioration, Dartmoor apparently became depopulated for some centuries until, in medieval times, new incomers established farms and villages.

From the 12th century, and possibly earlier, the working of tin was an important Dartmoor industry. Initially this was by surface streaming, but later tin-bearing material was worked out of the ground. Smelting was done on the moor. The tinners became an organised body, customary law securing for them certain privileges. Dues had to be paid to the Crown on tin sold, for which four Stannary Towns were appointed: Tavistock, Chagford, Ashburton, and Plympton. Over the years tin-working had spells of decline, but mining of tin continued into the early 20th century. (See: Greeves, T.A.P., 'The Great Courts of Parliaments of the Devon tinners 1484–1786' *Transactions of the Devonshire Association 119,* 1987, and also Greeves, T., *Tin mines and miners of Dartmoor,* 2nd edit., Devon Books, 1993. Also Newman, Phil, *The Dartmoor tin industry*, a field guide, Chercombe Press, 1998, also Gerrard, S., *Dartmoor*, English Heritage and Batsford, 1977. Also numerous other works by these and other authors.)

In the latter part of the 18th century roads over the moor were improved and farming and other schemes were being optimistically planned and tried. A leading pioneer was Thomas Tyrwhitt, friend of the Prince of Wales, holder of the Duchy lands and later King George IV. Amongst other developments, Tyrwhitt established Princetown. A prison was built in the early 1800s, to accommodate war prisoners, and this, after a period of disuse, became a civil prison in the 1850s, as it has remained.

Ecclesiastically, the parish church of the Forest dwellers was the one at Lydford. This meant carrying corpses long distances across the moor for burial, and a route known as the Lich Path, or Lich Way, became established. (In the 13th century the bishop granted permission for occupiers of certain more remote eastern settlements to attend Widecombe church instead of Lydford.) In later times other churches have been built on the moor. The church at Princetown (St Michael & All Angels) was built in the early 1800s by war prisoners. After falling into disrepair it has undergone restoration, to be used for other purposes. (Princetown is currently an ecclesiastical parish without a church.) Huccaby chapel (St Raphael) and Postbridge chapel (St Gabriel) were built around 1869 as daughter churches of Princetown.

Further reading: Bellamy, Reg, *Postbridge, the heart of Dartmoor*, Halsgrove, 1998
Gardner-Thorpe, Dr, *The book of Princetown*, Halsgrove, 2003
Stanbrook, Elizabeth, *Dartmoor's War Prison & Church 1805–1817*, Quay Publications, 2002

There is a vast collection of works on Dartmoor, and readers wanting more information are advised to seek the guidance of libraries and booksellers for advice on particular fields of interest.

Societies: The Dartmoor Preservation Association
The Dartmoor Society
The Dartmoor Tinworking Research Group
Princetown & District Local History Club

The High Dartmoor Information Centre at Princetown, run by the Dartmoor National Park Authority, is open throughout the year, and others are open at various points during the season.

DARTMOUTH (G10) South Hams
Pop. 5512 (1901: Dartmouth: 3702 Townstall: 2726)

The town of Dartmouth stands about a mile from the open sea on the west side of the mouth of the River Dart, on ground that rises steeply to almost 500 ft. Until the 13th century the name applied only to the actual river mouth, but then two settlements, on either side of an inlet called the Mill Pool – Hardness to the north and Clifton on the south – were combined and the whole area became known as Dartmouth. Later the pool was filled in, giving an area of flat ground to the centre of the town. The former separate parish of Townstall, up on the hill, has been united with Dartmouth since 1891.

The advantage of a sheltered deep-water harbour caused Dartmouth's early development as a port. This involved both military and commercial traffic. It served as a departure point for the Crusades in the 12th century and for subsequent campaigns. Trade of many kinds came through the port of Dartmouth, notably of products from the continent. A leading merchant and shipmaster of the 14th century was John Hawley, whose influence brought prosperity to the town. Later, in the late 16th and early 17th centuries, Dartmouth was involved with the Newfoundland fishing trade, and the town saw further building developments, including the New Quay on the river frontage in 1584–5, and buildings in the vicinity of the butterwalk, dating from 1635–40. During the Civil War Dartmouth was garrisoned for Parliament before falling to the Royalists, but finally, after siege, fell to Fairfax in January 1646.

As overseas trade declined in the 18th century Dartmouth's fortunes fell. Catering for passenger ships developed, but as vessels became bigger the port was disadvantaged by its narrow entrance, and business went elsewhere. In 1857 plans were made for extending the railway from Torquay to Dartmouth, and the first stages, to Paignton and Churston, were opened in 1859 and 1861 respectively. Problems delayed completion, however, including Dartmouth's position on the far side of the Dart, and it was decided to terminate the railway at Kingswear and to provide the final link by ferry. Dartmouth therefore acquired a railway station, but without rails, and the lack of actual railway connection had a lasting adverse effect. Ship-building and repairing continued however, and the establishment of the Royal Naval College in the early 20th century brought a new importance to the town, as has the increasing popularity

Dartmouth viewed across the Dart from Kingswear.

of fishing and sailing. Despite the lack of beaches, Dartmouth is indeed a delightful place for inhabitants and visitors.

At the actual mouth of the river is the square defence tower, built by Hawley, known as Dartmouth Castle. From here a chain could be extended across the water to Kingswear Castle to protect the harbour entrance. Within the castle's area is the church of St Petrox, dating from the 12th century and rebuilt in the 1640s. It has a Norman font. Dartmouth's parish church (St Saviour), in the town, dates from the 14th century, dedicated by Bishop Brantingham in 1372. It underwent extensive changes in the 15th century, when the wood screens and stone pulpit were added, and in the 17th century when the fine gallery was installed. With so much wood in the structure one can almost sense the atmosphere of a sailing ship in this church, where an air of sacred tranquillity prevails. Dartmouth's other surviving church is that of St Clement at Townstall. Also dating from the 13th century, its high altar was dedicated by Bishop Stapledon in 1318. It contains traces of Norman work but was heavily restored in the 19th century. The former church of St Barnabas, in the south area of the town, is now redundant.

Also along the south shore are the Old Quay and Bayard's Cove, with remains of a castle built as a defence by Henry VIII in 1537 and the nearby Custom House. Dartmouth was the home town of Thomas Newcomen (1663–1729), inventor of the atmospheric steam engine. One of Newcomen's engines, dating from the 1720s, with a 22in cylinder, was installed in a building in Royal Avenue Gardens, near the town centre, by the Newcomen Society in 1963, to commemorate the 300th anniversary of his birth.

Dartmouth is reached by the A 3122 and A 379 roads, or via the ferry from Kingswear.

Further reading:	Freeman, Ray, *Dartmouth: a new history of the port and its people*, Harbour Books, 1983, (and numerous other works by the same author)
Museum:	Dartmouth Town Museum, Butterwalk
Local societies:	Dartmouth History Research Group
	Dartmouth & Kingswear Society

DAWLISH (H8) Teignbridge Pop. 12,819 (1901: 4584)

Red sandstone cliffs on the south Devon coast, west of Dawlish. A main line train emerges from the Holcombe tunnel.

Dawlish is a fairly large parish on the English Channel coast with a long south-east waterfront boundary that extends from Sprey Point, on the outskirts of Teignmouth, east to Langstone Rock – almost 4 miles, continues around the delta-like spit of Dawlish Warren at the mouth of the Exe, and then runs for a further mile up the Exe estuary. The coastline is marked by red sandstone cliffs and sandy beaches, and the Warren and shore of the Exe are noted for their flora and fauna and for the wide range of bird life, particularly in winter. The nature of the beaches also makes this a sought-after seaside area in summer.

The pleasant town is situated centrally on the coast. Behind it the land rises, reaching 729 ft at the ancient earthworks of Castle Dyke on Little Haldon in the west. The east and west sectors of the parish are divided by the valley of the Dawlish Water, which flows through the town over man-made waterfalls with ponds (adorned usually by black swans) on its way to the sea. The stream anciently called Deflise, meaning a black stream, was recorded in a charter of 1044 and gave its name to the town.

The main A 379 coastal road from Exeter passes through the town, as does the main railway, which runs between the town and the beach. The line is carried on a low granite viaduct near the station which enables access. Constructed by Brunel as the South Devon Railway in 1846, this stretch of line is one of the most spectacular in the country as it proceeds close to the shore and through tunnels in the cliffs. It is also one that is costly to maintain due to its vulnerability to stormy seas.

Dawlish, c.1911. COURTESY THE BOOK OF DAWLISH

Lack of a secure harbour has limited Dawlish's development as a fishing port, although boats have always been moored on the beach and at Boat Cove to the west. The town had several mills and was busy with local industries including ironworking, brewing and cider-making.

The church (St Gregory) is located in the older, landward area of the town. It originates from at least as early as 1301 and still retains its 14th-century sandstone tower, but the main structure was largely rebuilt in 1824, and further altered in 1897. The United Reformed Church, with its spire, stands in the main street, nearer the sea. There is also the church of St George at Holcombe, a village to the west, close to the coast to which there is access via Smugglers' Lane and a railway underpass to a walkway. From here the waves can be watched and the stack known as the Parson & Clerk viewed, as well as the nearby tunnel through which trains frequently come and go. At the other, extreme east, end of the parish, near the old fishing hamlet of Cockwood on the estuary, is the church of St Mary, formerly an ancient chapel dating from the 14th century, which was restored in 1839 after becoming ruinous. There is also a Church Room used for Anglican worship at Dawlish Warren.

The Luscombe estate, west of the town, was bought by the banker Charles Hoare in the late 17th century. He engaged John Nash to design the house, known as Luscombe Castle, and Humphrey Repton to lay out the parkland. Shorelands, built nearby as the dower house c.1820, was lived in by the civil engineer John Rennie.

Further reading: Griffiths, Grace, *The book of Dawlish*, Barracuda Books, 1984
Pearce, Frank, *The book of Dawlish, a pictorial celebration*, Halsgrove, 2001
Local society: Dawlish Local History Society
Museum: Dawlish Museum, Barton Terrace

DEAN PRIOR (F9) South Hams Pop. 183 (1901: 259)

Dean Prior's formerly quietly-situated St George's Church now has the A 38 expressway in close proximity.

Having previously belonged to the family of Fitz Stephen, in Henry II's reign, Dean was given to the Priory of Plympton, thus acquiring the 'Prior' in its name. At the Dissolution the parish was bought from the Crown by a member of the Giles family, from Bowden, Totnes.

The church (St George the Martyr), stands close beside the road to Plymouth 2 miles SW of Buckfastleigh. It was reconciled by Bishop Stapledon in 1323. The present building dates largely from the 15th century, with subsequent alteration, enlargement and restoration. The poet Robert Herrick was vicar here 1629–47. Until the 1960s 'Dean church town' was connected to Lower Dean by a straight-mile avenue of chestnut trees which were removed for construction of the A 38 dual carriageway. The old coach road runs a little to the north. Dean Court was built as a large mansion by Sir Edward Giles in Tudor times, later becoming a farmhouse.

From rich farmland the parish rises westwards towards Dartmoor, taking in Dean Wood and Dean Moor, to Pupers Hill. The Dean Burn, tributary of the Dart, forms part of the eastern boundary, while the Western Wella Brook, the Avon, and the Harborne define lengths on the west.

On Dean Moor are many signs of prehistoric habitation. A settlement that was archaeologically investigated before construction in the 1950s of the Avon Reservoir, on the parish border, was submerged by its waters, as was a medieval farmstead. There are remains from tinning, including a mill that was also flooded and other, later, workings on the moor, including Huntingdon Mine.

DENBURY see TORBRYAN

DIPTFORD (F10) South Hams Pop. 503 (1901: 502)

Diptford parish is located E of the River Avon, which mainly marks the western boundary, and extends eastwards to tributaries of the Harbourne. It is a fairly hilly parish with land that rises to 605 ft in the north. The village is 17 miles E of Plymouth and 5 miles SW of Totnes, served by minor roads from the A 38 and A 385 in the north, and the A 381 on the east.

The church originates from 1226 when the parish was known as Dupeford. The present building (St Mary the Virgin), which has a spire, dates from the 15th century. The arcades are of granite and the church was restored in 1870. Ecclesiastically the parish is now linked with North Huish, and also includes St James' Chapel at Avonwick. Beenleigh in the east, and Curtisknowle and Farleigh in the south, were

Domesday manors. The former Kingsbridge branch railway, opened in 1893 and closed in 1963, ran close on the western boundary with a station at Gara Bridge.

Local society: Diptford & North Huish History Society

DITTISHAM (G10) South Hams Pop. 424 (1901: 549)

Dittisham is situated on the west side of the widening River Dart immediately upstream from Dartmouth. The eastern boundary from Dittisham Creek follows the curve of the river to Old Mill Creek in the south, with tributaries that feed into the creeks forming the boundaries on north and south. Most of the land is fairly high, reaching 640 ft in the south-west.

The village is located beside the creek, in the north. A favoured place for those with sailing vessels, it is virtually easier to reach by boat than over land, the approach being by minor roads from the A 3122 to Dartmouth, which turns off the A 381 Totnes-Kingsbridge road at Halwell. The area is very attractive, and in the past noted for its plums.

It is believed that a Saxon church may have preceded a Norman church on the site, which in turn was replaced by the present building (St George), constructed of local slate in the 14th century and dedicated by Bishop Grandisson in 1333. There is a Norman red sandstone font, a fine 15th-century pulpit, and a 15th-century screen that extends across the church. Bosomzeal, south of the village, is a medieval hall house, altered in the 16th-century.

DODDISCOMBSLEIGH (G7) Teignbridge Pop. 278 (1901: 210)

Doddiscombsleigh, 5½ miles SW of Exeter, is a hilly parish west of Haldon on the east side of the valley of the River Teign, which forms the western boundary. The land is steeply undulating and rises to c.650 ft on the eastern boundary with Dunchideock. The parish is served by minor roads from the B 3193 Teign valley road which connects with the A 38 south-west of Chudleigh. The railway also ran through Doddiscombsleigh in past times when, in 1903, the Exeter Railway connected with the Teign Valley line which had been constructed from Heathfield, north of Newton Abbot, to Ashton in 1882. The line closed in the 1950s, but during its years of service it at times carried main line trains as an alternative to the coastal route between Exeter and Newton Abbot.

The church (St Michael) which is of 15th-century construction, contains exceptionally fine medieval stained glass in the windows of the north aisle. Town Barton, which borders the churchyard, was formerly the manor house, built in 1604. In ancient times the manor was held by the Doddiscombes. In the 19th century there were several manganese mines in the parish.

DOLTON D4 Torridge Pop. 806 (1901: 621)

Dolton, which lies 6½ miles SE of Torrington, is bordered on the west by the meandering River Torridge and on the east mainly by the Torrington-Exeter road (A 3124). It is a parish of undulating land and attractive small streams, with the fairly large village in more or less central position.

The church (St Edmund) dates from the 14th century but was mainly rebuilt in 1848 and restored in 1862 and 1874. It has a most interesting and unusual Saxon font; square in shape, this consists of two sections from the shaft of an Anglo-Saxon cross set one above the other, the upper block being inverted and hollowed out. The sides are ornamented with serpents and dragons and the face of a man.

Stafford, in the south-east, was a Domesday manor, and home of the family of the same name. Iddlecott and Charnbeer were also Domesday manors.

DOWLAND (D4) Torridge Pop. 93 (1901: 119)

Dowland parish, 4 miles NNE of Hatherleigh, has just a narrow frontage on the River Torridge – its western boundary – but the parish broadens out eastwards over rising land, to include Dowland Moor.

This is a quiet parish without a real village centre. The 14th-century church (St Peter) stands beside a crossway on the rather narrow B 3217 road, with Dowland Barton and some pleasantly mature cottages nearby.

Further reading: Ellis, D.A., *Dowland past and present*, 1992

DOWN ST MARY (F5) Mid Devon Pop. 316 (1901: 337)

Down St Mary lies 6 miles NW of Crediton, between the A 377 Exeter-Barnstaple road and the A 3072 which forks from it at Copplestone. A length of the A 3072 forms the southern boundary, and the River Yeo and a tributary the boundary on the north-west.

The well-kept church (St Mary the Virgin) dates from the 12th century, but there is little to see of the early building. The tower is a 15th-century reconstruction. The body of the church, which was rebuilt in 1871, retains fine carved wood bench ends. Chaffcombe was a Domesday manor and Wolfin a Domesday estate. Lammacott was mentioned in 1170.

The megalithic denuded chamber tomb in Drewsteignton parish, known as Spinster's Rock.

Further reading: Browne, Peter, ed., *Down St Mary: a parish and its people*, Down St Mary Parish Council, 2002

DREWSTEIGNTON (F6) West Devon Pop. 818 (1901: 693)

Drewsteignton lies to the NE of Dartmoor, roughly 12 miles from Exeter and 10 miles from Okehampton. The parish is bounded on the south by the River Teign in its deeply wooded valley, by tributary streams on the east and west, and in the north by the line of the old A 30 road from near Crockernwell to Whiddon Down.

The centrally situated village is pleasant and open. The church (Holy Trinity) is built of large squared granite blocks in perpendicular style. The south aisle is of the late 14th century and the tower possibly a 15th-century rebuilding. There is a priest's room over the porch. The chancel and clergy vestry were rebuilt in 1862 and the nave repaired in 1918. A former gallery – where a barrel organ was played – was removed in 1907. The central block of fine wood pews was a replacement in 1936; produced by Herbert Read of Exeter the bench ends have carvings of wildlife. The other pews date from the 19th century and the pulpit from 1944. Out in the parish, Drascombe and Parford in the east were documented in the 8th century, and Coombe Hall, Fursham, Martin, Shilstone, and Thornbury were Domesday manors.

The parish has several features of archaeological interest. Just east of the A 382 road as it passes through on the west is a megalithic denuded chamber tomb, known as Spinster's Rock; the previously collapsed stones were re-positioned in the 19th century. The impressive Iron Age hill fort, Prestonbury Castle, is situated in the south above a bend in the Teign, a fine example of its kind. The granite Fingle Bridge, just below, dates from the 15th and 16th centuries.

Dunchideock's church of St Michael & All Angels stands on the north-eastern slopes of the Haldon Hills.

A much more modern construction of note is that of the unique Castle Drogo, which stands on an eminence in the south-west. Designed by Lutyens it was built entirely of granite between 1911 and 1930 for Mr Julius Drewe, founder of the Home & Colonial Stores, as a most impressive private residence. It is, in fact, the last castle to be built in England, although it has never seen battle. It is now owned by the National Trust.

DUNCHIDEOCK (G7) Teignbridge Pop. 262 (1901: 134)

Dunchideock is a small parish on the north-eastern slopes of the Haldon Hills, 4 miles SW of Exeter, on the upper reaches of the River Kenn which flows on to the Exe estuary. The land rises westwards from the valley, and to the north, reaching 679 ft on the west and 713 ft in the north-east. Approach from Exeter is via the Alphington A 30 roundabout and the village of Ide, or from the A 38 via the Haldon road.

This is a parish of scattered habitations rather than one with a compact village. The church (St Michael & All Angels) originates from at least as early as 1308 but the present building dates from the late 14th century. The main structure underwent rebuilding at various times – the chancel aisle and nave arcade in 1669, the chancel in 1889 – and other restoration in the late 19th century. Pillars are of red sandstone and there is much carved woodwork, including a very beautiful rood screen and pulpit, and a fine font of c.1400.

Dunkeswell – Millennium presentation of Dunkeswell parish in St Nicholas' Church.

DUNKESWELL (K5) East Devon Pop. 1553 (1901: 288)

Much of the Blackdown Hills parish of Dunkeswell stands at over 800 ft. The western boundary follows the top of the escarpment in the hills which gives way to a fairly high level expanse. To the north, east and south levels descend and rise again, with steep valleys and streams, rough ground and woodland. During the Second World War the plateau area was developed as an aerodrome for large military aircraft – mainly American – which thundered along the runways. It is now a private air centre, catering largely for leisure pursuits and civil aircraft basic training.

The parish is fairly large, and the centrally situated village is approximately 5 miles NNW of Honiton and 7½ miles E of Cullompton. The approach is by minor roads. The pleasant parish church (St Nicholas) which originated at an early but unknown date, was rebuilt in 1817 and again in 1868. It has a Norman carved font which includes a rare representation of an elephant. In 1201 a Cistercian abbey was founded near the Madford River in the north of the parish and colonised from Ford Abbey (near Chard). There are various wall remains of the early buildings. In 1842 Holy Trinity Church was built on the site of Dunkeswell Abbey by philanthropist Elizabeth Simcoe, widow of Lt General John Graves Simcoe, hero of the American War of Independence and Lieutenant Governor of Upper Canada (Ontario). The couple had purchased the Wolford estate, in the south of the parish, and built Wolford Lodge in the 1780s as their home. The abbey church of Holy Trinity is still used for worship.

Part of the remains of Dunkeswell's Cistercian abbey.

Further reading: Broad, Richard, *Dunkeswell, parish and people*, 1994
Also, obtainable from Holy Trinity Church: *A short history of Dunkeswell Abbey*

DUNSFORD (G7) Teignbridge Pop. 688 (1901: 633)

Dunsford, 7 miles WSW of Exeter, is located N of the River Teign, which forms the parish's southern boundary, with tributary streams marking those on east and west. The land is hilly, rising to over 600 ft at points across the north. The B 3212 Exeter-Moretonhampstead road passes through the south, crossing the Teign at Steps Bridge, a beautiful area noted for the splendour of wild daffodils in springtime. The attractive village, which has many thatched houses, stands just north of the B 3212 and is also connected by minor roads to the A 30 in the north.

The church (St Mary) dates from the 14th and 15th centuries. Pillars and screen are of white stone. The chancel was rebuilt and the church restored in the 19th century. There is a gallery.

In the north-west of the parish is the mansion of Great Fulford, Domesday manor and home of the Fulford family – one of Devon's oldest – from the 12th century to the present day in continuous male succession. The family has a distinguished record of military service, through medieval times from the Crusaders to the Civil War – in which the house was garrisoned for the king and bombarded by Fairfax – and in later times. The impressive house, in its park with tranquil lake, dates from the late 15th and early 16th centuries, built around a quadrangle.

Clifford Barton in the west, and Halstone in the north were also Domesday manors.

The Exeter Railway continuation from Ashton of the Teign Valley line, constructed in 1903, passed through the east of the parish, with a tunnel beneath Cotley Wood and the western section of the Longdown Tunnel. There was a halt for Dunsford and a station for Longdown. The railway closed in 1958.

Archway of the Tudor quadrangle of Great Fulford, Dunsford, home of the Fulford family in unbroken male succession from the 12th century to the present day.

DUNTERTON (B8) West Devon Pop. 51 (1901: 100)

The small parish of Dunterton lies on the very edge of West Devon. Deep meanders of the River Tamar immediately downstream from Greystone Bridge define the parish's western and southern boundaries and divide it, and the county, from Cornwall. This must have been a sensitive area in the time when the Saxons were pushing Celts back across the river. Frontier earthworks on the hillside above the Tamar are believed to be of Early Iron Age origin.

Standing in isolated simplicity, near the Tavistock-Launceston road (B 3662) as it begins to descend to the bridge, is the church (All Saints). Mainly of 15th-century construction, it retains some 14th-century features. Ecclesiastically the parish is united with Milton Abbot.

EAST ALLINGTON (F11) South Hams Pop. 596 (1901:396)

East Allington village and the church of St Andrew were among those compulsorily vacated for wartime exercises 1943–4.

East Allington is a rather stretched-out parish, extending from Halwell in the north to Stokenham in the south-east. The land is undulating, rising to 604 ft on the west, with several small streams, including the one that feeds into Slapton Ley which defines the parish's south-east boundary. The village is situated 3½ miles NNE of Kingsbridge, and a mile east of the A 381 Kingsbridge-Totnes road.

The church (St Andrew) is of ancient foundation. The first rector was presented in 1268 and the high altar dedicated by Bishop Grandisson in 1333. The present building dates from the 15th and 16th centuries, and there is a 16th-century screen. After becoming dilapidated the church was restored in the 1870s. The font, of Devon marble, is modern. Fallapit, west of the village, was home to a branch of the Fortescue family from the 15th to the 19th century. The earlier house was rebuilt in the 19th century.

The parish was amongst those that were evacuated of their inhabitants between November 1943 and late 1944, to enable allied forces to carry out exercises in preparation for the D-Day landings in Europe. There is a memorial on Slapton beach.

EAST ANSTEY (G3) North Devon Pop. 261 (1901: 216)

In outline, East Anstey parish, centred 10 miles E of South Molton, rather resembles a right-facing boot. The northern boundary, which follows the Danes Brook (top of the 'boot') and that on the east coincide with the Devon-Somerset county border, following which, in the south-east, the route takes an apparent ingression into Oakford parish (the 'toe' of the 'boot'). The southern and western boundaries follow a somewhat indeterminate course, eventually following a tributary of the River Yeo to the heights of East Anstey Common which rise to 1100 ft near Anstey Barrow.

The village stands near the eastern boundary, 1½ miles north of the old Taunton-Barnstaple main road (now the B 3227). The small church (St Michael) was rebuilt, except for the tower and porch, in 1870. The former East Anstey railway station on the Taunton-Barnstaple line (opened 1873, closed 1965) was located just south of the village.

EAST AND WEST BUCKLAND (E2) North Devon Pop. 456 (1901: East Buckland 96, West Buckland 277)

For civil purposes these two parishes are combined. They are located in the hilly country between Barnstaple and South Molton, north of the A 361 North Devon Link road, from which they are accessible by minor roads, and west of the River Bray. Between the two small villages is the independent West Buckland School, founded in 1858, whose numbers account for the higher than average population figures.

East Buckland church (St Michael) was rebuilt, except for the tower, in 1860. Brayley Barton, Middlecott, and Tossell's Barton were Domesday manors.

West Buckland church (St Peter) was also rebuilt, apart from its tower, in the early 1860s. Furze and Stoodleigh were Domesday estates.

EAST BUDLEIGH (J7) East Devon Pop. 769 (1901: 2653, including Budleigh Salterton)

East Budleigh parish extends from the valley of the River Otter on the east to East Budleigh Common, with land rising to over 400 ft on the west. This attractive village is located on the eastern side, 10½ miles SE of Exeter and 2 miles N of Budleigh

Salterton on the coast. (Budleigh Salterton was part of East Budleigh until 1894.) It was a market town, and also a port until, after the 15th century, the Otter estuary became silted. The fine Tudor house of Hayes Barton, a mile west of the village, was the birthplace of Sir Walter Raleigh in 1552.

The church (All Saints) dates from at least as early as 1200. The present 15th-century building, of red sandstone with arcades of Beer stone, contains many features of interest. It was restored in the 1880s. The parish is united ecclesiastically with St Mary, Bicton.

The former Budleigh Salterton branch line from the London & South Western Railway, opened in 1897, ran through the parish along the Otter valley, with a station for East Budleigh. It closed in the 1960s.

Hayes Barton, East Budleigh, the birthplace of Sir Walter Raleigh.

EAST DOWN (D1) North Devon Pop. 209 (1901: 326)

The roughly diamond-shaped parish of East Down, 6 miles NNE of Barnstaple, is one of high ground, steep valleys and streams. The little River Yeo marks some of the length of the eastern boundary, which also keeps company with the sharply bending A 39 Barnstaple-Lynton road. The village is located just W of this road.

The church (St John the Baptist), rebuilt in the 1880s, is rather hard to find, situated at the end of a path near East Down Manor. There is a south aisle and a 15th-century screen, carved pews, and a small marble font on a carved wood shaft. The parish is united ecclesiastically with that of St James, Arlington.

Churchill, Bugford, and Northcote were Domesday manors; Northcote, now a farm, was the ancestral home of the Northcote family, earls of Iddesleigh.

EAST PORTLEMOUTH (F12) South Hams Pop. 166 (1901: 264)

Situated on the east side of the mouth of the Kingsbridge estuary, opposite Salcombe, East Portlemouth is surrounded by water on three sides: South Pool Creek to the north, the main estuary on the west, and the sea in the south. Altitudes rise steeply around the inner shores and the coastal cliffs to a 400 ft plateau, with a highest central point of 440 ft. There are fine views in all directions. The village is in the east, 3½ miles due SSE of Kingsbridge, but several miles farther for travellers via the A 379 Kingsbridge-Dartmouth road and the web of minor roads leading from it. (Approach by boat could be easier.)

The church (St Winwalloe Onocaus) stands half a mile up from the waterside. It dates from the 15th century, with a fine 15th-century carved rood screen. The building was quite drastically restored in 1887, with further restoration of the screen in 1934.

The sea coast strip is owned by the National Trust. The beautiful rocky cliffs shelter some small coves which are sandy at low tide.

EAST PUTFORD (B4) Torridge Pop. 103 (1901: 125)

The parish of East Putford rises to a level of 700 ft on Melbury Hill, from the east bank of the River Torridge, which forms its entire boundary on the west, downstream from Kismeldon Bridge on the Bideford-Bradworthy road.

Tumuli (burial mounds) on the higher ground are indications of early habitation on what was once rough moorland. The church (St Philip and St James the Less), rebuilt in the late 19th century on an earlier foundation, became redundant and has been de-consecrated and sold, the parish being united ecclesiastically with West Putford, as Putford. The building and small churchyard are now overgrown.

Mambury, now a farm, dates as an estate from the 12th century. Winslade, in the north of the parish, was the home of father and son John and William Wynslade who featured in the Western Rebellion of 1549. Powler's Piece is a crossroads hamlet on the north-west.

EAST WORLINGTON (F4) North Devon Pop. 241 (1901: East 173, West 154)

The parishes of East and West Worlington were united as one civil parish in 1885 and named jointly as East Worlington, although the two are separate ecclesiastically.

A former small parish of Affeton existed up to the early 16th century when it was merged with West Worlington. The Little Dart River flows east-west through the parish, close to East and West Worlington villages and Affeton Barton. The parish is hilly, with much of the land at c.600 ft and reaching 737 ft at the northern boundary, near Burrow Cross and close to several tumuli. The South Molton-Witheridge road (B 3137) passes through the parish's north-eastern extremity and the B 3042 from Witheridge runs westward across the south.

When the parishes were originally created, in the mid 12th century, churches were built for both East and West Worlington, each dedicated to St Mary. Records of rectors in both churches date from 1261. Both Worlington churches still exist, although East Worlington was rebuilt in 1879. West Worlington church is of 14th and 15th-century construction, with a twisted spire above its early tower. It is approached through an arch in cottages that adjoin the churchyard. In 1439 Affeton church became reduced to a chapel appurtenance by Hugh Stucley, successor to the Affeton family who acquired Affeton in the late 12th century from previous Courtenay ownership. Some time after the mid 16th century Affeton church – or chapel – was demolished and no sign of it remains. The family lived in castellated Affeton Castle, built c.1400, which itself no longer exists although the substantial gatehouse, built probably in the later years of the 15th century, still stands, restored and preserved. Affeton is still a home and farm of the Stucleys (see also HARTLAND parish).

Further reading: 'A Devon parish lost', Presidential address by Sir Denis Stucley Bt
In *Transactions of the Devonshire Association* Vol 108 1976

EGGESFORD (E4) Mid Devon Pop. 66 (1901: 126)

Eggesford is located on the west side of the River Taw approximately half way between Exeter and Barnstaple. The Taw forms the eastern boundary, the stream flowing through the Hayne valley defines it on the north-west, and another Taw tributary partially marks it in the south. There is no village; the church (All Saints, united with Wembworthy) stands serenely in a field above the valley. It was originally the church for the Eggesford estate, which was owned by the Coplestones in the 16th century and passed to the Chichesters through marriage in 1606. There are family monuments in the church, which was partially rebuilt in 1867.

In 1718 the estate was bought by William Fellowes. In 1832 the original Eggesford House was demolished when the Hon. Newton Fellowes built a new, larger residence, again called Eggesford House but in Wembworthy parish (see there). The former walled garden is now a plant nursery.

The Exeter-Barnstaple road (A 377) passes along the western boundary, as does the railway (opened in 1854). Eggesford Station, which became a convenient livestock auction centre, is actually just out of the parish and in Chawleigh, being on the east side of the river.

ERMINGTON (E10) South Hams
Pop. 850 (1901: 2034 including part of Ivybridge)

Situated 10 miles E of Plymouth and 8 miles NW of Kingsbridge, Ermington parish includes the valley of the River Erme which flows close to the village, on its east side. The village stands on a slight rise just N of the A 379 Plymouth-Kingsbridge road and the A 3121 that branches from it for Avonwick. A much used minor road that is tortuous and in places narrow connects northwards with the A 38 at Ivybridge. Land rises on either side of the valley, reaching 475 ft north-west of the village.

The 15th-century twisted spire of Ermington's church of St Peter & St Paul.

The church (St Peter & St Paul) is large and light. Although there is no record of a church here in Saxon times it is likely that there was one, possibly of wood, as Ermington was by then in existence. A church was, however, built in Norman times, some of whose stonework remains in the present building. The Norman tower was demolished in the 14th century when the main part of the present church was built, and the spire was among 15th-century additions. The church is famous for its twisted spire, due to unseasoned wood being used in the construction which caused uneven settlement of the stonework. The church is blessed with much glorious carved woodwork. Most of this, notably the very fine pulpit with figures that depict the lives of St Peter and St Paul, and the reredos, are by three sisters: Mary Rashleigh and Esther and Violet Pinwill, daughters of the Revd Edmund Pinwill, vicar here in the late 19th century. After learning the skill they (latterly only Violet) carried out much work not only here but for over 100 other churches, mainly in Devon and Cornwall. There is a Jacobean screen, and carved bench ends not by the sisters.

Ermington was a royal manor at Domesday, and Worthele in the north-west was also a Domesday manor. The name of Penquit, in the north-east, suggests an early Celtic association.

EXBOURNE (E5) West Devon Pop. 318 (1901: 382)

The village of Exbourne is situated 8½ miles NNE of Okehampton, in quiet countryside at the intersection of the A 3072 and B 3217 roads. The River Okement forms most of the parish boundary on the west.

The church (St Mary) was constructed on an earlier foundation in the 15th century. It has a notable rood screen dating from the same period.

EXETER (H6) Exeter City Council Pop. 111,076 (1901: 47,185)

Exeter history goes back to Roman times when, in the late 40s AD, forces advancing into the country of the Celtic Dumnonii halted at the plateau above the east bank of the River Exe and established the settlement and fort that they named Isca. Here they enclosed their town with impressive walls, built of purplish volcanic rock from the summit mass. Remaining lengths of these walls can still be followed, and relics of the Roman occupation seen in the city's museum. Isca appears to have begun a decline in the late 4th century and little is known of the immediate post-Roman period until the arrival of the Saxons from the 7th century. Incursions by the Danes in the late 9th century were repelled by the forces of King Alfred who made Exeter a burh, or fortified place, as a means of defence and preconception of later administration. Developments took a new turn after the Norman Conquest, marked by the building by William I of Rougemont Castle in 1068, whose dry moat and building remains of red Permian sandstone, including a tower, are seen in today's Rougemont Gardens.

Also dating from early Norman times, with its magnificent early 12th-century twin towers, is Exeter Cathedral (now dedicated to St Peter). Christian worship in Exeter had been well established from at least as early as 670, when a monastery existed, and a minster church was built under Athelstan in 932. It was destroyed by the Danes but rebuilt in 1019 by King Canute. Under Edward the Confessor government of the diocese was transferred from Crediton to Exeter and Loefric installed as its first bishop in 1050. Building of the cathedral proceeded, including the impressive Norman twin towers for which much Salcombe (Regis) stone was used, with consecration in 1153. Rebuilding of the church itself was begun by Bishop Bronescombe in the 13th century, with completion in the time of Bishop Stapledon. Among the cathedral's beautiful features are the image screen of the west front (seen from outside) with its representations of angels, prophets, kings and soldiers, and the glorious 'palm' vaulting of the nave – the longest stretch of Gothic vaulting in the world. The ribs of the vaulting and their smaller bosses are amongst many parts of the construction for which stone from the quarries at Beer (see p.15) was employed.

By the time the cathedral was completed Exeter had acquired a mayor (in 1205), was increasing in importance and gaining other churches and buildings of note, including the Guildhall. Devon's industry was growing and Exeter, situated at the head of the Exe estuary and at the river's lowest crossing point, developed as an important port. It was one of the places from where tin, worked on Dartmoor, was exported, and with the woollen industry booming across the county, Exeter became a centre for manufacturing and marketing of the finished cloth. The Tuckers' Hall, in Fore Street, was built in 1471 as the chapel of the Gild of Weavers, Fullers (Tuckers) and Shearmen. Between 1190 and 1210 a multi-arched bridge was built across the Exe. This was partially demolished when a new bridge was constructed in 1778, and the remaining arches later buried or built over. They were revealed during clearance work for flood protection and a new bridge and road system in the late 1960s, and are now preserved in situ for all to see as an example of one of Britain's earliest surviving bridge structures, and scheduled as an Ancient Monument. Exeter's water needs in the 14th century were met by the cathedral and city authorities who cut tunnels and channels along which water from wells and springs at the head of the Longbrook valley could flow by gravity to the centre of habitation. These, the 'Underground Passages', still survive and are open to visitors from an entrance in the High Street.

Exeter's port facility was greatly hampered in the 13th and 14th centuries when weirs were built across the river by members of the Courtenay family of the earls of Devon. These at first restricted the passage of boats up to Exeter and eventually caused total blockage, necessitating transport of goods between Exeter and Topsham by road. Exeter Corporation succeeded in getting the weirs removed but still the river was not fully navigable, and so the problem was solved by construction of the Exeter Canal on the west side of the river. It was opened in 1566 and, after subsequent extensions, eventually reached 5 miles in length upstream from Turf. The canal remained in commercial use up to the 20th century but, still owned by Exeter City Council, has now been adapted for amenity uses. Besides providing the outlet for woollen cloths, the canal was the way in for short wools imported from south-east England and Spain. The area of Exeter's Quay, with the Custom House of c.1680, has been improved in recent years and is now a pleasant recreational area.

Dating from c.1200 and partially demolished in the 18th century, the northern end of Exeter's former multi-arched bridge across the Exe was buried under buildings until revealed by clearance work in the 1960s.

Exeter has faced attacks at various times: in 1497 from Cornish rebels, and shortly after from Perkin Warbeck, and in 1549 was besieged by Prayer Book rebels for five weeks. In the Civil War Exeter was for Parliament, but following siege fell to the Royalists, after which the city gave the King its support before eventually surrendering. In 1644 Charles I visited Exeter where his Queen, Henrietta Maria, had recently given birth to their daughter.

During the 18th century many elegant terraces and crescents were built to dignify the central area, and in the 19th century boundaries extended farther to the surrounding countryside as new transport developments came upon the scene. A new age began when, on 1 May 1844, the first train on Isambard Kingdom Brunel's broad gauge Bristol & Exeter Railway arrived at Exeter. Projection of the line to Plymouth as the South Devon Railway quickly followed, as did connecting routes all over the county.

Exeter Cathedral's twin towers date from the early 12th century. The image screen on the west front was completed in the 14th century.

The 20th century brought even more acceleration of change. Among the effects caused by the two World Wars was the Blitz on the night of 3–4 May 1942 which caused much loss of life and the destruction, mainly by fire, of a great many buildings. Fortunately the Cathedral and the 14th-century Guildhall were among those that sustained only limited damage. Always, from the time of the Romans, a centre of routes, Exeter has seen major developments in its road system to cope with increasing traffic. To ease inner-city congestion the Exeter bypass was constructed on the east in 1936, and an inner relief road was cut through in the 1960s. Later, as existing systems became inadequate for modern needs, the M5 motorway was constructed, and completed to connect with the improved A 38 just south of the city in 1977. Linking with the M5 to east and west is the A 30, now also remade and modernised. Since 1937 Exeter has also had its own airport on the eastern side, which is of recognised international status.

Besides having a variety of industries Exeter is the administrative centre for the county, with County Hall opened in 1964. The University of Exeter became established during the 20th century, with its foundation stone laid on land of the Streatham estate, north of the city, in 1927.

Despite the war, Exeter still has some small ancient churches in the city centre, such as the Norman St Mary Arches, and those of St Olave, St Petroc, St Pancras, St Stephen and St Mary Steps. Others of ancient foundation that serve ecclesiastical parishes within the city include those of St David, St James, St Leonard, and St Sidwell. St Thomas, on the west, came within the city on its incorporation in 1905, and St Michael & All Angels, Heavitree, similarly in 1911. The boundary award of 1965 brought Alphington, Pinhoe, and Topsham with their respective churches of St Michael & All Angels, St Michael, and St Margaret, within city bounds. Meanwhile numerous new churches have been built in recent centuries to serve changing concentrations of population, while a few others have been declared redundant. The church of St Mary Major, with its spire, which stood close to the Cathedral's west front, was demolished in 1971.

One of the delights of Exeter is the nature of its location and the fact that, despite developments, the surrounding rural and coastal areas are easily accessible. This, and the continuation of Exeter's livestock market, help to bring a unity to city and countryside.

(See also separate entries for ALPHINGTON, PINHOE, and TOPSHAM.)

There is a wide range of literature pertaining to Exeter, and also numerous societies including the Exeter branch of the Devonshire Association, and Exeter Local History Society, also Heavitree Local History Society. Those wishing for further information are advised to consult the Westcountry Studies Library, or other libraries, or bookshops.

EXMINSTER (H7) Teignbridge Pop. 3310 (1901: 2560)

Located immediately S of Exeter, with its eastern boundary marked by the Exe estuary, Exminster has steadily become a commuting parish for the city. Road developments have also increased the busy-ness. In summertime particularly, traffic is heavy on the A 379 road which runs through from north to south, bypassing the village, to the coastal resorts as far as Teignmouth. In addition, the M5 motorway, completed to Exeter in 1977, passes through the north of the parish, from the Exe viaduct – the longest bridge in Devon – to its terminal point at junction 31 where it meets the A 38 and A 30.

Exminster has also borne the weight of earlier transport initiatives. In 1566 the Exeter Canal was opened from Exeter Quay along the west bank of the Exe to a point opposite Topsham, and in 1827 extended two miles farther downstream to Turf Lock. The canal is now unused commercially, but maintained for pleasure craft. And, by 1846, Brunel's South Devon Railway (initially powered by atmospheric propulsion) had been constructed southward from Exeter over Exminster marshes as far as Teignmouth on its way to Plymouth. This is still the South West's major railway route, leading to one of the most scenic stretches on the system.

The large village is of Saxon origin and the red sandstone church (St Martin) also dates from early times. The present building is of 15th-century construction, with the chancel rebuilt and other works carried out in the 19th century. Peamore and Matford were Domesday manors, and Kenbury was recorded in 1083.

Local society: Exminster Local History Society

EXMOUTH (J7) East Devon Pop. 32,972 (1901: 10,485)

Exmouth seafront. COURTESY THE BOOK OF EXMOUTH

The seaside town of Exmouth stands on the east side of the mouth of the Exe, 9 miles SSE of Exeter, to which it is connected by the A 376 road and also by the railway which reached here in 1861. At the time of the Norman Conquest the area now occupied by the town was simply a fishing village known originally as Exanmutha, but from the early 13th century Exmouth developed as a port. Then, from the early 18th century, when the health-giving properties of the sea were becoming recognised, as well as the scenic delights of this particular place, visitors started arriving, and gradually the town grew to accommodate them. At first they were mainly from the upper strata of society, but after the coming of the railway in 1861 (which extended to Budleigh Salterton in 1903) the range broadened as families came to enjoy the pleasant surroundings and sandy beach. Such was the spread and development of the town that in 1895 Exmouth Urban District Council was formed out of the ancient parishes of Littleham and Withycombe Raleigh.

Littleham (near Exmouth, to differentiate it from the Littleham near Bideford) is on the east and still retains some countryside. It is ecclesiastically united with Exmouth, with the church of St Margaret; originating from the 13th century, most of the building is of the 15th and 16th centuries, restored in 1884. The church of Holy Trinity is a successor to a medieval chapel of Holy Trinity dating from 1412 on Chapel Hill, which was rebuilt in 1779. To accommodate the growing population a new Holy Trinity church was built in the 1820s, and this rebuilt 1905–7.

Withycombe Raleigh comprises much of the northern part of the present town. The manor was owned by Walter de Claville at the time of Domesday, and the former parish was later home to branches of the Drake and Raleigh families. The original church was that of St John in the Wilderness, a 15th-century structure that fell into disrepair and was rebuilt between 1926 and 1937. The church of St John the Evangelist was built in 1864, and there is also the church of All Saints.

Exmouth's sea wall was built by John Smeaton in the early 1840s, extended in 1870, and eventually extended farther eastwards to Orcombe Point. Besides giving protection to the town this also provides an excellent promenade for recreation. Boat building and repairing was a local industry up to the early 1900s, and Exmouth remained a small commercial port until the end of the century. Many sailing boats are now moored here while the surrounding area has been largely redeveloped for housing.

With many retired people living in the area in addition to the working population Exmouth is a lively place with numerous flourishing societies. They include:

The Exmouth Society
Exmouth Family History Club
Exmouth Historical and Archaeological Society

Further reading: There are numerous books on Exmouth, and among the most recent:
Pascoe, Harry, *The book of Exmouth*, Halsgrove, 2002
Boyles, Chris, *The book of Withycombe*, Halsgrove, 2003

Museum: Exmouth Museum, Sheppard Row

There has been a church at Farringdon from Saxon times. The present building dates from the 14th century, reconstructed in 1871.

FARRINGDON (J6) East Devon Pop. 309 (1901: 216)

Farringdon, 6 miles E of Exeter, lies mainly to the north of the A 3052 Exeter-Lyme Regis road, its border dipping south just as far as the Grindle Brook, west flowing tributary of the River Clyst. Another tributary flows across the north. The land is of low level, rising to only 250 ft south of the village.

There has been a church here since Saxon times. The present building (St Petrock & St Barnabas) dates from the 14th century, but was rebuilt in 1871. It has a small tower and shingled spire, and retains a Norman font. The walls are of stone externally, and of red brick within. The pews are of cedar wood from the former Farringdon House estate, installed to commemorate the Diamond Jubilee of Queen Victoria in 1897. The stained-glass window above the altar was designed by Bishop Stapledon of Exeter in 1321.

At the time of Domesday Farringdon was held by the chief bow-bearer, Fulchur Archibalistarius. Creely Barton was a Domesday manor, it is now the site of an adventure park. Farringdon House was rebuilt in 1889.

Further reading: Senar, Howard, *Farringdon with Bishop's Court: a Devon church and parish*, 1988

The Norman font in Farringdon church.

FARWAY (K6) East Devon Pop. 254 (1901: 233)

Farway, 3 miles SSE of Honiton, is a steeply undulating parish with altitudes that reach 823 ft near tumuli at the western boundary on Farway Hill. It is the source of various east-flowing streams that contribute to the River Coly.

The church (St Michael & All Angels), which stands a mile north-west of the main village, was in existence from at least as early as the 12th century, although most of the present structure dates from the early 14th century, with the tower built in the 15th century and the north aisle in the 17th century. The north arcade has impressive Norman piers. The church was restored in 1877. The manor of Netherton formerly belonged to Canonsleigh Priory; it was bought by Sir Edward Prideaux who built Netherton Hall – in the east – in 1607.

FENITON (J6) East Devon Pop. 1796 (1901: 387)

Feniton village is located in the south-east of the parish, 3½ miles WSW of Honiton.

South of the village the boundary touches the River Otter at Fenny Bridges on the old A 30 road. The modern A 30 dual-carriageway here runs close to the older road, as does the Waterloo-Exeter railway line. The railway's former Sidmouth Junction, now Feniton Station, and its housing development, is within the parish on the west. The River Tale forms the western boundary while in the north the parish extends to the edge of Hembury fort, at a point over 700 ft.

The church (St Andrew) is of early origin. It is believed that a Saxon chapel existed on the site. Building of the church began in the 12th century, after William Malherbe became lord of the manor, and the list of rectors starts in the early 13th century. The original building was cruciform, until the south aisle was added in the 15th century. The screen is believed to have come from Dunkeswell Abbey following the Dissolution. Curscombe Farm, in the north, was a Domesday manor. Colesworthy, on the west, dates from the 12th century.

Standing beside the road from Fenny Bridges to Feniton, just north of the new A30 embankment, is a memorial stone set up by Honiton History Society in 2000 to commemorate the Battle of Fenny Bridges on 29 July 1549 in which, during the Prayer Book Rebellion, 'men from Cornwall and Devon fought and died to preserve their religious faith and practice and the language in which they had been brought up'. Feniton Court was the birthplace in 1827 of John Coleridge Patteson, the first missionary bishop of Melanesia, where he was murdered in 1871. Commemorated in Exeter Cathedral, his name is revered by Melanesian Christians.

Commemoration of the Battle of Fenny Bridges during the Prayer Book Rebellion of 1549.

FILLEIGH (E3) North Devon Pop. 260 (1901: 319)

Filleigh, approximately 8 miles from Barnstaple and 3 miles from South Molton, largely comprises the Fortescue estate of Castle Hill. The former Filleigh Manor, owned originally by the Filleigh family, came to the Fortescues through marriage in the 15th century. The Fortescues were already an established Devon family; according to legend the name was acquired due to an ancestor, Richard, having three times saved the life of William I at the Battle of Hastings being described as a 'strong shield' – in French: fort escu. Filleigh Manor was demolished in 1684 and Castle Hill built in its place, followed by development of the park and its landscape features. In 1934 a fire severely damaged the house which was subsequently rebuilt, the top floor – added in Victorian times – being dispensed with and the former Palladian design restored.

The adapted Filleigh viaduct of the former Taunton-Barnstaple railway now carries the A 361 North Devon Link road across the Bray valley.

The 5th Earl Fortescue died in 1958. His only son was killed at Alamein in the Second World War and the title passed to another branch of the family. However, Lord Fortescue's elder daughter, Lady Margaret, inherited Castle Hill, which she has now passed to her daughter, the Countess of Arran. (Castle Hill is not normally open to the public.)

The present church (St Paul) originally stood south-west of the house, but because of new developments was rebuilt at its present roadside site in 1732 and remodelled in 1877. Built in Norman style it has a pleasant and welcoming atmosphere.

The former Barnstaple-South Molton main road runs through the parish. Pressure on this is relieved by construction in 1987 of the North Devon Link road which passed north of the house. In this area the new road follows closely the route of the former Taunton-Barnstaple railway (opened in 1873 and closed in 1966); for this purpose the former spectacular viaduct across the valley of the River Bray was utilised, with its piers extended in height to carry the pre-stressed concrete road deck at high level.

Further reading: Fortescue, Lady Margaret, 'Recollections of the Fortescue family', Presidential address, *Transactions of the Devonshire Association 131*, 1999

Local society: Filleigh History Society

FREMINGTON (D2) North Devon Pop. 9744 (1901: 1194)

Fremington includes a large section of land bordering the south side of the Taw estuary between Barnstaple and Instow, with the Taw forming the parish's northern boundary. Also included are the villages and residential area of Bickington and Yelland. From the sandbanks and saltmarshes altitude rises to the farming country inland.

The former railway line at Fremington's old quay on the Taw is now a cycle route, and its station (right) *a visitor centre.*

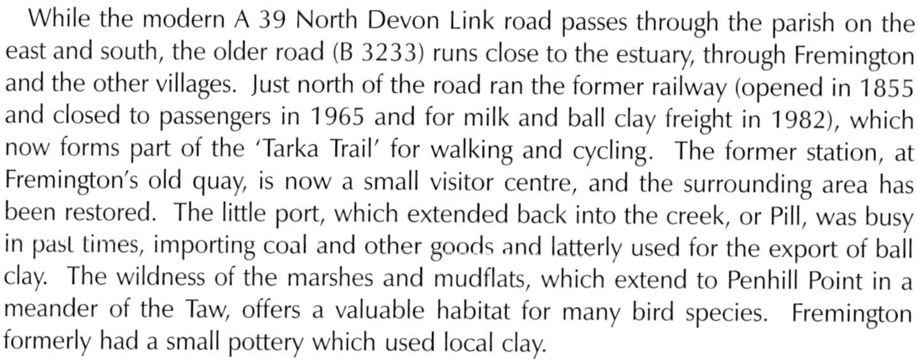

While the modern A 39 North Devon Link road passes through the parish on the east and south, the older road (B 3233) runs close to the estuary, through Fremington and the other villages. Just north of the road ran the former railway (opened in 1855 and closed to passengers in 1965 and for milk and ball clay freight in 1982), which now forms part of the 'Tarka Trail' for walking and cycling. The former station, at Fremington's old quay, is now a small visitor centre, and the surrounding area has been restored. The little port, which extended back into the creek, or Pill, was busy in past times, importing coal and other goods and latterly used for the export of ball clay. The wildness of the marshes and mudflats, which extend to Penhill Point in a meander of the Taw, offers a valuable habitat for many bird species. Fremington formerly had a small pottery which used local clay.

Of ancient origin, Fremington was named in Domesday as Fremantone – (Freeman's town). The manor was given by William I to Geoffrey, Bishop of Coutence, his lieutenant at the Battle of Hastings. The church (St Peter) dates from Norman times and there is a Norman stoup on the right side of the porch entrance. In 1189 the church was among possessions of Hartland Abbey. The oldest part of the present building is the north wall, other work dates from the 14th century, when a spire which formerly topped the tower was removed. The sanctuary is wide, and there is a south aisle, and a carved stone screen and pulpit. The church was restored in 1866 and the pulpit, much mutilated, was found beneath the floor of the nave. It dates from the 15th century, is of Beer stone and carved with the figures of Christ and the four evangelists. The altar is Elizabethan. There is also the church of St Andrew at Bickington.

FRITHELSTOCK (C4) Torridge Pop. 366 (1901: 429)

The remains of Frithelstock Priory, which was in existence from the 13th to 16th century.

Frithelstock parish is bounded by the meandering River Torridge and tributary streams on the east and south, and by the Duntz on the west. The Holsworthy-Bideford road (A 388) runs northwards through the parish, with a crossroads at Frithelstock Stone. The village is located a mile to the east, 2 miles W of Great Torrington, along the minor road which connects with the Torrington-Bideford road (A 386).

Close to the village stands the church (St Mary & St Gregory), which was rebuilt and enlarged in the 15th century and underwent some restoration c.1870. Nearby are remains of the priory which was founded here in the early 13th century by Robert de Beauchamp and continued in existence until being dissolved in the 16th century. The house of Austin canons was a subsidiary of Hartland Abbey, and dedicated to St Gregory. Horwood Barton, site of an ancient farm, is located just west of the A 388 immediately north of Frithelstock Stone.

FROGMORE AND SHERFORD (F11) South Hams Pop. 417 (1901: Sherford 342)

The parish of Frogmore and Sherford lies E and NE of Kingsbridge, Sherford village being 3 miles E of the town. The village of Frogmore is in the south, on the A 379 Kingsbridge-Dartmouth road and at the head of the long tidal Frogmore Creek from the Kingsbridge estuary. The undulating land rises to 487 ft on the northern boundary.

Sherford church (St Martin) dates from at least as early as the 15th century. It is built of slate from the quarries at nearby Charleton and has a fine carved rood screen. Ecclesiastically the parish is united with Stokenham. Malston and Stancombe in the north, and Keynedon in the south, were Domesday manors. This was one of the parishes that were evacuated of their inhabitants between December 1943 and late 1944 to enable allied forces to carry out exercises in preparation for the D-Day landings in Europe.

GEORGEHAM (C2) North Devon Pop. 1487 (1901: 689)

Georgeham, 3 miles NW of Braunton, was recorded as Ham in Domesday. With the church being dedicated to St George certainly from the 14th century (rebuilt except for the tower in the 1870s) the name is still locally often pronounced 'George Ham'.

Although Georgeham village lies inland, the parish extends westwards to the sea, including the old village of Croyde (where there is also the church of St Mary Magdalene). Croyde has been greatly developed with holiday facilities. There is a small beach at Croyde Bay where the Atlantic rollers roar in and there are strong currents, and another at Putsborough. Between them is the wild headland of Baggy Point, where the land rises to 311 ft; the point is owned by the National Trust and carries the South West coastal footpath. Many flints and chert artefacts have been found in the area dating from the Mesolithic period. The parish also includes the hamlet of North Buckland which, together with Croyde, Hole, and Pickwell, were Domesday manors.

Henry Williamson, author of the Tarka books, lived at Georgeham.

Further reading: Balfour, H. Stevenson, *The history of Georgeham and Croyde*, 1989

GEORGE NYMPTON (F3) North Devon Pop. 149 (1901: 170)

George Nympton, 2 miles SSW of South Molton, is bounded by the River Mole and a tributary stream on the south and west, and by a short upstream stretch of the Mole on the east, beyond Queens Nympton. Ecclesiastically George Nympton (also known as Nymet St George) has absorbed the small parish of Queens Nympton and is itself united with South Molton. The church (St George) probably originated in the 13th century, but the present building dates mainly from the late 15th century. The nave is of this date, the tower was rebuilt after collapsing – possibly due to a fire – c.1608, and the chancel rebuilt during restoration in the 1880s.

Further reading: George Nympton Working Group, *George Nympton, a Devon parish and its people*, 1995

Local society: George Nympton History Project Group

GERMANSWEEK (C6) West Devon Pop. 159 (1901: 204)

The upper area of Roadford Reservoir (viewed from the viaduct that carries the road to Germansweek) occupies a portion of the parish.

The small parish of Germansweek, 9 miles W of Okehampton, surrounds the south-west-flowing River Wolf. Between 1984 and 1990 works were carried out in the construction of Roadford Reservoir, to impound the Wolf water, which resulted in a large area of Germansweek and neighbouring Broadwoodwidger being flooded, the submerging of some farms, and diversion of certain roads. Thorough archaeological investigations of the properties were made before this was done. Having a capacity of 37,000 megalitres (8,140 million gallons) the reservoir, the largest in South West England, fulfils an important role in supplying Devon's water, and is also a valued reserve for wildlife and centre for water recreations.

Germansweek village stands well above the waterline. The church (St German) is of Early English date, the south transept and later added north aisle suggesting that it was possibly originally cruciform. It was restored in 1874. Germansweek and South Week were Domesday manors. The Seccombe family has owned and lived at Seccombe Farm since the 13th century.

Further reading: Fielding, Leslie, *Germansweek and its parish church: a history of the village of Germansweek and the parish church of St Germans*, 1977

Turton, S.D., *Roadford Reservoir project: documentary history of Hennard*

Turton, S.D., *Roadford Reservoir project: documentary history of West Wortha*, both Exeter Museum Archaeological Field Unit, 1988

GIDLEIGH (E7) West Devon Pop. 116 (1901: 114)

Gidleigh is a remote parish on the north-east of Dartmoor which, in its southern area, includes a length of the North Teign River and its Wallabrook tributary. Gidleigh Common rises westwards to heights well over 1400 ft. Prehistoric remains abound on the moorland and include the impressive Scorhill stone circle. The Teign and Wallabrook valleys were worked by the tinners.

The village is small, approached by long, narrow, winding lanes from Chagford, the A 382, or the old A 30 road in the north. The church (Holy Trinity) dates from the 16th century, with some later rebuilding. Rectors are recorded fom 1259. There is a fine rood screen. There are no pews, seating is on chairs, and the flooring parquet. Near the church are the remains of Gidleigh Castle, a fortified manor house of c.1300. The parish's northern boundary is defined by the Forder Brook and there are several interesting old houses in the area, including West Chapple, an early longhouse now restored.

Further reading: Grumley-Grennan, *Gidleigh*, Glebe Pub., 2000

GITTISHAM (K6) East Devon Pop. 582 (1901: 314)

Part of the attractive village of Gittisham near Honiton.

Gittisham is the next parish to Honiton on the west, with its very attractive village situated 2 miles SW of the town. The A 375 Honiton-Sidmouth road runs south on the eastern side, and the A 30, and also the railway, along the north.

The parish is dominated by lofty hills on the east and south, with the land rising from c.200 ft along the River Otter, which forms the northern boundary, to 769 ft in the south-west and 782 ft on Gittisham Hill on the east, where there are tumuli from the Bronze Age. A portion of land between the village and Gittisham Hill comprises the park of Combe House, built in the 16th century by Henry Beaumont and now a hotel.

There is reference to a church in 'Giddesham' in 1244, and the earliest recording of a rector is in 1279. The church was rebuilt in 1321 in flint; there was a thatched roof until this was replaced with slates c.1500. The interior has a distinct 18th-century feel, with box pews installed in 1715 and a west gallery dating from 1701, and there are many features of interest. Close to the churchyard are three cottages converted from the former village school, built in 1720 as a gift to the poor by Sir Thomas Pitt of Combe.

Rapshayes, in the south-west, was a Domesday manor.

GOODLEIGH (D2) North Devon Pop. 428 (1901: 253)

Goodleigh is located 3 miles E of Barnstaple on an unclassified road which branches from the road to Bratton Fleming in the west of the parish, and, proceeding eastwards eventually connects with the A 399 at Brayford. The parish is bounded on the north-west by the River Yeo and by tributaries to north and south.

Being at a convenient distance from Barnstaple, Goodleigh has attracted new residents in later years, but still retains its country character.

The ancient church (St Gregory) was rebuilt in the 1880s.

Further reading: Fice, J.E., *The history of Goodleigh, a north Devon village*, 1982

GREAT TORRINGTON (C4) Torridge Pop. 5279 (1901: 3241)

The town of Great Torrington, or just 'Torrington' as it is generally known, has an imposing situation high above the steep-sided north bank of the River Torridge as it completes the winding last few miles of its course before reaching the estuary at Bideford, and the sea. The view of Torrington from the opposite hills south of the river has been likened to that of Jerusalem across Kidron, and indeed a certain similarity does exist. The reverse view, looking south from the town's car park is amongst the most impressive in Devon, with the river below and the pattern of fields and hills rising in the distance.

Rivers and streams form most of the parish boundaries: the water from Gammaton on the north-west, the Torridge on the south-west, and the stream coming down through Stevenstone on the south-east. A brief over land course from tumuli on Darracott Moor to the ancient earthworks of Berry Castle completes the circuit.

Torrington was created a borough in the late 12th century and in the same period the town acquired common lands which still survive. Early in the 13th century a castle was constructed at a strategic point on the south-facing escarpment, its site later occupied by a bowling green. Torrington was an early market town and in 1554 was granted a charter of incorporation.

The position of Great Torrington, high above the Torridge, has been likened to views of Jerusalem.

The town was the scene of the last major battle fought in Devon during the Civil War, which virtually ended the hopes of the Royalists of ending the war militarily. In February 1646 Lord Hopton, commander of the King's Western Army, seeking to reach Exeter from north-west Devon, advanced to Torrington. A few days later the force was met by the Parliamentary New Model Army under Sir Thomas Fairfax. A fierce battle ensued in which the Cavaliers were defeated. Their supplies of gunpowder, which had been stored in the church, were blown up, resulting in the deaths of around 200 Royalist prisoners inside, and destruction of the building. The church (St Michael) was rebuilt in 1651, and restored in 1864.

Torrington was a centre of the woollen industry in 1538, and the making of baize became a speciality. The trade eventually declined c.1800. Glove-making was a home industry from the 16th century, and after the wool finished the skiving and dressing of chamois became established in the early 19th century, with skins being sent away for glove-making in London and elsewhere. Tanning had become a flourishing business by the 17th century, and in the mid 19th century the town still had five fully operational tanneries. Torrington was the home of Thomas Fowler (1777–1843), mathematician and inventor, who devised the first calculating machine, exhibited in London in 1844, which led on to modern computers.

The reverse view, southwards from the town of Torrington to hills that rise from the Torridge valley. Taddiport on the right.

An important industry in Torrington for over a century from 1874 was the Torridge Vale butter factory, sited near the Town Bridge at Taddiport. Milk was bought from farmers in the surrounding area for manufacture. The work expanded during the 1920s and operations greatly increased during the Second World War and following years when Torridge Vale Dairies played an important role in helping to maintain the nation's food supplies.

An industry established in later years is that of Dartington Crystal glassworks, products of which have achieved worldwide reputation.

In the 19th century the Torrington or Rolle Canal was built to convey limestone and coal from the Torridge estuary to kilns along the river and at Torrington, inspired by local landowner Lord Rolle. Opened in 1827 it was entered by a tide-lock near Landcross and had one inclined plane on its 6-mile length. The Torridge was crossed by an impressive five-arched aqueduct, which was later adapted as an entrance to the drive to Beam. At Taddiport limekilns and warehouses were served by the canal which then continued a further mile to a specially-built New Manor Mill, a substantial crenellated structure. Also at this point New Bridge was built across the Torridge, opened in 1843. The canal closed c.1876, with the railway arriving on the scene and offering better transport prospects.

The Torrington railway extension from Bideford was opened in 1872, with the station close to the town's 15th-century Rothern Bridge over the Torridge. Another railway route, that of the North Devon & Cornwall Junction Light Railway from Torrington to Halwill, was opened in 1925. On both this line and the one from

Torrington to Bideford and Barnstaple passenger services ceased in 1965 although transport for milk and clay continued until 1982. The line is now a walking and cycling route.

Further reading: Alexander J.J. and Hooper, W.R., *The history of Great Torrington in the county of Devon*, Sutton, 1948
Local society: Torrington Local History Society
Museum: Torrington has a fine museum, adjacent to The Square

GULWORTHY (C8) West Devon Pop. 488 (1901 N/A)

The present-day parish of Gulworthy, which extends from the outskirts of Tavistock westwards to the River Tamar, corresponds approximately to the former parish known as Tavistock Hamlets. Originally, from the time of Tavistock Abbey and the succeeding Bedford estate, the whole area comprised one parish, but in 1895 it was divided into two civil parishes: Tavistock and Tavistock Hamlets. In the late 20th century some boundary changes were made and the western part became Gulworthy. It still remains largely a pleasant area of hamlets and scattered farms, bordered by the 'great divide' of the Tamar valley, with the main Tavistock-Callington road (A 390) passing through.

Springtime in Gulworthy churchyard.

Morwell, a 15th-century quadrangular house overlooking the Tamar, was the country seat of the abbots of Tavistock. It was restored by the Duke of Bedford and is now a farm. Below it, beside the river, is Morwellham (pronounced 'Morwell Ham'), a small village that was Tavistock's ancient port. During the 19th century Morwellham took on a new importance due to the mining boom. The Tavistock Canal (constructed 1803–17) predominantly brought ores from inland Mary Tavy, delivered to the quay by inclined plane, while manganese ore was also carted here. Later, following the discovery in 1844 of rich copper lodes on the Duke of Bedford's land 4 miles away, the quays were extended and became extremely busy in storing and exporting the ore. With the closure of the copper mine in 1901 Morwellham became disused and gradually fell into decay, the docks silted up. Restored from the 1970s it is now an open-air museum and visitor centre. A small hydro station generates electricity from the canal water as it descends to the river.

The mine that brought prosperity to the duke was upstream from Morwellham at Blanchdown, and was known as Devon Great Consols. By the 1860s the mine was a substantial producer of the world's copper supplies. The various workings covered a wide area, much of it eventually rendered sterile due to the by-product arsenic extracted latterly. Part of the area is now afforested.

There is no actual village of Gulworthy, but it has an attractive church (St Paul) built by the Duke of Bedford in the 1850s. The churchyard is an array of primroses and daffodils in springtime.

Further reading: Booker, Frank, *The Industrial Archaeology of the Tamar Valley*, David & Charles, 1967
Local society: The Friends of Morwellham

HACCOMBE WITH COMBE (G8) Teignbridge Pop: 729 (1901: 415)

The parish of Haccombe with Combe is situated immediately E of Newton Abbot, bordered on the north by the shore of the Teign estuary. Included are the villages of Netherton and Combeinteignhead, with its church, and the mansion and church of Haccombe. The south-west parish boundary follows the line of the unclassified 'back road' between Newton Abbot and St Marychurch (Torquay) and in so doing cuts through the ancient earthwork of Milber Down hill fort (see under COFFINSWELL).

Combeinteignhead village is in the north, half a mile inland at the head of a valley (combe). The church (All Saints) is of ancient origin, two altars having been dedicated here by Bishop Bronescombe in 1259, with the high altar dedicated in 1339. The present building dates from the 14th and 15th centuries, restored in the 1880s. It has a 12th-century font and a fine rood screen. Nearby are red sandstone almshouses, given by William Bourchin in 1620; they are now artists' studios.

Coombe Cellars, directly north on the estuary's edge, is a pleasant spot, an early base for the local fishing industry when it was equipped with storage facilities. It was also a place for smugglers. Buckland Barton, in the north-west, was a Domesday manor and seat of the Hockmores. Netherton was an estate, believed to date from the 12th century.

The present early 19th-century house at Haccombe occupies the site of the early dwelling of the Haccombes, who held the manor in the 12th and 13th centuries. Later it passed to the Courtenays, and the Carews. Having been used for a girls' school in the 20th century, it is now divided into flats. Haccombe church (St Blaise) dates from the early 14th century, with dedications by Bishop Grandisson in 1328. In 1337 a community of chantry priests was founded here, forming a collegiate church. Most of the present building comprises the original red sandstone structure. Noted for its brasses and effigies, the church contains medieval Seville tiles and glass, while internal stonework results from restoration in the 1820s. Its one bell is said to be the oldest in the country.

Further reading: Boyd, Martin H.A., *Haccombe with Combeinteignhead parish history*, 1986

HALBERTON (J4) Mid Devon Pop. 1573 (1901: 1238)

Halberton village lies 3 miles due E of Tiverton, while the parish extends east to the valley of the River Culm and south of Tiverton to the Exe in the south-west. South of the village are the hamlets of Curham, Ash Thomas and Brithembottom. Served by the former A 373 (now unclassified) road to the A 38 in the east, the parish is now cut through on the eastern side by the M5 motorway, and is touched in the north by the A 361 North Devon Link road. There is also a network of minor roads. The land is undulating, ranging from c.200 ft in the south-east to 600 ft in the south-west. The changes of level caused problems for the engineer John Rennie in the construction of the Grand Western Canal (see TIVERTON) in 1810–14, necessitating expensive cutting and provision of an embankment to carry the canal north of the village. In 1844 the main railway line from Paddington via Bristol to Exeter came into operation throught the east of the parish, and from 1848 to 1967 a branch line connected from it to Tiverton with an intermediate station at Halberton.

The pond at Halberton is reputedly fed by warm springs that prevent it freezing.

The church (St Andrew) dates from the 15th century, restored in 1848. It has a notable screen and pulpit, dating from 1420. There is an Anglican chapel (St Thomas) at Ash Thomas. Besides Halberton itself, Ash Thomas, Leonard Farm, East and West Manley, Muxbere, Sellake, Sutton, and Moorstone Barton were settled pre-1066. East Manley was the home of the Manleys from the 13th to the 19th centuries and many people of that name still live in the area. Bridwell, on the eastern boundary with Uffculme, is a late 18th-century mansion built on the site of a medieval chapel.

The village is in two parts: Higher Town and Lower Town; between them is a pond, reputedly fed by warm springs which prevent the water freezing.

HALWELL (includes MORELEIGH) (F10) South Hams Pop. 393 (1901: Halwell 246, Moreleigh 104)

Halwell, 5 miles SSW of Totnes and 6 miles NNE of Kingsbridge, lies on the route of the A 381 road which connects the two towns and is the turn-off point for the A 3122 to Dartmouth. Minor roads from the west also connect here. Flowing northwards is the small River Wash which, with a tributary, joins the Harbourne in Bow Creek at Tuckenhay. The land is undulating, rising to 706 ft in the south where there are tumuli and an earthworks known as Stanborough Camp, believed to date from the Iron Age. Half a mile east of the village was another such camp, now mainly destroyed.

Halwell was one of Devon's four burhs in the 10th century, until superseded by Totnes. The church (St Leonard) dates from at least as early as the 13th century. The present building, which has a slate tower, dates from the 15th century. Poulston and Washbourne, both in the north, were Domesday manors.

For civil purposes Halwell and neighbouring Moreleigh, on the west, are now combined under the name of Halwell, although the two are still separate ecclesiastically. Moreleigh church (All Saints) dates from the 14th century, restored in the 17th century. It has a painted pulpit with sounding board, and chairs in place of pews. Nearby Place Barton was the site of the former manor house.

HALWILL (C6) Torridge Pop. 822 (1901: 434)

Harberton's church of St Andrew.

Halwill, 10 miles NW of Okehampton, covers a tract of Culm Measures moor and grassland, possessing – certainly in the past – an air of remoteness and wildness. The River Carey forms most of the western boundary, with the remainder running somewhat indirectly across land, the easternmost point being the ancient site known as Henderbarrow on the Okehampton-Holsworthy road (A 3079). The occurrence of barrows and tumuli are indications of early habitation in the parish, some areas of which are now afforested.

The village lies in the south-west, with the church (St Peter & St James). Dating from the 14th century, the church was partly reconstructed, and north and south transepts added in the 1870s. The tower is the original.

A mile or so to the north-east is Halwill Junction, on the A 3079. This developed with 19th and 20th-century railway construction. In 1879 the London & South Western Railway line from Meldon Junction, near Okehampton, to Holsworthy came through here (extended to Bude in 1898), then, in 1892 a link between Halwill and Launceston, down the Carey valley, was provided. Finally, in 1925, Devon's last railway to be constructed, the North Devon & Cornwall Junction Light Railway, enabled a 22-mile connection between Torrington and Halwill. Halwill Junction naturally developed as a somewhat isolated trading centre. Although the railways closed in the 1960s the name remains, and housing developments with limited shopping and other facilities continue.

In 1871 panels of Harberton church's 15th-century screen were replaced by depictions of various figures painted on to metal sheets.

HARBERTON (F10) South Hams Pop. 1285 (1901: 1170)

Harberton parish adjoins Totnes, its village being 2 miles SW of the town, with access by minor roads from the A 381 (Totnes-Kingsbridge) and from the A 38 and Avonwick-Totnes roads to the north. The River Harbourne, which gave the parish its name, flows through, west of the village and through the village of Harbertonford in the south. The land is undulating, pleasant and fertile, rising to 539 ft towards the north.

There has been a church on the site of the present one (St Andrew) since c.1100, the red sandstone girdle font, with its Byzantine design, being practically the only remnant. A vicar was first recorded here in 1235. The present building is of 14th and 15th-century construction, restored in the 1860s and 70s. Panels of the very fine 15th- century rood screen were replaced in 1871 by painted sheets of metal, depicting various figures. The beautiful carved stone pulpit dates from the 15th century. There are box pews in the nave. The roof of the vaulted nave bears eight bosses. Near the church is the ancient Church House Inn.

The former woollen mill at Harbertonford, now partly converted to residential accommodation.

Harbertonford was made a separate ecclesiastical parish in 1860 and its church (St Peter) then built. This is an attractive cruciform building with a small bell turret and spire at the intersection of the transepts and aisles, and woodwork forming the ceiling of the sanctuary. The A 381 road passes through, crossing the Harbourne by an ancient bridge. This was formerly a minor industrial place with a woollen mill near the village, a works for agricultural implements farther upstream at Hill Mills, and a slate quarry at Englebourne.

Great Englebourne and – farther north on the west – East and West Leigh, and Hazard, were Domesday manors.

The main railway passes through the north of the parish.

HARFORD (E10) South Hams Pop. 77 (1901: 198)

Harford parish, in the area of Dartmoor National Park, in outline is rather like a very long-necked bottle. It extends for 6 miles N from Ivybridge to a short boundary with the Forest of Dartmoor on the Red Lake, tributary of the River Erme which forms the western boundary. The northern, moorland area, which rises to over 1450 ft, is rich in Bronze Age remains of every description, particularly along the valley of the Erme. Here, too, towards the south, is one of the remnants of Dartmoor's ancient oak woods, known as Piles Copse. There are also remains of tinners' activity, including those of tinners' mills. In the early 20th century china clay was worked in the far north, served by the 7½ mile Redlake Mineral Railway, which meandered in and out of the parish.

There is no actual village but a narrow 2-mile lane extends north from Ivybridge to the church (St Petroc) in its almost solitary and unspoilt location, just east of an ancient bridge on the old road from Plympton to South Brent. An old way-marking cross now stands in a corner of the churchyard.

It is believed that a church existed here at the time of the Norman Conquest. The earliest record of a rector is in 1262. The present building, constructed of granite, dates mainly from the 15th and 16th centuries, although the tower may be older. There is an ancient font, believed to be Saxon, as well as one from c.1500. The church was restored in 1879 and 1920.

HARPFORD see NEWTON POPPLEFORD AND HARPFORD

HARTLAND (A3) Torridge Pop. 1676 (1901: 1634)

Hard sharp rocks extend spectacularly from Hartland's shores.

Hartland, one of Devon's largest parishes, appears outstandingly on the map as the county's 'top left-hand corner'. It is almost rectangular, surrounded by the sea on two sides, with the north-west prominence of Hartland Point marking the approach to Barnstaple-Bideford Bay, and the Bristol Channel. The parish's long coastline, wild and rocky, has through the ages demanded respect from seafarers and has been the scene of countless shipwrecks.

It is, however, a coastline of stunning beauty. The tall cliffs, which display impressive geological folds due to interbedded sandstone and Culm Measures shales, are, above, bright and fragrant in season with wildflowers – gorse and primroses, bluebells and sea-pinks. Seaward, ribs of hard rock project west, their treacherous sharpness constantly washed by white-foamed waves that break over them. In the air, seabirds soar and add their cries to the wave-sounds.

Inland the parish is one of many farms and winding lanes. Much of the land is rough, and trees that withstand the Atlantic gales are often bent permanently away from the west. This was an area of early inhabitation. Tumuli (burial mounds) which occur on Welsford and Bursdon Moors in the south are probably evidence of Bronze Age occupation. Windberry Point in the north-east, and Embury Beacon in the south-west are each marked on maps as 'Camp' – possibly Iron Age. The Saxons knew Hartland – it was a royal estate in the possession of King Alfred and his successors.

Tall cliffs and rocky beach at Hartland in the far north-west of the county. The cliffs display geological folds due to interbedded sandstone and Culm Measures shales. Remains of the former quay are on the right.

One of the many Celtic saints who had come this way, in the 5th and 6th centuries, was Nectan. He is reputed to have established a hermitage beside a well, a short distance from the site of the present church. Although it seems likely that a Nectan cult persisted, immediate subsequent history is obscure until 1050, when a collegiate church of 12 secular canons was built by Countess Gytha, mother of King Harold and wife of Godwin, Earl of Wessex, who held the manor of Hartland. Nothing is known of the location of this building, which was replaced in the 12th century by Hartland Abbey, under the religious order of St Augustine of Hippo.

The present church (St Nectan) is situated at Stoke, ½ mile inland from the coast at Hartland Quay. It dates from the 14th century and is large and lovely, restored in 1848. The tower is the second highest church tower in Devon – it can be seen from well out to sea. Although there are both north and south transepts the building is not truly cruciform, as these are adjuncts to the aisles. The wagon roofs are of high quality, and partly ceiled, with paintings of saints. A prominent feature is the very fine rood screen, and the font is Norman. There is a room over the north porch, used as a museum. In medieval times there were also numerous small chapels throughout the parish.

The main village is fairly large, situated 2½ miles inland and approached by turnings off the A 39 road. It was an ancient borough from 1290 and was granted charters for markets and fairs, but these ceased in later times. Hartland Abbey, in its valley, was eventually rebuilt, and only fragments of the original remain in the present house (of the same name). After the Dissolution the house passed to a succession of owners before being acquired by the Stucleys, by whom it is still owned. In the season it is opened to visitors.

The lighthouse, opened in 1874, is a vital feature at Hartland Point. The quay, ½ mile south, now has a museum, hotel, and shop. Originating from the 16th century the quay is no longer in use as such due to ravages of the sea which attacked and destroyed the structures in the late 19th century. There is a small rocky pebble beach. A mile down the coast from the quay is Speke's Mill, where there are grassy levels and an impressive waterfall.

Further reading: Chope, R.P., *The book of Hartland*, Devonshire Press, 1940
Local society: Hartland Society
Museum: Hartland Quay Museum, the Quay

The evocative 'Sheep', sculpted by Roger Dean of Exeter in the 1990s, stands near the entrance to Hatherleigh Market.

HATHERLEIGH (D5) West Devon Pop. 1306 (1901: 1293)

The ancient town of Hatherleigh, 6½ miles NNW of Okehampton, rises from the east bank of the River Lew. (This is not the same Lew as the Tamar tributary, to the south-west.) The Rivers Torridge and Okement form the parish boundary in the north, and the Okement also that on the east. Elsewhere the somewhat indirect boundary route is again often defined by streams. Large areas of the parish comprise land that is moory and poorish in quality, but pockets of the more favourable New Red Sandstone also occur.

Hatherleigh was one of the endowments given to Tavistock Abbey in the 10th century, and known as Hadreleia. The manor of Hatherleigh included also the present parish of Jacobstowe and part of Monkokehampton. It was not, however, among the properties granted by the king to the Russells at the Dissolution, but was sold to the Arscotts. East of Hartherleigh town is the wide expanse of Hatherleigh Moor, of approximately 400 acres. The moor was granted by the abbot to the local burgesses, with rights of common for the people, after Hatherleigh had been made a borough in the 13th century. These rights still continue under a management committee of 15 members including three from the Town Council. Grazing rights are held by 'potboilers', a term unique to Hatherleigh and referring to households, whether owner or tenant, residing within the borough bounds. (The ancient borough relates to a smaller area than the actual parish.) In order to manage the moor with adequate stocking levels grazing is invited from outsiders, on payment, but without the same rights as potboilers. During the Second World War the moor had to be ploughed for food cropping, but the requirement now is for its return to the natural state.

The church (St John the Baptist), of ancient foundation, was built in the 15th century. During exceptional storms in January 1990 the tall spire was at first weakened by the strong winds, and then crashed down. The destruction was followed by complete restoration.

There are several notable buildings in the town, including the medieval Church House, still used for meetings, and the George Hotel, a coaching inn possibly dating from c.1500. The town suffered a severe fire c.1840 which caused much damage. Rebuilding followed, with certain improvements to the streets. The town's main street is very steep, with a sharp bend near the top, and as traffic increased Hatherleigh suffered from jams. This problem has been greatly reduced by the provision of a bypass road.

Like many Devon towns, Hatherleigh played a part in the woollen industry. For long recognised as a centre for the selling of cattle and other livestock, Hatherleigh still has a busy market, on Mondays for cattle, Tuesdays for stalls, and Wednesdays for sheep, and well appointed premises on the edge of the town, close to the river and new roundabout. Sadly, however, due to recent crises in farming and changes in systems its long-term future is uncertain.

Ancient houses and farms in the parish include: Deckport, Essworthy, Fishleigh, Pulsworthy, Hannaborough, Passaford, Upcott and Great Velliford.

Further reading: Hatherleigh History Society, *The story of Hatherleigh*, 1999
Local society: Hatherleigh Local History Society

HAWKCHURCH (M6) East Devon Pop. 477

Hawkchurch's 12th-century Norman north arcade. The walls and roof of the church were raised and the clerestory provided in the 1860s.

The triangular parish of Hawkchurch is surrounded on two of its three sides by the county of Dorset, from which it was transferred to Devon in 1896. The western boundary is defined by the River Axe and a north-flowing tributary. From just over 100 ft near the Axe the land rises eastwards, reaching 841 ft at Lambert's Castle, an Iron Age fort. The B 3165 Axminster-Crewkerne road runs along the southern boundary, with minor roads leading off it to the village.

The church (St John the Baptist), which remains within the Diocese of Salisbury, is of ancient origin. The name of the parish means Hafoc's church, which may indicate the existence of a church here from Saxon times, possibly accounting for the Saxon font. The present building dates from the 12th century, and has many fine features including a Norman north arcade and chancel arch piers which date from that time. The first rector was instituted in 1295, when the church belonged to Cerne Abbey. The tower dates from the 15th century, reconditioned in 1957. The church was restored, with much rebuilding, in the early 1860s; the walls and roof were raised and a clerestory provided. On 25 January 1990 a severe storm caused great damage to the church, including lifting its roof, which necessitated costly repairs.

Wyld Court, in the north-east of the village, built c.1593, was the home of the Moore family, and originally E-shaped.

Further reading: Pullman, George P.R., *The book of the Axe,* 1969

HEANTON PUNCHARDON (D2) North Devon Pop. 1812 (1901: 404)

Heanton Punchardon lies along the north bank of the Taw estuary, between Barnstaple and Braunton, with land that rises from marshland to 450 ft a short distance inland. The A 361 road passes through, as did the railway to Ilfracombe between 1874 and 1970.

The manor of Heanton was formerly held by the Punchardon family, hence the double name. The church (St Augustine), situated on the end of the high ground, dates from c.1500, with 19th-century restoration. The church was re-ordered in 2000, the fine chancel screen moved eastward and the combined pulpit-lectern from south to north. There is now a nave altar, with removable communion rails, and the former sanctuary is now a prayer chapel. There are fine views from the churchyard to the Taw and the mouth of the Taw-Torridge estuary and the sea. Heanton Court, close to the shoreline, was a residence of a branch of the Basset family.

The parish includes the former hamlets of Wrafton, West Ashford, and Chivenor. At Chivenor, the site of a 13th-century settlement and later a farm, a small aerodrome was developed in the early 20th century. During the Second World War the potential in the expanse of level ground, bulging out into a loop of the Taw, was realised for construction of an RAF station. This continued after the war on a diminishing scale until being transferred to the Royal Marines, with just an RAF search and rescue unit being retained.

Hemyock's church of St Mary dates from the 12th century.

HEMYOCK (K4) Mid Devon Pop. 1821 (1901: 806)

The parish of Hemyock is situated on the southern slopes of the Blackdown Hills (designated as an Area of Outstanding Natural Beauty) with its northern boundary defined by the Somerset-Devon county border. This border is marked by the unclassified road along the edge at over 800 ft, from where there are very fine views. The River Culm flows westwards through the south, at a level of c.400 ft, and the land rises southwards to heights of from 700-800 ft. The parish's highest point of 880 ft is reached on Culm Davy Hill in the north-west. The surrounding area was evidently known to prehistoric peoples, and iron was smelted on the hills between 750BC and 100AD.

The last goods train to leave Hemyock, 1975. COURTESY THE BOOK OF HEMYOCK

The village lies south of the river, approached from the west by the B 3391 road and from the south by an unclassified road from Honiton. Hemyock originated in Saxon times and building evidence at the base of the church tower suggests the existence of a substantial structure of c.1100. Written records of the church (St Mary) date from 1268; Norman arches within the building date from that period, and there is a Norman font. Further work was carried out at later stages and in 1846–7 a major restoration. There is also the chapel of St Mary, dating from the 15th century, at the hamlet of Culm Davy. From the late 17th century Quakers and Baptists were active in Hemyock, and the Baptist Church, its present building opened in 1865, still flourishes.

Hemyock Castle, a privately-owned Ancient Monument located south-west of the church, originates from the 12th century, when the de Hydon family were lords of the manor, or possibly earlier. Although more probably a fortified manor house, the castle was the scene of skirmishes during the Civil War when it was used as a stronghold in turn by each side. In later times a succession of owners included Lieutenant General John Graves Simcoe, hero of the American War of Independence and the first governor of Upper Canada (Ontario). Much of the structure became ruinous over the years, but restoration and renovation, combined with archaeological investigations and surveys, have proceeded from the early 1980s.

In 1876 the Culm Valley Light Railway was constructed from Tiverton Junction, with Hemyock the eastern terminus. It closed in 1963. Also in the 1870s a consortium of Hemyock dairy farmers initiated the establishment of a milk factory to deal with the production of local farms. This began in a small way but grew rapidly as a farmers' co-operative, particularly due to the advantage of the railway for enabling quick transport to London. Many people were employed and butter and dried milk were among the products. Sadly the decision was taken in 1999 by the then owners, Unigate, to cease production at Hemyock, and the factory is no more.

Farming has always been a strong feature of this countryside, and in 1920 what started as a Calf Club for young farming people became the first Young Farmers' Club, in a movement that soon spread throughout the country. The club still flourishes as the Culm Valley YFC.

Of the farms and hamlets Culm Davy, Culm Pyne Barton and Gorwell were mentioned in Domesday.

Further reading: Clist, Brian, and Dracott, Chris, *The book of Hemyock*, Halsgrove, 2001
Local society: Hemyock Local History Group

HENNOCK (G7) Teignbridge Pop. 1626 (1901: 746)

In St Mary's Church, Hennock, the predominantly blue ceilure above the rood screen was restored in 1975.

Hennock is located 9 miles SSW of Exeter and 6½ miles NNW of Newton Abbot, in the hilly country between the Teign valley on the east and the Bovey valley on the west. The A 38 expressway passes through the extreme south, while the Teign and Bovey valleys respectively carry the B 3193 and A 382 roads. Altitudes rise from less than 100 ft on the heathland around the village of Chudleigh Knighton in the south, which is included in the civil parish, to over 800 ft in places in the north where the rock changes to granite. This northern section, which includes Hennock village, is within Dartmoor National Park, and part of Tottiford Reservoir lies within the parish.

It is believed that there has been a church here for over 1000 years. The present building (St Mary) dates from the 15th century, the tower possibly dating from 1250. There is a Norman font. Restoration of the rood screen was carried out in 1956 and c.1980. Above the rood is a striking ceilure, predominantly blue in colour, which was restored in 1975. Chudleigh Knighton is a separate ecclesiastical parish with its own church (St Paul), formerly a chapel-of-ease built in 1841–2, an ancient episcopal chapel having earlier been relegated to a barn.

The original name of the village was Hainoc, mentioned in Domesday. Warmhill, to the south-east, and Chudleigh Knighton were Domesday manors.

Deposits of pottery or ball clay, the product of granite decomposition and erosion, carried down from Dartmoor by natural forces to settle at lower levels, have been worked on Chudleigh Knighton heath since the early 18th century. In the higher north other extractive industries prevailed. Small quantities of lead and silver were produced in the area above Teign Village, and micaceous haematite – a form of iron ore used in rust-resisting paint – was worked at Bowden Hill, and at Great Rock which opened in the 1800s and was the last Dartmoor working mine before it closed in 1969. The large Trusham dolerite quarry on the west side of the B 3193, is actually on the extreme west of Hennock parish. Teign Village on the hillside above was developed for quarry workers in the early 20th century.

HIGH BICKINGTON (D3) Torridge Pop. 742 (1901: 539)

High Bickington is a parish of steep wooded valleys and high ground, as its name suggests. The eastern boundary is formed by the River Taw, in its meandering stage, from where the land rises steeply to achieve an altitude of nearly 600 ft at the village, and 643 ft on the western boundary. The other boundaries cross land, sometimes following roads or streams. These streams are mainly tributaries which combine to form the Langley Brook, which is crossed at Langridgeford – just outside the parish on the north-west – by the Torrington-South Molton road (B 3227). The B 3217 road runs north-south through the parish and village, and the Exeter-Barnstaple road (A 377) passes along the eastern boundary, adjacent to the river. The railway also shares the valley route.

It is believed that High Bickington's origins go back probably more than 1000 years, to the time of the Saxons. Named in Domesday as Bichentone, it is presumed to have been the settlement of Beocca. The farm names of Dadland, Seckington, Snape, Stowford, Shuteley, Yelland and Deptford are all suggestive of their having originated in the Saxon age.

The church (St Mary) is of great antiquity. It was founded and endowed in 930 by King Athelstan, grandson of Alfred the Great, who at the time was staying at nearby Umberleigh. The original church building, which would have been of wood and thatch, was rebuilt on the same site with stone walls following the Norman Conquest. Remains of those walls survive in the present structure, and the original Norman font remains in use. In 1450 the church was enlarged to its present size and a new tower built. The remains of the Norman tower still exist as a rather curious feature of the construction, now used as the vestry. A further restoration was carried out in 1873. Greatly treasured in the church are the 70 or so magnificent carved pew ends.

High Bickington's Methodist Zion Chapel was built in 1834, originally for the Bible Christians. The former Brethren Chapel in North Road is now a community centre.

Further reading: Stone, Avril, *The book of High Bickington, a ridgeway village*, Halsgrove, 2000

High Bickington, aerial view 1988.
COURTESY THE BOOK OF HIGH BICKINGTON

HIGHAMPTON (C5) West Devon Pop. 196 (1901: 219)

Highampton, on the wet moory land of the Culm Measures, is bounded on the north by the River Torridge and on the south-west by the Wagaford Water. Elsewhere the boundary passes over land or along tributary streams. Situated 3½ miles W of Hatherleigh, the village stands just north of the Hatherleigh–Holsworthy road (A 3072) which runs east-west through the parish. There are fine views to the south.

The church (Holy Cross) was inaugurated in 1270, and the inner south doorway is Norman, while the font with its bowl motif of crosses, saltire and stars, has been here since 1270. Apart from the tower, which dates from 1489, the 15th-century building was largely rebuilt in the 1830s when the north aisle was added; the two slender pillars on this side are of Dartmoor granite, there is no vaulting.

Burdon was in the family of the Burdons from the late 12th century for 650 years. It has been greatly re-shaped and is no longer a private dwelling; for some years a nursing home it is now an adolescent rehabilitation unit. Totleigh Barton, close to the Torridge in the north, which retains signs of a moat, was probably the site of the 13th-century Zouch manor house, ancient seat in the 13th and 14th centuries of the Zouch and Fitzwarren families.

The line of the North Devon and Cornwall Junction Light Railway from Torrington to Halwill Junction ran through the parish, close to the main road. Opened in 1925, this section closed in 1965.

HIGH BRAY see BRAYFORD

HITTISLEIGH (F6) Mid Devon Pop. 113 (1901: 107)

The parish of Hittisleigh lies 9 miles E of Okehampton and 8½ miles SW of Crediton. The western and northern boundaries are defined by the small River Troney, tributary of the Yeo which flows eastwards to join the Creedy. The minor road from Whiddon Down to Yeoford and Crediton runs through the parish. The land is hilly, rising to 680 ft in the west.

The church (St Andrew) dates from the 14th century, enlarged in the 15th century. There is a Norman font.

Hockworthy's church of St Simon & St Jude is of ancient origin, rebuilt in the mid 19th century.

HOCKWORTHY (J4) Mid Devon Pop. 163 (1901: 244)

Hockworthy, 7 miles NE of Tiverton, is bounded on the north-east by the Somerset county border and by the upper waters of the River Lowman, tributary of the Exe, on the west. The land is hilly, reaching 876 ft on Chimney Down, west of the village, from where there are fine views.

The church (St Simon & St Jude) is of early origin. The tower was rebuilt in 1848 and the remainder of the church in 1863–5. The font is Norman, and the pulpit is of Beer stone with a marble stem and inlaid work.

HOLBETON (E10) South Hams Pop. 579 (1901: 850)

Holbeton is a pleasant parish with a fine stretch of coastline and the west bank of the lovely River Erme estuary, which form the south and east boundaries respectively. The land is undulating, much of it rising to 250-350 ft with 370 ft attained on the northern boundary. Located 9 miles ESE of Plymouth it is served by minor roads from the A 379 Plymouth-Kingsbridge road which skirts the parish in the north.

The village is centrally situated. The church (All Saints) is of early foundation. The church itself, the high altar and another altar were dedicated by Bishop Grandisson in 1336. The present 15th-century cruciform building, with its tower and spire, contains much finely carved woodwork, including the 15th-century screen. Besides an ancient Norman font there is a large elaborate font of Devon marble dating from restoration of the church in 1885.

In the north of the parish, in parkland, is Flete, an estate which dates from Saxon times and was named in Domesday. The Elizabethan mansion of Flete was the seat of the Hele family until 1716 when it passed to the Bulteels. A Bulteel daughter married Henry Bingham Mildmay, who subsequently became Flete's owner. Their son, Francis, became the 1st Lord Mildmay of Flete, whose son, Anthony, the 2nd Lord Mildmay, was well known in National Hunt racing; he died in 1950 at the age of 41. The house was much altered and remodelled in the 1830s, and at the end of the 19th century. During the Second World War it became a maternity home for Plymouth. It has since comprised apartments for the elderly.

Lambside and Battisborough were also Domesday estates. Mothecombe, near the mouth of the Erme, is also an ancient site and its house another home of the Mildmays. In the past, before the estuary became silted, 70-ton barges brought coal and limestone for burning in kilns. For coastal walkers, the estuary can be forded at low tide between Mothecombe and Wonwell by wading, to save a long trek around by road.

Further reading: Sayers, Arnold, *A history of Holbeton*, 1977

Holcombe Burnell church, of ancient origin, stands in peaceful hill country just west of Exeter.

HOLCOMBE BURNELL (G6) Teignbridge Pop. 575 (1901: 167)

Holcombe Burnell is located immediately W of Exeter, a hilly parish with much land rising to 500-600 ft and attaining 654 ft just north of Longdown. The Alphin Brook flows through the north-east to be joined by the Nadder Brook which forms the boundary in that sector. The B 3212 Exeter-Moretonhampstead road, running west, partly marks the southern boundary, with the village of Longdown upon it. Holcombe Burnell does not have a village in that name, but a 'church town' a mile north-west of Longdown. Access is by minor roads from the B 3212 or from the old A 30 road to the north.

The church (St John the Baptist) is set peacefully in a dip of the surrounding hills and woodlands. This is an early Christian site marked originally by a Saxon cross, and the first church was here in the 12th century. The original tower, granite arcades, and south doorway survive in the present structure which results from substantial rebuilding in the late 15th century and further restoration, including re-roofing, in 1843. The present neat smooth pews replaced Victorian box pews in the 1960s. The Beer stone 10-sided font dates from the 15th century, as also – it is believed – does the rare Easter Sepulchre in the north wall of the sanctuary, which depicts Christ rising from the tomb. The church has a light and pleasing atmosphere.

The rare Easter Sepulchre on the north wall of the sanctuary in Holcombe Burnell church, which depicts Christ rising from the tomb, is believed to date from the 15th century.

At the time of Domesday Holcombe belonged to Queen Matilda. On her death it was given to Tetbald Fitzbernel, one of William I's knights, from whom comes the 'Burnel' in the name. The Barton, near the church, was formerly the manor house of Sir Thomas Dennis, a notable figure in the country in the 16th century.

The Exeter railway continuation from Ashton of the Teign Valley line, constructed in 1903, passed through the south of the parish, including the eastern section of the Longdown tunnel. The railway closed in 1958.

HOLCOMBE ROGUS (J4) Mid Devon Pop. 503 (1901: 607)

The parish of Holcombe Rogus, 7½ miles NE of Tiverton, is bounded on the east and north by the Somerset county border, which on the east is partially defined by the River Tone and in the north by a tributary, the Marcombe Lake. The main means of approach are by minor roads to the north of the M5 motorway.

The undulating land rises to 600 ft in the north. In the south, mainly on the border with Burlescombe parish, are extensive limestone quarries. These were important in the construction of the Grand Western Canal (see TIVERTON) which was commenced here in 1810 – oddly in the middle of its planned route – in order to take advantage of the large potential trade in lime and limestone between the Canonsleigh Quarries in Burlescombe, and Tiverton and the farming area between. Conveniently, as the canal was being cut, springs were discovered in its bed at Lowdwells, close to the county border, which were successfully exploited for the canal's water supply.

The very fine Tudor Holcombe Court was built in the 16th century by Sir Roger Bluett.

The church (All Saints) dates from the early 13th century, the present building being of 15th-century construction. Holcombe Court nearby is a very fine Tudor house,

The church of St Petroc, with its saddleback tower, at Hollacombe, near Holsworthy.

built in the 16th century by Sir Roger Bluett, and the Bluetts lived here until 1858, when the estate was sold to new owners. (It was on the land of Peter Bluett Esq that the first turf of the canal was cut, with due ceremony typical of the time.) Near the church is the early 16th-century Church House, recently restored.

HOLLACOMBE (B5) Torridge Pop. 59 (1901: 69)

The small parish of Hollacombe, SE of Holsworthy, is one of just a few farms. It is reached from either Whimble Cross on the A 388 Launceston-Holsworthy road, or from Anvil Corner on the road from Holsworthy to Hatherleigh (A 3072).

The church (St Petroc) dates from the 14th century and was heavily restored in 1887. It has an unusual saddleback tower.

HOLNE (F9) South Hams Pop. 273 (1901: 273)

The parish of Holne, in the south-east of Dartmoor National Park, is quiet, beautiful and unspoilt. Situated 3 miles W of the A 38 expressway and approached from Ashburton or Buckfastleigh, it is served by a network of tortuous minor roads, many of whose hedges are thick with primroses in springtime. The land rises from the wooded banks of the River Dart, which forms the boundary on east and north – partly encircling in a wide loop the area of Holne Chase – to high moorland. This extends to the boundary with the Forest of Dartmoor on the west, where the highest point, 1690 ft, is reached at Petre's boundstone on Ryder's Hill; here Holne, the Forest, and Buckfastleigh's northern extremity all meet. The O Brook marks the boundary on the north-west, and the Holy Brook that on the south. Holne Moor abounds with the remains of prehistoric cairns, roundhouses and enclosures, and a system of reaves (land boundaries dating from the Bronze Age). There are also remains of 19th-century tin mining at Ringleshutes and Wheal Cumston. Venford Reservoir was constructed in 1907, initially to supply water to Paignton. In Holne Chase a small tin mine was worked in the 1870s, just south of a circular earthworks dating from the Iron Age. Holne Bridge and (Holne) New Bridge over the Dart both date from the early 15th century. Stoke, in the north, was a Domesday manor.

Primroses abound on Holne hedges in springtime.

The church (St Mary the Virgin), including the tower, was built c.1300. The first known priest was here in 1240. Originally the church was cruciform but two centuries later it was enlarged, with north and south aisles replacing the transepts. There are granite arcades, a screen, and an early 16th-century carved pulpit. In 1819 the writer Charles Kingsley was born in the vicarage during a spell when his father was curate in charge of the parish. Close to the church is the 14th-century Church House Inn. Archbishop Michael Ramsey of Canterbury and his wife used to spend their holidays here.

Further reading: *A history of Holne*, written in the year of the Silver Jubilee, 1977

HOLSWORTHY (B5) Torridge Pop. 2256 (1901: 2076)

Holsworthy, market town for a large area of West Devon, lies on the heavy, cold, wet, acid clay soils known as the Culm Measures. Much given to the growth of rushes and other indigenous plants, many areas were improved by careful management during the Second World War and post-war years for the production of grass and other needed crops. Since then their conservation value has been recognised and protective measures taken in certain cases.

The church (St Peter & St Paul) is of Norman foundation, the former, smaller building occupying the site of the present nave. Jambs of a Norman doorway date from c.1130. Most of the present structure is from the 14th and 15th centuries; the south nave pillars were built in 1430 and the tower c.1450. The remainder is Victorian. Here, at the annual Peter's Fair in July, in an ancient tradition, the town's 'Pretty Maid' is chosen for her virtuous conduct. Methodism is strong in the Holsworthy district and besides the church in Bodmin Street there are several chapels in the surrounding area. Thorne, and also Chilsworthy, were Domesday manors. Arscott was the home of the

Arscotts from the time of Henry III, and Soldon was a manor house in the 17th century.

Holsworthy's description as a Port Town dates from Saxon times when the word was not confined to a sea-port, and signified any enclosed town used for the harbouring of goods. It had, and still appoints a Portreeve – a governor or steward, and is one of only a few places where the office continues. The Court Leet, dating from the 12th century, is also one of a few remaining in the country; it meets on the eve of Peter's Fair. During much of the 19th century Holsworthy could, however, in a small way have been considered a port in the more accepted sense, with its own navigable waterway to the sea. Holsworthy was served by the Bude Canal, which was constructed mainly for carrying sea-sand for land improvement, as well as other goods. The tub-boat canal reached Holsworthy in 1823 with a terminus at Blagdonmoor wharf, 2 miles east of the town, the changes in levels having been accomplished by an ingenious system of six water-powered inclined planes, on which boats fitted with wheels travelled on rails. The coming of the railway to Holsworthy in 1879, to be followed by its extension to Bude in 1898, killed the canal trade, and the Holsworthy branch was closed in 1891. The railway to Holsworthy was itself later to be closed – in 1966; still remaining are the prominent stone-built eight-arch viaduct just east of the town and the impressive 50 ft high concrete viaduct west at Derriton, which crosses the valley of the River Deer.

Wednesday is market day in Holsworthy, when the Square fills with stalls and shoppers.

Rushes are a force to be reckoned with for farmers on the Culm Measures land around Holsworthy, which tends to be wet and heavy.

Further reading: Holsworthy Local History Centre, *Holsworthy: the passing years*, 1989
Harris, Helen, and Ellis, Monica, *The Bude Canal*, 1972
Local societies: Holsworthy Local History Society
Holsworthy Museum Society
Museum: Holsworthy Museum, Manor Offices

HOLSWORTHY HAMLETS (B5) Torridge Pop. 821

Although ecclesiastically one, Holsworthy and Holsworthy Hamlets are two separate civil parishes. The area of the hamlets covers the farming country north, east and south of the town. It includes such hamlets or farms as Thorne, Chilsworthy, Youldon, Honeycroft, Vognacott (adjoins Milton Damerel at Holsworthy Beacon), Merryfield, South Arscott, Herdwick, Staddon and Chasty. (See also HOLSWORTHY.)

HONEYCHURCH see SAMPFORD COURTENAY

HONITON (K5) East Devon Pop. 10,857 (1901: 3271)

Honiton, the administrative centre for East Devon, is a pleasant small town with a wide, long, straight main street. This was the early highway along which the town developed, which became the A 30. On summer Saturdays, in particular, the street was frequently the scene of holiday traffic jams until the town was bypassed on the north by the present-day A 30 dual carriageway.

The area of the parish is of only average size, and roughly pear-shaped, with the narrow southern tip reaching to Sidmouth's northern boundary. Honiton's northern boundary is marked by the River Otter, and that on the west by an Otter tributary before the line follows the eastern summit of Gittisham Hill at an altitude of 750 ft. After the intervening valley of another Otter tributary, flowing north from the parish's southern point, the land again rises steeply to the eastern boundary where points reach 808 ft and 835 ft. The area at the north end of the valley, on high ground immediately south of the town, was that of the early settlement, and possibly the home or farm of 'Huna' whose name became that of the town. The ancient church of St Michael is located here, a fine building dating from the 15th century, which was severely damaged by fire in 1911. Although still used for worship it is no longer the parish church since the Norman style St Paul's was built down in the town in 1835–8.

Besides having been a busy market town from early days Honiton participated in Devon's woollen cloth industry, notably in the 18th and 19th centuries, and is reputed to have been the first place in the county where serge was made. The town was also noted for lacemaking from the 16th century and became the centre of the trade for numerous surrounding towns and villages. Honiton has also long been noted for its attractive pottery.

In 1672 the town suffered a severe fire which destroyed many of the ancient buildings. However, the Honiton and Allhallows Museum in the High Street incorporates a notable part of Honiton's history. Early records indicate the existence of Allhallows Chapel here from the early 14th century. With the old parish church being on the hill above the town it is possible that Allhallows served as a chapel-of-ease. In the early 18th century it had fallen into disrepair. Part was then demolished and an extension built, and it became Allhallows School. This continued, with further building, for 200 years until in 1938 Allhallows School was moved to Rousdon near Axminster. (See COMBPYNE ROUSDON.) From 1946 the old chapel and adjacent former dining hall have housed Honiton Museum.

In the mid 19th century the London & South Western Railway reached Honiton, the line to Exeter being opened in 1860. Skilful engineering was necessary in this hilly terrain, including construction of the 1353 yd Honiton Tunnel, 2 miles north-east of the town.

Further reading: Edmunds, M., *Honiton: an old Devon market town*, Westcountry Books, 1993

There are numerous other useful books on Honiton, several of them published in recent years. Readers are recommended to consult bookshops or libraries according to their particular lines of interest.

Local society: Honiton History Society
Museum: Honiton and Allhallows Museum, High Street

HORRABRIDGE (D9) West Devon Pop. 2189

The civil parish of Horrabridge was formed in 1950. Previously the ancient bridge over the Walkham marked the boundary of three parishes: Whitchurch, Sampford Spiney and Buckland Monachorum.

The small but populous parish of Horrabridge did not exist as such until quite recent times. The name, from Anglo-Saxon *har* meaning boundary, indicated the meeting point of three parishes, Buckland Monachorum, Whitchurch and Sampford Spiney, at the bridge, named as Horebrigge in 1345 Assize Rolls. The present parish, located 3 miles SE of Tavistock on the A 386 road to Plymouth, was formed from small portions of the three older parishes (and included an enclave of Peter Tavy) as an ecclesiastical district in 1867, the church (St John) having been built in 1835 but not consecrated until 1866. The civil parish of Horrabridge was formed in 1950. The River Walkham flows through the centre of the village.

The area upstream from the bridge has associations with Dartmoor tin working. Downstream, to the north and west, copper was mined in the 19th century. The biggest copper mine was Wheal Franco, worked between 1823 and 1870. Horrabridge also had mills for various purposes including wool processing, and cloth making in the 19th century.

Further reading: Rowe, John, *Horrabridge as it was*, Yelverton & District LHS, 1989
Local society: Yelverton & District Local History Society

HORWOOD, LOVACOTT & NEWTON TRACEY (D3) North Devon Pop. 449 (1901: Horwood 102, Newton Tracey 127)

For civil purposes the ecclesiastical parishes of Horwood and Newton Tracey, and the hamlet of Lovacott are combined in one, incorporating the names of the three. They are located in the hilly country between Torrington and Barnstaple, with Newton Tracey village situated on the B 3232 road. Horwood lies to the west.

The parish of Horwood dates from the time of Edward the Confessor, and the first rector is named in 1275. St Michael's well in a field near the church was reputedly curative for sore eyes. The present church building (St Michael) dates from c.1500. There is a north aisle with five bays, one extending to the chancel. There are 16th-century bench ends, a fine pulpit and a Norman font.

Newton Tracey church (St Thomas à Becket), and its font, are believed to date from the late 12th century. Much Ham stone (from Somerset) was used in the construction, transported probably via Bridgwater, the Bristol Channel and the Taw estuary. The chancel arch is Early English, suggesting an addition to an existing nave. The original north aisle was built in the 13th century and rebuilt in 1868 when the church was restored. The tower was probably added in the 15th century. Date of the earliest recorded rector is 1282.

The two parishes are separate ecclesiastically.

HUISH (D4) Torridge Pop. 49 (1901: 76)

The small parish of Huish is bounded on the east by the north-flowing River Torridge, and on the west by the Mere, and tributary Little Mere. Most of the area comprises parkland of Heanton Sarchville, home of Lord Clinton, located 4 miles N of Hatherleigh on the A 386 road to Torrington.

The church (St James the Less) is on an ancient foundation. The tower is the only remaining part of the c.1100 church, restored in the 19th century. By this time the church had fallen into disrepair, it was rebuilt by Lord Clinton with walls of local stone and re-opened in 1873. Carved oak woodwork includes a hammer beam roof, and the font and pulpit are of carved Caen stone. The church path is of cobbles, with a central diamond pattern, similar to those at neighbouring Merton and Meeth.

The house of Heanton Satchville has suffered fires. One occurred in the early 1800s, after which the house was rebuilt, and another in 1932 which was again followed by rebuilding.

The parish includes the hamlet of Newbridge.

HUNTSHAM (H3) Mid Devon Pop. 138 (1901: 222)

Huntsham, 5½ miles NE of Tiverton, is bounded on the east by the River Lowman, tributary of the Exe, and on the north-west by the minor road over Bampton Down which reaches an altitude of 914 ft. The parish is one of hills, streams and woods.

The church (All Saints), which occupies a site hidden by trees just north of the village crossroads, was restored and enlarged in 1856, and the north transept lengthened in 1871. The building contains carved woodwork from the 16th century. Huntsham Castle, on the border with Tiverton in the south, was an Iron Age hill fort.

Huntsham Post Office in the village centre.

HUNTSHAW (D3) Torridge Pop. 120 (1901: 143)

Huntshaw parish is located 4 miles SE of Bideford on mainly high ground that rises to 677 ft at Huntshaw Cross on the B 3232 road, where the tall radio mast provides a well-known landmark. An indication of early inhabitation is the earthworks of Berry Castle, in a wooded area close to the parish's western boundary, which is marked by a stream coming down from Gammaton Moor.

The church (St Mary Magdalene) dates from the 14th century, reconstructed in the 15th century and restored in the 1860s.

HUXHAM (H6) East Devon Pop. 78 (1901: 136)

Huxham is a small low-lying parish 4 miles NE from the centre of Exeter, ½ mile E from Stoke Canon on the Exeter-Tiverton road (A 396). Partially wooded in the south, it is edged by the waters of the River Culm in the north-west. The small church (St Mary the Virgin) is of early 14th-century construction, largely rebuilt in the late 1860s. It has a fine Norman font. (The benefice is united with Poltimore.)

Local society: the Five Parishes Local History Society

IDDESLEIGH (D5) West Devon Pop. 198 (1901: 335)

Iddesleigh, located 3 miles NE of Hatherleigh and 8 miles N of Okehampton, is served north-south by the rather narrow and twisty B 3217 road. The River Torridge forms the western boundary, from Bramblecombe south to the confluence with the River Okement. The Okement, and then a tributary stream, mark the southern boundary.

On the east and north the line runs over land and in places follows streams. The terrain rises from west to east to a level just under 600 ft. Various streams flow down through the parish lands to feed into the Torridge.

The village is small but attractive, with houses of cob and thatch. The church (St James) stands prominently on the east side of the road. Dating from the 15th century it was renovated and partly rebuilt c.1840, and restored in the 1870s.

Further reading: Iddesleigh Society, *Iddesleigh: a parish in Devon*, 1983

IDE (G6) Teignbridge Pop. 547 (1901: 681)

Ide lies immediately W of Exeter, with land that becomes more hilly towards the west, where it rises to 713 ft. The village is served by minor roads which connect from the Alphington roundabout on the A 30, or from the B 3212 to Moretonhampstead. The disused track of the former Exeter Railway, opened in 1903 to link Exeter with the Teign Valley line, runs through; it closed in 1958.

The church (St Ida) is of 15th-century construction, rebuilt in 1834. The tower is of red sandstone, the main building being externally plastered. There is a gallery, and a screen dated 1930. Ide Bridge, over the small River Alphin (near the Twisted Oak) was noted in 1244.

Further reading: Burnett, Donald, *A history of the people and parish of Ide,* 1992

IDEFORD (G8) Teignbridge Pop. 342 (1901: 254)

Located 9½ miles SSW of Exeter and 4½ miles NNE of Newton Abbot, Ideford includes the southern extremity of the Haldon Hills, with land rising in the north to 750 ft. The western boundary is marked by the modern A 380 Exeter-Newton Abbot road and in stretches by its earlier course. The village is connected by minor routes with various points on the main road.

The church (St Mary the Virgin) dates from the 15th century, restored in 1852 and partly rebuilt c.1890. Ecclesiastically it is united with the church at Luton (St John) which lies east of the boundary in the civil parish of Bishopsteignton.

ILFRACOMBE (D1) North Devon Pop. 10,840 (1901: 8557)

Ilfracombe is bounded in the north by the steep and rocky coastline of the Bristol Channel, from Lee Bay in the west to Watermouth in the east, and on the south by hill country which rises to over 800 ft. Various roads from the south converge on the town including the A 361 from Barnstaple.

In 1998 the twin towers of the Landmark Theatre rose on the site of the former impressive Victorian hotel.

In early days Ilfracombe was a port of some significance. The Bourchier family, lords of the manor, were active in the Crusades. In the reign of Edward III six ships went from here to the siege of Calais (Liverpool, a smaller port then, sent just one). Later, however, Ilfracombe's importance declined, the town for some time retained its market but the port suffered reduced overseas trade while keeping its fishing, which in the 19th century largely involved herrings.

From early Victorian times the situation changed. The town developed as a fashionable resort, acquiring a reputation for its health giving benefits, and boosted by the arrival of the railway in 1874. Much of the town's building work dates from this period. Coal was formerly brought in from South Wales, but as demand reduced the trade declined. The town was a regular port of call for pleasure boats and for passengers crossing to Wales, served by the *Bristol Queen* and *Cardiff Queen* in the post-war years. Regular services ended in 1968 although vessels still bring visitors from across the water, and there are plans for reviving the harbour and port facilities. The railway closed in 1970. While the town itself has many of the attractions common to seaside towns, the scenery around is attractive and dramatic.

The ancient parish church (Holy Trinity), which stands at the west end of the town, dates from the 12th century, the present building being mainly of 14th and 15th-century construction. The Norman tower was partly enclosed within the north aisle when this was added. There is also the church of St Peter. A short distance north-east is the church of St Philip and St James, built in 1857. At the entrance to the harbour, on Lantern Hill, stands the former chapel of St Nicholas, a 15th-century building that provided a landmark for seafarers and where prayers could be said for them, before it became a lighthouse. A prominent building added to the scene in 1998 is the Landmark Theatre, with its twin towers. It occupies the site of the former impressive Ilfracombe Hotel built in the 19th century, which became outdated and was demolished in 1976.

The village of Lee is a separate ecclesiastical parish with its own church (St Matthew) built in 1833.

Lincombe was a Domesday manor. The large parish of Ilfracombe has many interesting farms, including Damage Barton and Chambercombe, both of which were originally medieval mansions.

Further reading: Lamplugh, Lois, *A history of Ilfracombe*, Phillimore, 1984
Local societies: Ilfracombe Local History Research Group
Ilfracombe Natural History and Field Society
Museum: Ilfracombe Museum, Wilder Road

ILSINGTON (F8) Teignbridge Pop. 2444 (1901: 886)

Ilsington – Sanctuary Cross, 1906.
COURTESY THE BOOK OF ILSINGTON

The parish of Ilsington lies on the eastern boundary of Dartmoor Natonal Park, between Bovey Tracey and Ashburton. Most of the parish is within the Park, but a portion extends south-east of the A 38 expressway, as far as the lower River Lemon where it includes the village of South Knighton amid steep rounded hills that rise to over 600 ft. The boundary proceeds east to the Drumbridges interchange from where, in flatter heathland terrain, it follows for a short distance the straight road to Bovey Tracey. In this area the village of Liverton is also included. Ilsington village is fairly centrally situated and from here, to both west and north, the land is that of the moor, rising to 1560 ft at Rippon Tor and 1490 ft at Hay Tor. Haytor Vale is another village of the parish, to the north of which is Haytor Down, site of a noted group of granite quarries worked extensively in the 19th century when granite was supplied for use in the rebuilding of London Bridge and for other important edifices. Transport for the stone was provided by the unique Haytor Granite Tramway, which had 'rails' made of granite and conveyed the material 8½ miles on a descent of 1300 ft to the Stover Canal, from where it travelled by boat to the Teign estuary and port of Teignmouth. Much of the tramway system can be followed over Haytor Down where it is classified as an Ancient Monument.

Ilsington as a settlement dates from Saxon times when the area was largely woodland. By 1066 much had been cleared and the village was becoming established

The unique Haytor Granite Tramway can be traced across Haytor Down in Ilsington parish.

with, it is believed, a church. The present church building (St Michael) dates from the 14th century, reconstructed in the 15th century, and restored in the 19th century. The interior has fine pillars of slender granite and a delicate ancient screen, with a pulpit carved in 1884 to blend with it. The font is also ancient. While Ilsington had its own manor house (demolished in the 1870s) near the church, there were also the Domesday manors of Bagtor, Ingsdon and Sigford.

Besides the working of granite, Ilsington has a history of mining. High on the moor, near the Haytor-Widecombe road, tin was extracted in the 19th century at Hemsworthy Mine, on the site of older workings. There was another tin mine at Bagtor. Iron was worked in the area south of Haytor Vale in the 19th century, and some tin, copper and arsenic were produced near here in the 1920s. Silverbrook Mine, south of the village, was a lead and silver mine, believed to have been worked in the 17th century and also in the 19th century.

Further reading: Wills, Dick, *The book of Ilsington*, Halsgrove, 2000
Articles on various aspects of Ilsington's history by Bill Ransom in *The Devon Historian* numbers 57, 60, 62, 63, 65 and 68, and in *Transactions of the Devonshire Association 131* (1999), *134* (2002) and *135* (2003)

Also: Harris, Helen, *The Haytor Granite Tramway and Stover Canal*, Peninsula Press, 2nd edit., 2002

INSTOW (C2) North Devon Pop. 786 (1901: 634)

The preserved and recently restored Instow signal box, on the former Barnstaple-Bideford railway, is a Grade II listed building.

The land of Instow parish rises from sea level at its tidal frontage to over 300 ft in the farming country on the east. The western boundary is formed by the estuary of the Torridge to the south, and that of the Taw to the north. They meet at Instow and flow west to the open sea. Consequently Instow enjoys fine prospects beyond its sandy beach: the view across the Torridge to Appledore, and the more distant outlook beyond the dunes to glistening waves breaking over Bideford Bar.

The B 3233 Bideford-Barnstaple road along the estuaries bypasses the waterfront at Instow, although the coastal route, which sometimes receives storm-blown sand, is accessible, and recommended for enjoyment of the views. The former railway, opened in 1855 and closed to passengers in 1965 (for milk and clay in 1982) also closely follows the estuaries. The route now forms part of the 'Tarka Trail' for walking and cycling, and, at the site of Instow Station (where there was a level crossing) the old signal box is preserved. For many years until the early 20th century Instow had a small commercial quay; a ferry boat still plies is way to Appledore and sailing has become increasingly popular. There is a quay, for oils and other commodities, at Yelland, at the mouth of the Taw.

The village stands on the rising ground. Formerly called Johnstow, its church (St John the Baptist) is of ancient foundation, situated to the north-east, slightly apart from the village. The present building is of mainly 14th-century construction, enlarged in the 16th century, and restored in 1873. There is also the church of All Saints, closer to the village. Johnstow, Bickleton, Worlington and Huish were named as manors in Domesday. The former mansion of Fullingscott dates from 1600.

Further reading: Grant, Alison and Others, *Instow, a history*, 1999

INWARDLEIGH (D6) West Devon Pop. 454 (1901: 421)

The fairly large parish of Inwardleigh is situated between Okehampton and Hatherleigh, with Inwardleigh centre 3½ miles NNW of Okehampton. The A 386 road connecting the towns passes northwards through the parish and beside the development of Folly Gate. Inwardleigh's 'church town' is in a quieter location off the main road, ¾ mile to the west, with just a few houses and a farm. The church, (St Petroc) which is approached through a double line of 12 beech trees, was built in the 16th century; at times during the second half of the 19th century it was repaired, partially rebuilt, and eventually fully restored. There is a Norman font. There are fine views from the churchyard.

The Medland Brook, tributary of the River Lew, flows north-westwards through the parish. Owner of the manor at Domesday was Inwar, who gave the parish its name. Curworthy, Oak and Widefield were also Domesday manors. The Barton, by the church, is built on the site of the ancient manor of the Coffin family, who held it from the 12th to the 14th century.

IPPLEPEN (G9) Teignbridge Pop. 2466 (1901: 813)

The parish of Ipplepen extends on either side of the A 381 Newton Abbot-Totnes road, approximately 4 miles from each town. The fairly large village is located on ascending land on the west, the generally undulating terrain reaching its maximum altitude of 442 ft on the south-east boundary. The small River Hems and a tributary form the boundary on the south-west. A stretch of the main railway line that includes the Dainton Tunnel, runs through the parish.

Tumuli in the northern extremity are an indication of early human habitation. The name of Dainton, a hill in the north-east on which there was an ancient settlement and, and of the nearby hamlet, appeared in a Saxon charter of 956. Dainton is now the scene of large quarries. Battleford and Combe Fishacre were Domesday manors. A cell of the Augustinian abbey of St Pierre at Fougeres, Brittany, was founded at Ipplepen c.1100. The church (St Andrew), standing at the top of the village and visible from a distance, dates from the 14th century, with the high altar dedicated by Bishop Stapledon in 1318. The parish is united ecclesiastically with Torbryan.

IVYBRIDGE (E10) South Hams Pop. 12,056

The small but mainly urbanised parish of Ivybridge has been a separate civil parish only since 1874, when it was carved out of Ermington and Ugborough with tiny portions also of Cornwood and Harford. Previously it had been a large village on the old road to Plymouth with an ancient bridge (evidently known for its ivy covering) over the River Erme. The Erme was already a useful source of power for corn mills when, in the 18th century, two paper mills were also established here to take advantage of the flow and clearness of Dartmoor water. Of the two paper mills, the higher, Stowford Mill, still survives. First built in 1787 the present impressive factory dates from 1862 and continues in paper-making.

The rapidly developed town of Ivybridge has grown from a village that took its name from the strategic bridge across the River Erme.

Ivybridge's industrial enterprises were further enhanced by the coming of the main railway line in the form of Brunel's South Devon Railway in 1849, and it was one of the places where construction of a viaduct was necessary. The stone piers which carried the former timber structure across the Erme valley can still be seen alongside the present viaduct east of the station.

In the small part of the parish originally within Cornwood a chapel-of-ease was built in 1790, and consecrated as a district church. It was replaced by the present church (St John the Evangelist), built farther south in 1882.

During the latter half of the 20th century Ivybridge made extremely rapid growth to become the small town that it is today, due largely to its suitability as a commuting base for Plymouth, and the accessibility of the rail and road systems. The town is now bypassed by the modern A 38 expressway.

Local society: Ivybridge Local History Society

JACOBSTOWE (D5) West Devon Pop. 118 (1901: 229)

The village of Jacobstowe, 4 miles N of Okehampton, is situated rather awkwardly at the intersection of the A 3072 with the B 3216 and minor roads. The countryside around is gently undulating and very pleasant, with the River Okement forming the parish boundary on the east and the tributary Merryland Stream that on the north. The land in the north is fairly rough, but farther south small streams and woodland abound.

The church (St James) dates from the 14th century, much altered subsequently – notably in the 19th century – and further restored in 1902. Broomford was a

Domesday manor, and Lower Cadham, in the north-east, was a 17th-century farmhouse on an earlier site.

KELLY (B7) West Devon Pop. 127 (1901: 167)

Set back to the north of the Tavistock-Launceston road (B 3662) and approached by winding lanes, the roughly triangular parish of Kelly gives the impression of having to some extent escaped the passage of time. Its quiet rural heart comprises just the church (St Mary), dating from the 15th century, and a few houses. One of these, Kelly House, has been the home of the Kelly family and their ancestors from the time of the Norman Conquest, the manor being held in the actual Kelly name from the time of Henry II. Thus the Kellys have the longest such occupancy of any family in Devon. Kelly House is Tudor, remodelled in the 18th century.

Ecclesiastically the parish is united with Bradstone.

KENN (H7) Teignbridge Pop. 968 (1901: 977)

Part of the very fine 15th-century screen in Kenn church. The rood was added in 1889 to replace the earlier banished original.

Kenn is a fairly large parish 4 miles S of Exeter. The small River Kenn flows through on its south-eastward route to the Exe estuary. From under 100 ft in the Kenn valley the land rises south-westwards to the largely wooded Greensand plateau of the Haldon Hills where the altitude reaches 827 ft, giving fine views. The M5 motorway terminates just short of the eastern boundary, but the main highway is carried westwards by the A 38 expressway, which bypasses the village of Kennford and then divides, with the A 38 continuing over Haldon, past Exeter Racecourse, to Plymouth, and the A 380 forking left for Telegraph Hill, Newton Abbot, and Torbay.

Kenn village is located in the valley, on the same-named river. There was a church here from at least as early as the mid 12th century. The present church (St Andrew), built of locally quarried red sandstone which gives a warm impression, dates from the early 14th century, enlarged in the 15th century. The tower, which also includes limestone and flint, is of earlier, possibly 13th century, construction. The 15th-century rood screen across the width of the church was restored in 1889 when the rood and figures, which were carved at Oberammergau in Germany, were added in replacement of the original rood, removed under the law in the late 16th century. The font is of Purbeck marble.

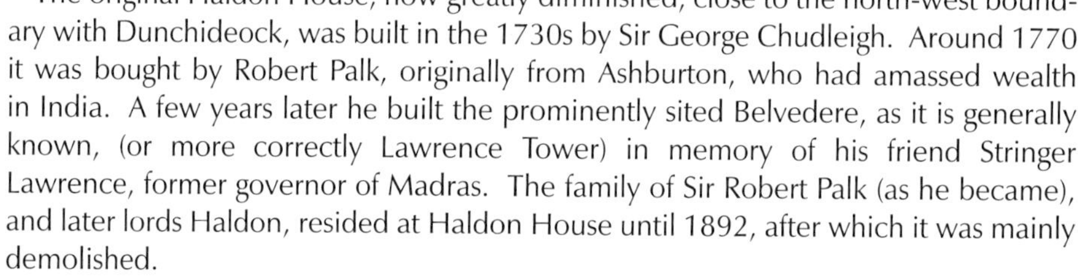

The original Haldon House, now greatly diminished, close to the north-west boundary with Dunchideock, was built in the 1730s by Sir George Chudleigh. Around 1770 it was bought by Robert Palk, originally from Ashburton, who had amassed wealth in India. A few years later he built the prominently sited Belvedere, as it is generally known, (or more correctly Lawrence Tower) in memory of his friend Stringer Lawrence, former governor of Madras. The family of Sir Robert Palk (as he became), and later lords Haldon, resided at Haldon House until 1892, after which it was mainly demolished.

KENNERLEIGH (G5) Mid Devon Pop. 80 (1901: 80)

Kennerleigh is a small parish, 4½ miles NNW of Crediton. Streams that form the south-western and eastern boundaries unite at the southern tip to form the River Creedy.

The pleasant village is located centrally on a minor road north of Crediton. The church (St John the Baptist) dates originally from the 14th century (at that time St Clement's). It was partially rebuilt and restored in 1847.

KENTISBEARE (J5) Mid Devon Pop. 878 (1901: 733)

Kentisbeare, 7½ miles NW of Honiton and 3 miles E of Cullompton, comprises fertile farming country on the fringe of the Blackdown Hills. The Stoford Water, tributary of the River Culm, flows westwards through the parish and land rises from c.250 ft to c.900 ft at Blackborough Beacon and on Ponchydown on the north-east.

The village is located centrally, conveniently approached from the A 373 Honiton-Cullompton road. The church (St Mary) dates from the 15th and 16th centuries and is large and interesting. It has a chequered tower, and internally a 16th-century screen and 17th-century gallery. Formerly there was a separate small parish church at Blackborough, but this is now part of Kentisbeare and the church (All Saints) which was rebuilt in 1838 no longer exists as such. In past centuries iron was worked in bell pits and the mining of whetstones (for sharpening tools) was carried out on the hills at Blackborough.

Priesthall, near the church, is a fine early church house. There were nine Domesday manors, and several of the farms have old and interesting houses.

Further reading: Barrett, Helen, *Our heritage: a history of Kentisbeare and Blackborough*, 1977

KENTISBURY (E1) North Devon Pop. 266 (1901: 304)

Kentisbury is located in the high open country of North Devon, a direct 8 miles NNE of Barnstaple and 4 miles S of the coast. The church, in the north, stands at 600 ft, and the land rises further, to 1105 ft on Kentisbury Down towards the eastern boundary at Blackmoor Gate. Tumuli here indicate early human presence.

The A 39 Barnstaple-Lynton road passes through the parish, with a small village centre at Kentisbury Ford. The 'church town' is a mile to the north. The church (St Thomas) dates from the 15th century and was restored in the 1870s.

Breadwick and Patchole were Domesday manors.

South West Water's Wistlandpound Reservoir, completed in 1855, is sited south of Blackmoor Gate.

Further reading: Kentisbury Steering Group, *The Kentisbury Catalogue*, c.2000

KENTON (H7) Teignbridge Pop. 1131 (1901: 1723)

From a short eastern border on the banks of the Exe estuary, Kenton broadens westwards and then narrows again towards the south-west boundary on the Haldon Hills where the land reaches over 800 ft. The small River Kenn approximately forms the parish's north-eastern boundary and passes just east of Kenton village, which is located 6½ miles SSE of Exeter on the A 379 Dawlish road. The main railway line runs between the road and the shoreline. A stream from Haldon also feeds into the Kenn, having run through the grounds of Oxton House, an estate dating from the 12th century which became the home of various Exeter merchants and later belonged to the Revd John Swete who built the present house and set out the grounds in the 1780s.

It is believed that a church existed here as early as 560 when St Petrock set up a simple building. The present church (All Saints) is thought to date from 1360–70, with several subsequent restorations. It is a particularly fine building of local red sandstone, spacious, with a high roof, and arcades of Beer stone. The extremely beautiful painted rood screen has been considered among the most notable of any in a parish church; dating from 1455 the central section was restored in 1899. The elaborately carved pulpit, which blends with the screen, is said to have been shaped from the trunk of an oak tree; it was thrown out in the 19th century but not destroyed, and on the instigation of the Revd S. Baring Gould, was repaired and replaced. The parish is united ecclesiastically with Mamhead.

Blending with Kenton's notable screen is the pulpit, said to have been shaped from the trunk of an oak tree. It was thrown out in the 19th century but rescued, repaired and replaced.

Local society: Kenton Local History Society

KILMINGTON (L6) East Devon Pop. 762 (1901: 523)

Kilmington, 2 miles W of Axminster, has the A 35 road passing through, with the village situated immediately to its south, on the junction of various older, now minor, roads. The Corry Brook, tributary of the River Yarty, flows through the north-east of the parish, with the Yarty, and then the Axe, forming approximately the eastern boundary. An area of land in the Axe valley, in the south-east, is common to the parishes of Axminster and

Kilmington. Land rises towards the west of the parish to c.500 ft.
The church (St Giles) dates from the 15th century, rebuilt, apart from the tower, in 1862.

Further reading: Elliot, G.M., *A brief history of Kilmington*, 1981
Berry, Les, and Gosling, Gerald, *The book of Axminster with Kilmington*, Halsgrove, 2004

KINGSBRIDGE (F11) South Hams
Pop. 5521 (1901: Dodbrooke 1183, Kingsbridge 1413)

Looking towards the head of Kingsbridge's waterfront and town.

The civil parish of Kingsbridge includes Dodbrooke (on the north-east), although the two are separate ecclesiastically. The area is served by the A 381 and A 379 roads.

The town stands at the head of the Kingsbridge estuary through which drain numerous small streams at the heads of various creeks. The breadth of the tidal waterway is, however, disproportionate to the normal modest outflow of the contributory streams for this is an outstanding example of a ria, or drowned valley, caused by the post-glacial rise in sea level.

For long a port and market town, Kingsbridge is now a busy and attractive centre, with its pleasant waterfront area and steep Fore Street, much sought by visitors and holidaymakers.

The name derives from a bridge that existed here in the 10th century which linked the royal estates of Alvington on the west and Chillington on the east – the king's bridge. A manor of Buckfast Abbey, the town developed, and acquired a market in 1219 and became a borough in 1238.

Kingsbridge's church (St Edmund, King and Martyr), with its spire, stands near the top of Fore Street. It dates from the 13th century, enlarged in the 15th century, and was restored in 1960. There is an ancient font and 15th-century screen. Dodbrooke's church (St Thomas of Canterbury) is mainly of 15th-century construction, with a fine screen and a square Norman font. Both places have had their industries: Kingsbridge had mills and a foundry, and Dodbrooke shipping, brewing and tanning.

Kingsbridge was the birthplace of William Cookworthy (1705–80) who discovered the product of granite decomposition – kaolin or china clay – and pioneered its use in the making of English porcelain. He is commemorated in the town's Cookworthy Museum, housed in the 17th-century grammar school, which also has exhibits of other local interest including pharmacy, Victorian kitchen equipment and farm vehicles.

In 1893 a branch railway from the main line at Brent reached Kingsbridge, with a station near the centre of the town. It closed in 1963.

Further reading: Born, Anne, and Turner, Kathy, *Kingsbridge, Devon*, 1986
Born, Anne, *A history of Kingsbridge & Salcombe*, Phillimore, 1986
Linton, Sue, *A pictorial history of Kingsbridge and the surrounding Area*, Orchard, 2003
Local society: Kingsbridge History Society
Museum: Cookworthy Museum, Fore Street

KINGSKERSWELL (G9) Teignbridge Pop. 4799 (1901: 1027)

Kingskerswell is situated 2–3 miles SSE of Newton Abbot on the busy A 380 road to Torquay, and is largely urbanised. The railway from Newton Abbot to Torbay branches from the main line to Plymouth in the north of the parish and passes through close to the village centre, just west of the A 380.

The church (St Mary), located west of the A 380 and the railway, dates from the early 14th century, enlarged a century later and restored in 1834 and 1874. On the higher side of the churchyard are extensive ruined walls of the early manor house. Held by the king at the time of Domesday, the manor was later in the hands of the Dinhams, who occupied the manor house, which was fortified.

Further reading: Various, *The book of Kingskerswell*, Halsgrove, 2003
Local society: Kingskerswell Local History Group

KINGS NYMPTON (E4) North Devon Pop. 377 (1901: 502)

Kings Nympton, 5 miles SSW of South Molton, is a parish of high ground which rises in several places to over 600 ft. The centrally situated village stands at over 500 ft. The River Mole defines the boundary on the north and west, and tributary streams partly those on the south and east.

The manor was anciently part of the royal demesne – which would account for 'King's' in the name. In the 13th century it was given by Henry III to Roger le Zouch. 'Nympton' derives from 'nemeton', meaning a sacred place or grove, which possibly indicates a Celtic presence here. In earlier times the parish was more wooded than today, with areas of rough moor, but these have mostly been brought into cultivation over the past 150 years.

The church, which has a spire, is entered by a granite step which was the shaft of a Celtic cross, possibly marking the spot as sacred before the church was built. The present structure dates mainly from the 15th century although the north wall is believed to be part of the earlier Saxon church. It was cruciform before the addition of the south aisle. There is a magnificent carved rood screen of c.1540. Above this is a richly decorated ceilure (restored in the 1960s) and the painting of the chancel roof is striking, depicting a huge gilt cross against a night sky with stars, moon and clouds. This dates from 1755. There are bosses on the nave roof. The altar rails, reredos and pulpit date from the 18th century. At the west end, where there was formerly a gallery, the last three rows of pews are tiered, and there are box pews in the north transept. Rectors are recorded from 1309.

Kings Nympton is not on any major road, but is best approached from the B 3226 road to South Molton, which forks off the A 377 at King's Nympton railway station. This station, on the Exeter-Barnstaple line, was known as South Molton Road until c.1950 when the name was changed.

KINGSTEIGNTON (G8) Teignbridge Pop. 10,615 (1901: 1942)

Kingsteignton lies E of the lower River Teign and N of its upper estuary, with the village centre 1½ miles NE of Newton Abbot. The modern A 390 road, which runs north-west through the parish, bypasses the village. Other routes radiate, including the A 381 eastwards to Teignmouth and the B 3193 to Chudleigh, besides the busy road into Newton Abbot. The main railway also passes through, close to the estuary shore. Land in the south is low-lying, with levels rising to 190 ft towards the north-east.

The former basin area of the Hackney, or Kingsteignton Canal, and clay cellars, now replaced by commercial redevelopment.

A predominating feature and major industry in the south and west of the parish is the working and processing of white pottery clay known as ball clay, resulting from the erosion of decomposed Dartmoor granite removed by natural forces to settle at the lower levels. In 1843 the ⅝ mile Hackney Canal was opened for carrying clay – previously carted to Hackney Quay – more conveniently from a basin to connect with the Teign. At the basin were clay cellars which remained for many years after the canal's disuse in 1928, but the area, immediately north-east of Newton Abbot Racecourse, is now completely altered with the growth of commercial buildings. The remains of the canal lock can, however, be seen by following a short footpath.

Kingsteignton has a long history, believed to date from c.700 when it was one of the Saxons' early footholds. The church (St Michael), of red sandstone with a limestone tower, originates from the early 14th century, its high altar having been dedicated by Bishop Stapledon c.1318. It was rebuilt in the 15th century.

Further reading: Harris, Richard, *King's Teignton: a parish history*, 1977

KINGSTON (E11) South Hams Pop. 399 (1901: 399)

Kingston parish is situated on the E side of the estuary of the River Erme, with the Erme forming the western boundary and the sea coast that on the south. The boundary on the east is marked by a small stream which enters the sea at Westcombe Beach.

The beautiful estuary of the River Erme, looking to distant Dartmoor, with Kingston parish on the right, Holbeton to the left.

The northern boundary is also defined by a stream, which joins the estuary at Clyng Mill. Both the estuary, which has a small beach at Wonwell, and the rugged coastline are lovely and unspoilt. Rising land reaches 450 ft in the far north-east.

The rather remote village is located centrally and approached from the A 379 Plymouth-Kingsbridge road, the B 3392, and country lanes. The church (St James the Less) is of ancient foundation. The present building dates from the 14th century. It had fallen into disrepair by the 19th century and was partly rebuilt before being reopened in 1893. The parish is now united ecclesiastically with Ringmore.

Further reading: Petter, Helen Mary, *Kingston remembered*, 1987
Kingston two hundred years ago, 1988
Kingston History Society, *Kingston: a South Hams village*, 1980
Local society: Kingston History Society

KINGSWEAR (G10) South Hams Pop. 1332 (1901: 841)

Kingswear is located on the north side of the River Dart estuary, occupying the southern part of the Berry Head peninsula. Only the northern boundary, which extends with a slight dip from Galmpton Creek to south of Sharpham Point, is across land, the parish being bounded on the west by the Dart and on the south and east by the sea. Land rises quite steeply, attaining 586 ft in the west, with an Iron Age earthwork occupying a strategic high point over-viewing the Dart. Road access is from the A 3022 near Churston Station, via the A 379 and B 3205. A ferry is also operated between the small town, which stands just inside the estuary mouth, and Dartmouth. When, in the early 1860s, plans for an extension from the Torquay branch of the South Devon Railway to serve Dartmouth were carried out, Kingswear was made the terminal rail point, the ferry providing the final connection. (After closure in the 1970s the line now carries steam trains from Kingswear to Paignton, run by the Dart Valley Company.)

The church (St Thomas of Canterbury) originates from the 12th century. It was rebuilt, apart from the tower, in 1845. There are very fine views from the upper part of the town, looking up the Dart and across to Dartmouth. (see p.58.)

Kingswear Castle, at the estuary mouth, was built as a defence c.1500 but abandoned as such in the mid 17th century due to the superiority of Dartmouth's castle across the water. It was, however, held for the king in the Civil War until captured by Fairfax in 1646. The National Trust property, Coleton Fishacre, established by the D'Oyly Cartes in the 1920s and built in the style of Lutyens from shale quarries on the site, is close to the coast on the south-east.

Local society: Dartmouth and Kingswear Society

KNOWSTONE (G3) North Devon Pop. 199 (1901: 343)

Knowstone, in the Exmoor foothills, situated 7½ miles NW of Tiverton, was a remote and quiet parish until in the 1980s the new North Devon Link road (A 361) was cut westwards over Hares Down and across the centre of Beaples Moor, causing a change to the rural scene. The parish boundary extends north almost to the former main road (now the B 3227) and in the south to the South Molton-Rackenford-Tiverton road. The Sturcombe River rises in the south-east. There are tumuli at various points and an ancient earthwork above the Crooked Oak valley. Near Beaples Moor the altitude reaches 881 ft; the village, a mile or so north, stands at 700 ft.

The village, in which there are numerous thatched houses, has managed to retain a certain detachment from the passing traffic to the south. In the 12th century the church was given to Hartland Abbey. The present building (St Peter) dates from the 15th century, but retains Norman features including the south door; some rebuilding was carried out in the 17th century. There is an unusual small pulpit. The list of vicars dates from 1280. One of them, the Revd John Froude (1777–1852), a 'hunting parson' of notorious reputation, succeeded his father here as vicar of Knowstone and Molland and was apparently a participant and instigator in episodes of lawlessness prevalent in Knowstone in the mid 19th century.

Wadham, in the north-west, was a Domesday manor and the early home of the founders of Wadham College, Oxford. Shapcott, on the east, was also a Domesday manor.

The name of the parish is pronounced 'now stone'.

Further reading: Rapley, Verna C., *Knowstone, a brief history of the parish*, 1983
Bhanji, S., 'Parson Froude – villain or victim?' *The Devon Historian 59*, October 1999

LAMERTON (C8) West Devon Pop. 737 (1901: 1028)

Lamerton, 2½ miles NW of Tavistock, is a parish of many farms and green fields, deep winding lanes and streams. The road to Launceston (B 3362) passes through, with the village centred just to its north. The small River Lumburn, tributary of the Tavy, rises south of the village, and later joins a feeder stream to form the parish's south-east boundary. At certain points around the boundary are either stone or metal markers. In the north, where, until 1880, the parish included part of present-day Brentor, an area of Heathfield – unenclosed moorland until the 1840s – is still retained within Lamerton. Here, adjacent to the boundary, are five tumuli – prehistoric burial places from c.2000BC.

Lamerton – early 1900s view.
COURTESY THE BOOK OF LAMERTON

The church (St Peter) originated in the 12th century and possibly earlier. The tower was consecrated in the 14th century and the building enlarged in the 15th century. In 1877 the church suffered a destructive fire; the tower was saved, and rebuilding soon followed, being completed two years later. An ancient building close to the church gate, known today as the church room, possibly dates from the 13th century. It was probably a church house, used at times by the people and by priests. Ecclesiastically the parish is united with Sydenham Damerel.

The parish includes the ancient hamlet of Chaddlehanger, and 16th-century Collacombe is one of several impressive houses.

Various mining ventures in the parish, for copper and lead, were mainly short-lived. Hurdwick Quarry, now disused, was worked to provide stone – a greyish-green volcanic ash – for buildings of Tavistock Abbey, subsequently by the Bedford estate, and until recent years. Mill Hill Quarry provided slate from the 1600s and is still in production for building and garden purposes.

Further reading: Cole, Ann, and Friends, *The book of Lamerton*, Halsgrove, 1999

LANDCROSS (C3) Torridge Pop. 70 (1901: 58)

The tiny parish of Landcross – the smallest in Devon – occupies a peninsula contained in a meander loop of the River Torridge, just under 2 miles SSE of Bideford. The Torridge forms the boundary on north, east and south, and, with the tributary Yeo forming most of the boundary on the west, Landcross is in fact almost completely surrounded by water, except for a small neck of land close to the junction of the Bideford-Torrington (A 386) and Bideford-Holsworthy (A 388) roads.

The small church (Holy Trinity) was rebuilt on an earlier foundation in 1435, with later work in the 1870s. The font is Norman. General George Monk, later 1st Duke of Albemarle, was baptised here in 1608.

The Torrington or Rolle Canal, opened in 1827, began its route from the Torridge by a tidal lock near Pillmouth and continued through Landcross into Monkleigh parish. In 1872 the extension of the London & South Western Railway from Bideford to Torrington was opened. Upstream from Bideford this crossed the Torridge by a bridge just above the entry of the Yeo and nearby limekilns at Pillmouth, then ran south-westwards through the edge of Landcross parish in a cutting parallel with the road.

LANDKEY (D2) North Devon Pop. 3181 (1901: 621)

Landkey is the next parish to the SE of Barnstaple, and inevitably has become a desirable residential area, particularly in the west. Both the A 361 North Devon Link road and its fore-runner (now unclassified) pass through the parish and close to the village, and there is a network of minor roads to east and west. The land is pleasantly undulating with much farming. There is a working quarry at Venn.

The village is in two parts: Landkey town, on the west, off the through road, where the church is located and there are old and newer houses, and Landkey Newland on the old road to South Molton. The church (St Paul) is of ancient origin. The present building dates from the 15th century, it was restored and partly rebuilt c.1870. The font dates from c.1400. Acland Barton, now a farmhouse, gave its name to the Acland family, by whom it was owned from the 12th to the 20th century.

Landkey was one of the Devon parishes famed for its mazzards, a specially luscious type of cherry known also for its abundant blossom. Memories are being revived by the planting of 60 new mazzard trees on Landkey's Millennium Green.

LANGTREE (C4) Torridge Pop. 621 (1901: 613)

Langtree parish, 7 miles due south of Bideford, is bounded in the north and east by two tributaries of the River Torridge, which merge at Watergate Bridge. The southern boundary extends across land to include in the west the hamlet of Stibb Cross, a crossroads on the Holsworthy-Bideford road (A 388). From here a rather winding minor road proceeds east to Torrington, and on this road Langtree village is located. The church (no dedication) is of 15th-century construction, restored 1856–6.

Further reading: Edgcombe, A. C., (comp.), *A short history of Langtree*, 1985

LAPFORD (F5) Mid Devon Pop. 993 (1901: 528)

Lapford parish, 16 miles NW of Exeter, includes the valley of the River Yeo before it joins the Taw. In places the Yeo and tributary streams form the parish boundary, but in the central area the river, the A 377 road, and the railway all come together. Here is located Lapford's small commercial area. From 1925 to 1974 it was the site of a large dairy factory which received milk from farms over a wide area. The village is situated on the hillside, nearly a mile north of the main road.

The church (St Thomas of Canterbury) probably stands on the site of a Saxon or Norman building. The present structure originates from c.1170, with the north aisle added c.1300. The south door, which has a sanctuary ring, dates from 1180. The building, including the tower, was largely rebuilt in the 15th century. There is much carved woodwork including the very fine rood screen which dates from the early 16th century; the calvary was added in 1929. The porch was rebuilt in 1871 and the church restored in 1882, with further work in the early 20th century.

Bury Barton, just south of the river – its name taken from an ancient earthwork – was a Domesday manor and for long the home of the Bury family. Eastleigh is a hamlet.

Further reading: Parry, Noel, *Lapford, the 2000 year story of a mid Devon village*, priv. pub., 1995

LEWTRENCHARD (C7) West Devon Pop. 172 (1901: 257)

Lewtrenchard is located 8½ miles N of Tavistock and includes a short stretch of the old pre-dual carriageway A 30 road, also part of the village of Lewdown on that road. The small River Lew, tributary of the Lyd and Tamar, flows westwards through the parish.

The 15th-century church (St Peter) contains much fine woodwork, including Tudor bench ends. This was the parish of the Revd Sabine Baring Gould, rector for 43 years, writer of hymns (including 'Onward Christian soldiers'), of theological and antiquarian works, and novels, and a collector of folk songs. From 1625 his family owned the estate and the impressive Lew House, which is now the Lewtrenchard Manor Hotel. Ecclesiastically Lewtrenchard is united with Thrushelton.

The former Lew House, home of the Baring Goulds, now the Lewtrenchard Manor Hotel.

LIFTON (B7) West Devon Pop. 976 (1901: 942)

Lifton, one of the 'last parishes' in Devon, is situated on the old A 30 road to Cornwall, and has become quieter since through traffic which formerly caused congestion now travels on the modern road just to the north. It is of ancient origin, of military importance due to its strategic position, founded by the Saxons and referred to as Liwtune in King Alfred's will of the 880s.

The parish is well-watered. The River Tamar and a tributary, the Carey, form the western boundary, while the Wolf and Lyd, forming part of the eastern boundary, unite at Tinhay and continue to join the Tamar south-west of the village.

The church (St Mary) is of 15th-century construction with some 14th-century work from a previous building. The pillars are of granite and there is a large 12th-century font. The church was restored in 1871.

Ashleigh was a Domesday manor. Wortham was a medieval mansion, and Tinhay and Gatherley are ancient farms. The house at Lifton Park, at the end of a long drive, was built in the early 19th century.

The factory near the site of the former railway station (on the former Lydford-Launceston line, opened in 1865, closed in the 1960s) was a large dairy founded in 1917 (Ambrosia). Now in different hands it is used for the manufacture of various food products.

Lifton, on the old A 30, is now far quieter since construction of the modern dual carriageway north of the village.

Local society: Lifton Local History Group

LITTLEHAM (near Bideford) (C3) Torridge Pop. 394 (1901: 302)

Two miles SSW of Bideford, Littleham is located between the A 39 and A 388 roads, and just north of the unclassified road to Bradworthy. The parish extends over rising ground north of the River Yeo, tributary of the Torridge, which forms the southern boundary. From Yeo Vale the boundary runs north and then follows streams for most of its route back to the south-east. The village has increased in size with modern housing and the church stands on the east, nearer the older part which formerly included a brewery.

The church (St Swithin), of 15th-century construction, incorporates interesting features, both early and modern, including some fine stained glass. There is a gold embossed screen. Recorded incumbents date from the 13th century. The tower appears to be built of bricks, purplish brown in colour, and of somewhat irregular size, similar to those in the construction of the towers at Monkleigh and Parkham.

Littlehempston's church of St John the Baptist.

LITTLEHEMPSTON (G9) South Hams Pop. 207 (1901: 182)

The small parish of Littlehempston surrounds the lower valley of the River Hems as it approaches the Dart. The confluence of the two rivers at the tip of a narrowing strip of land marks the parish's southernmost point, with the Dart and the Hems here defining the boundaries. From the river valleys levels rise to a maximum 300 ft. The A 381 Totnes-Newton Abbot road passes through the parish as does the main railway line.

At the time of Domesday the manor of Littlehempston, known as Hemistona, belonged to the king, but was later held by the Arundel family. Earliest records of a church here date from the 13th century, with the first rector appointed in 1264. The church (St John the Baptist) was largely built in the 15th century and extensively altered in the 19th century. The fine 15th-century rood screen remains, and the north chancel window contains 15th-century glass. The Purbeck stone floor flags were brought by sea to Bridgetown quay and set in place in 1734.

The fine former manor house, later known as the Old Parsonage, was built in the late 14th century.

Besides Little Torrington's parish church, the tiny church of St Mary Magdalene beside the Torridge at Taddiport is still used. It was the chapel of a 13th-century leper hospital.

LITTLE TORRINGTON (C4) Torridge Pop. 420 (1901: 407)

Little Torrington, whose village is situated 1½ miles due S of the town of Great Torrington, is bordered on the north and east by the deeply wooded looped course of the River Torridge, and on the south and west mainly by tributaries. The Hatherleigh-Torrington road (A 386) passes through the parish, with the village at high level just off the road to the east. From this point the road follows a long descent to cross the river at New Bridge.

The original Saxon settlement here was called Toritona. The first church was built in the early 11th century, and the first recorded vicar noted in 1259. The tower was rebuilt and the present church (St Giles) constructed in the 15th century, later renovated in 1755 in Georgian style. Subsequent major renovations were carried out in 1857, 1866, and in 1898 on the tower, with screen, new pews and marble reredos added. The large font, which dates from the 11th or 12th centuries, is of unusual cushion shape cut into four divisions. It stands on a 15th-century base.

The minor road from Langtree to Great Torrington runs through the north-west of the parish to cross the river ¾ mile downstream from New Bridge at the hamlet of Taddiport, which was the location from the 13th century of a leper hospital. Its tiny chapel of St Mary Magdalene is still used for worship, united with Little Torrington. The substantial 3-arched Taddiport Bridge is believed to date from the 17th century.

Frizenham, Hollam and Smytham were named in Domesday.

LODDISWELL (F11) South Hams Pop. 891 (1901: 650)

Loddiswell is a rather long parish from north to south, with the eastern boundary defined almost entirely by the River Avon, before the river turns westwards to run through the south of the parish. The undulating land reaches 416 ft at Coldharbour Cross in the north, near which is the ancient site known as Loddiswell Rings or Blackdown Camp. This appears to relate to two different periods of construction, possibly a hill fort from the Iron Age, and an early Norman castle built within it, with remains of a mound and an outer and an inner bailey.

The village is in the south, a mile NNW of Kingsbridge, and standing high above the Avon. It can be approached from the north by the A 3196 road which connects with the A 38, and in the south by minor roads leading from the system around Kingsbridge. The church (St Michael & All Angels) dates from the 13th and 16th centuries. The font is of red sandstone and bears unusual scrolls, and there are hagioscopes in the north and south transepts. The church was restored in 1866.

The Kingsbridge branch railway, opened in 1893 and closed in 1963, ran southwards from Brent – on the main line – down the parish's eastern boundary, crossing and re-crossing the Avon. Loddiswell had a station ½ mile SE of the village.

Further reading: Various, *The book of Loddiswell*, Halsgrove, 1999

LOXBEARE (H4) Mid Devon Pop. 165 (1901: Loxbeare 100, Calverleigh 69)

The civil parish of Loxbeare, 3½ miles NW of Tiverton, also includes the ecclesiastical parish of Calverleigh. The Tiverton-Rackenford road passes through – with Loxbeare village just off the road to the east – as also does the A 361 North Devon Link road, constructed in the 1980s. A tributary of the River Exe flows through the south. The land is mostly of 500-600 ft altitude, rising to 824 ft on the southern boundary.

Loxbeare church (St Michael & All Angels) dates from the 12th century, restored in 1832. Leigh Barton was the Domesday manor of Lega. Calverleigh church (St Mary the Virgin) retains part of the 14th-century construction, with rebuilding from the early 16th century, and restoration in the 19th century.

Further reading: Vickery, Richard, ed., *The Loxbeare Journal*, Loxbeare PCC, 2002

LOXHORE (E2) North Devon Pop. 153 (1901: 202)

Loxhore, 5 miles NE of Barnstaple, is almost entirely bounded by the partially wooded valleys of streams – the River Yeo on the south, its tributary the Woolley Water on the west, and other tributaries on north and east.

The church (St Michael) dates from the 15th century, restored in the late 19th century. There is a slender screen, and the north arcade is supported, unusually, by two pillars of oak.

Loxhore is not served directly by a major road but is reached either east from Shirwell Cross on the A 39, or north from the unclassified road from Barnstaple to Bratton Fleming.

Further reading: Payne, Jessie K., *A little history of Loxhore*, 1987

LUFFINCOTT (B6) Torridge Pop. 45 (1901: 62)

This tiny parish of Luffincott is located 6 miles S of Holsworthy, to the west of the Holsworthy-Launceston road (A 388). It is bordered on the west by the River Tamar and on the north and south by tributary streams. The church (St James) has been unused since the 1970s and is now redundant, cared for by the Churches Conservation Trust. The parish is united ecclesiastically with Tetcott.

LUNDY (A1) Torridge

To speak of 'Lundy Island' is actually incorrect because the name 'Lund-ey' is itself Norse for 'puffin island'. Located 10 miles NW of Hartland Point and 18 miles due W of Morte Point, where the Atlantic meets the Bristol Channel, the island measures 3 miles from north to south and ½ mile in width. Composed almost entirely of granite, and rising to 471 ft, it forms a grassy plateau with rugged cliffs beaten by the elements on the west, and a slightly more temperate coastline of combes and varied plant life on the east.

Lundy ponies on the slopes of the island's wild west-facing coastline.

The island provides a habitat for many bird species, including nesting sites for colonies of seabirds in late spring, although, sadly, numbers of puffins have declined. It is a stopping-off point for migrant birds in both spring and autumn. Rabbits and deer graze the grassland as well as ponies and sheep, while the surrounding waters are rich in marine life.

Lundy bears signs of human presence from the Neolithic Age in the form of flint flakes and scrapers, and of late prehistoric times with remains of hut bases and burial sites. It became a stronghold of robbers and of Scandinavian pirates from the 12th century when possessed by the Marisco family. The so-called Marisco Castle, in the south-east, was actually built after their downfall, by Henry III. Its remains, in which three fishermen's cottages were incorporated in the 19th century, and the square keep, still exist. During the Civil War the island was fortified for the king. Leased in the 18th century to the notorious Bidefordian Thomas Benson, it was used by him for landing convicts destined for the New World, whom he engaged in wall building, and for smuggling. After being held by a succession of individuals, in 1834 Lundy was sold to William Hudson Heaven (who succeeded in making the island free of mainland jurisdiction, earning for it the description: 'Kingdom of Heaven'). During his lifetime, from 1863–8, granite quarries were worked on the island's eastern side under lease by the Lundy Granite Company, signs of which are prominent, while those of an associated tramway are still visible along the cliff top. W.H. Heaven's son, the Revd Hudson Grossett Heaven, in 1889 built the church (St Helen) in the south, a replacement for the ancient ruined chapel of the same dedication.

Sold in 1925 to A.L. Christie, Lundy was bought in 1954 by Martin Coles Harman who made it a sanctuary for wildlife. Since 1969 the island has been owned by the National Trust and financed, administered and maintained by the Landmark Trust. Visitors are now encouraged, with sailings mainly from Bideford and Ilfracombe, and occasionally from Clovelly. Helicopter flights are also possible.

Lundy's first ('The Old') lighthouse was erected on the highest point, in the south-west in 1819. Often obscured by fog, it was replaced in 1897 by the North Light and the South Light, which continue in operation.

Further reading: Etherton, P.T. and Barlow, Vernon, *Tempestuous Isle*, 1950
Langham, A. and M., *Lundy*, David & Charles, 1970

LUPPITT (K5) East Devon Pop. 444 (1901: 467)

The 10th-century font in Luppitt Church.

The diamond-shaped parish of Luppitt is one of hills and valleys, lying 4 miles N of Honiton. The village itself stands on a hillside at c.500 ft and altitudes reach over 800 ft at various points, including Dumpdon Hill (856 ft) in the south-east, a probable Iron Age hill fort. The village is approached by minor roads north from the A 30. Tributaries of the River Otter flow eastwards through the parish, one of them forming the boundary on the south-west while the Otter itself defines it on the south-east. The north-western boundary follows the ancient high road, bending from it to include Luppitt Common.

The church (St Mary) is of early origin, the present building dating from the 14th century, restored in the late 1880s and in 1923. The font is of Salcombe (Regis) stone, carved to a most unusual barbaric design. There is a list of its rectors and vicars from 1247.

Greenway, Mohuns Ottery and Shapcombe were named in Domesday. Mohuns Ottery was the home of the Carews from c.1300 to the late 16th century. The house suffered a fire in 1868.

Further reading: Sage, John, *St Mary's Church, Luppitt*, Devon, 1992
Local society: Luppitt Local History Group

LUSTLEIGH (F7) Teignbridge Pop. 626 (1901: 394)

Lustleigh is situated within the area of Dartmoor National Park, 11 miles SW of Exeter and 4 miles SSE of Moretonhampstead. The village lies just under a mile west of the A 382 Bovey Tracey-Moretonhampstead road which forms most of the eastern parish boundary. The River Bovey defines much of the boundary on the west, with an extended loop in the south-west to take in Trendlebere Down from which there are fine views. This is a parish of winding lanes and woodland. Along the east bank of the Bovey is the steep ascent of Lustleigh Cleave, where moorland which bears remains of Bronze Age hut circles rises to 1063 ft near Hunters Tor and an adjacent Iron Age hill fort.

Said to have been known earlier as Sutreworde, in Anglo-Saxon meaning 'south of the wood', the manor of Lustleigh was granted by William I to Ansgar, who had held it since the time of Edward the Confessor. It is believed that the churchyard may have been a Celtic burial ground as a Celtic gravestone, called Datuidic's Stone, for long existed in the church porch floor, until moved inside to stand against the west wall of the north aisle where it remains. Building of the present church (St John the Baptist) began c.1250, and lancet windows of the chancel and a few other features remain from then. The list of clergy dates from 1262. The building was enlarged in the 14th

View of Lustleigh. COURTESY THE BOOK OF LUSTLEIGH

century which involved demolition of some of the earlier structure. The tower was added slightly later and in the late 15th century the north aisle was added. The vestry is a 19th-century addition. The ancient Church House stands across the road to the east of the church.

In 1866 the railway came to Lustleigh when the line from Newton Abbot to Moretonhampstead was opened. This brought numbers of visitors to the parish which, up to that time, had been relatively isolated and devoted almost entirely to farming. With the delights of the surroundings becoming realised more people eventually came, and many settled, often on retirement. The railway closed to passengers in 1959 and for freight in 1964.

Lustleigh men were among those engaged in the mining of micaceous haematite, a form of iron ore known as 'shiny ore', used for various purposes including, latterly, in the manufacture of grey paint for warships and bridges. Nearest to Lustleigh, although just outside the parish boundary, being immediately east of the A 382, was Kelly Mine. Working is believed to date from 1797, although apparently rather intermittently for a century or so. Regular production began soon after 1900 and continued until c.1950. Work has been proceeding since 1984 in preserving the site by the Kelly Mine Preservation Society.

Further reading: Crowdy, Joe, comp., *Lustleigh, portrait of a Dartmoor parish,* Halsgrove, 2001
Also various books, papers etc. relating to Wreyland and Lustleigh by Cecil Torr
Local society: Lustleigh Society

LYDFORD (D7) West Devon Pop. 394 (1901: 2812)

A view of the castle as it appears in the 21st century. COURTESY THE BOOK OF LYDFORD

The present Lydford parish is much reduced in size from earlier days when it included the whole of the Forest of Dartmoor and as such was Devon's largest parish. Since 1987 the two have been separate civil parishes and Lydford is restricted to the narrow western section. Part of the southern boundary is defined by the River Lyd which flows south-westwards with momentum, passing through dramatic Lydford Gorge, a National Trust property.

Lydford has a long history. It was one of four burhs established by King Alfred as defence against the Danes, and became a Domesday borough. A massive earthen rampart was made where the land to the western end of the village forms a promontory, and can still be seen. The Saxon influence is also evident in the layout of early streets on a 'grid' plan. From 973 to 1050 Lydford had a mint, producing large numbers of coins of which many have found their way to Scandinavian countries.

In the 11th century, possibly involving the destruction of several dwellings, a castle was built on the top of the promontory defences, now marked, it is believed, by a mound and ditch. This was superseded in 1195 by the existing substantial keep, seen close to the Castle Inn. It was not, however, a castle, but a prison for offenders against

Forest and Stannary law. Conditions are believed to have been extremely harsh, with prisoners dumped in the dungeons and, under 'Lydford Law' being 'hanged first and tried afterwards'.

The church (St Petrock) is of early foundation, consecrated by Bishop Bronescombe in 1261. The present building is of mainly 15th-century construction. A north aisle was added in 1890. There are stairs to a former rood screen and a hagioscope. The present screen was carved by the Misses Pinwill of Ermington and the pews were renewed in the 1920s. The west window, depicting the crucifixion, was formerly in Princetown church. The reredos shows St Petrock with a wolf, which reputedly accompanied him. On the north wall is the recently restored watchmaker's tombstone, brought in from outside for protection from weathering, which carries interesting wording.

Further reading: Weeks, Barbara, *The book of Lydford*, Halsgrove, 2004

The cliff railway which connects Lynton and Lynmouth operates by counterbalance, with water providing the weight ballast.

LYMPSTONE (H7) East Devon Pop. 1754 (1901: 1012)

Lympstone is a fairly small, narrow parish, running inland from low red sandstone cliffs on the east side of the Exe estuary, 7 miles SE of Exeter and 2 miles N of Exmouth. The parish's narrowing eastern extremity terminates at c.400 ft on Lympstone Common. The A 376 Exeter-Exmouth road passes through the parish, as does the railway which dates from 1861, with a station. The pleasant village lies between the railway on the shoreline, and the road a mile inland.

Lympstone was a Saxon manor. The church (Nativity of the Blessed Virgin Mary) is of early 15th-century date, rebuilt, except for the tower, in 1864 and enlarged in 1928. The parish is united ecclesiastically with St Swithun, Woodbury, and there is also St Andrew's Church at Exton. For long a fishing village, Lympstone developed an overseas trade, particularly with Newfoundland from the 16th century, and ship building and repair work from the 17th century. (See 'Economic developments in Lympstone and Nutwell in the eighteenth century' by Rosemary Smith in *The Devon Historian 58,* April 1999.)

The Commando Training Centre of the Royal Marines is located at Lympstone.

Local Society: The Lympstone Society

LYNTON AND LYNMOUTH (F1) North Devon Pop. 1513 (1901: 1641)

For civil purposes Lynton and Lynmouth have long been combined, although ecclesiastically Lynmouth is united with Countisbury. They are served by the A 39 road between Barnstaple and Minehead, which is tortuous with steep gradients in this area, and by the B 3223 to Simonsbath on Exmoor.

This is a large parish, bounded by North Devon's Bristol Channel shore on the north. South from the coast the land rises steeply and is very dramatic, reaching 1000 ft from sea level in less than a mile, and over 1350 ft on the border with Somerset. The Hoaroak Water, flowing off Exmoor, defines the boundary on the south-east. Tumuli and hut circles occur in several locations, providing evidence of early habitation. The East and West Lyn Rivers, flowing through beautiful wooded valleys, meet to enter the sea at Lynmouth, which has a small harbour and in the past was noted for herring-fishing. Great tragedy struck Lynmouth on the night of 15 August 1952 when unprecedented rainfall on the area of Exmoor called The Chains caused a huge rapid rise in the levels of the Lyn rivers, and consequent disastrous flooding to the hamlet of Barbrook, and to Lynmouth itself. Thirty-one lives were lost, and immense damage caused to many properties, bridges and roads. Considerable reconstruction had to be carried out, in which measures for protection from future flooding were incorporated.

The town of Lynton stands at the higher level, c.600 ft. Besides being joined by the steep road, Lynmouth and Lynton are connected by a cliff railway, which is unique in being powered entirely by water. Designed by George Marks, built by Robert Jones, it was financed largely by publisher and local benefactor George Newnes. The cliff railway was opened in 1890 and continues in operation throughout the year – except for a brief winter maintenance spell – carrying a maximum of 40 passengers on each journey and rising 430 ft with a gradient of 1 in 1¾. The service's vehicles work on a system of counterbalance: the one at the top takes on 700 gallons of stream water which provides weight for the descent, during which the other vehicle, having discharged its water ballast, rises.

Sir George Newnes was also a promoter of the narrow gauge Lynton & Barnstaple Railway, opened in 1898 and closed in 1935, which is currently undergoing restoration by volunteers working from Woody Bay Station, 3 miles to the west.

Lynton church (St Mary the Virgin) dates from the 14th century but was mainly rebuilt (apart from the tower) in the 1860s. It has a Norman font. There is also the church of St Bartholomew at Barbrook which was built as a mission chapel in 1875. Lynmouth's church (St John the Baptist) was built in 1870.

West from the town of Lynton, close to the coast, is the awesome Valley of Rocks, with its impressive rock formations, in which dwells a herd of wild goats. Lee Abbey, at the far end, was earlier the site of a small house, the seat of the Wichelhalse family, until 1713. The present name was given when a new house was built in the mid 19th century. Later it became a hotel, but is now a Christian conference and retreat centre.

Coffins Heanton, Ilkerton, East Lyn, and West Lyn, were Domesday manors.

Further reading: Delderfield, Eric, *The book of Lynton and Lynmouth*, 1981
Mold, Ernest, *Lynton and its coast, a brief history*, 1992
Travis, John, *An illustrated history of Lynton and Lynmouth 1770–1914*, Breedon, 1995
Local society: Lynton & Barnstaple Railway Association
Museum: Lynton & Exmoor Museum, Market Street

MALBOROUGH (F12) South Hams Pop. 898 (1901: 2167)

Malborough is a fairly high and open parish 3½ miles SSW of Kingsbridge from where it is reached by the A 381 road. The south-western boundary lies along the English Channel coastline and includes at its east and west ends the promontories of Bolt Head and Bolt Tail, the latter bearing the remains of an Iron Age hill fort. The coastline strip along this stretch, including Bolberry Down and Soar Mill Cove, is owned by the National Trust and is natural and unspoilt. Inner Hope village, at Hope Cove, north of Bolt Tail, is within Malborough parish. The parish is also bounded on the north-east, by a short length of the Kingsbridge estuary in the Ilton area north of Salcombe. The highest altitudes of up to 437 ft are reached in the cliff-top areas of the south.

The village is located centrally. The large church (All Saints), with its spire that provides a landmark from far away, originates from c.1200. Much of the present structure is from the 15th century, with a 15th-century screen. The font is late Norman. The parish is united ecclesiastically with Galmpton and Hope Cove in South Huish. Alston and Ilton in the north-east, Collaton in the east, and Sewer in the south, were Domesday manors.

Local society: Hope Archive Group

MAMHEAD (H7) Teignbridge Pop. 99 (1901: 178)

The small parish of Mamhead, 7 miles S of Exeter, is on the eastern slopes of the Haldon Hills, with land rising to 821 ft. The unclassified road from the A 380, eastwards to Starcross, forms the northern boundary and access is from this or from other minor roads in the south. The parish is centred on Mamhead Park, which contains many fine trees and gives splendid views out to sea. The church (St Thomas the Apostle) is set within the park and is remote from the small village to the east. It is of mainly 15th-century construction, partly rebuilt in the 1830s. The parish is united ecclesiastically with Kenton.

The Mamhead obelisk, erected in 1743 as a guide for seafarers. It is now surrounded by woodlands.

The estate was bought from Sir Peter Carew in the early 17th century by Giles Ball, in whose family it remained until sold to the Newmans in 1823. An earlier mansion, which had been garrisoned for the king in the Civil War, was rebuilt by his son Sir Peter Ball. His grandson, Thomas Ball, added numerous exotic trees, gathered on his travels, to the park, and also, in 1743, erected a tall obelisk on the hill above as a guide to seafarers. The house was again rebuilt, on a new site, by the Newmans in 1830. Although the main area is private, the obelisk, now surrounded by trees, is accessible to walkers by forest paths.

MANATON (F7) Teignbridge Pop. 351 (1901: 315)

View from the green, Manaton, 1999. COURTESY THE BOOK OF MANATON

Situated on the east side of Dartmoor, within the Dartmoor National Park, the parish of Manaton somewhat resembles in outline a map of the Indian sub-continent, with a long broadening area stretching out westwards which at its extremity meets the Dartmoor Forest boundary. On the east the Manaton boundary is marked by the River Bovey as it flows south-eastwards between the steep wooded slopes of Neadon Cleave, and of Lustleigh Cleave, as far as the confluence with the Becka Brook, which it then briefly follows westwards. However, before reaching the renowned Becky Falls, where the brook descends 70 ft in a spectacular waterfall over granite boulders, the boundary swings south, to encompass the northern area of Haytor Down at an altitude of 1332 ft. Beyond this comes progression to the southern apex in the area of Holwell and a fairly acute turn again north-westwards. Wilder moorland and higher elevations are encountered in the western extension, including Hameldown Tor (1736 ft) and the parish's highest point at Broad Barrow (1750 ft). The boundary rounds the area of Challacombe Down, with its early farm system marked by lynchets, and Soussons Down, where the Golden Dagger tin mine – part of the Birch Tor-Vitifer area – was worked between 1879 and 1914. Proceeding back along the north, the boundary passes through Grimspound, an enclosed Bronze Age settlement which includes some of the many hut circles and other prehistoric remains with which Manaton abounds. On its final lap the boundary passes just north of Easdon Tor (1439 ft). Among the numerous other natural and ancient features with which Manaton is endowed is the centrally located Bowermans Nose, a prominent tor on Hayne Down, which has legendary associations, and, farther south, Hound Tor, with the nearby remains of its medieval village settlement.

Manaton's small village is situated in the north-east of the parish, beside the minor road that winds its way from the B 3212 across Dartmoor to Bovey Tracey, with, half a mile along towards Bovey, the hamlet of Water. At Manaton there are some attractive houses and the village green, also the church (St Winifred). The church, dating from the late 15th century, is built of granite and has a very fine screen of c.1490. The building suffered in a severe storm in 1779 which split the tower. Repairs were subsequently carried out, and later a major restoration in 1924.

Manaton, Langstone, Neadon, and Houndtor were Domesday manors – Houndtor being held by the abbot of Tavistock Abbey. Neadon Upper Hall dates from the 15th century; it was restored in the 1980s with its medieval features retained.

Further reading: Compiled by the people of the parish, *The book of Manaton*, Halsgrove, 1999

MARIANSLEIGH (F3) North Devon Pop. 155 (1901: 205)

Three miles SE of South Molton, the roughly triangular parish of Mariansleigh (often pronounced ' Mary Ansleigh') lies between the Crooked Oak Brook and another tributary of the River Mole. Flowing westwards they converge and meet the river at Alswear, a small village on the edge of the parish beside the South Molton-Witheridge road (B 3137), which runs south-eastwards close to the parish boundary.

Mariansleigh village is situated centrally, at an altitude of c.600 ft. The church (St Mary) is of ancient foundation, the first incumbent noted in 1259. The 15th-century building was burnt down in 1932 and subsequently reconstructed.

Further reading: Tull, Christopher S., *Mariansleigh Church and people*, 1981
Mariansleigh Millennium Group: Mariansleigh

MARLDON (G9) South Hams Pop. 2023 (1901: 506)

Marldon is situated on the western fringe of the Torquay conurbation, with the modern ring road running north through the parish, immediately east of the village. The land is hilly, rising to 643 ft at Beacon Hill on the southern boundary.

There is a mention of a church here in 1348, and the still-existing early tower dates from c.1400. The present church (St John the Baptist) is of 15th and early 16th-century construction, built of limestone, red sandstone, and granite, with Beer stone arcades, window tracery and doorways. Its main builders were Otho Gilbert and his wife Elizabeth, to whom there are memorials. The Gilbert family dwelt at Compton Castle, in the north of the parish, the building of which commenced in the early 14th century by Geoffrey Gilbert who had married the Compton heiress. Some traces of the building still exist, but most of the present house dates from the mid 15th century, with additions from the late 16th century. It is a very fine example of a fortified manor house. Remaining in the same family until 1800, it was the home of Sir Humphrey Gilbert, explorer and colonist. After passing into other hands, Compton Castle was bought back by a family descendant, Commander W.R. Gilbert, restored, and later given to the National Trust.

MARTINHOE (E1) North Devon Pop. 104 (1901: 174)

Martinhoe extends from Heddons Mouth to Lee Bay (west of Lynton) on North Devon's Bristol Channel coastline and includes the descriptively named Woody Bay. The western boundary is defined by the River Heddon, and in the south of the parish includes a short length of the A 39 Barnstaple-Lynton road at Martinhoe Cross. Levels rise in the south to c.1000 ft, and there are steep descents to the sea with spectacular cliffs. Near the Beacon are earthwork remains of a Roman coastal fortlet or watch point dating from the 1st century AD, part of the series of defences established by the Romans during their advance.

The village, in the north, is reached by minor roads from the A 39. The church (St Martin), dating from the 13th century, was enlarged in the 1860s. Killington was a Domesday manor.

A recently-restored section of the former Lynton & Barnstaple Railway (narrow gauge) is located in the south of the parish. Carried out by volunteers operating as a charitable trust company, the work on this railway, which originally opened in 1898 and closed in 1935, has been proceeding in recent years from a base at Woody Bay Station, near the A 39 at Martinhoe Cross. Facilities for visitors have been developed.

Woody Bay Station from where work is proceeding to restore part of the former Lynton & Barnstaple Railway.

Further reading: Bridle, Harriet, *Woody Bay*, 1990

MARWOOD (D2) North Devon Pop. 762 (1901: 681)

The village of Marwood stands 3 miles NNW of Barnstaple, the parish comprising undulating country that rises northwards to 780 ft on Metcombe Down and to 859 ft at Hewish Down Beacon in the north-east. The Bradiford Water forms the eastern boundary. A minor road to Ilfracombe runs north through the parish and the eastern side of the village.

The church (St Michael & All Angels) is of ancient origin, with the first recorded rector named in 1263. Part of the 13th-century building is incorporated in the present structure which dates from the 15th century. There is a north aisle separated from the nave by a 5-bay arcade, and a south transept. A section of the very fine 16th-century rood screen, with rood loft, remains (the rest having been destroyed c.1850). Although a Norman font is kept in a corner, the font in current use is pseudo- medieval in design, with a large sculptured cover depicting Simeon blessing the boy Jesus. There is a Berry sundial (1762) on the porch which tells the time for Marwood, Jerusalem, and some European countries.

The parish bears an air of antiquity and remoteness, with several farms having originated in Saxon times, and a number of names recorded in Domesday: Marwood, Blakewell, Kingsheanton, Metcombe, Varley, Westcott Barton, Whiddon, and

Whitefield Barton. Muddiford and Milltown are hamlets on the B 3230 road through the Bradiford valley.

MARYSTOWE (C7) West Devon Pop. 196 (1901: 255)

Marystowe's church of St Mary and the church room stand in tranquil setting.

Marystowe lies in the countryside 6 miles NNW of Tavistock, approximately equidistant from Tavistock and Launceston, and approached by minor roads. The River Lyd flows north-westwards through the parish, joined here by the Lew on its course to join the Tamar.

There is no actual village. The church (St Mary the Virgin) stands in the extreme south-east of the parish, in an elevated position with fine views to the south. The structure dates from the 12th century, with alterations. It contains a very fine Norman font, also a large Renaissance monument to Sir Thomas Wise.

Sir Thomas Wise, knighted by James I in 1603, acquired possession of the manor of Sydenham and built the large and beautiful Jacobean house in tranquil surroundings close to the river. Sydenham passed to the Tremaynes in 1675. The house is visible from the minor road through the ironwork of its gates but is in private hands and not open to the public.

MARY TAVY (D8) West Devon Pop. 865 (1901: 717)

The busy A 386 road runs through Mary Tavy village, with the War Memorial and recently restored Methodist Church, dated 1835, on either side.

Mary Tavy lies on the western fringe of Dartmoor and is crossed south-north by the main Tavistock-Okehampton road (A 386). The inverted pear-shaped parish is defined in the south by the River Tavy on the east, and by its tributary the Burn on the west – their confluence being at the 'pear's' southern tip. In the north is the expanse of Black Down, rising to 1158 ft on Gibbet Hill.

The church (St Mary), built on the site of an early Norman church, is of 15th-century construction, enlarged from the original and restored, in accordance with High Church tradition, in the late 19th century. Mary Tavy, Wringworthy, North and South Warne, and Burntown were all Domesday manors.

From the 18th century until the early 20th century the parish was much involved in mining. Wheal Friendship, in the village area, had deep and extensive underground workings. From 1714 copper and lead were raised, and the mine reopened on a larger scale in 1796. Following construction of the Tavistock Canal in the early 19th century ores from Mary Tavy, carted to Tavistock, were conveyed on the canal to the port of Morwellham on the Tamar. Water was the mine's main power source – 17 waterwheels were in use in 1875. After copper ceased to be profitable arsenic was extracted from the waste; remains of the refining plant still exist. The shell of the fine old Wheal Betsy engine house with its stack stands beside the road on Blackdown. Lead and copper, arsenic and silver were mined here during the 19th century. The site of another former small mine, South Friendship, in the south of the village, is now occupied by a hydro-electric station, owned by South West Water and fed by water brought by leat from the Tavy, which supplies power into the National Grid.

Further reading: Sargent, F. Gerry, *Tavy St Mary parish, a kaleidoscopic history and guide*, 1992

MEAVY (D9) West Devon Pop. 624 (1901: 261)

Located on the Dartmoor fringe, Meavy – as its name suggests – is watered by the River Meavy which rises on the moor and continues south and west from Burrator Reservoir. The south-west section of the reservoir is within the parish boundary, which proceeds north and west, skirting Yennadon Down, including the residential Dousland, and passing south of Yelverton to rejoin the river southwards to its confluence with the Plym. The Plym, upstream, then forms the southern boundary. From Brisworthy the route turns north, crosses country and is then realigned with the Meavy south of the reservoir.

Wigford Down, in the south, is particularly rich in Bronze Age remains, and the summit of Dewerstone Rock is the possible site of an Iron Age fort. Some of the

Meavy village green, c.1912.
COURTESY THE BOOK OF MEAVY

earliest, 12th century, records for tin working refer to the vicinity of Brisworthy, beside the Plym, east of Cadover Bridge. In the 19th century iron ore was worked on Yennadon Down, and a ferro-ceramic mine existed near Shaugh Bridge. Dewerstone Quarry produced granite, and the east side of Wigford Down yielded china clay, worked near Brisworthy and processed at Cadover Bridge. The Princetown Railway, which closed in 1956, ran through the north of the parish, giving spectacular views over Burrator Reservoir which dates from 1898.

Meavy church (St Peter) has records of incumbents and chaplains from 1121, when in the care of monks from Plympton Priory. Structure of the building dates from Norman times to the early 16th century. Near the church is the Royal Oak Inn, beside which stands the famous Meavy Oak, a magnificent tree now partly propped, which is reckoned to be well over 900 years old.

Hoo Meavy is a hamlet. Goodameavy House, a 16th-century manor, underwent rebuilding in the 18th century. Marchant's Cross, ½ mile south-east of the village, is a fine wayside granite cross recorded in 1291.

Further reading: Hemery, Pauline, *The book of Meavy*, Halsgrove, 1999
Local society: Yelverton & District Local History Society

MEETH (D5) West Devon Pop. 171 (1901: 203)

Meeth is located 2½ miles N of Hatherleigh, on the twisty A 386 Hatherleigh-Torrington road. The River Torridge forms the boundary on south and east, and it is here that that long river, which so far has flowed south-east from its source – just 3 miles from the North Devon coast on Hartland's Welsford Moor – takes a decisive turn northwards, on its way to join the waters of that same coastline at Bideford. The parish's northern and western boundaries follow land routes and tributary streams.

The church (St Michael & All Angels), which contains Saxon work in its structure, dates mainly from the 12th century, although parts were later rebuilt. The path through the churchyard is cobbled, with a central diamond pattern, similar to those at Huish and Merton. Meeth, Hele, Stockleigh and Woolladon were all named in Domesday. Crocker's Hele and Friar's Hele are ancient farms.

Ball clay, used in ceramics, electrical porcelain, and sanitary ware, is worked in open pits on Woolladon Moor. This area and industry were served by the North Devon & Cornwall Junction Light Railway from Torrington to Halwill, which opened in 1925 and closed in 1982. The railway crossed the road just south of Meeth village by an unmanned level crossing. The clay is now transported by road.

MEMBURY (L5) East Devon Pop. 503 (1901: 603)

Membury is a parish of pleasant countryside with land that rises to c.650 ft, with

Membury's church of St John the Baptist, parts of which date from the 13th century.

the village located 3 miles NW of Axminster. The River Yarty marks the western boundary and the Somerset county border that on the north-east. The parish is served by a network of minor roads that connect with the A 35 and A 358 from Axminster.

The church (St John the Baptist) dates from the 13th century with the surviving chancel, other parts are of 15th and 16th-century construction. Membury Castle, on the east side of the village, is a hill fort, believed to be from the late Iron Age when it would have served as a defence against invaders from Dorset. A field near Membury Court, a mile north-west of the village, was the site of a Roman villa, excavated in 1914.

Further reading: Craddock, Ron, *Around and about Membury*
Local society: Membury & District Local History Society

MERTON (D4) Torridge Pop. 331 (1901: 507)

In due direction, Merton lies 5 miles SSE of Torrington, but the travelling journey is longer because of the many corners on the A 386 Hatherleigh-Torrington road which passes through the village. The parish boundaries are defined by the widely-looped course of the River Torridge on the east and north and by the Mere on the west and south.

The church (All Saints) stands on the west side of the village square, approached by a long path edged with yew trees. The path is cobbled with a central diamond pattern, similar to the church paths at neighbouring Huish and Meeth. The list of rectors dates from 1261, the present building from c.1400. There is a south transept and north aisle with slim granite arcade pillars. The church was restored in 1875.

Merton was the birthplace of Walter de Merton, founder of Merton College, Oxford. Speccott and Potheridge, in the north, were Domesday manors. Great Potheridge is notable as having been the ancestral home of General George Monk, whose part in the Restoration of the Monarchy in 1660 resulted in his being created Duke of Albemarle and Baron Torrington.

Ball clay, for the brick and ceramics industries, has been extracted on Merton Moor for some years. The North Devon & Cornwall Junction Light Railway, opened in 1925 and closed in 1982, which served the various clayworks, ran briefly through the west of the parish and included Dunsbeer Halt.

MESHAW (F4) North Devon Pop. 151 (1901: 181)

Meshaw is situated 5 miles SE of South Molton on the B 3137 South Molton-Witheridge-Tiverton road. This is a fairly small parish with land that rises to over 700 ft, some of it fairly rough or reclaimed moorland. There is a tumulus on Meshaw Moor, in the south.

The church (St John the Baptist) dates from the 16th century but was rebuilt, except for the tower, in 1838. Irishcombe, in the south-east, was a Domesday manor.

Further reading: Smith, P., and Headon, J. and H., *Meshaw, a north Devon parish*, 1991

MILTON ABBOT (C8) West Devon Pop. 737 (1901: 719)

Milton Abbot, 5½ miles NW of Tavistock on the road to Launceston (B 3662), stretches from the River Tamar on the south-west to the Lyd in the north-east, where it includes the village of Chillaton. Hills in the farming country between rise to over 900 ft.

As part of the estates of Tavistock Abbey from c.974, Milton Abbot passed at the Dissolution to the Russell family and succeeding dukes of Bedford. In 1810 the 6th Duke and his second wife Georgiana built Endsleigh, a 'cottage' retreat on land running down to the Tamar. Architect Jeffry Wyattville and landscape gardener Humphrey Repton designed the house and grounds – the latter laid out in the style of the 'picturesque' movement. Later becoming a hotel, the house and gardens have undergone restoration in the hands of the Endsleigh Trust.

The attractive, former Endsleigh estate, buildings of Milton Abbot School.

The church (St Constantine), standing close by the road through the village, dates from at least as early as the 12th century. The present building is of mainly 15th-century construction, built of green Hurdwick stone. It underwent considerable necessary restoration in 2002–3. Ecclesiastically the parish is united with Dunterton. The village includes many attractive Bedford buildings.

Edgcumbe was the home of the Edgcumbes from the 13th century. Leigh Barton was a Domesday manor.

The village of Chillaton was a centre for small-scale manganese mining in the late 19th century. Ores from the nearby Hogstor mines and from small workings in neighbouring parishes were brought to the Chillaton centre for recording and processing before being carted to Morwellham quays on the Tamar.

Local society: Milton Abbot Discoverers

MILTON DAMEREL (B4) Torridge Pop. 428 (1901: 442)

Milton Damerel, 5 miles NNE of Holsworthy, has its south-western boundary at Holsworthy Beacon. From here the line proceeds briefly west and then northwards along south and north tributaries of the River Waldon, before turning eastwards to reach the Torridge near Woodford Bridge. This river then forms the north-eastern border until a turn westwards and a short overland section bring it to the Waldon, which is followed before a final overland length back to the Beacon.

The Holsworthy-Bideford road (A 388) passes through, with the village crossroads at Venngreen, half a mile north-west of the church (Holy Trinity), a restored early 14th-century structure.

The parish is mainly agricultural. Wonford and Whitebeer are hamlets in the south and north.

Further reading: Harris, George. O., *A glance back to some history of Milton Damerel,* 1991

MODBURY (E10) South Hams Pop. 1454 (1901: 1330)

Modbury has many interesting houses, some slate-hung, as seen here in Brownston Street.

Modbury may be recalled by many people as the small town with the steep street on the road from Plymouth to Kingsbridge (A 379) where several other minor routes converge. The area of the parish, however, is quite large, extending from the head of the River Erme estuary north-westwards to a tributary of the Avon and boundaries with Ugborough and North Huish. Altitudes reach 400-500 ft, and 550 ft on the north and south-east boundaries. This is the heartland of the fertile farming country and grass hills known as the South Hams, home territory of the large golden brown breed of South Devon cattle. Farming has long been the traditional occupation – already a borough, Modbury was granted a weekly market and two annual fairs in 1238. In 1643 Modbury was the scene of a Civil War conflict, and in the 17th and 18th centuries was a centre of woollen manufacture.

The town, located 12 miles ESE of Plymouth and 7 miles NW of Kingsbridge, has a pleasant atmosphere, with many slate-hung houses. The church (St George), with its angle-buttressed tower and spire, stands high, south-west of the town and is seen prominently from the road to Kingsbridge. It is of ancient foundation. There was a Benedictine priory here in the 12th century, and there are remains of an early church in the structure of the present building, which dates from the 13th century, dedicated in 1320. It was reconstructed in the 14th and 15th centuries and suffered at the hands of Cromwell's soldiers.

The Champernownes were lords of the manor from the early 14th century until 1700. Great Orcheton in the south-west, home of the Prideaux family for 13 generations, was a Domesday manor, as also were Shilston Barton and Spriddlescombe in the north, and Leigh in the east.

Local society: Modbury Local History Society, which has produced booklets on the history of the town

Molland's ancient church has a striking interior, with Georgian developments that include high box pews and a north aisle pulpit.

MOLLAND (G3) North Devon Pop. 203 (1901: 397)

Located 6½ miles ENE of South Molton, to the north of the old South Molton-Taunton road (now B3227), Molland is a spectacularly beautiful parish on the southern edge of Exmoor, with high ground that rises northwards to 1239 ft at Round Hill on Molland Common. Near this point are tumuli that indicate early human presence on these moors. The southern boundary is mainly marked by the River Yeo, although the line extends south beyond the river to include an area in the south-east. The eastern boundary, following first a Yeo tributary and then running over land, reaches the Danes Brook defining the Somerset border, which it follows for a spell before the parish boundary heads away south, to catch up with another, western, tributary which it takes back to the Yeo.

The village is situated in the valley country that fringes the wild moorland. The church (St Mary) dates from the 15th and 16th centuries, with a Norman font from an earlier church. The building has a most striking interior with a flagstone floor sloping at all angles and arches that have developed a 'lean'. Splendid examples of the Georgian (1740s) developments are the 44 tall box pews with doors, from which the altar and three-decker pulpit in the north aisle can just be seen by sitting adults. West of the village are two ancient mansions, now farmhouses: West Molland near the parish boundary, and Champson which dates from the 16th century.

From the end of the 18th century farmer Francis Quartley of Great Champson was responsible for improvement of the red (North) Devon breed of cattle, the survival of which had been in danger. He bought all the best females at local markets, preferring them small-boned and neat rather than heavy, and used mainly his own reputable bulls. In subsequent years Champson cattle achieved high reputation and were increasingly sought as foundation stock for herds elsewhere.

East of the village, near Bremley and Gourt, there are some remains of mining for iron and copper which began in the 17th century. Copper was last produced in 1867 and iron in 1894.

The former Taunton-Barnstaple railway (opened in 1873, closed 1965) ran through the parish's southern extremity, Bishops Nympton & Molland Station being 2 miles from the village.

Monkleigh's substantial Annery limekilns stand close to the River Torridge and the route of the former Rolle Canal.

MONKLEIGH (C3) Torridge Pop. 399 (1901: 358)

Except for brief connecting stretches in the north and south, Monkleigh parish is entirely bordered by rivers and streams, chiefly the River Torridge to the east, the Yeo in the north, and the Duntz on the west. The village is situated in the south, 4 miles S of Bideford, at a sharp bend in the Holsworthy-Bideford road (A 388). The Torrington-Bideford road (A 386) winds through the east of the parish. The church (St George) stands close to the village, on the east. Its main structure results from a rebuilding in the 15th century, with restoration in the 1860s. The substantial tower appears to be built of bricks of slightly irregular size, brownish purple in colour, similar to those in the towers at Littleham and Parkham.

Along the road to Bideford is the hamlet of Saltrens, the name derived from one of the parish's notable families of the past, which has grown from just a few cottages in the mid 20th century. Farther on is Annery, situated high above the Torridge, which stands on an ancient foundation. It was the early seat of the Stapledons, and birthplace of Walter de Stapledon, Bishop of Exeter 1307–26. Later it passed to the Hankfords, Sir William Hankford who died here in 1422 was previously Lord Chief Justice. The house was greatly altered c.1800.

Loading incline at the rear of the Annery kilns.

The Torrington or Rolle Canal, opened in 1827, ran close to the parish's eastern river border, from the Landcross boundary, where there was a sea lock, to the Beam aqueduct which carried it into Weare Giffard. This length of its route included the canal's one inclined plane, which was located close to the Torridge on the south side of the minor road to Weare Giffard, following its turn off from the A 386. The canal passed under this road, immediately west of the substantial Annery limekilns. The canal was superseded by the Bideford-Torrington railway, opened in 1872, which crossed and re-crossed the boundary in its route.

MONKOKEHAMPTON (D5) West Devon Pop. 121 (1901: 177)

Monkokehampton is a small parish lying on the east side of the River Okement, 6½ miles N of Okehampton, on the B 3217 road. A tributary of the Okement forms the northern parish boundary, another partly that on the east, and further streams flow through the parish.

The church (All Saints), which stands on the west side of the village, is of ancient origin. It was rebuilt in 1855 except for the early tower, which remains.

MONKTON (K5) East Devon Pop. 176 (1901: 106)

Monkton is a small parish located from 1 to 3 miles NE of Honiton along the east bank of the River Otter which forms the western boundary. Land levels rise eastwards to over 700 ft. The A 30 road runs through the parish; this section is not dualled, so heavy transport thunders through the village.

The church (St Mary Magdalene) dates from the 13th century; it was entirely rebuilt, except for the tower, after a fire in 1863.

MORCHARD BISHOP (F5) Mid Devon Pop. 975 (1901: 985)

This row of thatched cottages at Morchard Bishop is believed to be the longest of its kind in England.

COURTESY THE BOOK OF MORCHARD BISHOP

Morchard Bishop is a large parish 7 miles NW of Crediton and on the east side of the valley that carries the A 377 Exeter-Barnstaple road and also the railway. Its western boundary is defined for a short distance by the River Yeo and a tributary stream, and the northern boundary is marked by another tributary, the River Dalch – Dalch being from the Celtic, meaning 'dark water'. It is an attractive parish of valleys and hills, with land rising to over 600 ft. The large centrally located village stands at 568 ft. It has numerous thatched houses, with, reputedly, the longest row of thatched houses in England.

The area was known to the Celts. This is evidenced by several Celtic place names – 'Morchard' itself derives from the Celtic 'Morchet', meaning great wood – and archaeological excavations carried out in the 1980s at Rudge confirmed the existence there of a Celtic site enclosed by a ditch. In the 7th century the Saxons arrived, and after defeating the Celts nearby took over Morchet and founded settlements. The manor belonged to Brictric before the Norman Conquest. Later, after being in the possession of the king, it was sold by Henry II to the Bishop of Exeter in 1165, which brought 'Bishop' into the name, although subsequently there were changes of ownership. For long it was known as Bishop's Morchard. Formerly on the stage coach route to Barnstaple the parish suffered when the turnpike road through the valley was developed c.1830, bypassing the village.

The church (St Mary) dates from Saxon times, and the first rector was installed in 1258. The present building is of late 15th-century and early 16th-century construction, although the chancel was rebuilt in the 18th century. The parish has one of the most complete set of registers in Devon, dating from 1660, with members of early-named Rice, Cann, and Webber families still residing.

Easton Barton was the home of the Eastons from the 13th to the 17th century. Oldborough, Middlecott, Woodgate, Frost, Redhill, and Leigh are hamlets.

Further reading: Kingaby, Jeff, *The book of Morchard Bishop*, Halsgrove, 1999

MOREBATH (H3) Mid Devon Pop. 322 (1901: 424)

Morebath is a remote parish 2 miles N of Bampton and 8 miles N of Tiverton. On the north it is bounded on the ridge by the Somerset county border, on the west by the River Exe, in the south by minor roads, and on the east mainly by the River Batherm and a tributary. The Shuttern Brook, tributary of the Batherm, flows southwards through the parish, in its progress forming a marsh or 'moory' basin near some slightly warm chalybeate springs. From these features the name Morebath is derived. This is Brendon foothill country with land in the parish attaining 733 ft and 747 ft in the south and 852 ft in the north.

Morebath's church of St George originates from c.1300. The former tower parapet was replaced by the gabled saddleback roof during 19th-century reconstruction.

Morebath was owned by King Harold until the Norman Conquest when it was taken over by William I. Later it was held by the monks of Barlynch until the priory there was dissolved by Henry VIII. The estate was subsequently split among several landowners.

The church (St George) is of ancient origin, the tower and base of the font dating from c.1300. The main building dates from the 15th century but was very largely rebuilt and restored in the mid 19th century. At this time the former tower parapet was replaced by a gabled 'saddleback' roof. The church is well-kept and obviously greatly cherished.

From 1873, when the railway from Taunton to Barnstaple was completed, Morebath had a station – actually located near Shillingford. And from 1884, when the Exe Valley line was opened from Tiverton (connecting from Tiverton to Exeter in 1885) to join the route, Morebath Junction also provided a platform just south of the village. These facilities were lost, however, when the Exe Valley line closed in 1963 and the Taunton-Barnstaple one in 1966, reducing greatly the ease of travel for Morebath residents without cars.

Further reading: Duffy, Eamon, *Voices of Morebath, reformation and rebellion in an English village*, Yale University Press, 2001

MORELEIGH see HALWELL

MORETONHAMPSTEAD (F7) Teignbridge Pop. 1536 (1901: 1527)

Moretonhampstead is situated on the east side of Dartmoor, 11 miles WSW of Exeter and 11 miles NW of Newton Abbot. The small town, although itself standing at c.600 ft, is surrounded on all sides by higher altitudes. Nearest are those to north and east, with several points over 1000 ft, including Butterdon Hill (1153 ft), Mardon Down, from where there are magnificent views (1169 ft) and Blackingstone (1100 ft). The River Teign in its meandering gorge forms the northern boundary, its steep sides deeply wooded. Strategic points here bear the remains of Cranbrook Castle, an Iron Age hill fort from the 1st century BC, and those of Wooston Castle 2 miles to the east. The Wray Brook, tributary of the River Bovey and ultimately of the Teign, flows southwards through the south-east.

Two roads cross in the town: the tortuous B 3212 from Exeter that continues across the moor to Tavistock, and the A 382 from Whiddon Down on the A 30 to the A 38 and Newton Abbot. Minor roads serve the outlying areas.

The large granite-built church (St Andrew), which comes prominently into view on the approach from the east, was constructed from the early 15th century and is large and beautiful. Not far away, beside this same road as it enters the town, there are 17th-century almshouses. There is also an Anglican chapel at Doccombe, a hamlet east of the town on the B 3212 which had a medieval mansion. Wray Barton, a Tudor house beside the twisty A 382 to the south, was a Domesday manor, and Lowton, on the west, was also named in Domesday.

Moretonhampstead, which suffered a series of destructive fires, was a participant in Devon's woollen industry for some centuries. Micaceous haematite, a form of iron ore, was mined near Wray and at Moorwood in the 1920s and 30s. The town was the terminus of the Moretonhampstead railway from Newton Abbot which opened in 1866 and closed to passengers in 1959 and for freight in 1965. The former station, on the road south, is now used for commercial purposes.

Further reading: Friend, George, *Memories of Moretonhampstead*, Devon Books, 1989
Heath, R.O., *Sparrowhawk: the story of Moretonhampstead*, 1977
Local society: Moretonhampstead and District Museum and Local History Society

MORTEHOE (C1) North Devon Pop. 1506 (1901: 788)

Mortehoe occupies the western extremity of the North Devon Bristol Channel coastline, terminating in the National Trust-owned Morte Point, rising to 451 ft, with Bull

Point and its lighthouse just to the north. The scenery is beautiful and spectacular, with sharp-edged rocks that spell hazards for shipping.

The fine Norman church (St Mary) was enlarged in the 13th century and again in the 16th century. Woolacombe has been a separate ecclesiastical parish since 1922, with the church (St Sabinus) built 1910–12. Woolacombe was a Domesday manor, and Oussaborough, Rodway, and Spreacombe were recorded in Domesday. Of these, Woolacombe, with its splendid beach, has developed greatly during the past century. Within living memory it was quiet, with a few hotels on the cliff road and the Barton Farm just inland from the beach; now it is a bustling holiday centre with cafés, surf shops and other amenities.

Mortehoe village is 2 miles on the seaward side from the former Mortehoe Station (on the old railway to Ilfracombe), beside the B 3343 road which connects east with the A 361 at Mullacott Cross.

Bull Point, with its lighthouse, is Mortehoe's northerly extremity.

Further reading: Bidgood, R.F., *Two villages: the story of Mortehoe and Woolacombe*, 4th edit., 1984
Reed, Margaret, *On the record*, 1997
Museum: Mortehoe Heritage Centre (through car park)

MUSBURY (L6) East Devon Pop. 550 (1901: 422)

Musbury, 3 miles SSW of Axminster, is situated east of the River Axe, on the A 358 road from Axminster, which connects with the B 3172 to Axmouth and the A 3052 between Seaton and Lyme Regis. From the valley the land rises eastwards to 500-600 ft around the site of Musbury Castle, an Iron Age hill fort and an Ancient Monument since 1924.

The church (St Michael) is of early origin, the first known rector having been instituted in 1204. The oldest part of the present building is the tower, dated 1420. Much of the church was rebuilt in the 1860s, and completed 1876–7. The huge Drake monument is a striking feature of the interior.

Ashe, a mile north near the Axminster road, was the ancient seat of the De Esse, or Ash, family, and later that of the Drakes. The house suffered in the Civil War and was rebuilt in the 1670s.

Further reading: Pulman, George P.R., *The book of the Axe*, Reprint 1969

NETHEREXE (H5) East Devon Pop. 47 (1901: 60)

Netherexe is a remote and peaceful parish lying in the valley of the River Exe 5 miles N of Exeter and 8 miles S of Tiverton. Most is on the east of the river, where the land is low and not above 100 ft, the small portion on the west rises slightly higher.

The small church (St John the Baptist) stands serenely in a field, close to the Exe. It dates from the 15th century and has a Norman font. Netherexe is not a separate ecclesiastical parish but comes under the care of Rewe.

St John the Baptist Church, Netherexe, stands serenely in a field in the Exe valley.

Local society: The Five Parishes Local History Society

NEWTON ABBOT (G8) Teignbridge Pop. 23,580 (1901: Highweek 2709, Wolborough 9720)

The busy town of Newton Abbot is located on the River Lemon at its confluence with the Teign (which forms the northern boundary) at the head of the Teign estuary. The village of Highweek to the north-west, and the residential area of Milber in the south-east, have been included in the town area since 1901. Although now bypassed on the east by the A 380 Exeter-Torquay road, the town is the hub of several road routes: the A 382 and A 383 connect to the A 38 on the west and the A 381 bears south for Totnes and east for Teignmouth. It also has a station on the main railway and became an important centre from the time when Brunel's South Devon Railway reached here in 1846, which caused the town to grow. As a market town Newton is the natural focal point for the surrounding country district. There were quays, including at Jetty Marsh on

Newton Abbot, viewed from Highweek churchyard.

the south side of the Whitelake, a tidal leat cut to drain marshland on the north-west of the town. A quarter-mile in length, this connected with the Teign, enabling vessels to come to the quay at high tide. It also provided exit for boats from the Stover Canal, which had two locks entered on the north side, and a quay (see TEIGNGRACE).

Early man certainly knew this area, evidenced by Neolithic tools found in the Bradley area. The hill fort here probably dates from the Iron Age, as does that on Milber Down (just beyond the parish boundary). Development of the town began on the banks of the Lemon from around 1200 in the manor of Wolborough, and was called Shireborne Newton, soon changed to Newton Abbot. Concurrently, in the manor of Teignwick, or Highweek, north of the Lemon, a new town was being formed which became known as Newton Bushel. Later the two combined under the name of Newton Abbot. As the town grew two types of building material predominated – limestone from quarries in the south and white bricks manufactured from ball clay extracted on the north-west from the 18th century.

Wolborough and Highweek have Newton Abbot's oldest churches. That at Wolborough (St Mary) on the hill, dates from the 15th and early 16th centuries and has particularly fine screens as well as other interesting features. St Paul's Church in Devon Square was built as a chapel-of-ease in 1862. Two other former churches in the parish are now redundant; that of St Leonard, built as a chapel-of-ease in 1836 to replace the 14th-century St Leonard's demolished that year (of which the tower in the main street is a remnant), and St Michael's. Highweek Parish church (All Saints) is also set on a hill and there are extensive views from the churchyard. Its tower dates from the 14th century and the main building from a century later, restored in the 19th century. Also in Highweek ecclesiastical parish, St Mary the Virgin, Abbotsbury, was built in the early years of the 20th century.

Another interesting 20th-century church is St Luke's, Milber. Unusual in form it was designed and built as the result of a dream experienced in 1931 by the Revd Keble Martin. Rector of Haccombe with Combe, he also helped at Milber where the population was growing. Initially a 'hut' was built as a hall for worship and Keble Martin felt there should be something better. On waking he recalled and noted details of his dream, which his architect brother put into effect. The foundation of the Lady Chapel was laid in 1936 and this section built first. War delayed full completion until 1942. In plan the building comprises a partial circle surrounding the sanctuary from where it fans out westward with three naves. It is so designed that all can see the altar, there is no chancel – the congregation are seated right up to the sanctuary, and there is no pulpit.

Forde House, now the headquarters of Teignbridge District Council, on the east end of the town, was built in 1610. Charles I stayed here in 1625 (it is believed possibly to have been the scene of W. Yeame's painting 'When did you last see your father?') and Prince William of Orange in 1688. Bradley Manor, Highweek, is a 15th-century manor house now owned by the National Trust.

From medieval times up to the 20th century Newton Abbot was engaged in the woollen industry, and in the working of leather from the 14th century. Iron ore in the form of brown haematite was worked between Wolborough and Abbotskerswell 1872–3. Tuckers' Maltings, in Teign Road, were established by Edwin Tucker, an Ashburton seeds merchant, in the 19th century, with the business developing here into malt production. The town has numerous modern industries.

Further reading: Unsworth, Harry, *A new look at old Newton Abbot*, 1933
Jones, Roger, *A book of Newton Abbot*, 3rd edit., 1986
Beavis, Derek, *Newton Abbot, the story of the town's past*, 1985
Local society: Newton Abbot Branch of the Devonshire Association
Museum: Newton Abbot Museum

NEWTON AND NOSS (D11) South Hams
Pop. 1743 (1901: Newton Ferrers 611, Revelstoke 405)

Newton and Noss civil parish comprises the separate entities of Newton Ferrers and Noss Mayo. Noss Mayo includes the ancient ecclesiastical parish of Revelstoke, the village area of Noss Mayo having been a fishing settlement from the 13th century.

More important as a port from that time as well as for fishing was Newton Ferrers.

The two are located 6 miles SE of Plymouth, on either side of an eastward creek of the River Yealm estuary, near its mouth in Wembury Bay. The long estuary shoreline and the coast form the western and southern boundaries, with lands rising to over 300 ft, including 362 ft reached in the south-west and 360 ft in the north-east. Newton Ferrers stands on the north side of the creek, extending west to overlook the Yealm itself, Noss Mayo is on the south. Residential development in the parish has increased in modern times and the estuary is a favoured haven for boats.

The church of Newton Ferrers (Holy Cross) dates from the 13th century, with early structure in the chancel, and the rest of the building of the 15th century. The altar is inclined slightly to the north. There are paintings on the pulpit and the elaborate font is of marble. Revelstoke's 14th-century church of St Peter the Poor Fisherman, situated on the cliff side north-east of Stoke Point, is now redundant. After falling into decay the ruined building was restored in the 1960s and since 1972 has been in the care of the Churches Conservation Trust. Regular worship takes place in the replacement church of St Peter, Revelstoke, built in Noss Mayo village in 1882.

Membland, in the east of Noss Mayo, was a Saxon estate recorded in Domesday. Membland Hall, rebuilt in the 1780s, was considerably enlarged in the late 19th century after being bought by Edward Baring, later the 1st Lord Revelstoke, banker and director of the Bank of England. A lavish lifestyle was enjoyed here until Barings Bank faced difficulties c.1890. There were subsequent changes of hands and in the First World War Membland Hall housed young Army officers in training as No. 1 Officer Cadet Battalion. After the war the Hall was demolished and its site redeveloped for modern residences.

Remains of the 14th-century church of St Peter the Poor Fisherman on the cliffs at Revelstoke.

Interior remains of Revelstoke's former church, now in the care of the Churches Conservation Trust.

Further reading: Clamp, Arthur L., *Newton Ferrers and Noss Mayo remembered,* 1986
Local society: Newton Ferrers & Noss Mayo History Group

NEWTON POPPLEFORD AND HARPFORD (J7 & J6) East Devon Pop. 2014 (1901: Newton Poppleford: 441, Harpford: 213)

The single civil parish of Newton Poppleford and Harpford is situated around the A 3052 Exeter-Lyme Regis road. Newton Poppleford village stretches along the road, and Harpford lies immediately north, the two being situated respectively west and east of the River Otter, 10½ miles E of Exeter and 4 miles S of Ottery St Mary.

Newton Poppleford, which was part of Aylesbeare until 1896, has several cob and thatched buildings along its village street. It was formerly notable for the manufacture of silk, and lacemaking. The church (St Luke) was originally a chantry chapel founded and endowed by Hugh, Lord Courtenay, in 1331. It was rebuilt, except for the sandstone tower, in 1875, and re-ordered internally in 2003.

Harpford is an attractive village beside the river. The manor, Court Place, was in early times held by the Dinham family. The church (St Gregory the Great) is of early origin. It was given to the abbey of Mont Michel in Normandy in 1205. The present structure dates from the 15th century, restored in the 1880s.

Venn Ottery, in the north-west, is within the civil parish. Its manor was held at Domesday by the Furneaux family, the parish's early name, Fenotri, denoting 'fen' or marshes. The church (St Gregory) which is of ancient foundation, has a Saxon tower of red sandstone. It was the only part to survive a fire c.1780 which destroyed much of the village. The church was subsequently rebuilt in Early English style. It is ecclesiastically united with Tipton St John. The present house of Venn Ottery Barton was built c.1530.

The former Sidmouth and Budleigh Salterton branch lines from the London & South Western Railway, opened respectively 1874 and 1897, ran through the parish; they closed in the 1960s.

Newton Poppleford and Harpford St Gregory's Church, Venn Ottery, has a Saxon sandstone tower. It is located in Newton Poppleford and Harpford civil parish but united ecclesiastically with Tipton St John.

Further reading: Tenney, G., *Peep into the past: Newton Poppleford and Harpford,* 1988

NEWTON ST CYRES (G6) Mid Devon Pop. 867 (1901: 700)

Newton St Cyres is situated 4 miles NW of Exeter and 3 miles SE of Crediton on the A 377 Exeter-Barnstaple road. The parish is one of rich pastures watered by the River

Creedy and its tributaries, with woodlands on rising ground in the south. The northern boundary is defined by the minor road that branches from the A 3072 Crediton-Tiverton road and proceeds towards Thorverton while the other boundaries run over land or follow small streams.

The church (St Cyr & St Julitta) is beautifully light. The building dates from the 13th century with 15th-century additions. Major alterations were carried out in the 1920s with the removal of box pews and gallery. The tower is probably the oldest part, arcades are of Beer stone. The mahogany pulpit and sounding board date from the 1700s. On the inner south wall are the arms of James II dated 1685 – a rarity because of the short reign. Below the arms is a stoup for holy water; plastered over during the Reformation, it was recently discovered. There is also the Anglican chapel of St Antony at Cowley.

The village has several attractive cob and thatch houses. The Quicke family has dwelt in the parish since the 16th century and in the present Newton House since its building c.1780. Hayne (south of the A 377), marked now by a 19th-century farmhouse, was acquired in the 16th century by John Northcote, a successful participant in Crediton's woollen industry. Bidwell Barton, in the north-east, was for generations the home of the Bidwells.

Manganese was worked in the parish (for use in the Potteries) for a spell from the 1790s. The railway to Barnstaple passes through, with a station just north of the village.

Further reading: Village residents, *Newton St Cyres, a village history*, 1999

NEWTON ST PETROCK (C4) Torridge Pop. 163 (1901: 179)

This roughly diamond-shaped parish lies between the River Torridge on the south-west and a tributary stream on the south-east. Northwards the parish extends to take in land just north-west of the Holsworthy-Bideford road (A 388). With land rising to 550 ft the parish has steep descents in the valleys.

The village, 7 miles SW of Great Torrington, lies E of the A 388; it has a small village green. The church (St Petrock) is of 14th and 15th-century construction and has a Norman font.

NEWTON TRACEY see HORWOOD, LOVACOTT AND NEWTON TRACEY

NORTHAM (C3) Torridge Pop. 11,604 (1901: 5355)

The parish of Northam forms a peninsula, immediately north-west of Bideford. The River Torridge estuary marks the eastern boundary, the combined Taw-Torridge estuary the north, and the open sea the west. Appledore, on the north-east, is part of the civil parish (although ecclesiastically they are two, comprising a united benefice, each with its own church), and Westward Ho!, again with its own church, is also within Northam.

The south of the parish is now crossed by the North Devon Link road, carrying traffic from the Torridge Bridge built in 1987. The small town of Northam stands on the hill to the north. The church (St Margaret) is also here, built mainly in the 16th century on the site of a believed 12th-century structure, and restored in the mid 19th century. Kenwith Castle is an earthwork a mile or so to the south-west, thought to be of medieval origin.

The seaward area of the parish has provided evidence of early habitation dating from the Mesolithic period. Archaeological investigations carried out just off-shore at the south end of Westward Ho! beach have revealed vegetation remains including tree stumps and also those of bones and a kitchen midden. From the evidence it is considered that there was also Neolithic and Romano-British activity here. Over the many years of erosion the coastline of the Burrows with its pebble ridge has receded some distance, and the remains described become accessible only at very low tides.

The pebble ridge is itself an impressive phenomenon. Formed, apparently, by erosion over the ages of the coastal rocks between here and Hartland Point, the

Westward Ho!'s wide 2-mile long beach is backed by the natural pebble ridge, which protects Northam Burrows from the sea.

pebbles have been washed this way by rough seas and become rounded in the process, flung on to the sandy shore and gradually built up into the ridge. This provides a protective barrier for the Burrows, the delta-like expanse of sand-dunes, saltmarshes and pasture which cover about 600 acres. The Burrows have for long been common land, carrying grazing rights for parishioners. Being dependent on the security of the pebble ridge to prevent flooding by seawater it became an annual custom for those who enjoyed the rights – called 'pot-wallopers' – to gather on Whit Monday and throw pebbles washed over in winter storms back on to the ridge. Northam Burrows is now a Country Park, lying within an area of Outstanding Natural Beauty. Part of the Burrows, at the southern end, comprises the course of the Royal North Devon Golf Club, the oldest links course in the country, established in 1864. Besides the beauties of the Burrows, the wide sandy beach, nearly 2 miles long, is one of the finest in Devon, and good for surfing.

The village of Westward Ho! has evolved only from the mid 19th century, following publication in 1855 of Charles Kingsley's book *Westward Ho!*, which brought visitors. A company was formed to develop the resort, and the name given. Also associated with the area was Rudyard Kipling, who was a pupil at the United Services College 1875–82. The church (Holy Trinity) was built in 1870.

The little port of Appledore has a long seafaring history, particularly associated with ship and boat building. On the road from Northam is a point known as Bloody Corner, reputedly the site of a battle c.1069 involving Harold's three illegitimate sons who had crossed from Ireland and faced opposition. (Conclusions reached in modern times by historians regarding Bloody Corner, and also Kenwith, are somewhat contrary to local legends.)

The name Appledore was known in 1335 but it was not until the 14th century that its trading reputation began to grow. By then it had an advantage over Bideford in being the first point on the Torridge where incoming vessels, having negotiated the dangerous sand bar, could tie up and disembark. Fishing and the ship work were important and continued, with new shipyards constructed in the 19th century. Trade with North America became considerable, involving large quantities of timber for ship building and other purposes. Fishing from Appledore still continues but on a reduced scale. Salmon netting has been a long-standing tradition. Shipbuilding has also been a continuing industry; the large dry dock of Appledore Shipbuilders, dating from the mid 20th century, is a prominent feature, although, sadly, work prospects fluctuate and 2003 brought the threat of closure.

Appledore church (St Mary) was built in 1838.

For a few years in the early 20th century the narrow gauge Bideford, Westward Ho! & Appledore Railway was in operation. Its route started on Bideford Quay and proceeded to Abbotsham cliffs, then followed the coast north-eastwards to Northam. This section was opened in 1901, and the extension to Appledore in 1908. The railway closed in 1917, its track and locomotives requisitioned by the government during the First World War.

Further reading: Davis, Corinna M., *A short history of Northam*, 1967
Mayo, Ronald, *The story of Westward Ho!* 2nd edit., 1981
Beara, John, *Appledore: handmaid of the sea*, 1976
Museum: North Devon Maritime Museum, Odin Road, Appledore

The medieval Bennetts Cross, which stands beside the Moretonhampstead-Postbridge road in North Bovey's moorland area. Birch Tor on the skyline.

NORTH BOVEY (F7) Teignbridge Pop. 274 (1901: 418)

North Bovey, 11 miles WSW of Exeter and 1½ miles SSW of Moretonhampstead, is within the area of Dartmoor National Park, situated on the high moor's eastern fringe. The village is one of the most attractive of those on and around Dartmoor, with the River Bovey, tributary of the Teign, passing close by on west and south. Approach is by minor roads either from Moretonhampstead itself or from the A 382 from Bovey Tracey, or the B 3212 road across the moor. The church (St John the Baptist) is built of granite and dates from the 14th century.

The common lands of the parish share a fairly long boundary with the Forest of Dartmoor and include many features of interest. Altitudes rise westwards to nearly 1600 ft, giving spectacular views. The area abounds in prehistoric remains of various kinds, including hut circles and barrows, and a stone row on Challacombe Down, while the southern boundary skirts the Bronze Age enclosed village of Grimspound. There are also remains of medieval and later farming systems. Besides signs of the earlier tinners' workings on the surrounding moorland, part of the former important tin mining area of Birch Tor and Vitifer lies within the parish. Deep scars on the hillside east of the B 3212 road, opposite the Warren House Inn, are the result of early tinners' extractive activities, while such remains as those of buildings, leats and wheelpits in the valley are from as late as the early 20th century.

Beeson and Shapley, in the north, were Saxon settlements and referred to in Domesday. The so-called Bovey Castle, south of the B 3212, was built 1905–7 as a seat for Viscount Hambledon, son of the newsagent W.H. Smith. Later it was bought by the Great Western Railway, and altered c.1930 to become the Manor House Hotel. During the Second World War it was used as a military hospital for officers. The hotel changed hands and also its name in 2003.

Further reading: much information concerning North Bovey can be found in many of the large number of books on Dartmoor.

St Mary's Church is now redundant and in the care of the Churches Conservation Trust.

NORTHCOTT (B6) Torridge Pop. 26 (1901: 60)

Located 7 miles S of Holsworthy, Northcott is bounded by the River Tamar on the west, by tributary streams to north and south, and by the Launceston-Holsworthy road (A 388) at Chapman's Well on the east. This is a hamlet, without a church, ecclesiastically linked to Boyton across the river in Cornwall.

NORTH HUISH (F10) South Hams Pop. 360 (1901: 317)

The outline of North Huish parish is not unlike, in miniature, that of Great Britain – minus the South West Peninsula. The parish is located 16 miles east of Plymouth and 6 miles south-west of Totnes, in hilly farming country that rises to 568 ft in the north-west. It is served by minor roads from the A 38 in the north, and from the A 3121 and B 3196 on the west. Most of the eastern boundary is defined by the River Avon, and the parish includes the village of Avonwick in the north. North Huish village is small. The church (St Mary) is redundant and now in the care of the Churches Conservation Trust. Dedicated by Bishop Grandisson in 1336 it is of 14th-century and 15th-century construction, with a spire, enlarged from cruciform by the addition of a south aisle. The font, bearing the date 1662, is still in place and there is a feeling that the church is still cherished. Ecclesiastically the parish is now united with Diptford, which includes St James's Chapel at Avonwick.

Huish, and Butterford in the north, Lupridge in the south, and Broadly on the east, were Saxon estates, named in Domesday. Bickham Bridge, over a beautiful stretch of the Avon, mentioned in a charter of 962, was on an important ancient route linking ridgeways. The present, probably 16th century, bridge now carries a minor road. Close by, to the west, is a bridge over the former Kingsbridge branch railway.

Local society: Diptford and North Huish History Society

NORTHLEIGH (K6) East Devon Pop. 149 (1901: 161)

Northleigh is a rather remote parish of streams and hills, rising in the north to 700 ft, in the country 4 miles SE of Honiton and 4 miles NW of Colyton, and served by a network of minor roads.

The village is pleasantly open, and neat. The church (St Giles) dates from the 14th century with later work, partially rebuilt c.1860 and restored in 1869. The font and south door are Norman. Smallicombe, in the north-east, was recorded in Domesday.

Further reading: Northleigh Parish Council: *Northleigh, a millennium history*

Ashbury is now part of Northlew parish. Its ancient church (St Mary) is now redundant but still cared for.

NORTHLEW (D6) West Devon Pop. 592 (1901: 629)

The parish of Northlew which includes the formerly separate parish of Ashbury, occupies high ground 5½ miles WNW of Okehampton and 4 miles SW of Hatherleigh. The Culm Measures land of cold wet clays rises in altitude in the south to over 800 ft, and Northlew village itself nears 500 ft. With fine views towards Dartmoor and exposure to the winds that blow from there, Northlew has acquired a legendary reputation for coldness.

The north-flowing River Lew, tributary of the Torridge, flows through the parish, which also has an abundance of other streams. The Wagaford Water and another brook form most of the north-west parish boundary, and others feature on the long circuitous route. The area has seen human habitation since ancient times, as indicated in the south by a tumulus on Wadland Down, another burial mound near Stoney Farm, and the reputed site of a medieval village near Scobchester. The name of Wadland Barton – in the Ashbury area – among the oldest of the farms, derives from that of Wadal, a Saxon landowner here.

Northlew village is centred around a large open square, formerly a green. In the past there were several shops and businesses here, but now services are provided by just the one combined shop and Post Office. In the north-west stands the village cross, dating from the 15th century and restored in 1850, on the site of an early preaching place. The church (St Thomas of Canterbury) is nearby. It is believed that there was possibly a church here from the 11th century, a rector is recorded in 1258, and the Norman font survives. The early church was enlarged in subsequent centuries – latterly in the 16th – but fell into neglect up to the 19th century until, in 1885, a restoration was completed. The church at Ashbury (St Mary) dates from the 13th century, restored c.1700 and rebuilt, except for the tower, in 1871. In 1876 the parishes of Northlew and Ashbury were united, and in 1991 Ashbury church was made redundant. It is now in the hands of the Woollcombe family whose distinguished forbears inhabited Ashbury House for centuries until the 1930s. Northlew Methodist Chapel also stands in the village square; built from 1811–15 it was extended in 1858 and 1889, and reopened after repairs in 1952.

Lew, Rutleigh, Gorhuish, Kimber, and Ashbury (Esseberie) were Domesday manors.

Cross and Church Gate Farm pre 1909, Northlew. COURTESY THE BOOK OF NORTHLEW WITH ASHBURY

Further reading: Northlew History Group: *The book of Northlew with Ashbury*, Halsgrove, 2002

NORTH MOLTON (F3) North Devon Pop. 1047 (1901: 1069)

The large Exmoor parish of North Molton is bounded on the north-east by the Devon-Somerset border, and on the west by a tributary of the River Bray and for a stretch by

Part of the stunning view southwards over Devon from the North Molton-Somerset border.

North Molton's village square. All Saints' Church was rebuilt on the site of an earlier one in the 14th century.

the Bray itself. The southern boundary follows a somewhat indeterminate course that includes, on the south-east, a short length of the River Mole. Land in the south rises to over 760 ft, and on the far north moorland to 1618 ft at Five Barrows. On a clear day a glorious view can be enjoyed from this point, or from the road just south of the county border, southward for many miles across Devon. The River Mole rises in the east of the parish and flows southwards, through the wooded valley at the hamlet of Heasley Mill, and on the east side of North Molton village. Farming is based mainly on beef cattle and sheep.

North Molton, formerly a royal manor, is quieter now than it would have been in the past. Not surprisingly, in such a 'sheepy' area, wool played an important part in local life, and in the early 18th century the parish had many combers and weavers, with several mills near Heasley. Mining was another industry here, initially in the 16th century, the workings being mainly in the Heasley Mill area. In the later period of activity Bampfylde Mine, located here on both sides of the Mole, produced iron, copper and manganese before closing in 1877. Its remains are obscured by woodland. A mile east was Florence Mine where lead, copper and iron ore were worked up to 1885. A 4-mile tramway was constructed in 1874 from the mine to South Molton Station on the Taunton-Barnstaple railway. Copper was also worked in the early 19th century near North Radworthy, and some gold was also found, but not in quantities that warranted extraction.

The substantial church (All Saints) was rebuilt on the site of an older one in the late 14th century. It contains many interesting and beautiful features. Ecclesiastically the parish is united with Twitchen. The 16th-century Court House, west of the church, was the home of the Parker family, forbears of the earls of Morley. Court Hall, east of the church, belonged to the Bampfyldes, later raised to the peerage as Lords Poltimore.

NORTH TAWTON (E5) West Devon Pop. 1570 (1901: 1529)

The small town of North Tawton lies 6½ miles NE of Okehampton and a mile N of the junction at de Bathe Cross of the A 3072 and A 3124 roads. The former, proceeding eastwards, meets the A 377 Exeter-Barnstaple road at Copplestone, and the latter leads south to join the A 30 dual carriageway at Whiddon Down. The north-flowing River Taw is crossed by two 15th-century bridges as it passes through the roughly triangular parish, one at Newland, and the other on the town's western outskirts. A section of the southern boundary follows the straight course of a former Roman road, which connected with a Roman fort. The site covered an area on either side of the A 3072 which includes private land at The Barton to the north, Newland Mill on the west, de Bathe Farm on the east, and a portion south of the railway. Although not yet properly excavated, aerial photography has indicated that the settlement was far more extensive and complex than originally thought.

The Romans were not, however, the earliest people here; evidence of Stone Age inhabitation and of Bronze Age occupation occurs at various points in the parish.

At the time of Domesday six manors were named, known today as Tawton (held by the king), Beere, Broadnymett, Crooke, Greenslade, and Nicholls Nymet. Newland Mill, on the south side of the A 3072 near the bridge dates from 1242 and was worked until the 20th century before becoming derelict and eventually undergoing renovation.

The church (St Peter) may have originated in Saxon times; a record indicates that it was certainly here by 1257 and the tower is of that period. The present building is mainly of 14th and 15th-century construction. It is located approximately in the centre of the town, just east of The Square from which radiate various streets and outgoing roads.

Set as it is in the heart of farming country, North Tawton was a market town. Granted to the lord of the manor in 1270, the market lapsed c.1720 but was revived in 1870 when a market hall was built, with livestock being sold in The Square. A further lapse, and restart, ensued, and removal to alternative sites before the market finally ended in 1986.

For centuries North Tawton has been an industrial town, particularly regarding wool. A fulling mill operated at Cottles Barton in 1558, dealing with cloth woven in local homes. In the 17th century serge making employed many hands. With the advance to mechanisation, in about 1800 a woollen factory was established on the town's edge near the Taw, powered by waterwheels, where all the processes from receiving the raw wool through to weaving were carried out. The business ended and the factory closed in 1930. For many of the subsequent years the buildings were used for storage of various materials, including, at times, wool.

Two modern industries feature in North Tawton. The transport business of the Gregory family, modestly founded in 1919, has grown to the extent of now employing c.1000 people, with the large Gregory Distribution vehicles, operating from the North Tawton depot, a common sight on the country's motorways. The other prominent establishment is the cheese factory, built in 1974, which produces cheese and whey powder and employs around 130 people.

Broadnymett, a Domesday manor in the east, was for centuries a tiny separate parish with its own church (St Martin). Dating from the 13th century the building was abandoned as a church in the 19th century, but has been partially restored. For ecclesiastical purposes Broadnymett is merged with Bow, but is part of North Tawton civil parish.

The London & South Western Railway, on its way to Okehampton, reached North Tawton in 1865. Occasional trains still use the line.

The Square, North Tawton, early 20th century. COURTESY THE BOOK OF NORTH TAWTON

Further reading: Mortimer, Walter, *The history of North Tawton,* 1969, rev. 1978
Baker, Alison; Hoare, David; and Shields, Jean, *The book of North Tawton*, Halsgrove, 2002

NYMET ROWLAND (F5) Mid Devon Pop. 98 (1901: 67)

Nymet Rowland is a small parish, roughly 16 miles NW of Exeter, to the west of the Exeter-Barnstaple road (A 377). It is bounded on the north by the River Taw and on the east by the Yeo; the confluence of the two rivers forms the parish's northern extremity. The railway to Barnstaple keeps company with the eastern boundary. The land is undulating, with the village at 400 ft.

The church (St Bartholomew) is of 15th-century construction, with some traces of the earlier 12th-century building, and other external and internal features of interest.

OAKFORD (H3) Mid Devon Pop. 340 (1901: 484)

The 15th-century builders of Oakford church (St Peter) had to cope with the village's steeply sloping situation.

Oakford parish, 6½ miles NNW of Tiverton, is defined on the north by the county border with Somerset. The River Exe marks the eastern boundary and the Iron Mill Stream that on the south, while the western boundary runs mainly over land. The former A 361 Taunton-Barnstaple road (now the B 3227) passes through the parish, with Oakford village, standing at 611 ft, situated just south of it and approached by minor roads. North of the B 3227 the land descends to ancient Oakford Bridge over the Exe. The parish land rises steeply, attaining 929 ft at Bickham Moor on the western boundary, and 866 ft on the parish's south-west corner, marked by a tumulus.

The church (St Peter), which stands on sloping land beside the village street, dates from the 15th century and, except for the tower, was rebuilt in the 1830s. Remote Spurway Mill was a Domesday manor, and home of the Spurways from the 13th century. Bickham Barton, Mildon, Woodburn, and East and West Tapps, were all mentioned in Domesday.

Further reading: Bentley, E.W., *Oakford, the history of a Devon parish*, 1982

OFFWELL (K6) East Devon Pop. 420 (1901: 304)

Offwell is the next parish to the east of Honiton, with its village located 2 miles ESE of the town. It is a parish of steep hills, partially wooded, rising to 773 ft on the west, with deep valleys, drained by the Offwell Brook, tributary of the River Coly. A north-west area of the parish, north of Widworthy, stretches to a short boundary with Stockland; the southern boundary of this arm is marked by the A 35 Honiton-Axminster road so that part of the village of Wilmington is in Offwell parish. Approach to Offwell village is by minor roads from the A 35.

Building of the church (St Mary) began in the 13th century, with completion including the tower, in the 15th century, the structure being of flint and Beer stone. Members of the Copleston family were rectors of the parish in continual succession from 1773 until 1954. The family's early home was at Copplestone (see that parish) and on the corner beside Offwell School is a replica of the ancient pillar that stands in the centre of Copplestone. Colwell Barton, Culbeer, and Wilmington were Domesday manors, and Glanvill Barton, in the south was known in 1173.

The origin of the parish's name is Offa, a Saxon settler here. It is thought that the village well – its source of water in past times – may possibly be the original in the name. The pump head was provided in 1830 by Dr Edward Copleston, Bishop of Llandaff and Rector of Offwell in the early 19th century. It was extensively repaired c.1950 and renovated, with grants, in 1999. An inscription reads: 'Whosoever drinks of this water shall thirst again'.

OGWELL (G8) Teignbridge Pop. 2753 (1901: East: 219, West: 27)

Located around 2 miles WSW of Newton Abbot and served by minor roads, the two former small parishes of East and West Ogwell were united as Ogwell in 1881.

The River Lemon forms the northern boundary, and a tributary, the Kester Brook, that on the west. Much of the land is on the 200 ft range but rises in the east to points of 390 ft and 425 ft. The National Trust woods of Bradley Manor border the Lemon in the north-east. Channings Wood Prison is situated in the south-west, close to Denbury village but actually in Ogwell parish.

Ogwell (formerly East Ogwell) church (St Bartholomew) was originally a cruciform building of the 14th century, enlarged by the addition of the north aisle in the 15th century. The former West Ogwell church, of unknown dedication, is now redundant. Holbeam, in the north-west, was a Domesday manor and home of the family of the same name for many generations.

Local society: Ogwell History Society

OKEHAMPTON (D6) West Devon
Pop. 5846 (1901, incl. Hamlets: 3223)

Okehampton lies below Dartmoor's northern edge, on the East and West Okement Rivers which come together here as they continue their flow north. Okehampton town is surrounded by a large rural parish, comprising numerous hamlets which now constitute a separate civil parish (see OKEHAMPTON HAMLETS).

The beginnings of Okehampton go back to prehistoric times and include association with the Roman occupation. There was a Saxon settlement, whose church, it is believed, occupied the site of the present parish church (All Saints) on the hill, half a mile west of the town. The town's real foundation was laid when Baldwin de Brionne, the Norman sheriff of Devon, built a castle here beside the West Okement shortly after the Norman Conquest, in which he established residence (see HAMLETS). A borough was created before Domesday, and also a market, with the town moving down from the hill to its present lower level. The church remained on the hill and was substantially built in the 15th century; in 1842 it was destroyed by fire, except for the tower, and subsequently rebuilt. Meanwhile, in the 14th century, the Chapel of St James was provided in the town for greater convenience of the people; this too was rebuilt, in 1862, and continues as the Church of St James.

The two branches of Methodism, which had grown into being since Methodist preaching was introduced into Okehampton in the late 18th century, were united in 1964 when the Fairplace Methodist Church, which had been opened in 1904, officially became Okehampton Methodist Church. In 1974 the United Reformed Church was included under covenant and henceforth the title became Okehampton United Church.

Like other towns, Okehampton participated in Devon's woollen industry, and the town also had tanneries. As a market town Okehampton became a centre for the farming area around, and as transport developed was a recognised staging post for horse-coaches. An advance in transport came in 1867 when the London & South

Fore Street, Okehampton, late 1920s. COURTESY THE BOOK OF OKEHAMPTON

Western Railway arrived with its station on the hill, which enabled direct travelling from Okehampton via Exeter to London, and shortly to Plymouth in the other direction. Regular services on the line ceased in 1972 but occasional quarry traffic still uses the line, as well as a few passenger trains at weekends in summer. Okehampton Station is also base for the attraction called 'Dartmoor Railway' in which passengers can travel by steam train the short scenic distance to Meldon viaduct.

Okehampton's livestock market sadly came to an end in 1958, after nearly 900 years of existence. By this time through traffic was becoming a problem for the town, especially on holiday Saturdays, with market stalls operating in the main street. Eventually, after many objections and delays, the town was bypassed in 1988 by the A 30 dual carriageway, constructed south of the town.

Further reading: Radford, Roy and Ursula, *The book of Okehampton*, Halsgrove, 2002
Endacott, Alan, *Tales of old Ockington*, Orchard, 2002
Local societies: Okehampton & District History Society
Okehampton Branch of the Devonshire Association
Museum: Okehampton & District Museum of Rural Life, 3 West Street

OKEHAMPTON HAMLETS (D6) West Devon Pop. 400

The 144 ft high Meldon viaduct, south-west of Okehampton, dates from 1874. It now carries walkers and cyclists.

Okehampton Hamlets parish covers an area around the town of Okehampton that includes agricultural land on the west, north, and east and in the south rises in its Common to cover a substantial stretch of northern Dartmoor, including the moor's highest points, High Willhays (2039 ft) and Yes Tor (2028 ft), and the Rivers East and West Okement.

Besides the manor of Okehampton itself (Ochementon) two other manors were named in Domesday: the present Kigbeare in the west, and Chichacott north-east of the town. Later there were others.

Meldon is an example of a considerable manor and hamlet of antiquity, named as Maledune in 1241 and held from the Courtenays by Robert de Maledune. In later times Meldon has become associated with various industries and developments. Limestone quarries near the West Okement were worked in the 18th century and stone burnt in two kilns. These, and the pool left by extractions, can still be seen. East of the hamlet a glass factory using granulite (aplite) from another quarry operated from 1885 to c.1920. In the late 19th century the continuing Meldon roadstone quarry (hornfels, including dolerite) was developed for supplying railway ballast. In 1874 the spectacular 144 ft high Meldon viaduct, of iron lattice girder spans, was brought into use for the London & South Western Railway – at 950 ft altitude the highest point on the LSWR and later Southern Railway. In 1972 completion of the Meldon Dam and Reservoir commenced the impounding of waters of the previously wildly beautiful West Okement.

The former deer park of Okehampton Castle was also 'invaded' for the construction of the A 30 Okehampton bypass opened in 1988.

Okehampton Castle, which was owned by the Courtenays, is located in the Hamlets, on the west bank of the West Okement. As already mentioned (see OKEHAMPTON) it was built soon after 1066. There are considerable impressive remains in an enchanting situation, including those of the keep, the great hall, kitchens and other rooms around the bailey. The castle is now in the hands of English Heritage and open to visitors.

A barn at Brightley, in the north, was formerly a chapel of a religious house founded here in the 1130s, which was used by monks from Waverley Abbey until, after just five years, they removed to the later Ford Abbey in Dorset (at that time in Devon).

OTTERTON (J7) East Devon Pop. 700 (1901: 622)

The elongated parish of Otterton has the English Channel coast for its eastern boundary, and the River Otter for its approximate boundary on the west. The two meet at a point just across the river mouth from Budleigh Salterton. The north-east boundary extends from Bridge End, on the A 3052 road by the Otter east of Newton

Poppleford, to the 512 ft Peak Hill on the coast. Along the coast, ¾ mile west from this point is High Peak, with the remains of an earthworks fortification, much of which, over centuries, has evidently eroded into the sea. Investigations have indicated that the site was occupied in the 4th millennium BC, and in the Roman period, but the fortifications which remain at a height of 500 ft are believed to date from the 6th–8th centuries AD.

The attractive village is situated in the south, on a minor road which runs from the A 3052 to the B 3178 near East Budleigh. A pleasant feature is a row of seven joined houses along the main street. The large church (St Michael) belonged to Mont St Michel in France at the time of Domesday, and a dependent priory was founded in the late 11th century. In 1414 its endowments were granted to Syon Abbey in Middlesex. At the Dissolution the manor of Otterton was bought by Richard Duke who converted part of the monastic buildings to a mansion which, divided into separate dwellings, is seen near the church. The church was rebuilt in 1871.

Otterton Mill, in the south of the village, was built in the 19th century on the site of the manor mills named in Domesday. After closing in 1959 it was restored in 1979 for milling using two waterwheels powered by a leat from the Otter. It is opened to the public.

Further reading: Millington, G. and Jones, B., *All about Otterton*

OTTERY ST MARY (K6) East Devon Pop. 7692 (1901: 3495)

St Mary's Church, Ottery St Mary.
COURTESY THE BOOK OF OTTERY ST MARY

Ottery St Mary is a large civil parish almost in the centre of East Devon. The River Otter flows southwards through the parish and on the west side of the town, which is located 11 miles ENE of Exeter and 5 miles SW of Honiton. It is approached by the B 3174 road from points on the A 30 to the north, and by minor roads from the A 375 on the east, the A 3052 in the south, and the B 3180 on the west.

The countryside is undulating and pleasant, rising to the ridge of East Hill and reaching 809 ft on the east, and to c.500 ft on the west. The town has a long history. In the mid 11th century Edward the Confessor gave the manor and Hundred to the cathedral of St Mary at Rouen. In 1334 it was retrieved through an exchange by Bishop Grandisson who used it to endow a college of secular priests which he established in 1337. The bishop enlarged the 13th-century church (St Mary), remodelling it on the lines of Exeter Cathedral which it resembles as a smaller version, and greatly beautified it for his college. Further enlarged in the 16th century and restored 1849–50 it is indeed among Devon's most splendid churches. Henry VIII suppressed the college in 1545 and the property was transferred to governors as owners and guardians of the church and churchyard. The property included the school house which was refounded as a grammar school, and still continues as The King's School.

For long a market town, Ottery St Mary was also a centre of the woollen industry. When Devon's trade was declining in the late 18th century a new factory was built on the site of earlier mills close to the river near St Saviour's Bridge in an effort to create new interest. Worsted thread was produced. Subsequently the mill changed hands at various times as did the type of manufacture, from silk spinning to other activities which have continued up to modern times (see 'Ottery St Mary's worsted factory' by Ronald F. Homer in *The Devon Historian 67,* October 2003). The town was also an important centre for lacemaking.

John Coleridge (1719–81) who was the vicar, and master of the grammar school, was the father of the poet Samuel Taylor Coleridge. The town suffered severe fires in 1767 and 1866 but retained many interesting buildings. A mile north-west of the town is Cadhay, a fine, pleasantly situated Tudor mansion built in the 16th century by John Haydon and latterly owned by the William-Powlett family.

The civil parish of Ottery St Mary, besides having its own parish church already described, incorporates other ecclesiastical parishes and their churches. Alfington, south of the A 30 in the north, has its own church of St James & St Anne. At Wiggaton, just south of the town, is the church of St Edward the Confessor, and farther south there is St John's at Tipton St John, a village that developed with the coming of the railway, and is now united ecclesiastically with St Gregory, Venn Ottery. On the west side, West Hill has the church of St Michael the Archangel.

From 1874 the Sidmouth branch from the London & South Western Railway ran south through Ottery St Mary parish, close to the river. The town had a station, as did Tipton St John's (sic.) where, from 1897 a branch led off to Budleigh Salterton. The Sidmouth branch closed in the late 1960s.

Further reading: There are several good books relevant to Ottery St Mary, including *Golden Jubilee book of Ottery St Mary* produced by Ottery St Mary Heritage Society in 2002.

PAIGNTON (G9) Torbay Unitary Authority (Pop. 1901: 8385)

Oldway Mansion, Paignton. COURTESY THE BOOK OF PAIGNTON

The seaside town of Paignton is located in the central area of Torbay of which it has been part since 1969 when the county borough was created, and a component of the unitary authority from 1995. It is reached from the M5 in the north by the A 380 road and from the A 38 and Totnes on the west by the A 385, while the A 3022 runs near the coastline and connects with neighbouring Torquay.

Paignton is the oldest of the Torbay towns. The early settlement was half a mile inland, while marshes bordered the sea. It is believed that Saxons established themselves here in the 7th century, farming the fertile land which attracted bishops of Exeter for the siting of a palace. Named in Domesday as Peintona, the manor continued in the hands of the bishops until 1644, a market and fair having been acquired in 1295, and a borough created. Some 15th-century remains of the palace can be seen near the church, including Bishop's Tower (also incorrectly known as Coverdale Tower) which was built as part of a coastal defence to protect the palace. There have been three churches on the site of the parish church (St John the Baptist). The first was built by the Saxons, probably of wood. The second church was built by the Normans c.1100, remains of which, comprising parts of the chancel walls, the west doorway, and the font, still exist. The third church was erected in the 13th century, initiated by Bishop Bronescombe of Exeter. Over the centuries this, the present church, has been altered and enlarged, restored after becoming ruinous in the 15th century and again, after neglect, in the 19th century.

Coverdale Tower or, more correctly, 'The Bishop's Tower'. COURTESY THE BOOK OF PAIGNTON

United now with St John the Baptist are the churches of St Andrew in Sands Road, which dates from 1875, and St Boniface, consecrated in 1961, in Belfield Road. There are also Christ Church, built in the 1880s, Goodrington Church (St George) consecrated in 1939, and that of St Paul at Preston, also established in the early 20th century.

The original town was near the parish church, and the surrounding land remained rural – famed for cider production and the growing of enormous cabbages. Paignton had its small harbour in the shelter of Roundham Head, where from the early 1800s cottages accommodated men of Customs and Excise who patrolled to prevent smuggling. As the population increased the resort developed, new streets stretched out into the countryside and the marshland was reclaimed. In 1859 the initial 3 miles of the proposed Dartmouth & Torbay Railway was completed to Paignton, which greatly increased the number of visitors. The railway was completed to Kingswear (for Dartmouth) in 1864; in 1973 the line west from Paignton was closed, but later restored by the Dart Valley Company which runs steam trains between Paignton and Kingswear. In the early 1900s Paignton also became linked to Torquay by a tramway system which survived until the early 1930s.

From the late 19th century the sea front – the sandy beach backed by the esplanade with its green – became the centre of summer activity. Houses already established were converted to hotels and new ones built. The pier, built in 1879, became a focus of attractions; it was destroyed by fire in 1919, but restored.

Goodrington, in the south, earlier named Godheringstone, where there is also a sandy beach, was developed as an adjoining resort to Paignton in the 1920s and 30s. Terraced walks were formed, with sea wall and rock gardens, and a swamp was formed into a park and lake. On the inland side, south of the Totnes road, are the extensive grounds of Paignton's Zoological and Botanical Gardens. To the north, Preston forms the coastal link between Paignton and Torquay. Here is the impressive

Oldway Mansion, built originally in 1874 by Isaac Singer, the sewing machine millionaire, and transformed by his son Paris Singer 1904–7. The triumphal arch is copied from the Trianon gateway at Versailles and the colonnaded east front from buildings in the Place de la Concorde in Paris. Inside are a marble staircase, a painted ceiling copied from Versailles, and a vast reproduction of the painting by J.L. David: *The crowning of Josephine by Napoleon*. Having had to flee America for France because of his philandering lifestyle, Isaac Singer married Isabelle Boyer who was later chosen to model for the Statue of Liberty. They came to England with their six children in the early 1870s and he and his family became great benefactors in the Torbay area. Oldway is now owned by Torbay Council and used as offices and for events and exhibitions.

On the west side of Paignton, forming Blatchcombe ward in the present local government system, are the areas of Blagdon and, in the south, Yalberton. Towards the centre is the church of St Mary the Virgin, Collaton, built in 1864–6 when the western part of Paignton became a separate parish.

Besides the involvement in tourism Paignton has various light industries.

Further reading: Pearce, Frank, *The book of Torbay*, Halsgrove, 1999
Pearce, Frank, *The book of Paignton*, Halsgrove, 2001
Local societies: Paignton & Preston Local History Group
Torbay Branch of the Devonshire Association

PANCRASWEEK (B5) Torridge Pop. 218 (1901: 277)

Pancrasweek's western boundary is mainly defined by the upper reaches of the River Tamar (which also marks the county border with Cornwall) northwards as far as (Lower) Tamar Lake, from where it proceeds east and south, eventually joining the tributary Small Brook westwards back to the Tamar.

The parish, located 3 miles WNW of Holsworthy, is scattered, with no real village centre. The church (St Pancras) with its impressive tower can be seen to the north of the Holsworthy-Bude road (A 3072). It is of 15th-century construction, with signs of earlier work. The parish is united ecclesiastically with Pyworthy. Dunsdon, Hamsworthy, and Virworthy were named in Domesday.

Lower Tamar Lake was formed in the early 1820s as the reservoir for the Bude Canal (see HOLSWORTHY). It is now cherished for its wild life, and for coarse fishing. The 4½ mile feeder channel from the reservoir connected near Brendon with the canal's Holsworthy branch, just east of its entry into Devon by an aqueduct across the Tamar. Here was the canal's 500 ft long Vealand inclined plane, which raised the boats 58 ft.

PARKHAM (B3) Torridge Pop. 742 (1901: 786)

Parkham is a fairly wide-ranging parish. In the south the land rises to 709 ft on Melbury Hill. On the west side of the hill streams rise which feed westwards into the upper course of the River Torridge before the river makes its wide detour southwards prior to returning north for Bideford Bay. A mile north of those springs rises the River Yeo which flows east to join the Torridge at its estuary stage – a river now of very different character. And in further contrast, the parish extends north to include a length of the coastline between the parishes of Woolsery and Alwington.

The Bideford-Bude road (A 39) passes through the north. The village, which stands 5 miles SW of Bideford, is also accessed from the unclassified road from Bideford to Bradworthy. The land of the parish comprises mainly scattered farms, with the pleasant village, which has an open centre and small green, in a fairly central elevated position above the Yeo valley. Occupying the site of an Anglo-Saxon church, the present one (St James) dates mostly from the 15th century and is large, light and beautiful. It retains a fine Norman doorway (inner door of south porch) and a Norman font which is surrounded by medieval 'Barum' floor tiles. The tower appears to be built of bricks, purplish-brown and of somewhat irregular size, similar to the towers at Littleham and Monkleigh. The arcade pillars are of Lundy granite, and of varying shape: the arches

Looking down into Parracombe village, with its Victorian church.

The interior of Parracombe's old church, with the Lord's Prayer, Ten Commandments and Apostles' Creed on panels above the screen.

on the south are older, and curved, those on the north are pointed. The north aisle is shorter than the south. The pulpit is 17th century. The church was restored in 1875, since when the chancel has had a bare roof, with carved angels looking down.

On the coast, between Bucks Mills and Peppercombe, are earthworks identified as 'camp', probably from the Iron Age. Halsbury, in the east of the parish, in the 12th century was the home of the Halsburys; later it passed through marriage to the eminent family of Giffard. The house dates from the mid 16th century. Ash, Horns Cross, East Goldsworthy, Hoops, and Newhaven are hamlets.

PARRACOMBE (E1) North Devon Pop. 294 (1901: 315)

Parracombe village lies in a dip of the steep hills 10 miles NE of Barnstaple and 4 miles SW of Lynton, with surrounding land rising to 974 ft at the Beacon in the north, and to 1575 ft on Parracombe Common at the south-east parish boundary point. Barrows in this boundary area, and elsewhere, are all indications of early habitation, while earthworks nearer to the village are remains of Holwell Castle. These remains, showing traces of motte and bailey, may date – it is believed – from soon after the Norman Conquest.

Parracombe's interesting old church (St Petrock), standing on high ground above the village, is of ancient origin. Domesday references provide evidence of a church here in the 11th century. The tower was added in the 12th century, and the chancel in 1252. The present building retains 13th-century elements despite being largely rebuilt in the early 16th century. On a solid tympanum above the screen the Lord's Prayer, Ten Commandments and Apostles' Creed are painted in four panels. St Petrock's was declared redundant in 1969 and vested in the Churches Conservation Trust in 1971. It is occasionally used for worship, mainly only in summer, a new church (Christ Church) having been built in the village in 1878.

Rowley Barton and East and West Middleton were Domesday manors.

The A 39 road to Lynton passes through the parish but takes a wide loop around the village to avoid the rather steep descents. Close to it ran the former narrow gauge Lynton & Barnstaple Railway, opened in 1898 and closed in 1935. A length of this is currently being restored by the Lynton & Barnstaple Railway Company Limited from a base at Woody Bay Station, just beyond the parish's north-east boundary on the A 39, where there is a visitor centre.

PAYHEMBURY (J5) East Devon Pop. 603 (1901: 415)

The parish of Payhembury, 5 miles WNW of Honiton and 7½ miles SE of Cullompton, lies mostly to the south of the A 373 Honiton-Cullompton road, but with a small extended area across it in the north-east that includes the site of Hembury Fort. The impressive earthworks, on a Greensand spur at 885 ft, dates from the Iron Age, although archaeological excavations in the 20th century have revealed Mesolithic and Neolithic occupations. Later, it is believed to have been occupied briefly by Roman forces. The River Tale, tributary of the Otter, flows southwards through the parish.

The beautiful church (St Mary the Virgin) contains many interesting features. Originating from the 12th century, when it was consecrated by Bishop Bronescombe, the present main structure dates from the 15th century. The arcades are of Beer stone, bench ends are finely carved, and the screen which dates from 1450 is richly carved and painted. There is also delicate pointing on the chancel roof with 12 bosses. Restoration was carried out c.1897 by the vicar, mainly at his own expense. An apparent clump of yew trees in the churchyard is believed to stem from just one which at some time split; it may be older than the church. A spring of water that still exists below the church may, it is thought, have given rise to the church being established here.

Higher and Lower Cheriton, in the south-east, comprised the manor of Charleton in Domesday, and Higher and Lower Tale, in the west, the manor of Tala.

Further reading: Payhembury Book Group, ed. Stanes, Robin, *Payhembury millennium book*, 2000

PETERS MARLAND (C4) Torridge Pop. 234 (1901: 286)

The small parish of Peters Marland is defined on the east by the little River Mere and tributaries. The village, situated 4 miles S of Great Torrington, is approximately in the centre. The ancient church (St Peter) was restored in the Early English style in 1865. Twigbear, Week, Winswell, and Winscott were estates before the Norman Conquest.

In the south-west workings on deposits of ball clay were established well before recent times, and until the 1940s a brick and tile works was in operation. The creamy-yellow bricks produced here are much in evidence in buildings in Torrington and other towns. Industry continues in extraction from pits of the raw material, for use in ceramics, electrical porcelain, and sanitary ware, much of it exported to European countries. To serve the works, in 1925 the North Devon & Cornwall Junction Light Railway was opened between Torrington and Halwill, a distance of 22 miles. It closed in 1982.

PETER TAVY (D8) West Devon Pop. 305 (1901: 293)

Peter Tavy Inn, 2000. COURTESY THE BOOK OF PETER TAVY

Peter Tavy, on the western side of Dartmoor, 3 miles NE of Tavistock and accessed from the A 386 road, includes a wide area of the moor. Its bounds are defined partly by the River Tavy on the west, the Walkham on the east, and by the Western Redlake, upper Tavy, Rattlebrook, Deadlake, Walla Brook and Lyd in the north. Elsewhere the boundary traverses country that is largely open and wild, embracing such major tors as Cox, Roos, Whit, Lynch, Hare, and Ger, and the dramatic gorge of remote Tavy Cleave.

The moorland abounds with prehistoric remains, mostly from the Bronze Age, although the enclosure of Whit Tor (Whittor) may be of Neolithic origin. Lines from early strip cultivation are apparent on some lower moorland slopes.

At the lower level are many farms, several of which originated in medieval times; Coxtor Farm is one of the oldest, possibly of pre-Norman origin. Willsworthy was a Saxon farmstead, referred to in Domesday; the present farmhouse possibly derives from that of the manor. Cudlipptown is a small hamlet within the parish, its name probably relating to that of the holder of lands here in Saxon days. It became an outlying holding of Tavistock Abbey, and later remained part of Tavistock parish until transferred to Peter Tavy in 1885.

The church (St Peter) includes features indicating its existence from Norman times, and there is reference to a priest here in 1185. The present building dates probably from c.1500, when the imposing tower was rebuilt and the porch added. There has been subsequent restoration.

Close by the church, in the village which is located in the parish's south-west, is the ancient Peter Tavy Inn. Possibly dating from the 15th century, it may have been established to accommodate builders engaged on the church.

Signs of the workings of early tinners proliferate on the moor and include the remains of tinners' mills beside the Walkham. There are also remains of later mining on the moorland fringe, including Devon United Mines, worked for copper, tin, and arsenic in the 19th and early 20th centuries. The Reddaford leat, cut from the Tavy c.1800 to serve mines at Mary Tavy, flows through part of the parish. Its water, and that brought from the Tavy by the Hillbridge leat, now supply a hydro-electric station at Mary Tavy. Ochre was worked on Smeardon in the mid 19th century.

Further reading: Peter Tavy Heritage Group, *The book of Peter Tavy with Cudlipptown,* Halsgrove, 2002

PETROCKSTOW (D5) Torridge Pop. 379 (1901: 385)

Petrockstow is a parish that includes woodland and moor. It extends southwards to a brief boundary with the River Torridge, and elsewhere is defined in several places by smaller streams.

The village is located 4 miles NNW of Hatherleigh, approached by minor roads from the A 386. The church (St Petroc) is on a foundation dating certainly from the

11th century, mainly rebuilt in the 14th century, with further rebuilding, except for the tower and north arcade, in 1875. It retains the 13th-century square font. Allisland, Heanton, Hele, Little Marland, and Varleys were Domesday manors.
Ash Moor, in the south-east, has been extensively worked for ball clay.

PINHOE (H6) Exeter City Council (Pop. 1901: 952)

Formerly a separate village 3 miles ENE of the city centre, Pinhoe has become part of Exeter's extended urbanisation during the past century. The parish is well served by road, being just west of the M5 motorway and the A 30 and on the route of the B 3181 which leads into the city. The railway from Exeter to Salisbury and Waterloo also passes through, with a station.
The church (St Michael & All Angels), situated NW of the village on a hill in quiet peaceful countryside, dates from the 14th century. The present building is of mainly 15th century construction, of red sandstone. There is a fine 15th-century carved screen with pulpit of similar date. The unusually styled font is believed to be very ancient. There is also a hall church licensed for worship.
In 1001 a battle was fought in which Danes defeated Saxons; the site is believed to have been in the Mincimore area.

Further reading: Woodley, Kathleen M., *Pinhoe*, 1982

PLYMOUTH (C10) Plymouth Unitary Authority Pop. 241,000 (1901: 107,636 not including Stoke Damerel (Devonport) 63,917 and East Stonehouse 15,111)

The view south from Plymouth Hoe must surely be one of the most impressive and inspiring in England, and one which embodies much of the nation's history. Looking out across the Sound and beyond the 2-mile distant breakwater to the English Channel, with Mount Batten and Staddon Heights on the east, and Maker and the park of Mount Edgcumbe, and Penlee Point on the Rame peninsula on the west (Cornish) side, one cannot fail to be aware of the great natural advantage to which this Devon port owes its existence. Located along a broad front between the estuary of the Plym on the east and the mighty Tamar on the west, Plymouth has known human habitation since before the Ice Age, although the coastline and water levels were different then. In Mesolithic times men hunted here with flint-topped weapons and the coast developed more into its present outline. Gradually immigrant farming people arrived, and stone was quarried for making axes. By the Bronze Age people were settling on Dartmoor and using a route from the coast northwards roughly on the line of today's road to Tavistock. In the Iron Age a settlement existed at Mount Batten, where gold and silver coins and other artefacts have been found, and a cemetery was sited on high ground nearby. Roman coins have also surfaced, indicating use made of the natural harbour as a trading place, and doubtless it was also used for building boats. On how the area developed during the Dark Ages we can only speculate, although it seems certain that missionary saints, such as Budoc, whose name is perpetuated in St Budeaux, came from across the Celtic Sea. By the 7th century the Saxons had reached Devon, and then many of the earlier inhabitants, the Dumnonii, retreated west across the Tamar to Cornwall.
The area to the north and north-east of the Hoe comprised a hamlet known to the Saxons as Sutton ('South town') and was part of a royal estate. As spaces were carved out of the surrounding woodland the king gave estates to chosen settlers, and so developed the manorial and parish system and the establishment of early parish churches. Sutton itself and various creek inlets developed with the growth of shipping, and Stonehouse is one of the names that appear in early records. Viking raids caused havoc in the region in the 10th century, and then came the Normans in 1066. Plympton Castle was one of those in Devon ordered by William I and given by him to Baldwin Redvers, Earl of Devon, while other manors went to various of the king's friends. Plympton, where a priory had been established in the time of Alfred, was already of some importance and accessible by shipping with tidal waters navigable up

to the castle walls. In 1328 Plympton was added to the three already appointed Stannary Towns dealing with tin from the industry on Dartmoor. In the 14th century waste washed down from the tinning caused silting of the Plym and the decline of Plympton as a port in favour of the fishing village of Sutton which, certainly from the 13th century, with the surrounding area became known as Plymouth.

The port of Plymouth developed in marketing and overseas trading, with wool and cloth among the exports and wine and iron coming in, and, from the time of war with France in the late 13th century, becoming a victualling port and naval base. The town suffered during the Hundred Years War with burning raids by the French. In the mid 14th century a square castle was built for Sutton, only little of which now remains in the area of the Barbican.

The Wars of the Roses had some effects on Plymouth, which was disturbed also by other events of the 15th and 16th centuries. In the 1530s Henry VIII had a system of coastal defences constructed. By the late 16th century, when England was at war with Spain, Plymouth had risen to considerable naval importance and there is the well-remembered account of Sir Francis Drake's decision in 1588 to finish his game of bowls on the Hoe before setting sail to defeat the Armada. Besides his ventures on the high seas Drake was much involved in Plymouth life. He had married Mary Newman in St Budeaux Church in 1569, lived for a time at Buckland Abbey, was elected mayor of Plymouth in 1581 and in 1584 was instrumental in authorising construction of a leat to bring water from the River Meavy on Dartmoor to Plymouth as the town's first supply, necessitated by the growth of population and the fleets of ships.

The Mayflower *replica, permanently moored at Plymouth, Massachusetts, USA. Built at Brixham, Devon, she sailed the Atlantic in 1957, the 350th anniversary year.*

By the 17th century Plymouth had developed a Puritan element and also an established merchant community, with trade largely involved in Newfoundland fisheries, and also the export of woollen cloth. Soon the American coast of New England was being explored and trade grew. In 1620 Plymouth Quay was the scene of departure for 102 religious dissidents who had left England for Holland in 1607 but were now seeking life across the Atlantic. After calling at Plymouth they – the Pilgrim Fathers as they became known – set sail in the *Mayflower*, eventually to land and establish themselves at a creek in Massachusetts that they named Plimoth. A memorial on the Barbican marks the approximate departure point.

Plymouth also faced problems during Charles I's war with Spain, and soon after, in 1663, saw intense fighting in the Civil War. Despite bloody battles and siege the Parliamentarians held out against the Royalists to the war's end. A relevant monument can be seen in Freedom Fields park. Following the restoration of the monarchy Charles II instigated the construction of huge protective measures of which the Citadel, completed in the 1670s, is one. It remains the finest example of 17th-century fortification still existing in Britain.

After the accession of William and Mary the need was seen for a new port in the country's south-west. After much consideration the Navy Board decided on Plymouth, and the stretch of the Tamar mouth known as the Hamoaze, in the ancient parish of Stoke Damerel, was chosen. Work on the construction began in 1691; the naval dockyard took shape and the foundation was laid for the town known initially as Plymouth Dock, or just Dock, which was later to become Devonport. In the 19th century Devonport, like Plymouth, became enhanced by buildings designed by the architect John Foulston. Stonehouse – the area between Plymouth and Devonport – was also seeing developments in the 19th century, including the building of the Royal William victualling yard, designed by John Rennie in the years 1824–35. The mile-long Plymouth breakwater was constructed 1812–40 and its lighthouse in 1844. There had been a succession of lighthouses farther out to sea (14 miles from the Hoe) from 1696, the first of which was destroyed by storms in 1703, the second burnt down in 1755, and the third (Smeaton's) becoming undercut by the sea. It was removed and re-erected on Plymouth Hoe (open to visitors). The present functional lighthouse was built in 1882.

In the 1860s, under Palmerston's government, several forts were built around Plymouth as defence against possible attack by Napoleon III. These forts included one at Crownhill which can be visited by the public.

Plymouth had its railway in 1848 when Brunel's South Devon Railway from Exeter reached Laira. The line was extended to Millbay in 1849 to serve commercial docks

Smeaton's lighthouse, replaced by the present Eddystone lighthouse in 1882, now stands on Plymouth Hoe. Mount Batten is seen in the distance.

there and packet ships, and in the 1850s was continued westwards, crossing the Tamar by Brunel's Royal Albert Bridge, opened in 1859 and still in use. A branch extended north to Tavistock in 1858 and one to Yealmpton in 1898 (both later closed). Meanwhile Plymouth had been joined to another railway, when in 1890 the Devonport and South Western Junction Railway completed the route from Exeter around the north of Dartmoor, although unlike the other main line this was to close in the late 20th century. Still surviving, however, is the Tamar Valley line from Gunnislake. During the busy railway years several small local lines served quays, docks, and the Dockyard.

By the early 20th century Plymouth, Devonport and Stonehouse – known as the Three Towns – had all grown considerably and there was sustained pressure for amalgamation. This was achieved, as the Corporation of Plymouth, in 1914. Fourteen years later, in 1928, Plymouth gained city status, and in 1935 acquired a Lord Mayor.

The two World Wars of the 20th century affected Plymouth deeply. As a naval base and Royal Dockyard Plymouth and Devonport were of course highly involved, and in the second war suffered greatly from severe German bombing raids which caused great loss of life and destruction. The raids started at the end of 1940. On two nights in March 1941 they reached a peak, with 336 people killed. The city centre was devastated, and destruction wrought by further attacks in April also severely affected Devonport.

After the war Plymouth started to tackle the enormous process of rebuilding which proceeded over several years. These have also seen other great developments and city expansion, including the urbanisation of various surrounding parishes. While Devonport Dockyard, now privatised, is still the biggest employer its workforce is considerably reduced, and other industries, including electronics, have come in.

The great increase in road traffic has necessitated new systems around and through the city. These have included the Tamar Bridge constructed 1956–61 and the 'Parkway' of the A 38. The port facilities at Millbay, used by ocean liners following the arrival of the railway, declined in mid-century until the ferry system with the continent developed from 1970. Millbay is now privatised under Associated British Ports. The fishing industry has benefited from Sutton Harbour Company's new fish quay, which replaced that on the Barbican in 1995. And a nearby attraction is the National Marine Aquarium opened in 1998.

Plymouth's airport at Roborough dates from 1931. Near it is Plymouth's Derriford Hospital, developed from the late 1970s and serving West Devon and East Cornwall, with well over 1000 beds. The former Plymouth Technical College progressed to

Polytechnic, and eventually became the University of Plymouth, now with its medical school, and the affiliated College of St Mark & St John.

Several of Plymouth's churches were destroyed in the Blitz attacks. The mother church (St Andrew) is of ancient origin, its first vicar named in 1087. The 14th–15th century building was gutted, but later rebuilt. One of the oldest church foundations (it has been suggested possibly early Saxon) is that at Pennycross – a Celtic name – dedicated to St Pancras, a boy who was martyred by the Romans in 304AD. St Budeaux Church has origins at least as early as the 11th century and Egg Buckland church (St Edward) dates from the 12th century, when the parish, like Plympton, Plymstock, and Tamerton Foliot, were rural parishes. Stoke Damerel, like the others, was an early manor – its church was enlarged in 1750 when the population was increasing. For the same reason – slightly earlier – Charles Church was built in the town's centre in the 1640s, named for the king whose permission enabled its construction. It suffered badly in the Blitz and its shell is preserved as a memorial to those who perished in the raids. Increasing population prompted the building of numerous other churches in Victorian times, some of which were lost in the war. Then, after the war, some demolition, and residential movements brought the need for new buildings. A particularly fine addition is Crownhill's Church of the Ascension, consecrated in 1958. Plymouth's Roman Catholic Cathedral of St Mary and St Boniface, with its tall spire, was built as a church in 1801 and raised to its present status in 1858.

Charles Church was destroyed during wartime bombing but its shell is preserved as a memorial to the many who perished in the attacks.

Under local government changes in 1998 Plymouth became a unitary authority with complete independence from Devon County Council. It is now divided into wards. For formerly separate parishes now included within the boundary, see entries for: PLYMPTON ST MARY, PLYMPTON ERLE or ST MAURICE, PLYMSTOCK, and TAMERTON FOLIOT.

Further reading: Gill, Crispin, *Plymouth a new history*, Devon Books, 1993
For advice on the many other books on Plymouth, readers are advised to consult the Local History section of Plymouth Library, or other libraries or bookshops.

Local societies: Old Plymouth Society
Plymouth Branch of the Devonshire Association
Plymouth & District Archaeological Society
Plymouth Mineral and Mining Club

Museum: Plymouth City Museum and Art Gallery, Drake Circus

PLYMPTON ERLE or PLYMPTON ST MAURICE (D10)
Plymouth Unitary Authority (Pop. 1901: 1117)

Plympton Erle, or Plympton St Maurice, comprises a quite small ecclesiastical parish, but as a ward now of Plymouth, covers a rather wider area. It is included here because of its interesting independent history, and continuing sense of local identity.

Located on the Plymouth authority's eastern extremity, the parish lies between the old A 38 road through Plympton St Mary and the modern A 38 expressway. The town originated in the 12th century, granted by Henry I to Richard de Redvers, who built the castle of which the motte and some stonework remain. The town grew up close by and in 1194 was made a borough with market and fair. In 1328 it was designated one of the four Stannary Towns to which tin from Dartmoor (in this case the south-west quarter) had to be brought for the official coinage sessions before being sold. For centuries the town was busy and prosperous with woolcombing, tanning and brewing among the industries. Although such activities declined, business today is stimulated by the closeness of Plymouth, while the place retains an air of quiet dignity. Fore Street has several interesting houses as well as the Guildhall, which dates from the late 17th century. The slightly earlier grammar school is strongly associated with the painter Sir Joshua Reynolds whose father was its master. Joshua was born here in 1723; the house, close to the school, has long been demolished but a plaque records the event.

The church (St Maurice) dates from the 14th century, when it was dedicated to Thomas Becket (changed c.1538). It was restored in 1879.

PLYMPTON ST MARY (D10) Plymouth Unitary Authority (Pop. 1901: 3837)

Although now part of Plymouth and so a constituent of the system of wards rather than civil parishes, Plympton St Mary is here given an individual entry because of its separate historical identity up to recent times. Included is the ward of Plympton Chaddlewood.

Situated on the eastern extremity of the Plymouth conurbation, on the lower reach of the River Plym, Plympton St Mary grew immensely during the 20th century. In the early years still separated from the city by countryside, and the centre of a rural district until 1974 (when Sparkwell became a separate parish), the development of housing and industries has virtually closed the gap. Located on the old main road to Plymouth, now the B 3417, it is by passed to the south by the modern A 38 expressway. The main railway also passes through.

Ecclesiastically the parish is large, and has a long history. A collegiate church of St Peter & St Paul existed here from the time of King Alfred, and in 1121 an Augustinian priory was founded, endowed by the Earl of Devon and others, situated just south of the present parish church. Parts of its walls still remain and the area is being cleared for conservation by members of Plympton Civic Society. Plympton Priory was richly endowed with properties that extended both east and west, where they included the site of today's Plymouth. The church (St Mary Blessed Virgin) was built on the site of the priory's chapel of St Catherine and dates from the 14th century, dedicated by Bishop Stapledon in 1311. It is large and beautiful, both the tower and main building being of granite. There were several Domesday manors in the parish, with land extending from fertile areas in the south northwards to the edge of Dartmoor. During the 19th century a few small mining ventures were operated on the moorland fringe: at Boringdon where lead, silver, arsenic and iron were produced, and at Bottle Hill and Wheal Sidney for tin. The Lee Moor Tramway, which carried china clay down to the Plymouth waterside, passed through Cann Woods in the north-west of the parish.

The house at Boringdon, in the north, rebuilt and now a hotel, dates from 1279; from the 16th century it became the home of the Parkers before they moved south in the parish to Saltram (now a property of the National Trust) in the early 18th century. Newnham was the seat of the Strodes.

Local society: Plympton Civic Society

PLYMSTOCK (D10) Plymouth Unitary Authority (Pop. 1901: 3195)

The area of Plymstock comprises the south-east section of the Plymouth conurbation, east of the Plym estuary, the Cattewater, and coast of the Sound, south of the A 379 Plymouth-Kingsbridge road. It is divided into Plymstock Radford and Plymstock Dunstone wards. Ecclesiastical boundaries do not completely correspond but involve the parishes of Plymstock, to which the Church of the Good Shepherd at Oreston is joined (and formerly that of the Holy Family at Staddiscombe, now redundant), Hooe (St John the Baptist), and Elburton (St Matthew).

Formerly a country area with a large village, Plymstock is now very much a busy suburb of Plymouth, although the coastal strip, from Turnchapel around the point of Mount Batten, and at Jennycliff Bay are interesting and pleasant.

Plymstock church (St Mary & All Saints) originates from Norman times, with the early font surviving. The present structure dates from the 14th and 15th centuries, with subsequent restoration work and adaptation. There is a fine 15th-century rood screen. This has been moved rather farther east in recent years to provide greater space and to accommodate a nave altar. The pulpit and sounding board date from 1666.

A Celtic burial ground has been located on the site of Stamford Fort and the finding of gold and silver coins and other artefacts at Mount Batten is evidence of habitation there from the Iron Age through to Roman times. Radford was the early seat of the Harris family; it was demolished in 1937 and the site redeveloped. The quarries at Oreston have been the source of much of the limestone used in building Plymouth.

In 1898 the Yealmpton branch railway was built by the GWR from Plymouth and included stations at Billacombe and Elburton, and a branch to Turnchapel. It closed initially in 1930, but reopened for a spell during the Second World War with final closure in 1951.

Local society: Plymstock Civic Society

PLYMTREE (J5) East Devon Pop. 605 (1901: 359)

Plymtree is a fairly small, squarish parish situated somewhat remotely 3½ miles SSE of Cullompton and 7 miles WNW of Honiton. It is approached by minor roads either southwards from the Honiton-Cullompton road (A 373) or from the unclassified road leading off the A 38 at Westcott (south of Cullompton) towards Ottery St Mary. Land levels rise from c.150 ft in the west to 450 ft in the east. The River Weaver, tributary of the Clyst, flows through. The parish comprises rich farming land, and agriculture has historically been the main occupation.

1907 postcard – church showing raised pavement, Plymtree. COURTESY THE BOOK OF PLYMTREE

The name Plymtree, is derived from the Saxon Plum-trei meaning 'place of springs'. The parish's origins in fact date from Saxon times when the three manors, eventually termed Plymtree, Clyst William, and Woodbeer, were each held by a Saxon lord. Before 1066 Plymtree was held by Bristric, Earl of Gloucester, but after the Norman Conquest it was given to Odo fitz Gamelin. The church (St John the Baptist) is recognised as being of Saxon origin.

In the late 1200s Plymtree church was regarded as the mother church of several others in the surrounding area which became a deanery until absorbed in Ottery St Mary in 1873. Rectors' names from the late 13th century are known. Rebuilding of the church followed in the late 1300s, and construction of the tower in the 1420s, followed shortly by further enlargement. In subsequent years furnishings and embellishments were added, including the noteworthy 15th-century fan-vaulted screen. Towards the end of the 19th century the church's structure showed signs of deterioration and restorative work proceeded in stages until well into the 20th century.

There are many ancient farmhouses and cottages in the parish, several of them thatched. Fordmoor (formerly just Ford) was the home of the Fords from the 12th to the late 18th century and there is a tradition that it was once stayed in by the Black Prince. The impressive Hayne House (now called Plymtree Manor) is of early Georgian date; the earlier dwelling on the site and its successor were home to the Harwards from the 16th–19th centuries.

In the past Plymtree participated, like many other villages, in the woollen industry, with spinning and weaving being done in cottages. From the late 1800s, for about a century, the production and repair of tools and machines for farming was a thriving business, centred on the hamlet of Normans Green. The parish now has various small light industries.

Further reading: Eames, Tony, comp. and ed., *The book of Plymtree*, Halsgrove, 1999
Carden, J.J., *The history of Plymtree*, 1981

POLTIMORE (H6) East Devon Pop. 297 (1901: 298)

Poltimore has a short length of boundary on the south-west with Exeter and on the west is bounded by Huxham. Elsewhere it is 'wrapped around' by Broadclyst, the eastern boundary being partly marked by the River Clyst and a tributary. From c.100 ft land rises on the west to 410 ft.

Poltimore church was built by John Bampfylde in the 14th century.

The cruciform church (St Mary the Virgin) was built by John Bampfylde who died in 1390, and restored c.1880. The Bampfyldes acquired the manor in 1303, and Poltimore remained their seat until 1921. The earliest part of Poltimore House was built in the late 1500s, it was improved in the late 17th century, enlarged in the 18th century, and altered by Lord Poltimore, in the early 19th century. After the family left the house served as a girls' school, a boys' school, a hospital, and a nursing home. Subsequently it fell into disrepair and was severely vandalised. Efforts are currently being made by the Poltimore House Trust, which bought Poltimore in 1999, to restore it for an appropriate purpose. The house has notable historical associations with the time of the Civil War; in 1646 the Treaty of Exeter was signed here, ending civil strife in Devon and Cornwall.

Further reading: Fortescue Foulkes, R.A., *A short history of Poltimore*, 1954
Local society: The Five Parishes Local History Society

POUGHILL (G5) Mid Devon Pop. 189 (1905: 222)

Poughill (pronounced: 'Poyle') is located in the fairly remote hill country 6½ miles SW of Tiverton and 5½ miles NNE of Crediton, served by a network of minor roads. It is bounded on the east and west by streams which form tributaries of the River Creedy. Land to the north of the village rises to 687 ft.

The parish anciently belonged to the Poughill or Poghill family. The church (St Michael & All Angels), which dates from the 14th century, was restored in 1856.

The red sandstone church of St Clement stands close to the Exe in the park of Powderham Castle.

POWDERHAM (H7) Teignbridge Pop. 100 (1901: 238)

Powderham, 6 miles SE of Exeter, lies on the west side of the Exe estuary which is a rich habitat for birds and an internationally recognised wintering area for a large number of species, including Brent geese and avocets. The River Kenn, which enters the estuary, approximately forms the south-western boundary.

The area in the south comprises the parkland of Powderham Castle, seat of the Courtenay family, the earls of Devon, since the 14th century. The late 14th-century Powderham – more a fortified manor house than a castle although with battlements – was garrisoned for the king in the Civil War. The Fairfax forces attacked it in 1645 but were repelled, upon which they retreated to Powderham church where they sustained Royalist attacks before the castle surrendered in 1646. Until the 18th century waters extended much nearer to the castle and at times must have almost lapped its walls. Considerable alterations were carried out on the house in the 18th century, and further extensive work a century later. Powderham Castle is opened to the public during spring and summer. The park contains a large herd of fallow deer which can usually be seen from the passing road and railway.

The A 379 Exeter-Dawlish road runs west of the castle but a minor road passes between it and the coast which gives a view of the park, as is also possible from the main line railway which is routed close to the shoreline. This road also leads to the small church (St Clement, Bishop and Martyr), a red sandstone building dating from the 15th century, which has arcades of Beer stone and numerous Courtenay monuments.

PUDDINGTON (G4) Mid Devon Pop. 212 (1901: 173)

Puddington is located in fairly remote country 3 miles SE of Witheridge and 6½ miles N of Crediton, south of the B 3137 Witheridge-Tiverton road. The parish narrows to the north to reach the River Dalch which forms a length of the boundary. The Binneford Water – which goes on to form the River Creedy – flows through the south-east. The village is situated centrally at an altitude of 675 ft. The church (St Thomas à Becket) was partly rebuilt in the 1830s.

Further reading: Voce, Eileen, *Gleanings from the history of Puddington*, 1989

PYWORTHY (B5) Torridge Pop. 689 (1901: 429)

Pyworthy, 2 miles WSW of Holsworthy, is bounded by the River Tamar in the south-west, extends narrowly north to ancient Ugworthy Barrows, and is defined by a tributary stream of the River Deer and by a reach of the Deer itself on the north-east. The Derrill Water rises in the parish and flows south to the Tamar. The Holsworthy-Bude road (A 3072) passes westwards through the north as, in past days, did the railway between the two towns. The Holsworthy branch of the Bude Canal also passed through, south of Parnacott.

The rather lengthy village has seen modern developments. The church (St Swithun) is of 14th-century construction, restored in the late 19th century. The sanctuary is very light, the nave darker despite tiny clerestory windows. There is a large octagonal granite font on modern pillars. Ecclesiastically the parish is united with St Pancras, Pancrasweek.

Bradford was a Domesday estate and the parish also included the hamlets of Derriton and Killatree.

QUEEN'S NYMPTON (F3) North Devon Pop. 32

Queen's Nympton, 2 miles S of South Molton and bounded on east and south by the River Mole, became a small civil parish in 1900; previously it had been a detached area of the borough of South Molton. Ecclesiastically, however, it was absorbed by George Nympton and united as a benefice with South Molton. The name given to the parish in 1900 was in honour of Queen Victoria.

RACKENFORD (G4) North Devon Pop. 335 (1901: 302; Creacombe 57)

Rackenford, 7 miles NW of Tiverton and connected by minor roads with the A 361, now includes for civil purposes the small parish of Creacombe to the north-west. The parish has areas of moorland, some of it reclaimed, including Rackenford Moor in the north. The Little Dart River rises on Rackenford Moor and flows south-westwards, passing just east of the village. Much of the land stands at c.700 ft, the highest point being 866 ft near a tumulus on the north-east boundary.

Besides an early market and fair, there was a church here at least from the 12th century. The present building (All Saints) dates from the 15th century. Creacombe Church (St Michael & All Angels), rebuilt in 1857, is ecclesiastically united with Witheridge. Backstone, Bulworthy, Sideham, and Worthy were Domesday manors.

RATTERY (F9) South Hams Pop. 449 (1901: 347)

Rattery village. COURTESY THE BOOK OF RATTERY

Rattery is a parish of rich hilly farmland with its village centred 5 miles W of Totnes. The village is accessed by minor roads from either the A 38, A 384, or A 385. The River Dart forms the boundary on the north-east, and the Harbourne flows eastward through the south.

Aerial photography of Hood Ball has shown likely cropmarks, suggesting possible prehistoric Romano-British occupation. The name Rattery, of which there are numerous ancient variations, is believed to be of Saxon origin, and there may have been a Saxon church. In the present cruciform church (The Blessed Virgin Mary) the font, nave, chancel and sanctuary are believed to be from the 12th century, the tower and aisles were added in the 13th century, and the chapels and possibly the spire in the 15th century. The Church House Inn, dating from the 16th century or possibly earlier, stands nearby.

Of numerous ancient farms, Luscombe was a Domesday manor, and Velwell existed by 1249. The manor of Rattery was bought in 1543 by Richard Savery, whose descendants' long association with the parish continues. The Saverys also acquired the manors of Willing and Marley, both of which later changed hands. In 1784 the manor of Marley was bought by William Palk, who built the imposing Adam-style mansion. His daughter married Sir Henry Carew. The Carew family remained in ownership until the 1920s when, after the deaths of the two elderly Carew sisters, Bessie and Beatrix, the estate was sold. The house was bought for a community of Bridgettine sisters and re-named Syon Abbey. In 1989, the sisters' numbers having dwindled, the house was sold. Used initially for occasional events it has subsequently undergone conversion to several individual quality dwellings.

The main line railway, built by Brunel and opened to Plymouth in 1848, runs through the south of the parish and includes a viaduct and part of the 689 yd Marley Tunnel. The tunnel's deeper western section is in South Brent parish, the Rattery length is of 'cut and cover' construction.

An iron mine was worked at Bulkamore from 1800, or earlier, until the 1880s.

Further reading: The people of the parish, comp., *The book of Rattery*, Halsgrove, 2001

REWE (H6) East Devon Pop. 378 (1901: 237)

Rewe is a small parish of irregular and somewhat 'stretched out' shape. Centred 4½ miles NNW of Exeter it extends north-westwards from a point east of the River Culm along a narrow and elongated length to the Exe and a border with Bickleigh. The A 396 Exeter-Tiverton road runs through the parish and village, and the main Exeter-Taunton-London railway also passes through, crossing beneath the road.

The church (St Mary the Virgin) dates from the 15th century. Upexe and Rudway in the north were Domesday estates. Upexe had a halt on the Exe Valley railway from its opening in 1885 until closure in 1963.

Local society: The Five Parishes Local History Society

RINGMORE (E11) South Hams Pop. 219 (1901: 204)

Ringmore church (All Hallows) is small and ancient. Its tower dates from the 13th century.

Ringmore (not to be confused with Ringmore in Shaldon parish) is a small but pleasant parish remotely situated on the coast, 5½ miles WNW of Kingsbridge. It is approached by minor routes from the A 379 Plymouth-Kingsbridge road and the B 3392. Land rises to 475 ft in the far north and steeply to c.300 ft on either side of a small stream which enters the sea at Ayrmer Cove. Farther east along the coast is the holiday village of Challaborough.

Ringmore village is about a mile inland. The church (All Hallows) is small and ancient. Its tower, on the south side, with small steeple, dates from the 13th century and a hagioscope from the north transept is possibly of Saxon date. Unusual coloured patterning on the chancel arch dates from medieval times. A rare sundial on the south porch is from the 18th century. The church underwent restoration in 1863. The parish is united ecclesiastically with Kingston.

Local society: Ringmore Historical Society

ROBOROUGH (D4) Torridge Pop. 255 (1901: 312)

Roborough stands on the hilly country between the Rivers Taw and Torridge and roughly equidistant from each. The village is served by minor roads from the A 3124, the B 3217 and the B 3227. The rather square-shaped parish contains no rivers. An earthworks identified as a camp, near a stream in a wooded area in the west, is an indication of early human activity.

The church (St Peter), constructed in the 15th century, was restored and largely rebuilt in 1868. Owlacombe, Villavin, and Barlington were Domesday manors and Coombe Barton dates from the early 16th century. Ebberley is a hamlet in the north.

ROCKBEARE (J6) East Devon Pop. 880 (1901: 404)

Rockbeare is a mainly low-lying parish, although land rises towards the eastern boundary, reaching 504 ft on Rockbeare Hill. West-flowing streams run through the parish to join the River Clyst.

The village, 6 miles ENE of Exeter, stands south of the former A 30 (now unclassified) road, the dual carriageway A 30 that replaced it in the 1990s running a mile to the south. Exeter International Airport lies immediately west.

The church (St Mary with St Andrew) dates from at least as early as 1316. It was largely rebuilt in the late 1880s. Rockbeare Manor, built in the 18th century, was the home of Sir John Duntze, Exeter woollen merchant and banker.

ROMANSLEIGH (F3) North Devon Pop. 98 (1901: 155)

Romansleigh, 3½ miles SSE of South Molton, is situated to the west of the South Molton-Witheridge road (B 3171), with tributaries of the River Mole defining the north-west, north, and east boundaries. Land on the southern boundary attains 755 ft, and the village, centrally located in this hilly parish, stands at just under 600 ft.

The ancient church (St Rumon), having fallen into considerable disrepair, was completely rebuilt in 1868. It now has a pleasant interior, the internal roof being particularly attractive. Rumon was a Celtic missionary who became bishop of Devon and Cornwall in the 7th century. His remains were enshrined in Tavistock's former Benedictine abbey, which was dedicated to the Blessed Virgin Mary and St Rumon. The abbey was endowed with an estate in the area of Romansleigh parish. North of the church is a well, called St Rumon's Well, heavily impregnated with iron. There are remains of an ancient cross in the churchyard.

ROSE ASH (F3) North Devon Pop. 294 (1901: 439)

Rose Ash, 5 miles SE of South Molton is located in the country to the north of the South Molton-Witheridge-Tiverton road (B 3137). Another, minor, road to Tiverton, via Rackenford, passes through the north of the parish. The land is hilly, with the village, which has an attractive village green, standing at 780 ft. The northern boundary is defined by the Crooked Oak Brook.

The church (St Peter) dates from the 15th and 16th centuries but was fully rebuilt, except for the tower, c.1890. Restorations were carried out in 1961 and 2000–1. Eight generations of the Southcombe family were rectors here continuously from 1675 to 1948. The only son of the last generation was killed in France in the First World War. Yard was a Domesday estate.

ST GILES-IN-THE-WOOD (D4) Torridge Pop. 566 (1901: 623)

St Giles-in-the-Wood is a large parish immediately east of Great Torrington, with its village 2½ miles due east of the town. In its south-west extremity the boundary with Torrington is defined by a Torridge tributary to the confluence at Town Mills, from where the St Giles boundary follows two loops of the main river before taking its own course eastwards and northwards. The parish reaches north to Cranford Cross and Huntshaw Cross before the boundary returns south. The land rises in altitude to over 600 ft at points on the north and east borders.

The large and well-kept church (St Giles) is in the fairly centrally placed village. Built in 1309 as a chapel of Torrington, it was restored in 1862. Stevenstone Park was part of the Rolle estate. The former Tudor house here was rebuilt in the 18th century and again in the 19th century but later became ruinous. The former stables are now residential apartments. Kingscott, High Bullen, Dodscott and Healand are hamlets within the parish. Whitsleigh, in the south-east, was a Domesday manor.

Rosemoor Gardens of the Royal Horticultural Society are located in the south-west, close to New Bridge over the Torridge on the A 386.

ST GILES-ON-THE-HEATH (B6) Torridge Pop. 617 (1901: 258)

St Giles' Church is small and neat, with a low tower and Norman font.

Shaped rather like an elongated heart, the parish of St Giles-on-the-Heath is bounded by the River Tamar on the west and the Carey on the east. Northcott hamlet, Luffincott and Ashwater adjoin to the north. The village centre, which was known in the past as Box's Shop, is located 8 miles S of Holsworthy on the Launceston-Holsworthy road (A 388).

The church (St Giles), which is situated remotely from the village, farther west and nearer the Tamar, dates from the 15th century. It is small and neat, with a low tower and a Norman font. Ecclesiastically the parish is in the diocese of Truro.

West Panson dates from the time of Domesday. Carey Barton marks the 12th-century home of the Carys, a notable Devon family.

SALCOMBE (F12) South Hams Pop. 1893

The parish of Salcombe occupies the west side of the lower Kingsbridge estuary, as far south as an eastward-flowing stream which enters the sea just north of Bolt Head. The indented nature of the shoreline and the narrowing of the waterway just before widening to the mouth have helped to make this a favourable harbour for boats, a minor port in past centuries with a notable fishing fleet and ship-building facilities, and in modern times an attractive centre for sailing. The somewhat tortuous road approach is via the A 381 from Kingsbridge. Steep ascents are a feature of the topography, with a swift rise through the town to 271 ft, and to 431 ft above the cliffs in the south. The length of coastline is owned by the National Trust, as is the property known as Sharpitor, or Overbecks, close to Salcombe itself. Needless to say, the general scene is very beautiful, with the southerly position creating at times an almost sub-tropical atmosphere. North and South Sands are pleasant beaches.

The civil parish was formed in 1894, Salcombe having previously been part of Malborough. The present church (Holy Trinity) stands on the high side of the town. From the 13th century the site was that of a chapel dedicated to St John the Baptist, but by the 17th century it had become ruinous and the present church was built in Early English style during the 19th century, completed in 1889. Batson, at the head of the creek north of the town, was recorded in Domesday. Just south of the town are the remains of a castle built as a defence by Henry VIII which underwent sieges during the Civil War.

Further reading: Born, Anne, *A history of Kingsbridge and Salcombe*, Phillimore, 1986
Local society: Salcombe Maritime and Local History Museum Society
Museum: Salcombe Maritime and Local History Museum, The Quay

SALCOMBE REGIS see SIDMOUTH

The small but delightful church of St Mary, Honeychurch, dates from the 12th century. The parish is now part of Sampford Courtenay.

SAMPFORD COURTENAY (E5) West Devon Pop. 509 (1901: 758)

Sampford Courtenay, which has included the ecclesiastical parish of Honeychurch since 1894, is situated 5 miles NE of Okehampton. The large parish is partly bounded on the east by the north-flowing River Taw. The A 3072 road east to Crediton passes along the village's southern edge, and the B 3215 which connects to this from Okehampton runs farther south, with a further road leading from it northwards to the village. The point at which this minor road takes off is called Belstone Corner, and is marked by the former Sampford Courtenay Station. The London & South Western Railway arrived here on its way to Okehampton in 1867. The line continues in use for quarry traffic and for some weekend passenger trains in summer.

The village of Sampford Courtenay is attractive and well kept, noted for its floral displays. The church (St Andrew) is very fine. On Whit Monday 1549, at the time of the Prayer Book Rebellion, it was the scene of a riot and a murder. The people of Sampford Courtenay were against the introduction of the new English Prayer Book and they insisted on their parish priest conducting Mass in the accustomed style. A riot ensued, and a local man who attempted to intercede was murdered.

The tiny church at Honeychurch (St Mary), a mile to the north, is in a quiet location, delightfully simple and peaceful. Dating from the 12th century it was enlarged in the 15th century, and retains a Norman font. Restoration was being carried out in 2003.

Sampford Courtenay originally belonged to the Courtenay family as part of the barony of Okehampton. Amongst the old established farms in the parish is Reddaway, near Sticklepath in the south, which has been owned and farmed by the Reddaway family for nearly eight centuries.

Further reading: Pouya, Stephanie, *The book of Sampford Courtenay with Honeychurch*, Halsgrove, 2003

SAMPFORD PEVERELL (J4) Mid Devon Pop. 1225 (1901: 612)

Sampford Peverell, 5 miles E of Tiverton, has a fairly large village, situated in the south. The parish, which broadens in the south, narrows in the north-west. The land, mainly agricultural, rises from 200-300 ft in the south to several higher points including 773 ft towards the north. The former A 373 (now unclassified) road from Tiverton passes through the village to join the old A 38, and now, more prominently, the M5 motorway just a mile away. Junction 27 on the motorway is on the parish's eastern boundary, where the North Devon Link road takes off, to pass north of Sampford Peverell village and west through the north of the parish.

The route of the Grand Western Canal (see TIVERTON) also passes through the village – where there was a wharf – and the south-east of the parish. Its construction caused considerable upheaval and in 1811 Sampford Peverell was the scene of a navvies' riot. The main railway line from Paddington via Bristol crossed through the parish's south-eastern tip when it became operational in 1844, and here Sampford Peverell had a station; this has now been redeveloped as Tiverton Parkway, conveniently close to the M5 Junction 27.

The church (St John the Baptist) originated in 1259 when it was dedicated by Bishop Bronescombe of Exeter. The present building dates from the 15th century although traces of the earlier church remain. It was restored in the 1860s. The village formerly had a fair, for cattle, sheep and horses and was also involved in the woollen industry.

SAMPFORD SPINEY (D8) West Devon Pop. 125 (1901: 478)

Bounded on the east and south by the River Walkham, Sampford Spiney lies closely against the western edge of Dartmoor, 3–4 miles SE of Tavistock, from where it is approached by minor roads. It is a quiet parish of farms, woods and clitter-strewn moorland.

The church (St Mary) seems almost to grow out of the surrounding moor; dating probably from the 14th century it was later enlarged. The parish has several ancient farmhouses, including some of the traditional Dartmoor longhouse type. Hall Farm, by the church, was the former manor house, rebuilt in 1607.

Sampford Spiney, with its church of St Mary, is located on the western edge of Dartmoor.

Local society: Yelverton & District Local History Society

SANDFORD (G5) Mid Devon Pop. 1280 (1901: 1248)

Sandford, 1½ miles N of Crediton, is bounded on the east by the River Creedy and a tributary, and on the south by the minor road which connects the A 377 road to Barnstaple with the A 3072 from Crediton to Tiverton. Extending westwards the border tapers to make contact with the A 377 north of Copplestone. Set in pleasant countryside, which includes Creedy Park – ancestral home of the Davie family and now divided into residential apartments – the large village occupies a hillside position near the Creedy valley. The large church (St Swithin) was mainly rebuilt in the 16th century, and restored and enlarged in the 1840s. It has a substantial gallery. At New Buildings, a hamlet in the east, there is also the small Beacon Church. Dowrich, in the north, was the home of the Dowrich family from c.1200 to the 18th century. Ruxford Barton, a mile west of the village, was mentioned in a charter of 930; the farmhouse was rebuilt in the early 17th century. East Village is a hamlet in the north-east.

Further reading: Munday, Daphne, *Sandford, a parish patchwork*

SATTERLEIGH AND WARKLEIGH (E3) North Devon Pop. 166 (1901: Satterleigh 55, Warkleigh 220)

Combined as one civil parish in 1894, and also united ecclesiastically, Satterleigh and Warkleigh are situated somewhat remotely in the hill country between the Rivers Taw and Mole, with the rivers forming the boundaries to west and east respectively.

Satterleigh, on the east, was a manor at the time of Domesday. Its small but interesting church (St Peter), which possibly originated in Saxon times, was mentioned in 1288. The present building dates mainly from the 15th century, and has a wooden bellcote. It is now redundant, in the care of the Churches Conservation Trust, and the holding of six services a year is permitted. Inside, the Ten Commandments are inscribed on either side of the east window, with the Lord's Prayer and Creed on the tympanum over the former screen.

Warkleigh church (St John), farther west, was mentioned in episcopal registers in 1276. The south aisle was a 15th-century addition to the previously built chancel, which was reconstructed in 1850. The church was restored in 1869 and 1965. A precious possession is the Warkleigh Tabernacle, a container for the Reserved Sacrament, dating from the third-quarter of the 15th century and discovered in the parish chest in 1888.

Further reading: Lethbridge, Richard, *The book of Chittlehampton, with Warkleigh and Satterleigh*, Halsgrove, 2002

SEATON (L7) East Devon Pop. 6798 (1901: 2443)

Seaton parish is bounded on the east by the estuary of the River Axe and on the south by the English Channel. The beach is of shingle, which also forms a bar across most of the estuary mouth. Land rises from the Axe marshland – now reclaimed from the formerly wider estuary – to 300-400 ft on Seaton Hill in the north-west. The town, 6½ miles SW of Axminster, lies south of the A 3052 Sidmouth-Lyme Regis road, to which it connects by the B 3174 to the west and the B 3172 via Axmouth to the east. A concrete bridge, one of the earliest in the country, was constructed here in 1877 to carry the road across the Axe, but a replacement was built on the upstream side in 1989–90 while the older one, scheduled as an Ancient Monument, now serves pedestrians only.

The Seaton Tramway, which operates passenger trams on the former branch railway route alongside the River Axe, from Seaton to Colyton.

An area known as Honeyditches, on the north-west edge of the town, which had been occupied by Neolithic, Bronze Age and Iron Age people, also became a Roman site of some significance. Archaeological investigations in the second half of the 19th century and in the 20th century have revealed remains of a villa complex, comprising two long parallel timber structures, a bathhouse and a possible barn, dating probably from the 2nd to 4th centuries AD. The remains were subsequently re-covered but the area is scheduled as an Ancient Monument.

It is believed that the Saxons reached the area c.600. Becoming known (until the 12th century) as Aut Fleote, Seaton was granted in 1005 by King Aethelred to a thane, Eadisge, on whose death it passed to the Prior of Horton, Dorset, which was united with Sherborne Abbey in 1122. After the Reformation it was sold into secular hands, to John Frye, then to the family of John Willoughby. In 1627 the fourth John Willoughby, who had reclaimed the marshes for grazing land, built a fortification in the form of a huge earthworks, just east of the sea front, as a defence against the French. This was called the Barrow, which became changed over years to Burrow. In the late 17th century the manor passed through marriage to the Trevelyans. Salt-making, which had been an industry on the estuary six centuries earlier, was revived by John Trevelyan in the early 18th century, but by 1755 had entirely ceased.

The coming of the railway in 1868 brought changes to quiet Seaton. By now there was a growing awareness of the delights of the sea-coast and gradually the town developed into a resort. The railway branch from Seaton Junction on the main Waterloo-Exeter line closed in 1966. In 1970 three miles of this line, from Seaton to Colyton, were adapted and re-opened as the Seaton Tramway, on which passenger

Seaton, 1895. COURTESY THE BOOK OF SEATON

trams run on the pleasant stretch alongside the River Axe.

The church (St Gregory) apparently originally belonged to the monastery of Horton and abbey of Sherborne. After the Dissolution the manor and church of Seaton were granted by Henry VIII to Katherine Parr, before being sold to John Frye. Vicars are recorded from 1260. It is believed that the church building dates from the 13th century. It was enlarged, with rebuilding in the 14th century, followed by further rebuilding and enlargement, and restoration in 1865. Seaton was formerly united with Beer (to the west) until the two were divided in 1905.

Further reading: Gosling, Ted, *The book of Seaton,* Halsgrove, 2002

SHALDON (H8) Teignbridge Pop. 1628 (1901: 1121)

The village of Shaldon, on the south side of the mouth of the Teign estuary, with the neighbouring village of Ringmore (not to be confused with the parish of Ringmore in South Hams) formerly comprised the parish of St Nicholas, but the two are now known as Shaldon parish which, since 1972, also extends south in a narrow strip along the English Channel coast towards Maidencombe on the border with Torbay.

Both villages, which in the past were much involved in the fishing industry, are attractive and interesting. Shaldon is connected to Teignmouth by Shaldon Bridge, which carries the A 379 road to Torquay. Built in 1827 as the second longest timber bridge in Europe, it was replaced a century later by the 24-arch structure of steel and concrete and operated as a toll bridge until 1948. The corroding effects of salt water and sea spray necessitate constant attention and periodic repairs.

The church of St Nicholas at Ringmore may possibly originate from the late 12th century. The building was fully restored in 1896 but retains a Norman font. The church of St Peter, close to the bridge, was built c.1900.

Local society: Teignmouth & Shaldon Museum and History Society

SHAUGH PRIOR (D9) South Hams Pop. 751 (1901: 783)

The village of Shaugh Prior is located between the western slopes of Dartmoor and the Plym valley woodlands.

Shaugh Prior is a fairly large parish on the south-east of Dartmoor, extending from the Plymouth boundary to that of Dartmoor Forest. Over the area the countryside varies from woods and valleys to high moorland with altitudes that rise to 1600 ft. The moorland areas are rich in Bronze Age remains, with many cairns and cists, and there is much evidence of tinners' activities in the area of the upper Plym and Blacka Brook. There was an iron mine west of the village in the 1870s. The area south of Cadover Bridge, which crosses the River Plym, comprising Shaugh Moor and Lee Moor, has in recent centuries been much worked for the extraction of china clay and for this reason is not included in Dartmoor National Park, unlike other parts of the parish. The village of Lee Moor has developed since the commencement of clayworking in the 1830s. The industry was served between 1858 and the 1940s by the Lee Moor Tramway which ran from the workings to quays at Plymouth. Parts of the moorland bordering the Plym were used in the past for the warrening of rabbits.

The River Plym defines the parish's boundary on the north and, after being joined by the Meavy at Shaugh Bridge, also on the west. The village is located in the west, on the edge of the moor and above the wooded Plym valley. It is reached by minor roads from the A 386 Plymouth-Tavistock road or from the B 3417 to Lee Moor.

The church (St Edward) dates from the 11th century. Its fine granite tower is a prominent feature. The present building dates from the 15th century. There is also a mission church at Lee Moor.

SHEBBEAR (C5) Torridge Pop. 858 (1901: 840)

Bounded on the south and west by the twisted lower course of the River Torridge, Shebbear lies in the country between Holsworthy and Torrington and is roughly equidistant from the two towns. Approach is by minor roads from either the A 3072 Hatherleigh-Holsworthy road, or from the A 388 Holsworthy-Bideford road.

An unusual piece of grey sandstone discovered in 1988 on land of Rowden Farm after deep ploughing was identified by Exeter Museum as an axe head of the Neolithic period, around 4000–2000BC, but larger than other axe heads found in Devon. Also in the northern part of the parish is Durpley Castle, a small Norman castle site with a motte and bailey surrounded by a ditch. Several of the parish's farms date from the 12th century.

The village is centred around a large square, with the church (St Michael) close by. Believed to be of Saxon origin the church contains Norman work, including the south doorway – one of the best Norman doorways in Devon. The present building dates mainly from the 14th century. Non-conformity has been strong in Shebbear, with four chapels in the early 20th century. The Bible Christian movement originated at Lake Farm in 1815 and the building of the first Lake Chapel followed. Shebbear College was established by the Bible Christians in 1841 as a school for boys and as a training college for their ministers. A new Lake Chapel was built in 1905 and in 1907 the Bible Christians became part of the United Methodist Church. From then ministers were no longer trained at Shebbear, but the college continues as a school.

Further reading: Ackland, Ron; Clark, Richard; and Lott, Ted; comp. *Shebbear*, 2000

SHEEPSTOR (D9) West Devon Pop. 53 (1901: 95)

The Dartmoor village with its church is seen centre. Sheep's Tor, which gave its name to the parish, is on the right and Burrator Reservoir on the left.

The moorland parish of Sheepstor includes prominent Sheeps Tor (1210 ft) from which it is named, and the southern length of Burrator Reservoir in the north. From Burrator the western boundary continues south along the River Meavy and a tributary, then over land to the Plym. This river, almost to its source, forms the south-eastern boundary before the line turns north-west for Eylesbarrow and proceeds to the Narrator Brook and Burrator.

This area of Dartmoor, which includes Ringmoor Down and Ditsworthy Warren, is extremely rich in Bronze Age remains, particularly along the Plym valley. It was also much worked for tin, from at least as early as the 12th century, along the Plym and smaller streams, and latterly in the 19th century when mines included Eylesbarrow, and the small Kit Mine near the village. For centuries until the 1900s parts of the moorland were worked as rabbit warrens. Burrator Reservoir was constructed in 1898 and enlarged by raising the dam in 1928.

The village is accessed by minor roads from the B 3212 Yelverton-Princetown road. The church (St Leonard) dates from the 15th century, built of granite with window mullions of Roborough elvan. It has a south aisle and small north transept. There is a very beautiful rood screen. The original screen was removed in a mid-19th-century restoration, but its detail was recalled by the Revd Sabine Baring Gould. Subsequently, in 1914, the then vicar, the Revd Hugh Breton, was responsible for installing the present replacement, copied meticulously from architectural drawings and including fragments saved from the original. The fine bench ends date from the 1920s, designed by the Misses Pinwill. Outside, high on the porch, is a small sculpture symbolising life after death, depicting a skull with ears of corn sprouting from it. A striking Aberdeen red granite tomb in the churchyard marks the grave of Sir James Brooke, Rajah of Sarawak, who lived at Burrator House in the mid 1800s.

Local society: Yelverton & District Local History Society

SHEEPWASH (C5) Torridge Pop. 254 (1901: 326)

Sheepwash, located 3½ miles WNW of Hatherleigh, and 1½ miles from Highampton on the Hatherleigh-Holsworthy road (A 3072), is served by minor routes. The parish is bounded almost entirely by watercourses: the River Torridge on the south, and tributary streams on west and east. In addition, the Mussel Brook, flowing down from Buckland Filleigh, passes through the centre of the parish on its way to the Torridge. Therefore it is not unreasonable to conjecture that, considering its name, Sheepwash was a place to which sheep were brought for washing before being shorn, in the days when the process was still carried out in Devon.

The parish has an attractive village centre with several thatched houses around the Square. The church (St Lawrence) dates from at least as early as the 13th century. The present building of 1880 is the third on the site, the first having fallen down and the second being destroyed by fire. There is a Norman font on a stone and cement pedestal.

SHELDON (K5) East Devon Pop. 167 (1901: 120)

The small parish of Sheldon is remotely situated on slopes of the Blackdown Hills, 5½ miles NNW of Honiton and 6 miles E of Cullompton, and approached only by minor roads. The land rises to 750 ft in the east and to 912 ft on the western boundary. A tributary of the River Culm rises in the south and flows northwards through the parish.

The church (St James the Greater) was originally dedicated in 1259 by Bishop Bronescombe. It was entirely rebuilt, except for the tower, in 1871. There is a Norman font. The manor was held by Dunkeswell Abbey, and later by the Bourchiers, and others.

SHERFORD see FROGMORE AND SHERFORD

SHILLINGFORD ST GEORGE (H7) Teignbridge Pop. 382 (1901: 63)

Shillingford St George is a small parish immediately SW of Exeter and on the north side of the River Kenn. A small tributary of the Exe flows eastwards, north of the village. The land is mainly fairly low-lying, rising to c.350 ft. The A 30 road skirts the north of the parish, just west of Junction 31 of the M5, the motorway's southern terminal point where it meets the A 38 and A 30. Access to the village is by minor roads either from the Exeter area of Alphington or from the Kennford turn-off on the A 38.

The red sandstone church (St George) dates from the 14th century, restored in the mid 1800s. It stands on the south side of the village in a quiet and lovely situation, and in the early autumn the churchyard is adorned with the flowers of tiny cyclamen.

SHIRWELL (D2) North Devon Pop. 333 (1901: 338)

Shirwell is a hilly parish 3½ miles north-east of Barnstaple, with the village situated just east of the A 39 Barnstaple-Lynton road. The parish is bounded on the west by the Bradiford Water and on the east by the River Yeo.

The church (St Peter) was constructed in the 15th century and later restored. The 18th-century Youlstone, located in parkland that rises to 651 ft, on the opposite side of the A 39 from the village, was, from the 15th century, the home of a branch of the Chichester family. Plaistow Barton, in the north-west, was a Domesday manor.

SHOBROOKE (G5) Mid Devon Pop. 540 (1901: 557)

Shobrooke parish lies immediately E of Crediton and extends on either side of the A 3072 Crediton-Tiverton road. The southern boundary is marked by the minor road which branches from the A 3072 towards Thorverton; northwards from this it climbs to over 750 ft on the Raddon Hills from where it proceeds west and north following a route across land. The stream known as Shobrooke Lake flows southwards through the parish to join the River Creedy.

The church (St Swithin) is of early origin and retains a 12th-century Norman doorway; it was restored c.1880. Shobrooke Park, formerly called Little Fulford, was owned in the late 16th and early 17th centuries by Sir William Periam, chief Baron of the Exchequer. The house was demolished c.1820 and a new one built by R. Hippisley Tuckfield, who called it Shobrooke Park. Later it became a school but was destroyed by fire in 1947. West Raddon, on the lower slopes of Raddon Hills, on the east, was a Domesday manor. In the 16th century it was bought by the Westcotes and here it was that Thomas Westcote, the antiquarian, was born in 1567 and later wrote his *View of Devonshire*.

The 16th-century Shute gatehouse, restored by the Landmark Trust in 1980.

SHUTE (L6) East Devon Pop. 589 (1901: 461)

Shute parish – its village located 3 miles WSW of Axminster – rises from the valley of the River Axe, in the south-east, to hilly country, falling again on the west to the Umborne Brook (tributary of the Coly), a stretch of which marks the boundary. The highest altitudes, up to 566 ft, are on the partially wooded Shute Hill, north-east of the village. The A 35 Axminster-Honiton road passes through the north of the parish, with a minor road from it running south through the village to Colyton and the A 3052. The main railway from Waterloo to Exeter is routed through the south, where the former Seaton Junction was sited during the existence of the branch line to Seaton (1868–1966).

In the early 13th century the church (St Michael) was cruciform in shape with a central tower. The form changed, however, when extensions were added in the 15th century. The north aisle was added in 1811. Restoration and renovation were carried out in 1863 and 1869, the sanctuary was refashioned and the Lady Chapel restored in 1967. There is also the church of St Mary at Cross, a mile south in the village of Whitford.

The manor of Shute was originally held by the Shute family, followed by the Pynes, Bonvilles, and Greys. In 1787 it was bought from Lord Petre by Sir John Pole whose family, which had included Sir William Pole, Master of Queen Anne's household, had in fact leased Shute from the 16th century. John Pole built Shute House in the late 1780s. Latterly it became a girls school for many years but is now divided as residential apartments. There is a fine gatehouse (restored by the Landmark Trust in 1980) to the old manor house; the house was partly demolished in 1787 and, now known as Shute Barton, is in the hands of the National Trust. (Open to visitors on certain days.)

SIDBURY see SIDMOUTH

SIDMOUTH (K7) East Devon Pop. 13,135 (1901: Sidmouth 4037, Sidbury 1076)

Sidmouth includes Sidbury with its Norman church, beneath which are remains of a Saxon crypt. The spire was added in 1895.

Sidmouth is a large civil parish that has a 3½ mile southern boundary along the English Channel coast and its northernmost boundary point 6 miles north of Sidmouth town. The A 3052 Exeter-Lyme Regis road runs west-east through the parish, crossed by the A 375 from Honiton at Sidford, ½ mile north of the town.

The River Sid, which enters the sea on the east side of the town, rises in the far north at c.700 ft and flows almost due south, at first through remote valleys and then the villages of Sidbury and Sidford. A large earthwork known as Sidbury Castle, a mile north of that village, was an Iron Age hill fort. The mouth of the Sid is marked by a distinct gap between the red sandstone cliffs that rise to over 500 ft, to east and west, which can be noted from viewpoints a great distance away. The beach is of shingle. Salcombe Regis, formerly a separate parish, is located on the east, with a pleasant village and yellow sandstone quarries which, from c.1100 and for some centuries, produced building stone that was widely used, including in the structure of Exeter Cathedral. The Norman Lockyer Observatory, for astronomical study, is on Sidmouth's West Hill.

In earlier days Sidmouth was a small market town with fishing an important activity up to the 19th century. By that time its mildness and beautiful surroundings, and the healthy qualities of the sea, had been discovered by discriminating visitors from the upper levels of society. The attraction was heightened by the restrictions on travel imposed by the Napoleonic Wars, and by the reputation gained from the stay of the Duke and Duchess of Kent with their infant daughter, later Queen Victoria, over the winter of 1819–20. Many well-to-do people established themselves here, building pleasant houses, for second residences or for retirement, which continue to enhance the scene.

Several ecclesiastical parishes and their churches are contained within the civil parish. The main parish church of the town of Sidmouth is that of St Giles & St Nicholas, which dates from the 15th century but was rebuilt, except for the arcades and tower, in 1859–60. The Victorian church of All Saints was built in the late 1830s. Woolbrook church (St Francis of Assissi) on the town's northern fringe, was consecrated in 1938.

In the united benefice of Sidbury with Sidford, Sidbury church (St Giles & St Peter) is of particularly early foundation. Beneath it are remains of a Saxon crypt, above which a Norman church comprising nave and chancel were built in the early 12th century. The tower and north and south aisles were added later in the century, and in the 13th century extensions were made. Considerable reconstruction followed in the 15th century, and repairs in the 17th century. In the 19th century the tower was rebuilt and the spire added in 1895. At Sidford there is the church of St Peter. Salcombe Regis church (also St Peter) dates from the 12th century. It was enlarged c.1300 and again in 1430 with addition of the tower.

Sidmouth people have mostly been anxious for the town to maintain its character and not to become a popularised seaside resort. For this reason the town managed to remain aloof from railway developments until the 1870s, when an 8½ mile branch from the London & South Western Railway was constructed but, ostensibly to avoid gradient problems, only as far as the top of the town. It was opened in 1874 and closed in the late 1960s.

Further reading: Various: *The book of Sidmouth*, Halsgrove, 2004
There are also many other publications which cover Sidmouth, Sidbury and Salcombe Regis. Readers are advised to investigate bookshops and libraries.

Local societies: Sidmouth Local History Group
Sid Vale Association
East Devon Branch of the Devonshire Association
Museum: Sidmouth Museum, Hope Cottage, Church Street

SILVERTON (H5) Mid Devon Pop. 1905 (1901: 1188)

The centre of Silverton village which has numerous thatched houses.

Silverton, 7½ miles NNE of Exeter and 6 miles S of Tiverton, is situated a mile east of the A 396 road that connects the two. The parish narrows towards the north. The River Culm forms most of the boundary on the south until the line crosses land towards the slopes of the Exe valley on the west, then to proceed northwards as far as Burn. Here the route follows the River Burn towards Butterleigh and the northward extension. The eastern boundary takes a rather tortuous course over land.

The village is pleasant with a large square and several cob and thatched buildings. It dates from Saxon times and became a market town, with two fairs long since declined. The church (St Mary) is of 15th and early 16th-century construction, rebuilt in 1863. A mile east of the village is Silverton Park, where the 4th Earl of Egremont started to build an immense mansion. He died in 1845 before the work was finished, and little structure now remains. Greenslinch and Yard in the east, and Burn on the west were recorded in Domesday.

Further reading: Various, *The book of Silverton*, Halsgrove, 2000
Local society: Silverton Local History Society

SLAPTON (G11) South Hams Pop. 473 (1901: 527)

Slapton parish extends inland from its long straight beach on the English Channel coast and includes the east end of Slapton Ley, a freshwater lake that is a National Nature Reserve, fed by a minor stream and separated from the sea by a raised beach of shingle and sand. The A 379 coast road from Torcross to Dartmouth runs along this beach where, in stormy weather, it is sometimes invaded by high seas. The stream to the Ley forms the boundary on the west, the Gara that on the east. Land rises to 530 ft in the north.

The village stands about a mile inland. The church (St James the Greater), which has a spire, dates from at least as early as the 14th century, the high altar being dedicated by Bishop Stapledon in 1318. In the mid 14th century a collegiate church was also established here (St Mary) whose tall tower remains a prominent feature.

Slapton was one of several South Hams parishes that were evacuated of their inhabitants between December 1943 and late 1944 to enable allied forces to carry out

The freshwater Slapton Ley, viewed from Torcross (Stokenham).

The monument on Slapton beach presented by the US Army in recognition of those who vacated their homes and farms in 1943–4.

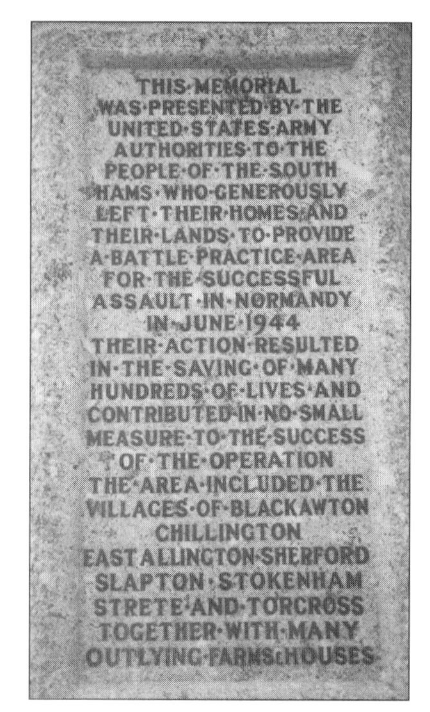

The monument's inscription.

exercises in preparation for the D-Day landings in Europe. People had just a month to vacate their homes and farms. Some damage was caused to Slapton church during the exercises. The evacuation is commemorated by a monument on the beach, presented by the US Army authorities to the people of the South Hams in gratitude for their sacrifice which helped ensure success of the eventual operation and reduced loss of life. Loss of life did occur, however, during the exercises, when, in April 1944, 700 American troops perished in an ill-fated incident.

Further reading: Charig, Peter, *Slapton, the village past and present*, 7th edit., 1990
Stanes, Robin, *A fortunate place, the history of Slapton in South Devon*, Field Studies Council, 1983

SOURTON D6 West Devon Pop. 406 (1901: 403)

(Including lands common to the parishes of Bridestowe and Sourton)

With its village centre 4½ miles SW of Okehampton, on the Okehampton-Tavistock road (A 386), Sourton, like its neighbour Bridestowe, ranges from farming land at lower levels to the high edge of Dartmoor, with land rising to over 1800 ft and Sourton Tors at 1446 ft. The common lands shared with Bridestowe adjoin the Dartmoor Forest boundary.

The church (St Thomas à Becket) is of granite, with clustered granite pillars and wagon roofs. The building dates from the 14th century, licensed by Bishop Brantingham in 1374. After falling into disrepair the chancel was rebuilt on new foundations in 1847, and the church was re-pewed and re-floored in 1880. There was formerly a rood loft, and also a gallery. The octagonal font is 15th century.

Lake and Collaven were ancient farms. Remains of an apparent early field system on Sourton Down were briefly examined by archaeologists in 1990, prior to the construction of the modern A 30. Including also signs of two longhouses and other features they were considered to be remnants of a medieval settlement, close to the Roman road to Cornwall. Close to the A 386, on the green below the church, is the base of an old cross, possibly a preaching cross. Near it is an incised stone, believed to be an early Christian memorial. It was discovered as a roof prop on a local farm and brought and erected here in the 1980s. There is also a stone cross on Sourton Down with an indistinct Latin inscription, beside the road to the caravan park.

A small copper mine, Torwood Mine, of unknown date, is marked by remains of shafts, ground disturbance and tips east of Lake Viaduct. The chimney of another small copper mine, Sourton Down Consols, or Alice Mine, can be seen south of the old A 30 road. The parish also had quarries. An unusual industry that functioned briefly in the late 19th century was an iceworks, located high on the moor just north of Sourton Tors. (See Harris, Helen, 'The Sourton Tors Iceworks, north-west Dartmoor 1874-86', *Transactions of the Devonshire Association 120*, 1988.) In 1874 the line of the London & South Western Railway was completed through the parish, including the fine 9-arched Lake Viaduct. (It is now a cycle track.) The Rattlebrook Peat Railway ascended (from Bridestowe Station) over the common lands to the high level peatworks.

The incised stone, found on a local farm and recently erected on Sourton's village green, is believed to be an early Christian memorial.

SOUTH BRENT (F10) South Hams Pop. 2847 (1901: 1360)

South Brent – or just Brent as it is generally known locally – is a fairly large parish that extends for a crows-flight distance of 7½ miles SE from the boundary with the Forest of Dartmoor, south of Huntingdon Warren, to the in-country just 3½ miles SW of Totnes. The large village is located 14 miles ENE of Plymouth and 4½ miles SSW of Buckfastleigh. The eastern parish boundary follows the River Avon (passing the Avon Dam, constructed in 1957) for a way before joining the Harbourne, along which it continues southwards before breaking away on a somewhat irregular course. Part of the western boundary is defined by the Glaze Brook, an Avon tributary. Several points of high altitude are reached; even in the farming country of the south levels rise to 500-600 ft, while northwards, on Brent Moor, they ascend to over 1500 ft, the highest being 1575 at Petres Cross on Western White Barrow. There is much evidence of prehistoric inhabitation on the moor in the form of hut circles and barrows, besides remains of tin-working and clay extraction.

The modern A 38 expressway runs through the parish (marking the boundary here of Dartmoor National Park), with the A 385 for Totnes branching from it at Marley. (The former A 385, via Avonwick to the south, is now unclassified.) The main railway also passes through, part of the Marley Tunnel being in the parish. The village is situated just north of the A 38, with several minor roads radiating from it, and with Brent Hill (1019 ft) rising steeply on the north-east. The River Avon flows by on the west side of the village.

The church (St Petroc) dates from pre-1066 and has been much altered over the centuries. It was originally cruciform in shape. In the 12th century the transepts were demolished and in the 13th century the nave and south and north transepts rebuilt. North and south aisles and the chancel were added in the 15th century. The font is of red sandstone. The rood screen was removed in a restoration of 1870. It is said that a vicar of the parish was murdered here, some centuries ago. The exceptionally heavy church door has a sanctuary ring on the outside by which, on reaching and holding, a fugitive could be given sanctuary within. From the 11th century the manor of Brent belonged to Buckfast Abbey, and at the Dissolution was bought by Sir William Petre. There was a Domesday manor at Harbourneford, a hamlet to the north-east on the old road to Dean and Buckfastleigh; although the Harbourne is now carried in a culvert under the road a small 4-arched clapper bridge remains from the time when it served as an essential footbridge. At Shipley Bridge, to the north, on the west side of the Avon are the remains of a building used in the production of naphtha from peat in the mid 19th century, and later as part of a clay treatment plant, further evidence of which can be seen on the hillside. There were mills on the Avon, just south of the village, and also, upstream, Lydia Mill, which was owned by the family of the Dartmoor writer William Crossing, who lived there in his early days.

SOUTH HUISH (E11) South Hams Pop. 560 (1901: 227)

South Huish is situated on the English Channel coast 4 miles SW of Kingsbridge and approached by minor roads from the A 381. Land rises to 376 ft in the south-east. On the short length of coastline at Hope Cove is the small village of Outer Hope, while adjoining, to the south and in Malborough parish, is Inner Hope. Hope has been a fishing village for centuries, in the past having facilities for storing and smoking fish. It was also doubtless a place for smugglers.

Ruins of South Huish's 13th-century church, replaced by a new Holy Trinity Church in Galmpton village in 1866–7.

The parish's main village is Galmpton, situated centrally. South Huish's early 13th-century church had fallen into disrepair by the mid 19th century and is now a ruin. It was replaced by a new church (Holy Trinity) built in Early English style at Galmpton in 1866–7. The buttressed tower has a pyramid cap. The 14th-century font and four bells from the former church were brought here. There is also the tiny church of St Clement at Hope Cove, which was originally the village school. The parish, and the two churches, are united ecclesiastically with Malborough.

Further reading: Le Cheminant, Richard, *Hope Cove, the history of a Devon fishing village*, 1999
Local society: Hope Archive Group

The beach at Hope Cove is in South Huish parish.

SOUTHLEIGH (L6) East Devon Pop. 193 (1901: 157)

Southleigh, 5½ miles SSE of Honiton and 2½ miles WSW of Colyton, is watered by a tributary of the River Coly, flowing through a deep partially wooded valley along the parish's south-eastern boundary where land reaches 589 ft. Towards the west levels rise to over 700 ft. The village, in the valley, is reached by minor roads, most nearly from the A 3052 Sidmouth-Lyme Regis road.

The church (St Lawrence) dates possibly from the 13th century, enlarged and partially rebuilt in the 19th century. An earlier house at Wiscombe belonged in the 13th century to the Bonvills. It was replaced by a new one in 1826. South of it is Blackbury Castle, a substantial Iron Age hill fort.

SOUTH MILTON (F11) South Hams Pop. 408 (1901: 287)

South Milton, 2½ miles WSW of Kingsbridge, and approached by a minor road from the A 381, stretches inland from a short western coastal boundary. Reaching 300 ft towards the village in the east, land on the seaward side is low-lying, forming, on the outflow of a small stream, large reed-beds that provide a habitat for many species of wild birds and are managed by Devon Birdwatching and Preservation Society. There is also a sandy beach.

The church (All Saints) dates from the 12th century, enlarged in the 13th and 14th centuries. The font is Norman and there is a Norman doorway. The 15th-century screen has been restored to reveal the original colouring.

SOUTH MOLTON (F3) North Devon Pop. 4093 (1901: 2892)

The parish of South Molton is bounded by the River Bray on the west, and by the River Mole on the east and for a short length on the south-west before the Bray-Mole confluence. The town stands towards the east, at higher level and half a mile from Mole Bridge over the river. With its broad main street and square South Molton is a busy market town and a trading and business centre for the wide surrounding area.

The town is located at the hub of several roads; the old A 361 from Barnstaple to Taunton passes through, and the B 3227 from Torrington, the B 3226 from Exeter, the B 3137 from Tiverton, and the unclassified road from North Molton and Exmoor, all converge here. Now, since the 1980s, South Molton has been bypassed on the north by the new A 361 – the North Devon Link road. From 1873 the town was also served by railway from Taunton to Barnstaple, and the onward connections this enabled, but the line was closed in 1966. The station, a mile north of the town, developed a much-used goods yard.

South Molton was in existence in the Saxon era, and there was a church here by the time of Domesday. Parts of the present large and beautiful church (St Mary Magdalene) are c.800 years old, the rest dates from the 15th century, enlarged in 1825, and the nave heightened in 1865 with a clerestory. Both the fine stone pulpit, which has figures of saints, and the font are from the 15th century. Spiral stairs remain from the rood screen, removed in 1757. There are no fewer than 18 stained-glass windows. North and South Aller, Blackpool, Bremridge, and Hacche were Domesday manors, and there are several other ancient farms. The parish also includes, in the west, the hamlets of Shallowford, Stags Head and Clapworthy Mill. South Molton was incorporated as a borough in 1590 and the charter was renewed in 1684.

The town was important in the woollen industry from medieval times up to the late 18th century, and subsequently to a lesser extent until c.1900. The former Mole woollen mill stands ½ mile E of the town on the W bank of the river, N of the B 3227. The town's former corn mill (earlier also wool) is on the opposite side of the road and river, and is actually in Bishops Nympton parish. The town also had a substantial tannery.

Further reading: Edmunds, Jonathon, *The book of South Molton*, Halsgrove, 2002
Local society: South Molton & District Archive and Local History Society
Museum: South Molton Museum, Guildhall, Market Street

SOUTH POOL (F11) South Hams Pop. 152 (1901: 296)

South Pool parish lies around the meandering creeks of the east side of the Kingsbridge estuary. The south shore of Frogmore Creek, in the north, falls within the parish, which then includes a shore of the main estuary before turning back inland to include the north and inner parts of Southpool Creek. Land rises to 284 ft just north of the village. The village lies 3 miles SE of Kingsbridge and access is from the A 379 Kingsbridge-Dartmouth road 1½ miles to the north.

The slate-built church (St Nicholas and St Cyriac) is of ancient foundation, dedicated after rebuilding by Bishop Stapledon in 1318. Much of the present structure dates from the 15th century, with careful restoration in the 19th century. The font is Norman and there is a very fine carved rood screen of c.1480.

Further reading: Shepherd, Doreen, *South Pool in the mid 20th century*, 1997

SOUTH TAWTON (E6) West Devon Pop. 1231 (1901: 1079)

South Tawton is a large parish, bordering the north of Dartmoor, with the village roughly 4 miles E of Okehampton. It is a parish of high ground, rising from 400 ft in the north to 1799 ft at Cosdon Beacon on the moor. The border on the west is defined by the River Taw, in the south by the Blackaton Brook, and by the Yeo in the northern length of the eastern border.

South Tawton has a long history of human habitation. Evidence of Bronze Age activity is provided by various remains around Cosdon on South Tawton Common in the form of hut settlements, cairns, stone rows and other features. Having been in royal possession since before the Norman Conquest, Tauetona, as it was then known, appeared in Domesday as a manor held by the king. Probably from the 13th century the upper Taw valley was worked for tin, and farming increased on the lower ground.

South Tawton Church House. COURTESY THE BOOK OF SOUTH TAWTON & SOUTH ZEAL WITH STICKLEPATH

Records indicate that South Tawton had a church by the 14th century; the present fine building (St Andrew), in the village, dates from the 15th century, and the Church House beside it from c.1500. The parish also has several fine ancient houses, including the 15th-century Wickington near Taw Green, North Wyke which dates from the 15th and 16th centuries (now a grassland and environmental research station) and West Week dated 1656. Oxenham, built in 1714, replaced the earlier home of the Oxenham family who dwelt here from the 16th to the 18th century.

The parish also includes the village of South Zeal, anciently a borough with a market and two fairs granted in 1298, through which passed the original road westwards. Viewed from above, the layout of 13th-century burgage plots at the rear of houses lining the street is clearly seen. The church (St Mary) which is united with that of South Tawton, was an ancient chapel, rebuilt in the 18th century, and restored in 1877. The inn, the Oxenham Arms, is built of granite and dates from the early 16th century.

Hamlets in the parish include Itton and Taw Green in the north, and Whiddon Down, Gooseford, Addiscott, and Ramsley in the south. Ramsley was the scene of one of South Tawton's mines; copper was worked here from about 1850–80 and again in the early 20th century up to 1909. The remains of its old chimney stack surmount the hill. The large limestone quarry just north of South Tawton village closed in the early 20th century, it is now partly wooded.

Traffic through South Zeal became reduced when the Okehampton Turnpike Trust, formed in 1760, built a new main road to the south. Even this became inadequate with the enormous growth of traffic and further relief for both road travellers and local residents came in the 1980s with the construction of the dual carriageway A 30, which passes immediately north of South Tawton village, touching the old quarry area.

Further reading: Radford, Roy and Ursula, *South Tawton and South Zeal with Sticklepath*, Halsgrove, 2000

SOUTH ZEAL see SOUTH TAWTON

SOWTON (H6) East Devon Pop. 639 (1901: 374)

Sowton is a low-lying parish directly E of Exeter, through which flows the River Clyst on its southward route to join the Exe. The parish is now completely dominated by major transport developments and other concomitants. The M5 motorway passes through from north to south, the modern A 30 road has a junction with the M5 at the northern border, and the complex Sandy Gate roundabout, junction with the A 3052 Lyme Regis road (and its connected routes) and one into Exeter city centre, as well as to the Sowton services stop-off, are in the south. The Waterloo-Exeter railway line also passes through the north, and aircraft landing and taking off from nearby Exeter

International Airport fly overhead. Sowton village, although trapped roughly in the centre, is however by no means overcome by its position. Protected perhaps by its now limited and somewhat difficult access, it retains a sense of quietness and remoteness, with buildings of character.

The church (St Michael & All Angels) dates from the 14th century, rebuilt in 1845 in Perpendicular style. Bishops Court, anciently called Clyst House, was a palace of the bishops of Exeter, dating from the 13th century. The estate was bought by Bishop Bronescombe who built the palace and a chapel. Altered in later years it is now privately owned. Men of Fairfax's army were garrisoned in the parish during the blockade of Exeter in the Civil War.

SPARKWELL (D10) South Hams Pop. 1246

Sparkwell, 7 miles E of Plymouth, has been a civil parish only since 1974, having previously been part of Plympton St Mary which is now within Plymouth Unitary Authority. It is a fairly large parish extending north to boundaries with Shaugh Prior and Cornwood, with moorland areas of clay working, and altitudes rising to over 700 ft. There is pleasant country around the village, while farther south modern developments have brought changes in recent years including new roads and the Langage industrial estate, construction of the modern A 38 expressway which passes through the south having been a contributory factor. The main line railway also passes through, south of the village.

Aerial view of Sparkwell. COURTESY THE BOOK OF SPARKWELL

The village of Lee Mill, on the River Yealm in the south-east, is included (although not the Lee Mill industrial estate and nearby superstore which are in Ermington). Lee Mill has existed from an early date and from 1833 was the site of a paper mill until its destruction by fire in 1908. Also within the parish is the hamlet of Hemerdon on the west. In the past there was clay working just to the north on Hemerdon Ball, and also mining for tin during the 19th century. The tungsten mineral wolfram was worked in a mine at Hemerdon Ball during the two World Wars.

Formerly Sparkwell was also part of Plympton St Mary ecclesiastically. In the 1850s an Anglican chapel was built in the village, which in 1884 became a parish church (All Saints) in its own right. The building was extended and restored in 1908.

Further reading: James, Pam, *The book of Sparkwell with Hemerdon and Lee Mill*, Halsgrove, 2001

SPREYTON (E6) West Devon Pop. 295 (1901: 360)

The parish of Spreyton consists of rising land with the village at 735 ft. Situated 7 miles E of Okehampton it is served by a minor road which connects Bow on the A 3072 with Whiddon Down on the A 30. It is pleasantly rural, with many farms. The River Yeo forms part of the western boundary and a tributary that on the east. The village is located roughly in the centre.

The manor of Spreyton was held originally by Exeter's monastery of St Andrew at Cowick. There was a church on the site in the 14th century but its actual date is not known. It is unlikely that any of the early structure remains in the present church (St Michael) although the two fonts are believed to have come from it. The tower is thought to be later. In 1922 the south wall had become dangerous and was restored by local craftsmen using Spreyton stone. During the work a Norman piscina was found. The altar is of granite. The rood screen was removed in 1760, its staircase was discovered in 1914. The pulpit dates from 1728.

The church path is bordered by an avenue of lime trees planted in 1856, at the same time as a yew tree. Also in the churchyard is the large hollow trunk of an ancient oak, which is reputed to mark the centre of Devon. Both Exmoor and Dartmoor and the towers of 24 other churches could be seen from Spreyton church tower before the growth of surrounding trees.

Spreyton was the home, and the churchyard the burial place, of the yeoman Tom Cobley, who with his friends in the well-known song rode the grey mare to Widecombe Fair.

Brunel's atmospheric pumping station at Starcross stands adjacent to the main railway and the Exe estuary (right).

STARCROSS (H7) Teignbridge Pop. 1780

The parish of Starcross, 8 miles SSE of Exeter, was formerly within Kenton parish. Bordered on the east by the Exe estuary, the land is low-lying, just rising at one point to 300 ft. The A 379 Exeter-Dawlish road passes through the village, which is adjacent to the shoreline, and there is a minor road eastwards over Haldon that connects with the A 380. In the village is the church (St Paul), built in 1826. It is a fairly large building with a gallery, and a bell, but no tower. Mowlish Farm, in the east, was mentioned in Domesday, and Cofford, in the south, was named in a charter dated 1044.

For centuries Starcross has shared with other places along the coast a strong fishing tradition, and this was also a place where fish could be stored in cellars. The village was put truly on the map in 1846 when Brunel's South Devon Railway (the broad gauge) came through, following the coastline. Initially trains on this stretch of line were propelled by atmospheric power, which involved a series of stationary engines connected to an iron pipe that was set between rails. Along the top of the pipe ran a slot with a flap cover which, when partially raised, enabled a rod from the train's leading carriage to connect with an elongated piston within the pipe. The vacuum created by the pumping engine, which caused heavier air pressure behind the piston provided the motive power. Sadly the system was not totally successful and was shortly abandoned in favour of steam locomotives. A surviving atmospheric pumping station still stands prominently at Starcross, close to the continuing main line railway; a Grade I listed building it is now the headquarters of Starcross Fishing and Sailing Club.

STAVERTON (F9) South Hams Pop. 717 (1901: 663)

The parish of Staverton is situated north-east of the River Dart and extends from the outskirts of Ashburton in the north-west nearly to Totnes in the south-east. Almost all the boundaries are marked by rivers: the Ashburn and the Dart on the west and south, and the Hems along the north-east. Only the short south-east boundary with Littlehempston is across land. The terrain is hilly, rising fairly steeply from the rivers to rounded hills of 400-500 ft, and attaining 620 ft at Halsworthy in the north-west. At the foot of this hill, at Pridhamsleigh, there are limestone caves.

Staverton Bridge across the Dart dates from 1413.

The A 38 expressway runs along the north-west boundary, with the A 384 for Totnes branching from it at Dart Bridge near Buckfastleigh. East and north of these the parish is served by a network of minor roads. Staverton village is in the south, close to the Dart which is crossed here by Staverton Bridge, dating from 1413. Woolston Green and Landscove are hamlets on the unclassified Staverton-Ashburton road. The medieval Austin's Bridge, in the south-west, carries a minor road across the Dart to Buckfastleigh.

The Totnes-Buckfastleigh railway line runs close to the Dart and in Staverton parish for most of its way. Opened in 1872 as a branch from Totnes to Buckfastleigh and Ashburton, it was closed to passengers in 1958 and for goods in 1962, but was later bought by the Dart Valley Light Railway Company and developed as a tourist attraction. It is leased to the South Devon Railway and steam trains are run during the season, with an intermediate station at Staverton.

The church (St Paul de Leon) is peaceful, grand and lovely. It dates from the 13th century, and the tower is of that time, most of the church having been rebuilt in the 14th century. There is a fine rood screen. Landscove, with its church (St Matthew) is a separate ecclesiastical parish within the civil parish of Staverton.

Further reading: Lavis, Pete, *The book of Staverton*, Halsgrove, 2002

STICKLEPATH (E6) West Devon Pop. 405

Until 1987 Sticklepath came within the parish of Sampford Courtenay, but then, in order to take account of certain new developments and to make for a more logical arrangement, Sticklepath was made an autonomous small parish. This was achieved by taking in a tiny piece of Belstone parish at Sticklepath's west end, and the area covered by just a few houses at the east end, and also by including in Sticklepath the extremity of Sampford Courtenay lying south of the modern A 30 dual carriageway road. Located 3 miles ESE of Okehampton, Sticklepath stands on the old A 30 where, as traffic increased, conditions became more and more disturbing and hazardous for local residents, especially at summer weekends and with heavy vehicles rumbling past within inches of house doors. Construction of the new road in the 1980s, which by passed the village on the north, came therefore as a considerable relief.

The origin of the village possibly dates from 1146 when, it is believed, a chantry chapel was established here, the siting of which is not precisely known. Certainly early inhabitants made use of the power afforded by the tumbling River Taw beside which the village stands, with mills built for various purposes. Western and Carnalls Mills, at the east end of the village street, were for corn, and for bone grinding, threshing, reed-combing, and winnowing. At the west end, near the road to Belstone, was Cleave Mill, at times a corn mill but also, from 1810–40, a woollen serge mill; modern apartments now occupy the site. A little downstream were the manor mills, one section of which was a corn mill and the other for woollen cloth. In 1814 a Mr Finch occupied the cloth mill and adapted it for the working of metal and making of tools for agriculture and the china clay industry. The trade flourished and continued in the Finch family until 1960 when the business closed and the mill became derelict. Due to family and other interests a programme of restoration ensued under a charitable trust. Subsequently the Finch Foundry was opened to the public and is now run by the National Trust. Visitors can see the working area and three restored waterwheels, and examples of the wide range of tools formerly made.

Ecclesiastically Sticklepath is in Belstone parish but has its own Anglican St Marys Chapel on the south side of the village street. The Methodist Chapel stands nearby. Quakers established a presence here in the 17th century, and their burial ground which in the 19th century became non-denominational is behind the Finch Foundry near the river.

Sticklepath Methodist Chapel. COURTESY THE BOOK OF SOUTH TAWTON AND SOUTH ZEAL WITH STICKLEPATH

Further reading: Radford, Roy and Ursula, *South Tawton and South Zeal with Sticklepath*, Halsgrove, 2000
Sticklepath Women's Institute, *The story of Sticklepath*, 1993

STOCKLAND (L5) East Devon Pop. 655 (1901: 772)

The parish of Stockland was transferred from Dorset to Devon in 1842. Squarish in outline, it is bounded on the east by the River Yarty, tributary of the Axe, and on the west by the Umborne Brook, tributary of the Coly. Between them the land rises dramatically in a series of hills, reaching in places 700-800 ft. Such is the suitability of the terrain that a site at 750 ft close to the straight north-south Stockland Hill road along the west was chosen for the Stockland radio and television transmitting station, opened in 1961. The area has, however, been a scene of human activity from far earlier times. Archaeologists have detected evidence of Mesolithic workings, while more prominent features – both in the south-west of the parish – are likely to date from the 1st millennium BC. These are Stockland Great Camp at 666 ft, an irregularly shaped enclosure partly bordered by bushy hedges, and Stockland Little Camp at c.550 ft, which is circular. Both are typical of Iron Age sites. Aerial photography has also shown two types of land enclosure – irregular fields of early origin, and regularly rectangular ones from parliamentary enclosure in the 1860s.

Access to the village, which lies 6 miles NE of Honiton and 5 miles NW of Axminster, is by minor roads from either the A 30 in the north or the A 35 in the south. The church (St Michael & All Angels) dates from the 14th century, with 15th-century alterations and enlargement. It stands at the end of a short narrow lane from the village centre, with no proper vehicle turning space at the end. Walking to it is therefore recommended!

STOCKLEIGH ENGLISH (G5) Mid Devon Pop. 63 (1901: 56)

Stockleigh English, located on minor roads 4 miles NNE of Crediton, is bounded on the west by the Binneford Water which becomes the River Creedy, and on the east by the

Seen from the Raddon Hills, lands of Stockleigh Pomeroy, and far beyond.

Holly Water, a Creedy tributary. The undulating land rises in the north to 553 ft.
The church (St Mary the Virgin) dates from the 15th century, restored c.1880. Stockleigh Court was the home, from the 16th century, of the Bellew family.

STOCKLEIGH POMEROY (G5) Mid Devon Pop. 121 (1901: 164)

Stockleigh Pomeroy is located 4 miles NE of Crediton and 7 miles SW of Tiverton on the A 3072 road which connects the two towns, with the village just off the road, to the east. Set around the waters of the stream known as Shobrooke Lake (lake is an old Devon word for stream), the scene is a combination of green valleys and steep hillsides. The land rises to over 700 ft on the Raddon Hills in the south-east, and to 818 ft at the northern boundary point with Cadbury.
The church (St Mary the Virgin) is of Norman origin, of which a doorway remains from the 15th-century rebuilding, and there was further reconstruction in the 1840s.

STOKE CANON (H6) East Devon Pop. 660 (1901: 383)

Stoke Canon, 4 miles NE of the centre of Exeter, lies close to the confluence of the Rivers Exe and Culm, and being low-lying is at times subject to flooding. The Exeter-Tiverton road (A 396), which runs through the village, crosses the two channels of the Culm by a causeway, the original bridge having been built in the 13th century. The main London-Taunton-Exeter railway passes just west. From 1885 connection was made here with the Exe Valley line to Tiverton and Morebath Junction, but this closed in 1963.
The church (St Mary Magdalen) is of early origin. It was totally rebuilt in 1836 except for the tower. It has a Norman font.

Further reading: Piper, G, and Piper, J, *Stoke Canon, a short history*, 1985
Local society: The Five Parishes Local History Society

STOKE FLEMING (G11) South Hams Pop. 1012 (1901: 708)

Stoke Fleming is situated adjacent to Dartmouth and west along the rocky and beautiful South Devon coast. The A 379 coastal road from Torcross to Dartmouth passes through. Around the village and to the north land rises steeply, reaching 600 ft in the north-west. The earthwork called Woodbury Camp in the north is probably of Iron Age origin. The parish owes its name to the Flemings, who were early inheritors of the manor.
The church (St Peter) originates from the 13th century and is recorded as having a rector in 1272. The building was enlarged in the 14th century with red sandstone arches standing on blue Purbeck stone piers. There is a Norman font. Major restoration was carried out in 1871–2 and re-ordering in 1991.

STOKE GABRIEL (G 10) South Hams Pop. 1205 (1901: 718)

Stoke Gabriel is a pleasant parish on the north-east bank of the River Dart in its meandering tidal stage, 2-5 miles downstream from Totnes. Land rises fairly steeply to rounded hills, reaching 539 ft on the northern boundary. The village is located in the south, on the shores of a creek which, partly dammed by a causeway, provided a pool which powered waterwheels of an ancient tidemill. The pool is now a delightful feature and the creek a haven for boats.
With Stoke being an Anglo-Saxon word meaning holy place it is possible that some kind of church existed here at an early date. Stoke Gabriel was listed as having a church at the time of Domesday. Also at that time reference was made to a yew tree outside the church, several hundred years old. The impressive yew tree seen in the churchyard today has been expertly estimated as being in existence from 1200 to 1500 years.
The present church building (St Gabriel) originates from the 13th century and retains the tower of that date. It was largely reconstructed in the 15th century, and

Stoke Gabriel stands in a delightful situation on a creek of the River Dart.

subsequently altered and restored. The 15th-century rood screen spans the nave and side aisles and the pulpit is of the same century. There is also a small church at Waddeton, on the east. This is in the vicinity of Waddeton Court, built in the early 19th century in Elizabethan style close to the site of its medieval predecessor. Sandridge, a little to the west, is the site of another mansion, dating from the 12th century and replaced by one built in Italian style by John Nash in 1805.

Excavations carried out in 1955 at Lower Well Farm, east of the village, revealed evidence of a farm dating from the Romano-British period, with remains of a farmhouse, surrounding ditch, and banks edging small fields.

Quarries in the east, beside Galmpton Creek, provided the red sandstone for Totnes church's tower.

Further reading: Birch, Sally, and others, *Stoke Gabriel*, 1991

STOKEINTEIGNHEAD (G9) Teignbridge Pop. 707 (1901: 614)

The parish of Stokeinteignhead is located south of the Teign estuary, and includes a short length of the waterfront in the north. The village is situated 4 miles N of Torquay, a mile inland from the coast, at the head of a valley. All around are hills which rise to 500 ft on the south.

The church (St Andrew) dates from the 14th century, the high altar dedicated by Bishop Grandisson in 1336. It was enlarged in the 15th century. Particularly notable are the capitals of the arcade, sculptured in Beer stone.

Fishing was important in past days; in the 16th century men from Stokeinteignhead worked the seas all along England's south and east coasts.

One of the sculptured Beer stone arcade capitals in Stokeinteignhead's St Andrew's Church.

STOKENHAM (G11) South Hams Pop. 1949 (1901: 1403)

Stokenham parish is situated on the South Devon coast, with a long eastern boundary following the coastline, which includes Start Point with its lighthouse built in 1836. Also within Stokenham, in the north, is the larger part of Slapton Ley, a freshwater lake separated from the sea by a raised beach of shingle and sand. The Ley provides a unique haven for birds and other wildlife and is a National Nature Reserve. Included also are the village of Chillington on the Kingsbridge-Dartmouth road, the hamlets of Beeson and Kellaton farther south, and at the south end of the Ley, the village of Torcross, also on the A 379. This low-lying stretch of Start Bay, which is very attractive, is vulnerable to encroachment by the sea when easterly storms coincide with high tides.

Stokenham has a long history of fishing, with manorial records that date from the 14th century, when mullet was a particularly sought-after catch. (See Fox, Harold,

An American Sherman tank that sank offshore in wartime operations and was recovered and restored in 1984 is kept on view in Torcross car park.

The inscription beside the tank.

The evolution of the fishing village, landscape and society along the south Devon coast, 1086–1550, Leopards House Press, 2001.) Fishing was also important at two other points on the coast: Hallsands and Beesands, where there were storage facilities known as cellars. Hallsands suffered a tragedy in 1917 when the hamlet was virtually swept away by the sea, caused by off-shore dredging which had weakened the protective pebble beach. (See Melia, Steve, *Hallsands – a village betrayed,* Forest, 2002.) Beesands sustained attack of a different kind during the Second World War when bombed from the air, which caused loss of life and property damage.

The village stands on rising ground, a mile or so inland from Torcross and the sea. The church (St Michael & All Angels) is believed to have originated in the 12th century, possibly established due to the proximity of a holy well. The present building dates from the 15th century with arcades of Beer stone and a 16th-century rood screen that extends across the church's width. Restoration was carried out in 1874 and 1890. There is a granite Norman font. There is also the church of St Andrew at Beesands, and the ecclesiastically united church of St Martin at Sherford.

Stokenham was one of the South Hams parishes that were evacuated of their inhabitants between December 1943 and late 1944 to enable allied forces to carry out exercises in preparation for the D-Day landings in Europe. This is marked by a memorial on Slapton beach. Some damage was caused to Stokenham church.

In the car park at Torcross is a restored Sherman DD tank that belonged to A Company, 70th Tank Battalion, US Army, that sank in 85 ft of water offshore during the wartime operations. It was recovered in 1984, given protective treatment, and placed in position as a monument.

Further reading: Rose-Price, Robin, *400 years in Torcross: a pictorial history*, Orchard, 2002

STOKE RIVERS (E2) North Devon Pop. 156 (1901: 174)

Located 5 miles ENE of Barnstaple, the parish of Stoke Rivers, in the Exmoor foothills, is bounded on north and south by tributaries of the River Yeo, while the eastern boundary runs over land. The small village is approached by unclassified roads from the Barnstaple-Bratton Fleming road, on the west, and the A 399 on the east.

The church (St Bartholomew) dates from the 15th century, with 19th-century rebuilding. Stoke, or Beara Castle, on the road east of the village was a small hill fort.

STOODLEIGH (H4) Mid Devon Pop. 298 (1901: 381)

St Margaret's Church, Stoodleigh, stands high above the Exe valley.

Stoodleigh, 4½ miles WNW of Tiverton, is a beautiful parish of hills, woods and streams. From its border with the River Exe on the north-east, and its northern boundary marked by the Iron Mill Stream, the land rises fairly steeply to levels of from 600-900 ft, and to 987 ft at Stoodleigh Beacon on the west.

The church (St Margaret) dates from the 15th century. Stoodleigh itself, and in the west Warbrightsleigh, West Whitnole, and Rifton were all Domesday estates.

STOWFORD (C7) West Devon Pop. 282 (1901: 323)

Situated 12 miles SW of Okehampton, between the old and modern A 30 roads, Stowford includes the hamlets of Sprytown and Portgate. The River Thrushel flows through the parish to join the Wolf, which forms the boundary on the west.

The church (St John) is of ancient foundation with rectors recorded from 1264. The oldest part of the present building – the east end of the nave and south aisle chapel – are of 14th-century construction. Other parts date from the 15th century with 16th-century alterations. The north aisle was added in 1874 when the whole building was very well restored by Sir Gilbert Scott. The altar inclines slightly to the south. The font is large and ancient. The roofs are adorned with carved faces, and the roof of the porch also has carvings. There is a sundial on the wall above the south entrance. On the right side of the churchyard gate, as one enters, under a chestnut tree is an ancient Ogham stone bearing a name which it appears may be GUNGLEI. One of just a few in Devon, it is believed to have marked an early Christian grave.

Hayne was the seat of the Harris family from the time of Henry VIII until 1864. The house was rebuilt by Wyatville in 1810 and has since been further restored by the present owners. Milford and Sprytown were Domesday manors. Milford is now the site of Dingles Steam Village, a collection of retired steam-powered vehicles.

The Ogham stone at Stowford which stands beside the church gate.

STRETE (G11) South Hams Pop. 520

Formerly part of Blackawton, Strete is a small coastal parish on the shores of the English Channel coast, with pleasant small coves and beaches. The stream called the Gara defines the boundary on the west and land rises steeply to 472 ft north of the village. The A 379 coastal road from Torcross to Dartmouth passes through. Strete with its church of St Michael, built in 1836, was made a separate ecclesiastical parish in 1881.

Strete was one of a group of South Hams parishes that were evacuated of their inhabitants between December 1943 and late 1944 to enable allied forces to carry out exercises in preparation for the D-Day landings in Europe. People had just a month to remove from their homes and farms.

Local society: Blackawton and Strete History Group

SUTCOMBE (B4) Torridge Pop. 299 (1901: 351)

Sutcombe is located 5½ miles N of Holsworthy, to the west of the Holsworthy-Bideford road (A 388). The River Waldon forms the north-western boundary which then extends south of the river, up a tributary and over land almost to Holsworthy Beacon. The line then proceeds northwards along tributaries south and north of the Waldon which flows south-eastwards through the centre of the parish. The northern boundary is across land.

The village is pleasant. There was a church here in the 12th century, of which a doorway remains. The present building (St Andrew) dates from the late 15th and early 16th centuries. The arcades are of granite and steps on the north side led to the former rood loft; only a partial screen remains. The pulpit is Jacobean, and the font is of granite. The 16th-century bench ends are finely carved; seating in the sanctuary is unusually arranged, set at right angles on either side of the aisle.

Thuborough, in the south of the parish, was a Domesday estate.

SWIMBRIDGE (E3) North Devon Pop. 1327 (1901: 1106)

Swimbridge, 4 miles SE of Barnstaple, stands on the old main road from Barnstaple to South Molton; there was a bridge over the stream that flows through the village from the time of Domesday. There is still an ancient packhorse bridge of uncertain date, upstream of the modern road bridge. The stream was evidently also forded here in the past and the site appears a possible place for sheepwashing. The village is quieter since the A 361 North Devon Link road was constructed in the 1980s, passing just north of the village. The land is undulating and rises to over 700 ft in the north.

The church (St James) was largely reconstructed in the 15th century, but the tower and lead-covered spire remain from the early 14th-century building. There is a late 15th-century carved stone pulpit and a fine rood screen of similar date. The carved font has a tall and most unusual carved wood cover, with tester and canopy, dating from the early 16th century. Incumbents date from 1443. They include the notable 19th-century Parson Jack Russell – incumbent here for 48 years – the hunting parson whose interest in dogs established the Jack Russell strain of terriers. He died in 1883 and is buried in the churchyard. There is also the Anglican chapel of the Holy Name at Gunn, in the north of the parish.

Besides Gunn (on the road east from Goodleigh), Cobbaton and Stowford are hamlets in the south. Stowford, March, and Hearson were former mansions, and Ernesborough (near the Hawkridge Brook which forms the parish's eastern boundary) was an ancient freehold estate recorded in 1175.

Swimbridge was long famed for the growing of large luscious cherries call mazards. Up to the 1930s consignments were sent in the season to London from five orchards. There was also a tannery which employed 60 people and in wartime produced leather soles for army boots.

SYDENHAM DAMEREL (C8) West Devon Pop. 259 (1901: 312)

The ancient Horse Bridge carries a minor road over the Tamar from Sydenham Damerel to Cornwall (left).

Sydenham Damerel, 4½ miles NW of Tavistock, is set in undulating country running down to the River Tamar which, with a tributary, forms the boundary on the west. The parish lands extend northwards to just beyond the Tavistock-Launceston road (B 3662).

An old route from Milton Abbot to Stoke Climsland in Cornwall passed through the parish crossing the Tamar at the hamlet of Horsebridge. The seven-span Horse Bridge probably originated at least as early as the 14th century; there are records of it being repaired or altered in 1437. It apparently suffered during the Civil War and was said to have been broken down in 1649. The bridge still carries the minor road.

The church (St Mary) is of 15th-century construction. It was badly damaged by fire in the mid 20th century but successfully restored. Ecclesiastically the parish is united with Lamerton.

TALATON (J6) East Devon Pop. 519 (1901: 415)

Talaton, 10 miles NE of Exeter and 6 miles W of Honiton, is bounded on the east by the River Tale, tributary of the Otter. The old A 30 road forms the southern boundary, with the modern A 30 running just north of it, within the parish. Most of the land is at 200-400 ft.

The church (St James the Apostle) was rebuilt, except for the tower, porch, east wall, and vestry, in 1859–60. The old roof was replaced and there is an oak screen.

Escot was first recorded in 1227. It is the site of a mansion built for Sir Walter Yonge in the 1680s in parkland of 4000 acres. In 1794 it was bought from Sir John Yonge, MP for Honiton, by Sir John Kennaway, the first baronet, after distinguished service in India. The house was destroyed by fire in 1808 and not rebuilt until c.1838, by the succeeding second Sir John. He also built the church of St Philip and St James at the southern end of the park where it became, in 1844, a separate small ecclesiastical parish, as it remains. The present Sir John Kennaway has created Escot Aqueculture as an attraction to help finance the restoration of the estate.

Westcott, Talewater, Larkbeare, and Fairmile are hamlets in the parish. The main railway from Waterloo to Exeter passes through the parish, just south of the village.

Further reading: Greenaway, Winifred O., 'The Kennaways of Escot' in *The Devon Historian 46*, April 1993

TAMERTON FOLIOT (C9) Plymouth Unitary Authority (Pop. 1901: 1102)

Located in the NW of the Plymouth area, Tamerton Foliot is of ancient origin, known to Celtic saints who apparently landed here in the 6th century. Foliot in the name was that of the family who held the manor in the 12th and 13th centuries. The large village is located at the head of the creek from the Tamar known as Tamerton Lake and is within the Plymouth Authority's Southway ward, bordering the South Hams parish of Bickleigh. Formerly Tamerton extended northwards, bordered by the River Tavy, but under boundary changes of 1974 this rural area was absorbed into Bickleigh parish.

The church (St Mary) dates from the 13th century, dedicated by Bishop Stapledon in 1318. The present building is of mainly 15th-century construction, with later rebuilding. The ecclesiastical parish does not follow the same borders as the civil ward, and Southway also has its church of The Holy Spirit.

Formerly a parish of many farms and market gardens, Tamerton Foliot is now very much a Plymouth suburb with the considerable development of Southway.

TAVISTOCK (C8) West Devon Pop. 11,018 (1901: 5841)

Standing on the banks of the River Tavy as it flows westwards from Dartmoor to join the Tamar, Tavistock has long supported human habitation. Possibly in the 8th century the Saxons established a settlement or stoc beside the river. Even before that a Celtic settlement existed on the hillside a mile north-east of the present town, where an irregular earthworks called the Trendle, that has yielded bronze tools and ornaments, can still be seen. Possibly also dating from pre-Saxon times are three inscribed stones, now in the Vicarage garden, one of which was discovered in Tavistock and the other two moved here from Buckland Monachorum.

In the late 10th century, as part of plans by the Saxon King Edgar to establish a series of Benedictine monasteries, the building of Tavistock Abbey was begun by Ordulf, the king's brother-in-law, in 974, and dedicated to Our Lady and the Cornish St Rumon. In 997 the initial structure – probably of wood – was burnt down by marauding Danes. Soon, rebuilt and richly endowed, the abbey prospered and continued as a benevolent influence until the Dissolution of the Monasteries in 1539. Following the Dissolution the site of the abbey and its lands and possessions were granted to John Russell, whose successors, the earls and dukes of Bedford held sway until the early 20th century. Although the main abbey structures were dismantled after the Dissolution, several of its features remain. They include a section of cloister wall in the churchyard, the court gate on the east side of Bedford Square, the now-named Abbey Chapel, and the ruin of the west gatehouse (known as 'Betsy Grimbal's tower').

Boehm's statue of Tavistock-born Sir Francis Drake, dated 1883.

There had been a small chapel dedicated to St Matthew in the town from Saxon times, but by 1200 the population had grown. Building of the parish church for the townspeople was begun, adjacent to the abbey church, in the early 13th century. It was reconstructed and enlarged in the early 14th century, and dedicated to St Eustachius, a Roman army officer who was converted to Christianity and martyred for his faith. The base of the tower and much of the walls date from this time. Major reconstruction was carried out in the second quarter of the 15th century, with the additional south aisle – the Clothworkers – added in 1445.

Tavistock is noted for its connection with Sir Francis Drake who was born at Crowndale, in a house no longer existing. His statue by Boehm, dating from 1883, stands at the west end of Plymouth Road.

With development of tin-working on Dartmoor, in 1305 Tavistock was designated one of the Stannary Towns to which tin smelted on the moor had to be brought during special sessions for coining and the paying of dues to the Crown. Later, the mining of copper on Bedford-owned land had profound effects upon the town. Following discovery of substantial copper deposits on the duke's land at Blanchdown near the Tamar in 1844, great profits were made. In 1850 Devon Great Consols Mine supplied a third, and later half the world's copper. The 7th Duke of Bedford (whose statue stands in Bedford Square) used proceeds to build model cottages for workers, an Anglican church in Italian style at Fitzford (now the church of the Roman Catholics) and for re-shaping the centre of the town. Much use was made of the greenish-grey Hurdwick stone, a volcanic ash quarried north of the town (Lamerton parish) which had been worked from abbey days.

Shillamill viaduct of the former Southern Railway still provides an outstanding feature between Tavistock and Bere Alston.

Tavistock had its woollen industry, which peaked here around 1500. Earlier produced cloths, which used mixed wools and were somewhat rough, were known as 'Tavistocks'; later finer kerseys were made. Foundries were developed in the 19th century to cater for the demands of mining and farming.

The 4-mile Tavistock Canal, from the Tavy at Abbey Bridge to Morwellham on the Tamar, was constructed 1803–17, mainly for conveying ores brought from the mines at Mary Tavy. Its water now powers a small hydro-electric station at Morwellham. Tavistock was served by two railways. The South Devon & Tavistock Railway (later GWR) reached the town from Plymouth in 1858 and closed in 1962, and the London & South Western (later Southern), which also connected to Plymouth from its station on the north of the town, arrived in 1890 and closed in 1968. The viaduct near the former North Station is preserved and is a public walkway.

In 1105 the town was granted a weekly market which still survives, and also, dating from the 16th century, a fair which continues as Goose Fair on the second Wednesday in October.

Further reading: Finberg, H.P.R., *Tavistock Abbey*, David & Charles, 1969
There are numerous other books on Tavistock, including several by Gerry Woodcock, among them, most recently: *The book of Tavistock*, Halsgrove, 2003
Local societies: Tavistock & District Local History Society
Tavistock Branch of the Devonshire Association
Museum: Tavistock Museum, Bedford Square

TAWSTOCK (D2) North Devon Pop. 2093 (1901: 1241)

Tawstock's fine cruciform church (St Peter) stands on the slopes of the lower valley of the River Taw.

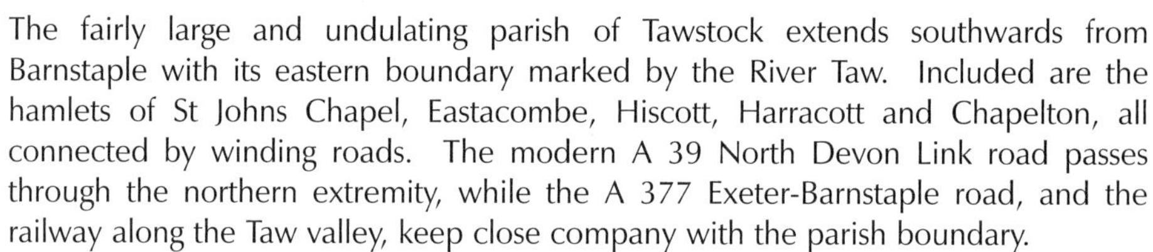

The fairly large and undulating parish of Tawstock extends southwards from Barnstaple with its eastern boundary marked by the River Taw. Included are the hamlets of St Johns Chapel, Eastacombe, Hiscott, Harracott and Chapelton, all connected by winding roads. The modern A 39 North Devon Link road passes through the northern extremity, while the A 377 Exeter-Barnstaple road, and the railway along the Taw valley, keep close company with the parish boundary.

In the north-east of the parish is historic Tawstock Court, and the parkland surrounding it. Owned from the 15th to the 17th century by the Bourchiers, it passed, through marriage of the heiress, to the Wreys. After being burnt down in 1787 the mansion was rebuilt in innovative style by Sir Bourchier Wrey. Later it became a school. The beautiful cruciform church (St Peter) stands nearby, dating from the 14th century it contains many interesting memorials. The prominent Tawstock Tower on the hilltop was an old look-out on the Wrey estate, it is now a private residence.

Further reading: Tawstock History Society, *The time of their lives*, 2000

TEDBURN ST MARY (G6) Teignbridge Pop. 1464 (1901: 475)

Tedburn St Mary, 6 miles W of Exeter, is an undulating parish with altitudes rising to c.650 ft on both east and west boundaries. Various streams water the valleys including those that feed the small River Culvery, northward-flowing tributary of the Yeo, south of Crediton. The village stands on the old A 30 road westwards from Exeter, while the modern dual carriageway A 30 passes close by to the south.

The church (St Mary), located at the church town half a mile north-west of the village, originates from at least as early as 1364. Most of the building dates from the following century. Alterations were carried out in the 17th century and restoration in the 19th century. Great Hackworthy and Upcott, south of the village, and Melhuish, in the south-west, were Domesday manors.

TEIGNGRACE (G8) Teignbridge Pop. 235 (1901: 190)

Teigngrace is a fairly small narrow parish lying in a north-west/south-east plane between the lower River Teign on the north-east, and Newton Abbot. The short north-west boundary coincides approximately with the A 38 expressway near Heathfield, with the longer western boundary marked for a distance by the A 382 road from Drumbridges to Newton Abbot. The River Bovey and then, irregularly, the Teign define the north-east boundary, and the parish tapers to the south-east.

In the north-west is the parkland of Stover, with its woods and lake, most of which now comprise a country park. A boarding school occupies Stover House, the mansion built by James Templer who purchased the Stover estate, which included heathland in the Bovey basin and the area of Hay Tor on Dartmoor, in 1765. Granite from the tor provided material for the house. From 1790–2 his son – also James – built the short Stover Canal from Ventiford in the parish to the Teign at Newton Abbot, initially for conveying pottery clay from the nearby area. His son, George, c.1820 constructed the Haytor Granite Tramway, which connected with the canal, for the transport of granite. (For fuller detail see: Harris, Helen, *The Haytor*

Granite Tramway and Stover Canal, Peninsula Press, 2nd edit., 2000.) The lower length of the later Moretonhampstead railway (constructed 1860s) still exists in Teigngrace parish, used at times for transporting clay.

There is no actual village apart from several attractive houses grouped close to the minor road, near the church, in the south. The church (St Peter & St Paul), which dates from the 15th century, was rebuilt by the Templers in 1787 and restored in 1872.

TEIGNMOUTH (H8) Teignbridge Pop. 14,413 (1901: 7366)

Tablet in Teignmouth commemorating George Templer's New Quay of 1821.

The star-shaped parish of Teignmouth stands on the north side of the mouth of the Teign estuary, with a reddish sandy beach along the English Channel shoreline and a sandy back beach behind the spit that protects the inner harbour. A large part of the parish is occupied by the town, behind which land rises to 658 ft on the northern boundary. The Teign marks the boundary to the south. The A 381 road connects the town with Newton Abbot, 5 miles to the west; the coast road from Exeter (A 379) crosses the estuary over Shaldon Bridge, to continue to Torquay, while the B 3192 heads over the hills north-westwards to join the A 380. Teignmouth has a station on the main railway which follows the coast road and estuary; it was its arrival here in 1846 as Brunel's South Devon Railway that caused the already established fashionable watering place to grow into a popular seaside resort.

Teignmouth was a port from early times, for fishing and for goods. Besides working seas near home, from the 1580s Teignmouth fishermen were going to Newfoundland waters for cod, and in the 18th century several Teignmouth boats were still active in that direction. An important commodity exported from Teignmouth from the 18th century has been pottery or ball clay, the product of workings in the Bovey Tracey-Kingsteignton areas. From the 1790s this was brought out in boats via the Stover Canal (see TEIGNGRACE) and down the estuary for loading on to bigger vessels. Between 1820 and 1859 granite from Haytor also travelled this route and in 1821 the canal's owner, George Templer, built the granite New Quay at Teignmouth to facilitate the off-loading. Teignmouth was also noted for shipbuilding. At times the town has been afflicted by attack and fire: in 1340 the port was burnt by the French, and in 1690 French forces severely bombarded and fired the town. It also suffered German hit-and-run air raids in the Second World War with much loss of life and many injured.

Formerly two separate towns, Teignmouth has two Anglican churches. East Teignmouth church (St Michael the Archangel) originates from Saxon times but was entirely rebuilt in the late 19th century. West Teignmouth church (St James) was also rebuilt, in octagonal form, earlier in the 19th century but retains its Norman tower, the oldest structure in Teignmouth. Christ Church, a small building in the west, used in the 20th century as a mission church but never consecrated, was made redundant and is now a dwelling.

Further reading: Griffiths, Grace, *History of Teignmouth*, rev. edit., 1989
Trump, Harold, *Teignmouth*, Phillimore, 1986
Local society: Teignmouth & Shaldon Museum and History Society
Museum: Teignmouth Museum, French Street

TEMPLETON (G4) Mid Devon Pop. 118 (1901: 175)

Templeton is a hilly parish 4 miles WNW of Tiverton, situated between the B 3137 Tiverton-Witheridge road and the road from Tiverton to Rackenford. Somewhat triangular in shape, the parish is bounded on the east and south largely by the River Dart (flowing to the Exe) and tributaries. The village stands at 764 ft and in the north the altitude reaches 889 ft where tumuli lie close to the border on Gibbet Moor. West of the village there is a steep descent to the Dart valley where Templeton Bridge carries a minor road.

The church (St Margaret) is of ancient foundation, rebuilt, except for the tower, in 1876. In early times the manor belonged to the Knights Templar – hence the name.

Tetcott's Holy Cross Church stands close to the manor house, in parkland half a mile from the village.

TETCOTT (B6) Torridge Pop. 110 (1901: 220)

Situated 5 miles S of Holsworthy, Tetcott has the River Tamar for its border on the west, while the Claw and other tributary streams partially provide the boundaries to north and south.

The Tetcott estate has been in the same family ownership since 1550, when it was bought from the Earl of Huntingdon by John Arscott, who built the present manor house and added the tower to the 14th-century Holy Cross Church. The property passed from father to son until 1788, then to the last John Arscott's cousin, Sir William Molesworth, forbear of the later Molesworth-St Aubyn family.

The church stands close to the manor house, ½ mile NW of the village, approached by a road through the park.

THELBRIDGE (F4) Mid Devon Pop. 258 (1901: 186)

Thelbridge is a scattered parish that spreads across the south-eastern border of Worlington and the south of Witheridge, 8½ miles NNW of Crediton and 10 miles W of Tiverton. The B 3042 road runs east-west through the parish. The land is open, much of it being well over 600 ft in altitude. The River Dalch (which joins the Yeo near Lapford) flows through the parish and forms much of the southern boundary; the northern boundary touches the Little Dart River.

There is no actual village. The church (St David) was rebuilt, with a new tower, in the 1870s. It is plain internally, but well cared for and obviously cherished. Middlewick was a Domesday manor.

THORNBURY (C5) Torridge Pop. 277 (1901: 291)

Thornbury, 5 miles NE of Holsworthy, is bounded in the north by the River Waldon, tributary of the Torridge. It is approached by minor roads from either the A 388 Holsworthy-Bideford road or the A 3072 Holsworthy-Hatherleigh road.

Remaining from the 12th-century church is a fine Norman south doorway of c.1150. The church (St Peter) was rebuilt c.1330 and much of the structure remains, restoration and raising of the tower by 5 ft having been done in 1876. An arch in the churchyard marks the entrance to the former village pound, used for securing stray animals.

Wonford and North Week farms were Domesday manors and Bagbeare gave its name to a long-lived family. Woodacott is a hamlet.

Further reading: Matthews, Gerry, *A history of Thornbury*, 1999

THORVERTON (H5) Mid Devon Pop. 771 (1901: 813)

Thorverton is a parish of beautiful countryside with a very pleasant large village, situated 6 miles N of Exeter and 7 miles SSW of Tiverton, 1½ miles west of the A 396 Exeter-Tiverton road. The River Exe in its luxuriant valley stage approximately forms the eastern boundary from which the land rises steeply to 773 ft at Raddon Top in the north-west, and to 800 ft on the border with Cadbury in the north. South of the village the fertile land levels out to around 100-200 ft.

In early times Thorverton was on a crossroads of routes, mainly of an ancient way from eastern England to Land's End via Uffculme, Bradninch, Crediton and Bow, and a north-south track which favoured high land rather than deeper valley ground. By medieval times it also had the advantage of a nearby bridge over the Exe. The broad square in the centre of the village is known as the Bury, or Berry, probably derived from the Anglo-Saxon burh, signifying a place of refuge where cattle could be secured at times of threat. It became the centre of regular cattle and sheep fairs and markets until they ceased c.1900.

The church (St Thomas of Canterbury) is mainly the result of rebuilding in the late 15th and early 16th centuries, although the nave was again rebuilt when the church underwent restoration in the 1830s. The village has numerous attractive houses, many of them thatched. Some are built of cob, others of the local Thorverton or Raddon stone, an igneous rock worked for centuries at Raddon Quarry a mile to the west, now long disused. Raddon Court was a Saxon estate and, besides Thorverton itself, East Raddon in the east and Treymill and Chilton in the north were medieval manors.

The former Exe Valley Railway, opened in 1885 from Exeter to Tiverton and continuing to connect with the Taunton-Barnstaple line at Morebath, ran northwards, close to the Exe, with Thorverton Station ½ mile from the village. It closed in 1963 although limited use for transporting grain from Stoke Canon to Thorverton continued until 1966.

Further reading: Stoyle, Ian, *Thorverton, Devon*, priv. pub., 1993
Local society: Thorverton & District Local History Society

THROWLEIGH (E6) West Devon Pop. 298 (1901: 241)

Throwleigh parish, on Dartmoor's north-east, is shaped rather like an inverted V, with the eastern leg enlarged at its foot where the more sheltered land descends to the River Teign and includes the hamlet of Murchington. The western leg narrows as it ascends the moorland of Throwleigh Common to meet the Forest boundary, reaching 1569 ft on Kennon Hill, and 1596 ft at the border with South Tawton. On the moorland are considerable prehistoric remains in the form of hut settlements and enclosures.

The small village is located centrally, near the V's upper apex, the boundary here being defined by the Blackaton Brook. Access is by minor roads south from the former A 30 (now unclassified) road between Whiddon Down and Sticklepath. The church (St Mary the Virgin) was rebuilt in granite in the 15th century, with the tower and north aisle added a little later; the Church House is also 15th century. In the churchyard is the shaft of an ancient cross found during excavations at Throwleigh Barton in 1977. The quiet area seems to have a quality of timelessness, which is reflected in the character of notable houses that date from the 16th and 17th centuries. They include Wonson Manor, North Wonson, and Higher Shilston – a fine example of a Dartmoor longhouse.

THRUSHELTON (C7) West Devon Pop. 195 (1901: 307)

Thrushelton lies roughly midway between Okehampton and Launceston, its southern area including part of the village of Lewdown. The River Thrushel flows south-westwards through the north of the parish to join the Wolf and the Lyd, and in places forms the parish boundary.

The church (St George) which dates from the 14th century, was enlarged in the 15th century. The corner-stones of the tower, and many of those of the whole building, are of substantial granite. The church paths are bordered by 20 tall lime trees. Ecclesiastically Thrushelton is united with Lewtrenchard.

The 'church town' of Thrushelton is located in quiet countryside north of the busy A 30 road in West Devon.

THURLESTONE (E11) South Hams Pop. 821 (1901: 354)

The name of Thurlestone derives from a pierced, or thurled stone, standing off shore, which was referred to as marking a boundary in a Saxon charter of 845. The parish is situated on the east side of the River Avon and extends to the boundary with South Milton. (The beach known as Thurlestone Sands is actually mainly in South Milton parish.) There is also a beach at Bantham, at the mouth of the estuary. The undulating land rises to 346 ft.

The village stands 4 miles WSW of Kingsbridge and ½ mile inland from the coast, approach being by minor roads from the A 379 Plymouth-Kingsbridge road. There was a fishing settlement here from the 16th century and some old buildings remain although there is considerable modern development.

A church was here in the early 12th century, of which the font remains in the present building (All Saints). This dates from the 13th century and was enlarged in the 15th century. It contains fine woodwork including a screen across the tower arch. Seating is now mainly on chairs. Buckland, north of the village, was a Domesday manor.

Further reading: McDonald, Kendall, *The story of Thurlestone, Bantham and West Buckland*, 1993

TIPTON ST JOHN see OTTERY ST MARY

TIVERTON (H4) Mid Devon Pop. 18,621 (1901: 10,382)

The civil parish – former borough – of Tiverton covers a large area. Standing on two rivers, the Exe and the Lowman, which unite just south of the town, it was originally Twyfordtown – the town of two fords. Fortunately these fords have now long been bridged, Exe Bridge being on the west of the main town area and that over the Lowman on the east. Beyond the urban area land stretches out to boundaries with Loxbeare, Washfield, Stoodleigh, Bampton, Huntsham, Uplowman, Halberton, Bickleigh, Cadeleigh, Cruwys Morchard, and Templeton, with beautiful countryside of rich farmland, and including the Exe valley to north and south with high hills and woodlands on either side.

Tiverton stands at the meeting place of roads: the A 396 coming from Exeter and continuing northwards, the former A 373 – now the B 3137 – coming from the west and continuing (unclassified) eastwards, and several minor routes. The 1980s brought some reclassification with the construction of the North Devon Link road from the M5, which, cutting through on the north, became the new A 361.

The area was of interest to early people. On a hill south of the town, which carried the old road to Exeter, are the scant remains of an Iron Age hill fort known as Cranmore Castle. And near Bolham the remains of a Roman fort dating from the 1st century AD were discovered and investigated by archaeologists prior to the new A 361 road's construction. The Tiverton settlement was founded as a royal estate in Saxon times, probably in the 7th century. A document of King Alfred's reign (c.880) referred to it as Twyforde. In 1066 the manor of Tiverton was in the hands of Gytha, widow of Earl Godwin and mother of Harold who was defeated by William I at Hastings. William then gave the manor to Baldwin de Brionis, and in 1106 Henry I commanded Baldwin's son, Richard de Redvers, to build Tiverton Castle on the high ground above the River Exe, close beside the church already established. Richard's son Baldwin was created Earl of Devon and Tiverton Castle continued as a residence of the succeeding de Redvers and Courtenay families until 1556.

In about 1250 a valued gift was made to the people of Tiverton by Isabella de

The River Exe at Tiverton, with St Peter's Church.

Fortibus, Countess of Devon in her own right, in the form of a supply of pure water. This flows from Norwood Common, 5 miles north of the town, through Chettiscombe and eventually Castle Street where it runs along a mid-road channel to Coggins Well in Fore Street. A ceremonial perambulation of the leat is made every seven years.

During the Civil War, in 1644, Tiverton was occupied by the Parliamentarians but later regained by the Royalists. However, in 1645 the Roundheads returned and attacked the castle, the Royalists' stronghold, and eventually took it. Parts of the castle which remain, including the round tower, still bear scars. A dwelling house now occupies most of the former site.

For long a busy market town, Tiverton also developed industrially, notably concerning textiles. In the late 15th century the manufacture of woollen kersey became established under merchants including John Greenway, John Waldron, and Peter Blundell, whose names have lived on. Greenway and Waldron established almshouses in the town, Peter Blundell founded Blundells School. The industry thrived in a big way, centred near the river in the area that became known as Westexe, until Devon's decline set in c.1800. In 1816 fortunes took a new turn when John Heathcoat, a lace manufacturer from Loughborough in Leicestershire, came south to avoid the Luddites and, bringing his workforce who walked the 200 miles, took over one of the old mills and re-established his business. Under considerate employers this thrived, developed, and diversified, and continues today, still under the John Heathcoat name. In the early 20th century the firm had around 2000 employees, numbers are reduced now to 550-600 but with a wide range of materials for modern purposes being produced. It was the founder's grandson, John Heathcoat Amory who built Knightshayes Court, designed by William Burges, which was bequeathed by his descendant, Sir John Amory, to the National Trust.

The town has been well provided with churches. The very fine St Peter's, near the castle, probably replacing an early Saxon wood structure, dates from the 11th century, consecrated by Leofric, Bishop of Exeter, in 1073. A Norman doorway survives in the 15th-century building, and further rebuilding was done 1853–6. The large Greenway chapel was added within the church in 1517. In 1714 the Georgian St George's Church was built to cater for increasing numbers, and in 1856 St Paul's Church, with its fine spire, was completed to serve the community of Westexe. A fourth church, St Andrew's, was built after the Second World War on the east side of the town for the increased population there. Also within the Tiverton boundary are the ecclesiastical parishes of Calverleigh (St Mary the Virgin, dating from the 14th century, restored in the 19th century), Chevithorne (St Thomas, built 1843) and Withleigh (St Catherine, 1846). Tiverton has also been strong in nonconformity, from Puritans in the 17th century, to preaching visits by John Wesley in the 18th century. The impressive Methodist Church dates from 1814, the United Reformed (formerly Congregational) Church was built in 1832, and the Baptist Church rebuilt on the site of an earlier foundation in 1877. The Roman Catholic St John's Church (1837) is on the town's north-western outskirts.

Passengers boarding the Tivertonian *on the Grand Western Canal, while the horse waits to provide the motive power.*

There are numerous hamlets in the town's extended area, and recorded in Domesday were: Bolham, Bradley, Chettiscombe, Chevithorne, Crazelowman, Patcott, and Peadhill.

In 1814 the first stage of the Grand Western Canal, which was originally intended to link with the Bristol and English Channels, was completed from the Somerset border to Tiverton, carrying mainly limestone and coal. An extension to the Bridgwater & Taunton Canal was completed in 1838, involving an ingenious system of seven vertical lifts and an inclined plane to negotiate the changes of level. The coming of the main railway in the 1840s brought decline in trade for the canal leading to closure of the Taunton length in 1864, while the Tiverton section continued in reduced state until the 1920s. Later, the Tiverton length was extensively restored, and as a country park owned by Devon County Council, offers recreation facilities which include a horse-boat service.

Tiverton was served by a branch railway line from Tiverton Junction from 1848 to 1967, and by the Exe Valley line, opened to Morebath Junction on the Tiverton-Barnstaple line in 1884 and to Exeter in 1885, which closed in 1963. There is now Tiverton Parkway Station on the main line.

Further reading: de la Mahotiere, Mary, *Tiverton and the Exe valley*, Phillimore, 1990
Harris, Helen, *The Grand Western Canal,* 2nd edit., Halsgrove, 1996
Local societies: Tiverton Archaeological Group
Tiverton Branch of the Devonshire Association
Museum: Tiverton Museum, St Andrews Street

TOPSHAM (H7) Exeter City Council (Pop. 1901: 2790)

Topsham occupies a very interesting location, 4 miles SE of Exeter city centre. Although within the Exeter authority, Topsham still very much retains its own character, influenced by close association with the tidal River Exe. Besides having a long western frontage on the estuary, Topsham is bounded on the east by the tributary River Clyst, and extends towards the confluence. The mudflats and marshes here are of international ornithological importance with large numbers of birds, including avocets, coming here in winter.

From early days Topsham was a port, possibly from Celtic times, but certainly after the arrival of the Romans who established it to serve Exeter in the 1st century AD and used it until c.400. From the 7th century new developments were wrought by the Saxons and in 937 it was given by Athelstan to the monastery of St Mary & St Peter in Exeter, although at the Norman Conquest it reverted to royal possession. The building of weirs across the Exe between Topsham and Exeter by the Courtenays in the 12th and 13th centuries prevented boats reaching Exeter and thus favoured Topsham, until construction of the Exeter Canal from 1564–6 restored the city's port ability to a certain extent, although much of the output of the woollen trade still used Topsham. This trade was largely with Holland, and Dutch bricks brought back as ballast provided building material for many of Topsham's houses. Shipbuilding and fishing – including for salmon – featured in the local trades. Gradually these have declined but the town has remained largely unspoilt despite residential developments. Views westward, across the estuary and towards the Haldon Hills, are glorious, especially at sunset.

The large church (St Margaret) dates from at least as early as 1152. It was rebuilt, except for the red sandstone tower, in 1876–8. The Norman font remains from the earlier building, used for baptisms from the 12th century. Its tall conical brass cover dates from 1888.

Since 1861 Topsham has had a station on the Exeter-Exmouth railway. A passenger ferry crosses the estuary to Turf on the Exeter Canal.

Further reading: Numerous books exist about different periods of Topsham's history
Local society: Topsham Local History Society
Museum: Topsham Museum, The Strand

TORBRYAN (G9) Teignbridge Pop. 841 (1901: 164)

Since the early 20th century the civil parish of Torbryan has included Denbury, although ecclesiastically the two are separate. The combined area is somewhat boot-shaped in outline, set obliquely, with the village of Denbury in the upper heel on the north-east, and Torbryans towards the toe in the south. Served by minor roads the parish lies west of the A 381, around 3 miles SW of Newton Abbot and 5 miles N of Totnes. Watered by tributaries of the small River Hems, destined for the Dart, the land is undulating, rising to rather more than 300 ft.

Torbryan's church (Holy Trinity) is now redundant, the former Torbryan ecclesiastical parish now being united with Ipplepen. The building dates from the early 15th century and its arcades are of Beer stone. It is a beautiful building, now in the hands of the Churches Conservation Trust, still consecrated and lovingly cared for. The Church House Inn nearby is of similar date and was formerly the Church House. Tornewton was the home, from the early 16th century, of the Petre family.

Denbury is a village of ancient origin. Its name is derived from the earthwork known as Denbury Camp, just south-west of the village. Its early name Defnas burg (the fort of the men of Devon) may indicate a stronghold of the Dumnonii against the Saxons. Between the 11th and 16th centuries the manor of Denbury was in the possession of Tavistock Abbey, and was granted a market and borough status. The church (St Mary the Virgin) originates from the 12th century, and the existing font probably dates from then. The present building was dedicated by Bishop Stapledon in 1318. Denbury House is Elizabethan.

TORQUAY (H9) Torbay Unitary Authority, total pop. 129,706 (Torquay 1901: 24,473)

Torquay occupies the hinterland of the northern shores of Torbay on the South Devon coast, served mainly by the A 380 road which connects with the M5 just south of Exeter. It includes the promontory that extends eastwards into the English Channel and terminates in the headland of Hopes Nose. In 1969 the town of Torquay became part of the newly created county borough of Torbay, in incorporation with neighbouring Paignton, Brixham, and Churston Ferrers (for which see separate entries). Another change came in 1998 when Torbay became a unitary authority, completely independent of Devon County Council.

Until the 18th century the area that is now densely populated Torquay was rural in character, based on the rocks that include limestone and New Red Sandstone. It comprised three ancient parishes: Cockington, St Marychurch, and Tormohun. Tormohun, whose name derives from the nearby hill and the 13th-century lords of the manor, included the remains of the 12th-century Torre Abbey and succeeding buildings on the site, and the sheltered harbour and small fish quay surrounded by fishermen's cottages. From the early years of the 19th century the beneficial effects of seawater were becoming recognised, as were the gentle climate and attractive scenery of Tor Bay. The arrival of the railway in 1848, as a branch from the South Devon Railway at Newton Abbot, brought increasing numbers of well-to-do visitors, and the town which became known as Torquay rapidly grew. Largely instrumental in the development was Sir Thomas Palk MP, who was mainly responsible for establishment of the Imperial Hotel, which encouraged many notable people to Torquay including, in 1877, the Prince of Wales (later King Edward VII) and his sons.

Since then growth has continued through the 20th century with houses replacing green fields and blocks of flats rising skywards. People have settled here from other parts of the country for their retirement, and holidays have become possible for a wide range of people, not only the more privileged. The type of holiday has changed; large and luxurious hotels continue to exist but many visitors seek bed and breakfast, or self-catering accommodation, and the town caters for what is now a main industry of tourism. For those who come there are still natural features to enjoy: the cliffs and sheltered beaches as well as man-made entertainments. Public gardens have been

View across Torquay Harbour, 1842. COURTESY THE BOOK OF TORBAY

created, the harbour area developed, and walks and drives defined along the coast which has been described as the 'English Riviera'.

Still existing are the churches of the three original parishes. The church of former Tormohun at Torre, St Saviour's, which dates from Norman times, is now however no longer used by Anglicans but since 1981 by the Greek Orthodox, and renamed St Andrew's. The present Anglican church at Torre, All Saints, was established in the late 19th century. The church at Cockington (St George & St Mary) is of ancient foundation. The tower of the present building dates from the 13th century, the main structure, with its rood screen, from the 14th and 15th centuries. Cockington Court in its beautiful park dates from the 16th and 17th centuries. It was the home of the Cary family from the 14th century and of the Mallocks from the 17th century. The house and parkland were bought by Torquay Corporation in 1935 and are now much visited for the attractions of the old village and forge, craft centre and other amenities. There is also at Cockington the church of St Matthew, dating from 1884, and, in the area of Lower Chelston, the church of St Peter (1962). The church of St Marychurch originates from the 11th century, on a site believed to have been established by Christian missionaries in the 7th century. Its high altar was dedicated in 1338–9. The church, apart form its tower, was rebuilt in 1861, but on Sunday 30 May 1943 the church was bombed by a German war plane, killing 45 people including 23 children assembled inside, injuring another 157 people and causing immense damage. The plane that dropped the bomb subsequently struck the spire of the nearby Roman Catholic Church and, damaged and in flames, crashed on a house, killing its woman occupant and also the pilot. The church was rebuilt and its tower, like its neighbour's spire, is a prominent landmark.

As Torquay's population grew many new places of worship were built. Of the Anglican churches, St John's, which stands high above the harbour area, was founded as a chapel in 1822, rebuilt in the 1860s, and completely renovated and refurbished in 1996. Others comprise: St Luke's (1862); All Saints, Babbacombe (1867); and at various dates, St Mary Magdalene, Upton; St Mathias; Christchurch, Ellacombe; and St John the Baptist, Shiphay Collaton. The church of St Martin, Barton, dates from 1928.

Torre Abbey, located in its parkland close to Abbey Sands, was founded in 1196 and prospered until the Dissolution. After passing into other hands it was bought in 1662 by the Cary family who established a country house here. Considerable remains of the abbey still exist, and the property was purchased in the 20th century by Torquay Corporation. The historic house and gallery are open to the public.

Torquay streets had trams from 1905, replaced by buses in 1934. At Babbacombe a cliff railway was opened in 1926 and still survives. The town has various light industries.

Further reading: Pearce, Frank, *The book of Torbay*, Halsgrove, 1999
Langmead, Sydney R., *The Ellacombe book*, Halsgrove, 1998
Born, Anne, *The Torbay towns*, Phillimore, 1989
Pike, John R., *Portrait of Torbay*, 1975
Pike, John R., *A Torbay century*, Breedon Books, 2003

Local societies: Torquay Museum Society
Torbay Branch of the Devonshire Association

Museum: Torquay Museum, Babbacombe Road

TOTNES (G9) South Hams Pop. 7444 (1901: 3116)

Situated just below the upper tidal limit of the River Dart, Totnes has enjoyed a strategic position and a long history. A settlement existed here from Saxon times, with the ridge position above the Dart becoming part of a system of fortified towns or burhs planned by King Alfred as defence against the Danes, and developed by his son Edward the Elder c.909. However, Totnes escaped any battle, and by the mid 10th century was minting coins. Following the Norman Conquest William I granted the royal burh to Judhael, who built the motte and bailey of Totnes Castle, which still stands prominently at the top of the town. Also largely still discernible are the town's walls built in the 12th century and the sites of their former gates, north, east, south, and west.

Commerce has played an important part in the development of Totnes, both through overseas trade and from the woollen cloth industry in which the town was involved up to the 17th century. Totnes was granted a fair in 1130, and a charter by King John in 1206, and it became a busy market town for the surrounding area. The first bridge was built in the early 13th century, and its successor remains the lowest crossing point of the Dart. Downstream from the bridge the quays were busy with exports and imports. Most traffic now is for pleasure including the vessels that take passengers down the beautiful river to Dartmouth, and former warehouses have been converted to other uses, including residential.

Fore Street and High Street, which run continuously, roughly east-west, and slightly uphill, are attractive, despite modern traffic problems. The former grammar school building, now called the Mansion House, is on the south side as is the town's museum in its Elizabethan house. The church (St Mary) stands on the north side of High Street and is very fine. It dates from the 11th century, rebuilt in the mid 15th century, with much use of red sandstone in the structure and of white Beer stone for the impressive screen. A Benedictine priory, founded in 1088, was built close to the church on the north; after the Dissolution it was demolished and the Guildhall erected on its site in the 16th and 17th centuries.

On the east side of the river across the bridge is Bridgetown, formerly an independent borough dating from the 13th century; it is now largely residential, with its own church (St John). Built in 1835 the church suffered a severe fire in the latter half of the 20th century but was rebuilt.

Totnes is served, north to Newton Abbot and south to Kingsbridge, by the A 381 road, while the A 385 runs east to Torbay and west to the A 38 near South Brent, with the A 384 branching from it for Buckfastleigh. It is on the main Exeter-Plymouth railway line, and also connects with the Dart Valley Light Railway, which operates steam trains from Buckfastleigh to Totnes in the summer season.

Further reading: Saunders, Kristin, *Totnes, a thousand years of history*, Totnes Museum Society for Totnes Museum Trust, 2000
(Also numerous other works)

Local societies: Totnes Museum Society
Totnes & District Society

Museum: Totnes Museum, Fore Street

TRENTISHOE (E1) North Devon Pop. 42 (1901: 68)

Located 8 miles E of Ilfracombe and 4½ miles W of Lynton, the boomerang-shaped parish of Trentishoe, thinly populated and wildly beautiful, includes a length of North Devon's Bristol Channel coast with cliffs that descend in half a mile from 1061 ft to the rocky sea. The south-east boundary is defined by a long tributary of the River Heddon which it joins at Hunters Inn. It then continues through a 1½ mile, partly wooded valley to the coast at awesome Heddon's Mouth, where there are remains of an old lime kiln.

The small church (St Peter) was rebuilt in 1861. It is approached by a lane extending from a minor road which connects with the A 399 Blackmoor Gate-Ilfracombe road. Tattiscombe was a Domesday manor.

TRUSHAM (G7) Teignbridge Pop. 144 (1901: 173)

Trusham is a small parish 8 miles SSW of Exeter on the south-western slopes of the Haldon Hills and on the east side of the River Teign which forms the western boundary. Land rises to 473 ft.

The name Trusham derives from Trisma meaning brushwood or fallen leaves. A church was listed here at the time of Domesday, probably a chapel of Buckfast Abbey whose abbot then held the manor. The present church (now St Michael the Archangel) was dedicated in 1259 by Bishop Bronescombe of Exeter and the remains of that early structure are incorporated in later rebuildings. The church was restored in 1865 and 1890. The inside of the roof is now ceiled. The font is Norman.

The oak pulpit in Trusham's ancient church (St Michael the Archangel) was carved by Herbert Read c.1900.

The former Teign Valley railway ran north along the western boundary, constructed from Heathfield, north of Newton Abbot, in 1882 and extended to Exeter in 1903. North of Christow the line closed in 1958 although some traffic continued on the southern section until 1965. For Trusham Quarry see HENNOCK.

Further reading: Cameron, Alick, *The book of Trusham, a parish patchwork*, Halsgrove, 1999

TWITCHEN (F2) North Devon Pop. 70 (1901: 163)

The remote moorland parish of Twitchen is bounded on the north by the Devon-Somerset border on Exmoor, and on the east by a tributary of the River Yeo that feeds into the Mole. Land in the south attains an altitude of 857 ft, and in the north 1360 ft.

Twitchen village is located close to the eastern boundary.

The church (St Peter) was rebuilt in 1844 but retains a Norman font. It is united ecclesiastically with North Molton. Praunsley and Pulham, west and south-west of the village, were recorded in Domesday.

Uffculme's Coldharbour Mill.

UFFCULME (J4) Mid Devon Pop. 2631 (1901: 1704)

Uffculme, 7 miles due E of Tiverton, has a large and ancient village, with fertile farming country on either side of the River Culm and southern tributaries. The land rises from c.200 ft on the west to 845 ft at Hackpen Hill on the eastern boundary. It is approached by the B 3440 and minor roads from the M5 and A 38 to the west. The parish includes the village of Ashill in the south-east and the parkland of Bradfield in the south-west.

A local centre of the woollen industry from at least as early as the 16th century, Uffculme still retains its Coldharbour textile mill, situated on the south side of the village and served by a leat from the Culm. With buildings dating from the 18th century when the industry was at its height, including one built by the Quaker Thomas Fox in 1799, the mill, although no longer in commercial production, retains a large waterwheel and machinery including steam engines – one of them a beam engine of 1867. After closing in 1981 the mill was reopened in 1982 as a working museum by the Coldharbour Mill Trust, and continues to welcome visitors.

The church (St Mary the Virgin) is of 15th-century construction but contains work from earlier. The tower and spire were rebuilt and the second south aisle added 1845–6. At Ashill there is the small church of St Stephen, and at Bradfield the small private chapel of All Saints. Religion has often been a matter of some consequence in Uffculme, strongly influenced not only by High Anglicanism but also by nonconformity such as that of the Quakers and Baptists. Research into ecclesiastical affairs has benefited from the parish having been a peculiar for three centuries from c.1545 during which it came under control of the Dean of Salisbury. This meant that records were kept at Trowbridge rather than Exeter where many church court probate records were destroyed in the wartime Blitz of 1942. Such good fortune, and other matters of local interest, have prompted recent writings about the parish (see below).

Bradfield was the home of the Walronds from the early 13th century. The present mansion dates from the late 16th century, restored c.1860. After becoming a special school in the 20th century it has undergone further developments and now comprises two residences.

Uffculme had a station on the Culm Valley Railway which provided connection with Tiverton Junction from 1876 to 1963.

Further reading: Payne, Gordon A., ed., *Uffculme: a Culm valley parish*, Uffculme Local History Group, 1st edit., 1988. The 2nd, revised edit., 2002, omits certain aspects from the earlier edition but includes new material.
Wyatt, Peter, and Stanes, Robin, *Uffculme a peculiar parish*, Uffculme Archive Group, 1997

Local society: Uffculme Local History Group

UGBOROUGH (E10) South Hams Pop. 1736 (1901: 1610)

Ugborough is a fairly large sprawling parish with a long narrow north-western arm which extends to Dartmoor and a short boundary with Dartmoor Forest. The southern part, in which the village is located, 11 miles E of Plymouth, lies to the south of the A 38 expressway and the B 3213 road at Bittaford, from which it is served by the A 3121 and minor roads. The area north of the A 38 lies within Dartmoor National Park.

The moorland area, which rises to 1522 ft at Three Barrows on the eastern boundary, is rich in Bronze Age remains particularly in the south. Also there are remains of tinners' workings, including ruined buildings, close to the East and West Glaze Brooks. The former 7½ mile, 3 ft gauge Redlake Mineral Railway, in use between 1911 and 1932, which carried men and supplies to clayworks at Redlake and Left Lake, ran northwards from Bittaford, with its course mainly over Ugborough Moor. The clay was conveyed by pipeline and aerial ropeway to treatment works at Cantrell. From quarries on the lower slopes of Western Beacon came granite used in constructing the viaducts at Ivybridge and Cornwood which carry the main railway.

The pleasant village is formed around a large square on the south side of which, at higher level, stands the church (St Peter). This is of ancient foundation, having been part of Plympton Convent in 1121. The high altar was dedicated by Bishop Stapledon in 1311 and the church in 1323. The only present remains from that date are the nave and font, the main structure having been enlarged in the 14th century. At that time the building of the side aisles acted as buttresses to prevent further outward leaning of the granite pillars, which are still seen to be inclined. The ceiling of the north aisle is also of that time. The chancel and screen (which only partially remains) date from the 15th century, and the present tower replaced a smaller one in the 16th century.

In addition to Ugborough itself, Broadaford, Langford Barton, Ludbrook, Peek, and Venn, were all manors named in Domesday.

UMBERLEIGH see CHITTLEHAMPTON

UPLOWMAN (J4) Mid Devon Pop. 278 (1901: 357)

Uplowman, lying 4 miles ENE of Tiverton, is approached by minor roads from the now unclassified (former A 373) road eastward from Tiverton to Halberton, or by turning off the modern A 361 North Devon Link road which skirts through the south of the parish. The village is in the extreme south-east, ½ mile east of the River Lowman (tributary of the Exe) which flows southwards through the parish. From c.400 ft in the south the land rises northwards and steeply on either side of the Lowman, attaining 800 ft in the north-east.

Part of the village of Uplowman, with St Peter's Church.

The church (St Peter) was dedicated by Bishop Stapledon of Exeter in 1318. The present building dates from c.1500, reputedly built by Margaret Beaumont, Countess of Richmond and mother of King Henry VII. It was restored in 1864. The manor of Uplowman originally belonged to the de Loman family; other Domesday manors were: Chieflowman, Coombe, Kidwell, Marley, and Whitnage.

UPLYME (M6) East Devon Pop. 1446 (1901: 798)

Uplyme is bounded on the east by the Dorset county border and on its short southern boundary by the English Channel coast. The large village is located in the south-east, on the B 3165 road north from Lyme Regis, 3½ miles SSE of Axminster. The A 3052 Sidmouth-Lyme Regis road passes through the south. The land is mainly fairly high, rising in the north to 690 ft.

The manor of Uplyme was given to Glastonbury Abbey by King Cynewulf in 774, and remained abbey property until the Dissolution. Later it passed to the Drake and Tucker families. Shapwick, meaning sheep farm, in the south of the parish, was a grange of Newenham Abbey at Axminster.

The church (St Peter & St Paul) is of ancient origin, with its list of rectors dating from 1259. The present building is of 14th-century construction; it possesses two fonts, the older being Saxon. There is a finely carved Jacobean pulpit. The north aisle and the

Uplyme's Jacobean pulpit. COURTESY THE BOOK OF UPLYME

gallery above it were added in 1827. At Holcombe, south-west of the village, a Roman villa was found in 1850.

Further reading: Gosling, Gerald, and Thomas, Jack, *The book of Uplyme, portrait of a devon village*, Halsgrove, 2004

UPOTTERY (L5) East Devon Pop. 679 (1901: 666)

As its name suggests, Upottery covers an area around the upper reaches of the River Otter, its valley lying between arms of the Blackdown Hills. The parish does not, however, extend to the Otter's source, which is still farther north on the Blackdowns in Somerset. A short stretch of the county border forms the parish's northern boundary. Upottery's land is high, much of it over 600 ft and rising to over 800 ft in places, including a point east of the village of 856 ft, and 840 ft on Beacon Hill just to the north. The village is located 5 miles NNE of Honiton and approximately 1 mile west of the A 30 road.

The church (St Mary the Virgin) is of 14th century foundation. The manor was given by William the Conqueror to Ralph de Pomeroy; subsequently it passed into other hands. Eventually it was bought by a Dr Addison whose son, Henry Addison, was Speaker of the House of Commons, and Prime Minister 1801-2, and who later became the 1st Viscount Sidmouth. He built a new Elizabethan-style manor house in the mid 19th century and contributed other pleasing features to the village. Rowridge, in the south, was also a Domesday manor.

UPTON HELLIONS (G5) Mid Devon Pop. 66 (1901: 109)

Upton Hellions, 2 miles NNE of Crediton, is bounded on the west by the River Creedy, on the north by a tributary stream, and on the south by the A 3072 Crediton-Tiverton road. There is no village. The church (St Mary the Virgin), which is located in pleasant quiet countryside, is approached by a long narrow lane. It dates from the 12th century, enlarged in the 15th century and with 15th-century windows. Lower Creedy (formerly Creedy Wiger) and Upton Hellions Barton were Tudor mansions.

UPTON PYNE (H6) East Devon Pop. 479 (1901: 355)

Upton Pyne lies close to the north-west of Exeter, mainly between the Rivers Exe and Creedy which meet at Cowley. Upton Pyne touches the Exe in the south-east and extends slightly across the Creedy on the south-west. Northwards, after narrowing in the centre, the parish broadens again towards an ancient east-west minor road that forms the northern boundary. The land is pleasantly undulating, with wooded areas, and rises to 300-400 ft. Tumuli in the north are evidence of likely Bronze Age habitation.

In 739 the area was part of a gift to the bishops of Sherborne, and in 944, as part of Brentefordland which included today's Brampford Speke, was sold by Edmund, King of Wessex, to Athelstan, Earl of East Anglia. Later the two parishes were divided, and from the early 12th century the manor was held by the Pynes for ten generations, then by the Larders, Coplestons and Staffords. In the 18th century it passed by marriage to the Northcotes, later earls of Iddesleigh. The present Pynes house dates from the 18th century, later enlarged.

The church (Church of Our Lady) was dedicated in 1328. The present building is mainly of 14th-century construction, with the north aisle added in 1833. The tower was undergoing extensive constructional repair work in 2003.

Manganese was worked in the parish (for use in the Potteries) from 1770–80. Cowley Bridge over the Creedy was built by the surveyor and engineer James Green in 1813–14. It is a scheduled Ancient Monument.

VENN OTTERY see NEWTON POPPLEFORD AND HARPFORD

VIRGINSTOW (B6) Torridge Pop. 115 (1901: 115)

The small parish of Virginstow, shaped like an elongated diamond, is located 7½ miles

SSE of Holsworthy. Its western boundary is marked by the River Carey, tributary of the Tamar. Access is from the unclassified road between St Giles-on-the-Heath on the A 388 (Launceston-Holsworthy) and the A 3079.

The church (St Bridget the Virgin) was rebuilt in the 1850s but retains its 12th-century font. Ecclesiastically the parish is in Truro Diocese.

Bradaford and Tilleslow were named in Domesday.

WALKHAMPTON (D8) West Devon Pop. 863 (1901: 584)

The large, roughly triangular parish of Walkhampton is bounded on the west by the River Walkham, flowing from the upper apex, where the parish adjoins Dartmoor Forest, southwards to the boundary with Horrabridge. An eastward cross-country route follows, passing through the length of Burrator Reservoir, and then defined by the Narrator Brook before crossing moorland, and swinging north to rejoin the Forest boundary at Eylesbarrow, 3 miles S of Princetown. The village, situated in the south-west, 4½ miles SE of Tavistock, is accessible by minor roads from either the A 386 or the B 3212 in the vicinity of Yelverton. The church (St Mary the Virgin from 1985) stands half a mile from the village, on an elevated ancient site to the north. It has a fairly slender tower with four prominent pinnacles. The present structure dates from the 15th century, with subsequent rebuilding and restoration. Close by is the Church House, which bears the date 1698. Opposite the house is a stone cross, reassembled from broken sections found in a hedge.

The route of the former Princetown Railway runs through part of Walkhampton's moorland area. It is now a cycle route.

The parish's large area of moorland is rich in prehistoric remains. They include the notable area south of the Tavistock-Princetown road (B 3357) east of Merrivale, where round house remains, stone rows, a standing stone, a stone circle, and other features can be seen in close proximity.

The valley of the Walkham was much worked by tinners and there are remains of tinners' mills, for crushing and smelting ore, beside both the Walkham and Meavy rivers. There were also small-scale copper mines north-west of the village. Walkhampton Common was an important source of granite, and large quarries at Foggintor, King Tor, and Swell Tor were in production through the 19th and early 20th centuries. The granite for Nelson's Column in London's Trafalgar Square came from Foggintor. Until its closure in 1956 the Princetown Railway passed close to the quarries on its winding ascent of the moor.

Further reading: Govier, L., *Walkhampton Church, Parish and Village*, 1984
Local society: Yelverton & District Local History Society

WARKLEIGH see SATTERLEIGH AND WARKLEIGH

WASHFIELD (H4) Mid Devon Pop. 362 (1901: 332)

Washfield, in the beautiful Exe valley, 2 miles NW of Tiverton, is a triangular-shaped parish having its long eastern boundary defined by the River Exe and its southern boundary marked partly by a tributary. The A 361 North Devon Link road, constructed in the 1980s, cuts through the south of the parish. This is a parish of fertile farmland and woodland with altitudes that rise to 900 ft in the west. An ancient camp called Castle Close stands at 685 ft in the north.

The church (St Mary the Virgin) is of mainly 15th-century construction. Worth House, in the south, was a Domesday manor and home of the Worth family from the 12th century to 1880. The house was rebuilt in the early 18th century and later altered.

Washfield village centre.

Further reading: Turner, John Maurice, *Washfield, the story of a Devonshire village,* 1947

WASHFORD PYNE (G4) Mid Devon Pop. 108 (1901: 150)

The small parish of Washford Pyne is located 1½ miles SSE of Witheridge and 8½ miles W of Tiverton. The River Dalch and a tributary form the northern boundary. The land is mainly high, rising to 682 ft on the south side of Washford Moor. The church hamlet

Washford Pyne's ancient church was mainly destroyed by fire in 1880, but rebuilt as a copy of the original.

is located in the north, and the parish includes the hamlet of Black Dog in the south.

The list of incumbents in the church (St Peter) dates from 1280. However, the earlier church was totally destroyed by fire in 1880, except for the tower base. It was rebuilt 1883–7 as a faithful copy of the original. The tower is capped by a small spire.

The manor formerly belonged to the Pyne, or Pyn family. The Washford part of the name may be an indication that in past centuries this was a point to which sheep might have been brought for washing in the stream before being shorn.

WEARE GIFFARD (C3) Torridge Pop. 354 (1901: 317)

Weare Giffard parish, midway between Great Torrington and Bideford, lies on the east bank of the River Torridge as it meanders in its final leisurely loops to meet the tidal waters that lead it to the sea. The village is very attractive, although sometimes afflicted by flooding. The river forms the parish's western boundary, and tributary streams provide the others, with a north-easterly point of over 400 ft at Gammaton Moor.

After the Norman Conquest the manor of Wera was granted to a Breton, Roald Adobak. Later it was held by the Giffards before passing to the Fortescues who built Weare Giffard Hall in the 15th century. The fine mansion with its gatehouse survives, although some outer walls were destroyed in the Civil War. The church (Holy Trinity) stands nearby, comprising 14th-century and 15th-century work. Huxhill and Little Weare were Domesday manors.

The parish had mills for corn and for wool, also quarries and kilns. The Torrington or Rolle Canal, opened in 1827, entered the parish from Monkleigh by the Beam aqueduct across the Torridge. This aqueduct later became the bridge that still carries the road to Beam. Kilns at Weare Giffard were among those using limestone and coal brought on the canal, which closed c.1871. The three-arched Halfpenny Bridge (downstream from Beam) was constructed in 1835, enabling connection with the recently completed turnpike road and access to the canal; a toll bridge until 1902, it also provided a more convenient route to Monkleigh and other places which had previously necessitated crossing the Torridge at Bideford or Torrington. The railway, which succeeded the canal, crossed over and back across the river boundary, on its route from Bideford to Torrington.

Further reading: *The story of Weare Giffard*, a millennium book written by the community, 2001

WELCOMBE (A4) Torridge Pop. 197 (1901: 150)

The small parish of Welcombe, 6 miles S of Hartland Point, and W of the Bideford-Bude road (A 39), is bounded on three sides by water – the Atlantic Ocean on the west, and westward-flowing streams on north and south, the latter also defining the county border with Cornwall. The land rises to over 500 ft, so the cliffs around the little beach – approached by narrow lanes – are impressive.

The name is a combination of combe (a valley, particularly one leading up from the sea) and wel which relates to a holy well near the church. Both well and church bear the name of St Nectan (as does Hartland church), who is believed to have been a 6th-century missionary. The small church was originally a chapel of Hartland Abbey, and was confirmed by name in a royal charter of 1189. It became a parish church in 1508, and was enlarged. The fine 14th-century rood screen is the oldest in Devon, the font is from the 11th century and the pulpit from the 16th century. The lectern is Jacobean. The vestry dates from c.1300, and the Revd Robert Stephen Hawker, noted 19th-century vicar of Morwenstowe, who also held the living here, used to leave the ancient door open during baptisms so that devils could depart. The church was restored in 1883–4 and the vestry rebuilt around the doorway in 1911. There is also the church of St Martin's at Bursdon Moor.

WEMBURY (D11) South Hams Pop. 2826 (1901: 501)

Situated on the coast, immediately SE of Plymouth and bounded by the Yealm estuary on the east, Wembury is a parish that has steadily increased in population over the

The sea at Wembury as winter dusk approaches, with the Great Mew Stone standing dark against the sunset.

past century, due to its proximity to the city and attractive coastline. The development has extended seawards from the old village, situated about a mile inland, so that the built-up area seems endless until one actually arrives at the coast. Here, however, there is the reward of a small unspoilt beach, with an old mill now used as a café, and the church (St Werburgh) standing on the cliff side where it has long provided a prominent landmark for seafarers. A mile or so offshore in Wembury Bay stands the Great Mew Stone, a small rock island which is part of the parish and a haven for birds.

A church of some kind existed on this site from the time of King Alfred in the 9th century. This was followed by the building of a Norman church in the early 12th century. Then, in the 14th, 15th (when the tower was added) and early 16th centuries, rebuilding was carried out and the present church took shape. The arcades were built of granite and there was a rood screen which no longer exists. The church was extensively restored in 1886. Two enormous monuments within the church are of note: one, which occupies the north side of the sanctuary, very close to the altar, commemorates Sir John Hele who died in 1608, and the other, in the south-west of the building, is to Dame Elizabeth Narbrough who died 1677–8. Outside, there is an ancient mass-dial above the west door. There is also the now redundant church of Holy Nativity west along the coast at Heybrook Bay.

Langdon in the west, was a Domesday manor, and there were others. In the village there are the 17th-century Hele Almshouses, gift of Sir Warwick Hele.

Local society: Wembury Local History Society

WEMBWORTHY (E5) Mid Devon Pop: 233 (1901: 315)

Wembworthy parish rises steeply from the west bank of the River Taw, c.20 miles S of Barnstaple and close to the unclassified road that connects the A 377 and A 3124. The Taw forms the eastern boundary, a tributary stream which meets the river at Bridge Reeve marks the north, and another tributary descending through the Hayne valley that on the south. The village stands at 500 ft and the altitude reaches 600 ft in the south-west. There are ancient earthworks in Heywood Wood in the north-east.

The short tower of the small church (St Michael) was rebuilt in 1626, and the main 15th-century building partly rebuilt and enlarged in the 1860s. This is a cheerful church with a specially light sanctuary, simply furnished but evidently cherished. Rectors are recorded from 1280. Ecclesiastically the parish is united with Eggesford.

Rashleigh, original home of the Rashleigh family, was a Domesday manor, later passing successively through marriage to the Clotworthys, and to the Tremaynes in whose ownership it continued until the 20th century.

Eggesford House was built in Wembworthy parish in 1932 by the Hon. Newton Fellowes, as a grander residence to replace the original which was in Eggesford.

Fellowes succeeded his brother as the 4th Earl of Portsmouth in 1853 but died the following year. In 1911 the 6th Earl, who rarely resided at Eggesford, put the house and grounds on the market. Not lived in again the house was gradually stripped of materials with the remaining structure falling into decay as a gaunt ruin. In later years restoration work and some reconstruction has been carried out by a new owner.

WEST ALVINGTON (F11) South Hams Pop. 535 (1901: 940)

West Alvington was an early settlement and it is believed that a church existed on this site in 909.

The parish of West Alvington lies directly SW of Kingsbridge, on the upper western shores of the Kingsbridge estuary. The village is in the north and the A 381 road from Kingsbridge passes through, bound for Malborough and Salcombe. Although the village is on a hill the land is mostly low-lying, rising in places to c.320 ft.

Origin of the settlement dates back to Saxon times. It was an estate of the king in 1066 and until the early 12th century, with a bridge that gave the name to the nearby town. In early days the parish was much larger, extending to the coast in the south-west.

It is believed that a church existed on the present site as early as 909 and some remains of 13th-century stonework exist. The list of vicars dates from 1309. The present church (All Saints), built of green slate, dates from the 15th century and has arcades of Beer stone. It was restored in the 1860s and the rood screen mostly removed. Bowringsleigh, in the north-west, was originally called Leigh, gaining its longer name from the Bowrings who dwelt here from the early 14th century to the late 15th. From the end of the 17th century it was the home of the Ilberts. It has been much altered over the years. Bagton and Woolston in the south were Domesday manors.

WEST ANSTEY (G3) North Devon Pop. 160 (1901: 192)

In outline the parish of West Anstey, centred 9 miles ENE of South Molton, somewhat resembles the shape of an elm tree, with a short broad trunk and close branches that soar upwards to a relatively flattened summit. The parish's southern boundary extends south centrally from the River Yeo and the hamlet of Yeo Mill to align with two tumuli on the course of a minor road. Northwards, both west and east boundaries partly follow the Yeo tributaries and then, in the far north, proceed over West Anstey Common to the Danesbrook which marks the border with Somerset. Altitudes rise to 1169 ft at West Anstey Barrows in the north, while the centrally situated village stands at c.700 ft.

The village is approached by minor roads from the B 3227 (north of the North Devon Link road). The church (St Petroc) dates from the 15th century, restored in 1880. It has a Norman font. Ringcombe, in the north-west, was a Domesday estate.

The former Taunton-Barnstaple railway, opened in 1873 and closed in 1965, ran through the south of the parish, with a halt at Yeo Mill.

WEST BUCKLAND see EAST AND WEST BUCKLAND

WEST DOWN (D1) North Devon Pop. 620 (1901: 553)

West Down, 4 miles S of Ilfracombe, is a steeply undulating parish. Much of the land is over 600 ft in altitude, and the northern boundary, marked by the A 3123 road, reaches over 800 ft. The River Caen separates the parish from Braunton in the south-east. Through the west runs the A 361 Barnstaple-Ilfracombe road. Near it along the valley, and then north-west via Mortehoe, from 1874 ran the railway to Ilfracombe, a line that was difficult to build because of ascending and descending gradients and sharp curves; it closed in 1970 and the Atlantic Coast Express can no longer be seen gliding by.

The fine cruciform church (St Calixtus) is of early origin, with its first recorded priest dated 1272. The present building dates from the 14th century, with subsequent rebuilding including the tower in 1712. The Norman font was buried in the churchyard at the time of Cromwell and not discovered until the 19th century. Aylescott, Bradwell, and West Stowford Barton were named in Domesday and Crackaway Barton recorded in 1242.

WESTLEIGH (C3) North Devon Pop. 328 (1901: 401)

The somewhat rectangular parish of Westleigh is situated 2 miles NE of Bideford, on the east side of the Torridge estuary which forms its western boundary, with tributary streams partly marking the boundaries on the north and south.

The village is located on the west. The church (St Peter) dates from the 13th century, enlarged later with north and south aisles. There are carved bench ends. West Leigh, East Leigh, and Tapeley were all Domesday manors, and Southcott an Elizabethan mansion. The Georgian mansion of Tapeley in its extensive grounds, owned formerly by the Clevlands and currently by the Christies, is opened to visitors.

The modern A 39 North Devon road passes through the south of the parish as it leads on to the high level Torridge Bridge constructed in 1987. The older road, now the B 3233, together with the former railway line – now the Tarka Trail walking and cycling route – follow the banks of the estuary.

The route of the former Barnstaple-Bideford railway beside the Torridge estuary in Westleigh parish is now a cycle track.

WEST PILTON (D2) North Devon Pop. 141

West Pilton is a civil parish only, as ecclesiastically it is combined with East Pilton (now within Barnstaple civil boundary), united with Ashford. The area is mainly rural, stretching around the north of Barnstaple and the River Yeo, eastwards from a short strip of access to the Taw estuary at the outflow of the Bradiford Water. The land is undulating, with steep hills, one of which was the site of a prehistoric camp. The A 39 road to Lynton passes through, with the branch from it of the old road to Ilfracombe (B 3230).

WEST PUTFORD (B4) Torridge Pop. 181 (1901: 216)

West Putford is located 8½ miles NNE of Holsworthy, west of the A 388 Holsworthy-Bideford road from which it is approached by minor routes. The parish is bounded mainly by the River Torridge on the north and east, although a section extends north-east of the river. Tumuli on the borders suggest early inhabitation. The parish includes Kismeldon Bridge over the Torridge, which originates from the 13th century.

The pleasant and well preserved cruciform church (St Stephen) dates from the early 14th century; the tower is believed to have been built c.1500. It has a Norman font. The church was reseated in 1930, the former bench ends having deteriorated, although two of them are preserved in the south transept. Ecclesiastically, by incorporating East Putford, the parish is now known just as Putford.

Churston House, in the village, was an Elizabethan manor; Cory Barton, a little to the north, is also Elizabethan. Colscott, Sessacott, Thriverton and Wedfield are hamlets.

WESTWARD HO! see NORTHAM

WHIMPLE (J6) East Devon Pop. 1642 (1901: 680)

Whimple, 8½ miles ENE of Exeter, is a parish of fertile soils for long noted for its orchards and cider-making. Land on the west is mainly low-lying, but levels rise to 508 ft on the eastern boundary. Tributaries of the River Clyst flow through. The village is connected by minor roads to the M5 and B 3181 (the former A 38) in the north-west, and the A 30 to the south. The main Waterloo-Exeter railway line passes through the parish, with a station in Whimple village.

It is believed that a church existed here from Saxon times, and the list of rectors dates from before 1258. The present building (St Mary) is of 15th-century foundation, but altered and extended in 1825, and then substantially rebuilt in the 1840s except for the 16th-century tower. Stone from quarries at Killerton and Beer feature in the reconstruction.

Local society: Whimple History Society

WHITCHURCH (C8) West Devon Pop. 514 (1901: 1508)

Valley of the Taviton Brook on the edge of Whitchurch Down. Cox, Roos, and Staple Tors on the skyline.

The somewhat elongated parish of Whitchurch adjoins Tavistock to the NW and extends north-eastwards from the River Tavy to a boundary defined by the River Walkham in the Merrivale area of Dartmoor. As the nature changes from valley, through woodland and enclosed farmland to open moorland, so there is an ascent in altitude of around 1400 ft from the Tavy to the summit of Great Staple Tor. Since 1935 part of the parish, including, somewhat anomalously, the village centre and church of St Andrew, has been absorbed into Tavistock, due to the town's expansion.

The church, built on a probable Saxon foundation, dates mainly from the 14th century, with some Norman features. The churchyard is a delight of natural beauty, particularly in spring, with successive drifts of snowdrops and crocuses, followed by daffodils, celandines, primroses and bluebells.

Of several interesting houses in the parish, Walreddon is built on the site of a Celtic settlement believed to date from the 7th century. It was in the ownership of a younger branch of the family of the Earl of Devon, the Courtenays, from the 17th to the 20th centuries. Since then the fine Elizabethan house has had a succession of owners. Holwell, on the edge of Whitchurch Down, was the seat of the Glanvilles from the late 1300s for over three centuries. The Priory, near the village, is a 19th-century house with a 14th-century entrance tower reputedly remaining from an ancient chantry. Sortridge was a detached part of Peter Tavy parish until coming within Whitchurch in 1884, but is now in Horrabridge. Grenofen, standing above the Walkham, was an ancient manor, the house was largely rebuilt in the early 19th century and is now divided into private apartments. Up on the moor, at the foot of Pew Tor, Moortown, one of the parish's oldest farmhouses, was the home of the Mooring family from the 14th century and possibly earlier.

Extractive industries have been active in Whitchurch. Tin was worked on the moor, in Beckamoor Combe and at Merrivale Bridge Mine, also, in the late 19th century, at Rixhill and Anderton, west of the village, and elsewhere. There were small trials for copper on the northern fringe of Whitchurch Down and on Plaster Down. On the slopes of Pew Tor and Staple Tor there is much evidence of the 19th-century working of surface granite. Around Staple Tor are numerous sett-makers' bankers – primitive benches made of slabs of granite where in the 1870s granite setts were cut for paving streets in Plymouth and elsewhere. (See Harris, Helen, 'Nineteenth-century granite working on Pew Tor and Staple Tor, western Dartmoor' *Transactions of the Devonshire Association 113*, 1981.) The nearby Merrivale Quarry, opened in 1875, closed in 1997. The village had a halt on the former railway from Tavistock to Plymouth, opened in 1858, closed in 1962.

Further reading: Tavistock & District Local History Society, *Whitchurch Down*, 2000
Cook, Ken, *Whitchurch Parish*, Tavistock & District LHS, 2002
Woodcock, Gerry, *The book of Whitchurch*, Halsgrove, 2004

WHITESTONE (G6) Teignbridge Pop. 699 (1901: 409)

Whitestone, immediately WNW of Exeter, is a rather sprawling parish of steep hills and valleys, a fair proportion of the hills being wooded. The Nadder Brook, tributary of the Alphin Brook and ultimately of the River Exe, flows south-eastwards through the parish. Just north of it is the church town, at an altitude of c.600 ft, with the land attaining 815 ft at Waddles Down half a mile to the north-west. The former A 30 road west from Exeter runs through the south with the village settlement alongside, and the modern A 30 passes parallel and in close proximity on the south.

The church (St Catherine) is of ancient foundation. The present building dates from the 15th century, restored in the 17th century. Various modifications have been carried out at later dates. The church tower can be seen from the mouth of the Exe and in the past provided a landmark for mariners. At Pathfinder Village (a development of park homes dating from the 1950s beside the old A 30 in the west) is the church of St John the Evangelist. Also under the care of Whitestone is the remote small church of St Thomas at Oldridge, in the north-west. This former chapel, which is believed to have belonged to the Courtenays in the 12th century (the date of the font) had become ruinous by 1798 when it was fully restored.

Besides Oldridge, Whitestone, Heath Barton, Halsford, Rowhorne and West Down all date from before the Norman Conquest.

WIDECOMBE-IN-THE-MOOR (F8) Teignbridge Pop. 562 (1901: 657)

Widecombe Church House.
COURTESY THE BOOK OF WIDECOMBE

There could hardly be a parish with a more accurately descriptive name than Widecombe-in-the-Moor. Viewed from the east, from the side of the hill on Bonehill Down, the village is clearly seen in the wide combe (valley), with the eastern Dartmoor moorland all around.

This is a large parish, bordering the Forest of Dartmoor on the west, where the boundary is defined by the Walla Brook and the East Dart River, with the Dart marking the southern boundary. The area is almost entirely moorland, partly open, partly enclosed and to a certain extent improved. Two smaller rivers flow southwards through the parish, the West Webburn, and the East Webburn, which is the stream of the wide combe, passing on the east side of the village. The Webburns unite near Leusdon, the East Webburn having for a short length marked the eastern boundary, which the combined stream continues until it joins the Dart near Holne Chase. Much of the land on the moor rises to 1000-1100 ft, with numerous high points including Sharp Tor (1254 ft), Corndon Tor (1415 ft), Chinkwell Tor (1504 ft) and Hameldown Beacon (1697 ft). The village is reached from the A 38 expressway by the A 382 road to Bovey Tracey, and the B 3387 via Haytor, and is also served by a network of minor roads.

The area of the parish has produced evidence of habitation from the depths of pre-history, including Mesolithic flints and arrowheads. Neolithic axe-heads and chambered tombs, and abundant relics from the Bronze Age are also to be found in the form of hut circles, cairns, barrows, stone rows and circles, and boundary reaves. There are indications, notably at Foales Arrishes, of occupation continuing into Iron Age times before a period of disinhabitation, due apparently to climate change. By the 10th century the Saxons had made incursions into the area; Bittleford is named in a Saxon charter of 956. Natsworthy, Dunstone, Spitchwick, Blackslade, Scobitor and Jordan were manors named in Domesday, although Widecombe itself was not mentioned at that time.

Farming and its ancillary activities developed as the enduring occupations of the people, although tinning involved many Widecombe men, and remaining signs of tin-working can be seen at various places.

The church (St Pancras), often referred to as the 'cathedral of the moor', with its bold granite tower, occupies a prominent position in the village. Of early origin, its list of rectors begins in 1253 and there is reference to a church in 1260. The present

Widecombe Fair. COURTESY THE BOOK OF WIDECOMBE

building is of 15th and early 16th-century construction. During the Sunday afternoon service on 21 October 1638 the church was struck by lightning, with 4 people killed and 62 injured. Close by in the village is the granite-built Church House which dates from c.1538 and is now owned by the National Trust. Leusdon, in the south of the civil parish, is a separate ecclesiastical parish with its small church (St John the Baptist) built and endowed in 1863 by Charlotte Rosamund Larpent.

Widecombe Fair, which evolved from a sheep fair dating from 1850, is a great annual event held on the second Tuesday in September. It attracts thousands of visitors from near and far, due largely to the familiarity of the traditional song of the same name.

Further reading: Woods, Stephen H., *Widecombe-in-the-Moor*, Halsgrove, 1996
Woods, Stephen, *Widecombe-in-the-Moor, Uncle Tom Cobley and All*, Halsgrove, 2000
Widecombe & District Local History Group, *All along, down long, Widecombe way*, Orchard Publications, 2003
Local society: Widecombe & District Local History Society

WIDWORTHY (L6) East Devon Pop. 300 (1901: 148)

The parish of Widworthy, 5½ miles W of Axminster and 3½ miles E of Honiton, is bounded on the north by the A 35 road, where it also includes part of the village of Wilmington. The Umborne Brook, tributary of the River Coly, forms the boundary on the east, and the Offwell Brook, another Coly tributary, that on the south-west. Land rises to 730 ft on Widworthy Hill, in the centre. In the north-west is the parkland of Widworthy Court, which includes Castle Hill, an earthwork of uncertain origin, but now considered probably a medieval fortification dating possibly from the 12th century.

Widworthy Court was built in 1830 for Edward Marwood Tucker. The former manor house to the south-west and close to the church then became Widworthy Barton. The situation of the small church (St Cuthbert) is very peaceful and beautiful, set in the rolling hills. The building dates from the 14th century. Sutton Barton, on the west, was a Domesday manor, near it is a disused quarry that produced white stone similar to that from Beer.

Further reading: Papers by Edwin Haydon from his studies of Widworthy parish in issues *48* (April 1994), *50* (April 1995) and *53* (October 1996) of *The Devon Historian*

WILLAND (J4) Mid Devon Pop. 2821 (1901: 418)

Willand is a small, oval-shaped parish lying between Halberton, Uffculme and Cullompton. The eastern boundary is formed mainly by waters of the River Culm and that on the west by a tributary, the Spratford Stream. The land is generally level at 200-250 ft.

The parish is dominated by transport systems. The main railway line passes through, and in earlier days was the site of Tiverton Junction Station. This was the connection, from 1848 until the 1960s, for the 5-mile branch line to Tiverton, and from 1876 to 1963 for the 7½ mile Culm Valley Railway to Hemyock. With the proximity also of the main road (A 38) the location was eminently suitable for the industrial developments that have taken place. The busy-ness was further increased with the construction of the M5 motorway, routed through here and completed from the Somerset county border to Exeter in 1977.

The village lies to the east. The church (St Mary the Virgin) dates from the 15th century, restored in 1863. It has a fine screen.

Further reading: Japes, F.E., *History of Willand*, 1969

WINKLEIGH (E5) Torridge Pop. 1401 (1901: 1079)

Winkleigh is a large parish in central Devon, located directly between Exeter and Torrington, and slightly nearer the latter. It is reached from Exeter on the A 377 and B 3220 roads and from Torrington on the A 3124.

The village, on a south-facing hillside, is large and of Saxon foundation. At Domesday the manor belonged to the Crown, and was settled on Matilda, queen of William I. Two small castles, or probably fortified manor houses, were here in Norman times: Croft Castle on the west side of the village, Court Castle on the east; only their named sites remain. The church (All Saints) is of ancient origin, its high altar dedicated by Bishop Grandisson in 1333. The present building dates from the 15th century, restored in 1873. It has been said that 24 other churches can be seen from the church tower.

Loosedon was a Domesday manor, and Court Barton and Southcott (seat of the Southcotts) were medieval mansions. The parish includes the hamlet of Hollocombe in the north.

During the Second World War an aerodrome was constructed on moory land north of the village. Heavy American aircraft operated from here in the later times of the conflict. The area is passed through by the road to Torrington.

Further reading: People of Winkleigh, *Winkleigh*, Beaford Centre, 1997

WITHERIDGE (G4) North Devon Pop. 1162 (1901: 1024)

Witheridge is situated 10 miles WNW of Tiverton and 10 miles SE of South Molton. The B 3137 road passes through the village. The parish is of mostly high ground, much of it c.600 ft and rising to 806 ft in the north-east. The Little Dart River flows westwards through the parish, joined by the Sturcombe from the north and other streams. Much of the farmland is reclaimed moor, of which Witheridge Moor on the east side and Dart Raffe Moor in the west still exist as such. Tumuli and standing stones on Witheridge Moor suggest a Bronze Age presence, while an earthwork known as Berry Castle at Queen Dart probably dates from Saxon times.

The church (St John the Baptist), which stands on the north side of the large village Square, is of early origin, with rectors from 1255. The present building dates from the early 14th century, rebuilt in the 15th century and restored in the late 1800s. A former spire was destroyed by lightning in 1840, and the tower was subsequently raised. There is very fine arcading, a carved font of c.1500 and a late 15th-century stone pulpit. Ecclesiastically the parish is united with Creacombe.

In 1248 Witheridge acquired a weekly market and a three-day fair, but these had ended by the early 20th century. Witheridge, Adworthy, Bradford Barton, Dart Raffe and Drayford were Domesday estates.

Further reading: Usmar, John, and Tout, Peter and Freda, comp., *Old Witheridge,* 1988
Usmar, John, and Tout, Peter and Freda. ed., *Witheridge memories*, 1999

	Various, *The book of Witheridge*, Halsgrove, 2003
Local society:	Witheridge Local History Group

WOODBURY (J7) East Devon Pop. 3466 (1901: 1527)

The fairly large parish of Woodbury, 7 miles SE of Exeter and 4 miles N of Exmouth, is bordered on the west by the estuary of the River Clyst, and then that of the Exe. Close to this runs the A 376 Exeter-Exmouth road, on which are the settlements of Ebford and Exton. Woodbury itself is on the B 3179, and in the north is the village of Woodbury Salterton.

In the east is the heathland of Woodbury Common, where land rises to 560 ft. At this high point is a large earthworks, from which Woodbury took its name. Sited on the ridgeway, Woodbury Castle as it is known is believed to date from the Iron Age when it would have been a defensive fort. There is still evidence of strong defences and ramparts, and the situation would have enabled good visibility of possible advancing forces from the sea. Because of this advantage it was also manned during the Napoleonic War. Today, besides often being used for military training, Woodbury Common is a popular place for recreation and valuable for many species of wildlife.

Woodbury village is believed to have originated in Saxon times, becoming a royal manor. The church (St Swithun) is of ancient origin, reconstructed in 1409 and restored with embellishments in the late 19th century. Ecclesiastically the parish is united with Lympstone and there is also the church of St Andrew at Exton. Woodbury Salterton church (Holy Trinity) which is united with Clyst St Mary, was built in 1845 in Doric style.

Nutwell Court, overlooking the estuary, was a Domesday manor and later a fortified house of the Dinhams. It was inherited in the 18th century by a branch of the Drake family and the medieval house demolished. The present house was built in 1810.

Up to the 19th century many women and children worked in making Honiton point lace. In 1861 the railway to Exmouth from the London & South Western Railway at Exeter was opened, running close to the shoreline with Woodbury Station sited at Exton.

Further reading:	Fox, Harold, 'The people of Woodbury in the fifteenth century' *The Devon Historian 56*, (April 1998)
	Stokes, Roger, *Woodbury: the twentieth century revisited*, Halsgrove, 1999
Local society:	Woodbury History Society

Woodbury early in the 20th-century.
COURTESY THE BOOK OF WOODBURY

WOODLAND (F9) Teignbridge Pop. 134 (1901: 170)

Woodland is situated just E of Ashburton and of the A 38 expressway, from which it is approached by minor roads.

The land is undulating, rising in the north-west to over 550 ft. The south-west boundary is marked by the little River Hems, whose tributary streams also water the parish. There is a disused slate quarry at Wickeridge, near the north-eastern boundary.

Until 1536 Woodland was part of Ipplepen before becoming a parish in its own right. At that time an early chapel here, licensed in 1424, was rebuilt as the parish church (St John the Baptist). The parish is now, however, united ecclesiastically with Broadhempston.

WOODLEIGH (F11) South Hams Pop. 151 (1901: 183)

Woodleigh, 3 miles N of Kingsbridge, consists of hilly land east of the River Avon which forms the western boundary, with levels that rise to 606 ft in the north. The village is in the south, standing above the Torr Brook, an Avon tributary. Access is by minor roads from the A 381 Totnes-Kingsbridge road and from the B 3196 at nearby Loddiswell.

The church (St Mary) stands on the site of a Saxon church and dates probably from the 13th century. It was restored in 1891, renovated in 1990, and is evidently lovingly cared for. In the north sanctuary wall there is a fine example of an Easter sepulchre.

Grimpstonsleigh, in the east, was a Domesday manor. Wood Barton, a mile north of the village, was the home of a branch of the Fortescues; a Cistercian monastery was established nearby in the early 20th century but was abandoned following the First World War.

St Mary's Church at Woodleigh is believed to have been built in the 13th century on the site of a Saxon church.

WOOLFARDISWORTHY (EAST) (G5) Mid Devon Pop. 166 (1901: 170) (Usually pronounced Woolsery)

Woolfardisworthy near Crediton is located 6 miles N of that town and 8 miles SW of Tiverton, served only by minor roads. The Binneford Water defines the eastern boundary, and an arm of the parish extends north-westwards to the River Dalch. The land is mainly fairly high, reaching 690 ft near Black Dog in the north, with pleasant valleys. The village is situated on the hillside, visible from across the valley to the south. The early church here was dedicated in 1261; the present one (St Mary) was entirely rebuilt in 1845.

WOOLFARDISWORTHY (WEST) (B3) Torridge Pop. 1123 (1901: 648) (Usually spoken, and written, as WOOLSERY)

Woolsery is one of those pleasantly wild and sometimes wind-swept parishes that border North Devon's spectacular coastline. The gently undulating land rises to over 650 ft, and tends to be wet and heavy. The infant River Torridge forms the southern boundary, and tributary streams those on west and east. In the north the boundary's overland course extends in the north-east to the coast, to include a length as far east as Bucks Mills. Ecclesiastically Bucks Mills forms a separate parish which also includes a portion of Parkham.

The village of Woolsery, 1½ miles S of the Bideford-Bude road (A 39), has old houses and modern developments surrounding the church (All Hallows). Originally a chapel of Hartland Abbey, Woolsery did not become a parish until the Reformation. The 12th-century structure was largely rebuilt in the 15th century but still retains a fine 12th-century south doorway with heavily engraved arch, and a 13th-century font with a square bowl supported on shafts. Bench ends are richly carved. Of the outlying farms Ashmansworthy and Almiston were named in Domesday.

Towards the coast the road down to Bucks Mills passes by the little church of St Anne, built around 1860 in the Early English style, and descends through a steep-sided valley to the hamlet. With just a few old cottages clinging to the cliff, Bucks Mills is smaller and less spectacular than neighbouring Clovelly, but shares some

Bucks Mills, with its ancient limekilns, was a fishing village on Woolsery's coastline.

of its character. Here one senses the quietness of a remote coastal settlement, resting in retirement from busier days of fishing and trading in lime. Until the mid 19th century it was known as Buckish Mills, but by 1878, when farmers were still bringing corn to a water mill it had become Bucks Mills. At that time there were around 300 inhabitants and the predominating surname was Braund; earlier it was said to have been almost exclusively so and the name became inseparable from the place. (It is to one of the last residing members of the Braund family, in 1970, that the author owes much of this information.)

In the early 19th century 16 fishing boats worked off Bucks Mills' small pebble shore. Herrings were caught from September to Christmas, also mackerel, whiting and other types. Having no jetty, Bucks Mills was not an easy place for landing returning boats. These, of heavy oak construction to withstand the pebbles, had to be beached on the open shore and winched, with women and children often also called upon to help. Sudden forceful winds could turn the boat sideways, necessitating use of a stern rope. Herrings were sold at 600 for half-a-crown (two shilling and sixpence in old money) and among buyers were farmers from the surrounding district who would collect quantities for pickling.

Two limekilns remain from times when limestone from South Wales was landed here and burnt for use on the land. The one on the west is of Elizabethan origin. That on the east, a tower-like structure, was probably built c.1760; from it a short steep inclined plane with narrow gauge rails enabled the burnt lime to be raised in skips, by a gin. This, powered by a horse with rope or chain attachments, walking around a circle, operated a winding drum. Pebbles were also carted from the beach, many to be cracked for road use. Sand was also taken up for the land, carried by donkeys with panniers.

Bucks Mills is now specially quiet in winter time as most of its cottages are holiday residences.

WORLINGTON – for both East and West Worlington see EAST WORLINGTON

YARCOMBE (L5) East Devon Pop. 530 (1901: 561)

Yarcombe village is located 7 miles NW of Axminster and 5 miles W of Chard; actual travelling distances are particularly greater in this case however due to the wandering character of the A 30 road on which the village stands, and the network of minor roads coming from the south. The parish is in Blackdown Hills country, with the River

Yarty, tributary of the Axe, forming the eastern boundary. It is very much a parish of hills and valleys, with altitudes reaching between 800 and 900 ft. The northern and north-eastern boundaries coincide with the Somerset county border.

The church (St John the Baptist) dates from at least as early as the 14th century. The present building is of 15th-century construction, retaining traces of the earlier one; it was rebuilt and restored c.1890. The manor was acquired by Sir Francis Drake in the late 16th century; Sheafhayne House, now much altered, was apparently the manor house at that time. Dennington was also a Domesdasy manor.

Further reading: Everitt, Ruth, *From monks to the millennium, a history of Yarcombe parish*, 1999

YARNSCOMBE (D3) Torridge Pop. 300 (1901: 273)

Yarnscombe is located 6½ miles due S of Barnstaple, on the high ground west of the Taw valley. The eastern boundary is marked for a short distance by the Langley Brook but elsewhere boundaries are mainly over land, extending westwards to just beyond Huntshaw Cross. The deep Langley valley is crossed at Langridge Ford by the Torrington-South Molton road (B 3227).

The village stands at a fairly high level of 450 ft, reached by minor roads from the A 377 or B 3232, south of Barnstaple. The church (St Andrew) dates from the 13th century when it replaced more centrally two earlier churches in the parish, although most of the present structure is of the 14th and 15th centuries. The building was restored in 1877.

Delley, in the west, was a Saxon estate.

The ancient TORENS or GORENS inscribed stone in Yealmpton churchyard.

YEALMPTON (D10) South Hams Pop. 1923 (1901: 937)

Yealmpton is a fairly extensive parish, named from the River Yealm which, having flowed form its source in the Penn Moor/Stall Moor area of southern Dartmoor, here approaches its tidal stage before entering the English Channel 4 miles SW in Wembury Bay. The Silverbridge Lake, tributary of the Yealm, forms the western boundary. From low level the undulating land rises to a mainly 200-350 ft range with 387 ft reached in the north.

The village, 6½ miles ESE of Plymouth, is located on the A 379 Plymouth-Kingsbridge road. It is certainly of Saxon origin and possibly earlier, referred to in Domesday as Elitona. In the churchyard, at the west end of the church building, is an inscribed stone bearing the word TORENS or GORENS. Of Cornish granite, it is believed to be a memorial to an ancient British chieftain who embraced Christianity 1500 years ago. It was erected in its present position in 1851 after being found lying on the north side of the churchyard. The first mention of a church occurs in a charter of 1225 and the list of incumbents shows the earliest at 1297. The old church fell into poor condition and the present one (St Bartholomew) is the result of total rebuilding in 1849–52. The Saxon font, still in existence, suggests that there may have been a church here long before the 1225 documentation. Much so-called marble used in the reconstruction, was actually a form of limestone (polished) obtained from local quarries.

The Kitley estate, centred west of the village was in the hands of the Pollexfens in the 16th century, and a mansion was built. This was reconstructed in the 18th century after passing through marriage to the Bastard family, and later remodelled by Repton. It is now a hotel. The nursery rhyme of Mother Hubbard originates from Yealmpton, its writer, Sarah Martin, having been staying at Kitley with her sister, Mrs Bastard, in the early 1800s. The tale is said to be modelled on the Kitley housekeeper of the time.

The basin of a Saxon font still in use in Yealmpton's St Bartholomew's Church.

There are limestone caves at Kitley. The parish includes the hamlet of Yealmbridge, on the A 379 to the east, and, just south of it, Dunstone. In 1898 the Yealmpton branch railway was opened from Plymouth which passed along the creeks of the Yealm and terminated at a station south of the village. After closing in 1930 it reopened from 1941–7 for the benefit of people who had moved out of wartime Plymouth.

YELVERTON see BUCKLAND MONACHORUM

ZEAL MONACHORUM (F5) Mid Devon Pop. 398 (1901: 316)

Zeal Monachorum is situated 1½ miles N of the Okehampton-Copplestone-Crediton road (A 3072), near Bow. The River Yeo flows northwards through the parish and in the north-east briefly forms the parish boundary. The boundary follows a somewhat wandering course, sometimes along tributaries, with an extension to the west to include a small patch of moorland.

The Monachorum in the name is due to this having been a manor of Buckfast Abbey from 1066. The church (St Peter) dates from the 14th and 15th centuries; it was restored in 1854 and again in 1913. Loosebeare in the north, and Lower Newton in the north-west were Domesday manors. Loosebeare, Burston and Tuckingmill, whose name indicates past involvement in the woollen industry, are hamlets.

Further reading: Adams, Ann, *Zeal Monachorum, a Devon rural parish, 1066–1801,* Pub. by the author, 2002